African Seats

African Seats

Edited by Sandro Bocola

with essays by Ezio Bassani, Sandro Bocola,
Hans Himmelheber, Lorenz Homberger, Piet Meyer,
Andrea Knecht Oti-Amoako and Roy Sieber

Photographs by Heini Schneebeli

Prestel

Munich · New York

First published in German on the occasion of the exhibition
"Afrikanische Sitze" (Chief Curator: Sandro Bocola),
organized by the Vitra Design Museum, Weil am Rhein, Germany,
in cooperation with the Africa Museum, Tervuren, Belgium, and shown at:
Vitra Design Museum, Weil am Rhein, Germany: 10 June – 25 September 1994
Musée National des Arts Africains et Océaniens, Paris: 18 October 1994 – January 1995
Villa Stuck, Munich: 1 February – 23 April 1995
Kunstmuseet Trapholt, Kolding, Denmark: 13 June – 3 September 1995
Museum für angewandte Kunst, Vienna: 13 December 1995 – 18 February 1996
Africa Museum, Tervuren, Belgium: 30 March – 29 May 1996

Picture research and design: Sandro Bocola
Design assistant: Bruno Moosbrugger
Translated from the German (essays by Sandro Bocola, Hans Himmelheber,
Lorenz Homberger and Piet Meyer, and Andrea Knecht Oti-Amoako) and
from the Italian (essay by Ezio Bassani) by Elizabeth Clegg
Copy-edited by Simon Haviland

Front cover: King's stool, Bamum, Cameroon (see cat. 75)
Back cover: Chief's chair, Tabwa, Zaire (see cat. 143)

Front endpaper: The Mangbetu chief Okondo waiting to perform his dance,
1913 (photograph on p. 110)
Back endpaper: A tribal prince in Kwahu, Ghana, with his court, *c.* 1888–96
(photograph on p. 53)

© Prestel Verlag, Munich · Berlin · London · New York 2002
© of the essay by Hans Himmelheber by Baessler-Archiv, Museum für Völkerkunde, Berlin
© of illustrated works by Pablo Picasso: Succession Picasso / VG Bild-Kunst, Bonn 2002

Photographic Sources and Acknowledgements on p. 200

Prestel Verlag
4 Bloomsbury Place, London WC1A 2QA
Tel. +44 (020) 7323-5004
Fax +44 (020) 7636-8004

175 Fifth Avenue, Suite 402
New York, NY 10010
Tel. +1 (212) 995-2720
Fax +1 (212) 995-2733

Königinstrasse 9, 80539 Munich
Tel. +49 (89) 38 17 09-0
Fax +49 (89) 38 17 09-35

Maps by Wolfgang Mohrbach, Munich
Typeset by Wagner GmbH, Nördlingen
Printed and bound by Gorenjski Tisk

Printed in Slovenia

ISBN 3-7913-2800-X

Contents

Foreword

African Seats offers the first survey of an aspect of the culture of everyday life in Africa that has long been neglected among Europeans. The study of African forms of seating introduces us to enormous variety: the examples presented here extend from simple seats hewn from a single block of wood to more complex chairs and thrones created under the influence of European models; from elementary forms of the purest 'functionality' to works richly decorated with ornaments and carvings of figures.

While certainly wide-ranging and representative, this survey does not attempt to be a systematic catalogue of familiar types; rather, it presents African seats as objects of great artistic value. The great elegance of the many types of body support that have an almost 'minimalist' impact encourages comparison with design in the West. Yet the so-called designer furniture of our culture, for all its variety of shapes, materials and colours, rarely attains a comparable aura. African seats may also prove to be the source of new ideas that will help us revise and reorient the design of our own household objects in response to global economic and ecological problems.

Travellers were already collecting African objects during the first voyages of exploration along the west coast of Africa in the sixteenth century. Brought back to Europe, and passing through ports and trade routes, these objects reached the few collectors of that period – rich public figures, sovereigns and the Church. These, of course, viewed such souvenirs as exotic curiosities rather than as the testimony of other cultures, and recognized in them neither intrinsic value nor even any artistic significance. Sadly, most of the objects that came to Europe in this early period disappeared during the following centuries.

These initial contacts also mark the start of trade between Europe and sub-Saharan Africa. African sculptors from along the coast of the Gulf of Guinea soon switched to working specifically for this trade. Objects made of ivory – including pipes and salt-cellars – were manufactured for use by Europeans and marketed to meet demand. Although these objects retained many formal characteristics that were essentially African, one can already detect the unmistakable first symptoms of what scholars were to term 'aculturation', the appropriation and incorporation of elements of an alien culture into one that has already reached maturity in a specific region.

The trade in traditional African objects remained very limited until the late nineteenth century. After 1880, however, collecting gradually became more systematic; the cultural significance of objects was recognized and they increasingly found their way into museums. Around the turn of the century European artists suddenly discovered the significance that African masks and carved figures could have for their own artistic work; and, from this point on, African carvings were also admired for their artistic value. Collectors initially focused their attention on masks and on ancestor figures and fertility statues, and soon also on smaller objects such as combs, neck-rests or brooches. Larger objects of everyday use, such as drums, cassava jars, canes and seating furniture, were not so highly valued except in so far as they were distinguished by figural or ornamental decoration.

It is only recently that various exhibitions have brought objects of everyday use to the centre of our attention. Even after the period between 1960 and 1970 – when masks and carved figures rose considerably in market value and they became hard to find in their countries of origin – there was hardly any demand from collectors for seats or pots. These objects remained modestly priced and it was still possible to find them where they had been made.

Our thanks are due to Sandro Bocola, who devised this exhibition and was also responsible, as editor, for its accompanying catalogue. When he proposed the project to the Vitra Design Museum in 1991, outlining its subject with the aid of a few photographs of objects and their places of origin, the Museum's director, Alexander von Vegesack, was immediately taken with the idea. Sandro Bocola was asked to act as the show's guest curator and, in this role, he has both selected the exhibits and played a large part in the project's practical organization.

We are also grateful to the private collectors and institutions who have lent objects to the exhibition and to the authors who have contributed texts to the catalogue.

Alexander von Vegesack
Vitra Design Museum, Weil am Rhein

Dirk F. E. Thys van den Audenaerde
Africa Museum, Tervuren

Jo-Anne Birnie Danzker
Museum Villa Stuck, Munich

Peter Noever
Österreichisches Museum für angewandte Kunst, Vienna

Sven Jøan Andersen
Kunstmuseet Trapholt, Kolding

Hubert Martin
Musée Nationale des Arts Africains et Océaniens, Paris

Lenders to the exhibition

Dr Thys van der Audenaerde, Director, and Dr Gustaaf Verswijver, Curator, Africa Museum, Tervuren

Dr Thomas Psota, Bernisches Historisches Museum, Berne

Galerie Walu, Zurich

Dr Peter Thiele, Director, and Dr Hermann Forkl, Curator, Linden-Museum, Stuttgart

Jean Paul Barbier, Musée Barbier-Mueller, Geneva

Henri Marchal, Director, and Etienne Féau, Curator, Musée National des Arts Africains et Océaniens, Paris

Professor Dr Armand Duchâteau, Museum für Völkerkunde, Vienna

Dr Eberhard Fischer, Director, and Lorenz Homberger, Curator, Museum Rietberg, Zurich

Dr Klaus Born, Rieß-Museum der Stadt Mannheim

Professor Dr Klaus Helfrich, Director, and Dr Hans-Joachim Koloß, Curator, Staatliche Museen zu Berlin, Preußischer Kulturbesitz, Museum für Völkerkunde

Professor Dr Walter Raunig, Director, and Dr Maria Kecskési, Curator, Staatliches Museum für Völkerkunde, Munich

Alexander von Vegesack, Vitra Design Museum, Weil am Rhein

Sandro Bocola, Zurich

Marie-Catherine Daffos, Jean-Luc Estournel, Paris

René and Denise David, Kilchberg

Dr Rolf Fehlbaum, Basle

Colette and Jean Pierre Ghysels, Brussels

Comte Baudouin de Grunne, Wezembeek-Oppem

Ingrid Hansen, Zurich

Udo and Waltraud Horstmann, Zug

Berthe Kofler-Erni, Riehen

Dr Michael Storrer, Zurich

Acknowledgements

Many individuals and institutions have contributed to the successful outcome of this project through their dedication, their generosity and their enthusiasm. I am especially grateful to Rolf Fehlbaum and Alexander von Vegesack, Director of the Vitra Design Museum, for their confidence and readiness in appointing me curator of the exhibition and editor of its catalogue. My thanks are also due to the collectors, institutions and museum directors listed opposite, who agreed to be separated from their unique objects for such a long period. A vital role was played by our partners in this project, Professor Dr Thys van den Audenaerde of the Africa Museum, Tervuren, and Jean Paul Barbier of the Musée Barbier-Mueller, Geneva: these institutions loaned a total of over sixty items, representing over a third of the exhibition's contents and including some of its high points.

I have particularly valued the contribution of all those who, with their specialist knowledge, their advice and the information they have been able to provide, have helped resolve problems as they arose and have found answers to unexpected questions: above all Lorenz Homberger (whose interest and sympathy have given me constant encouragement), Ezio Bassani, René David, Christraud Geary, Maria Kecskési and Laurence Mattet. I should also like to thank the following for their contributions to the catalogue: Ezio Bassani, Hans Himmelheber, Lorenz Homberger, Andrea Knecht Oti-Amoako, Piet Meyer and Roy Sieber. My own text has benefited from the comments of my friend Fritz Billeter.

A decisive contribution to the realization of our project was made by those colleagues with whom I worked most closely. The exhibition designer, Dieter Thiel, created settings in which the objects could be shown to optimum effect. The photographer, Heini Schneebeli, travelled extensively in order to record over 250 African seats, both in private collections and in museums. His colour photographs convey the sculptural power and the magical aura of these objects. Bruno Moosbrugger was of great help with the design of the catalogue; and Boguslav Ubik, Jutta Oldiges and Sixta Quassdorf were responsible for the administrative and technical aspects of the project. To all these I am deeply grateful.

For kindly supplying additional photographs and other material for illustrations, I am indebted to Jean Paul and Monique Barbier, René Gardi, E. Ablade Glover, Hans Himmelheber, Lorenz Homberger, Hans-Joachim Koloß, Malcolm D. McLeod and Piet Meyer, as also to the Africa Museum in Tervuren, the American Museum of Natural History in New York, the Basler Mission in Basle, the Frobenius-Institut in Frankfurt am Main, the Ghana Information Service in Accra, the Musée de l'Homme in Paris, the Museum für Völkerkunde in Vienna, and the National Museum of African Art, Smithsonian Institution, in Washington, D. C.

Lastly, I should like to thank my companion, Yvonne Wilen, for her patience and sympathy throughout two long and often difficult years.

Sandro Bocola

Sandro Bocola

Introduction

Almost a century has passed since Matisse, Braque and Vlaminck, in purchasing their first African masks, and Picasso, with his painting *Les Demoiselles d'Avignon*, brought 'l'art nègre' into the artistic awareness of the West. Since then, interest in African tribal art has not ceased to grow; and countless exhibitions and publications have assured it an unquestioned place in the pantheon of world art.

The interest and admiration of the Western observer were primarily focused on items in the form of figures, such as masks, crests, ancestral figures and ritual objects, all of these evoking a magical world of supernatural beings and powers. Articles of everyday use, meanwhile, such as furniture and vessels, chests, bowls and baskets, textiles, eating utensils, weapons and tools, were hardly ever considered from an aesthetic point of view. Only with the celebrated exhibition of 1980, *African Furniture and Household Objects*, devised by Roy Sieber, was a wider public introduced to the sculptural power and wealth of forms to be found among these simple objects, which were often completely abstract – dispensing, that is to say, with any figurative elements. In Sieber's view, these traditional practical utensils impart a deeper and more comprehensive insight into the African aesthetic than do those items at which almost all previous attention and research on African art has been directed.

African Seats presents both aspects of African 'sculpture'. Our subject, unlike any other, allows us to do justice to both the figurative and the non-figurative in African artists' inventiveness, and so to reveal the full range of their creativity. No other non-European culture can boast such a variety of seats. Alongside a multitude of stools for everyday use and unique to a particular group (objects that fascinate above all through their formal rigour), there are ritual seats decorated with symbolic motifs and stools for special occasions. We also encounter chairs influenced by European designs and used by the heads of families and of villages, as well as seats and thrones signalling the high rank of chiefs and kings. Especially notable among the latter are the caryatid stools of the Luba and the Songye, which are regarded as some of the most striking examples of African art.

For the first time we are able to offer an extensive, if not exhaustive, survey of aspects of a material culture that is even now approaching extinction. The objects on display come exclusively from sub-Saharan Africa, and date mostly from the first half of this century; a few pieces are slightly older.

Like almost every venture of this kind, our project reflects two distinct ways of regarding objects – the ethnological and the aesthetic. Although ethnological input is duly taken into account, our interest is centred on the artistic dimension of the seating culture of Africa: the manner in which African carvers have sculpturally realized the practical, ritual or ceremonial functions of any given seat. The exhibits have therefore been selected from a predominantly aesthetic point of view, and are presented accordingly.

This procedure has lately been criticized by many ethnologists. They point out that when non-European artefacts are displayed in exhibitions as works of art – placed on pedestals, protected by glass cases, and illuminated with spotlights – they are thereby disengaged from the significance implicit in their original context, rendering impossible any deeper understanding of their essential character.

This, however, is only partly true. The meaning of ceremonial or ritual objects is not limited to their specific function or to their symbolic role. It is realized, rather, in their organization in plastic and formal terms, for it is this that gives expression to the particular awareness of life, the values and the image of the world and of man that defines their creators and users. The same is true of everyday objects. Through its aesthetic dimension, material culture secures a community's collective identity, and thereby fulfils an important social function, albeit one of which the community is hardly aware. In other words, the ethnological view requires the complement of an aesthetic approach.

The latter is, of course, entirely alien to the societies from which these objects come. Even in our own culture, the ability to remove a given artefact from its socio-cultural context and to regard it primarily from a sculptural and aesthetic point of view are skills only recently acquired. They first emerged during the High Renaissance but were not universally acknowledged until the twentieth century and the advent of Modernism as the expression of a transformed understanding of art. They ensured that our civilization was the first in history to appreciate the artistic creations of entirely alien cultures, but also that we were able to recognize the aesthetic significance of the everyday objects of our own culture. I am thinking here not only of Marcel Duchamp's readymades, of Pop Art and Minimal Art, but also of the Design Collection which opened at the Museum of Modern Art in New York in 1934, or of the 1500-strong collection of chairs in the Vitra Design Museum.

Essays

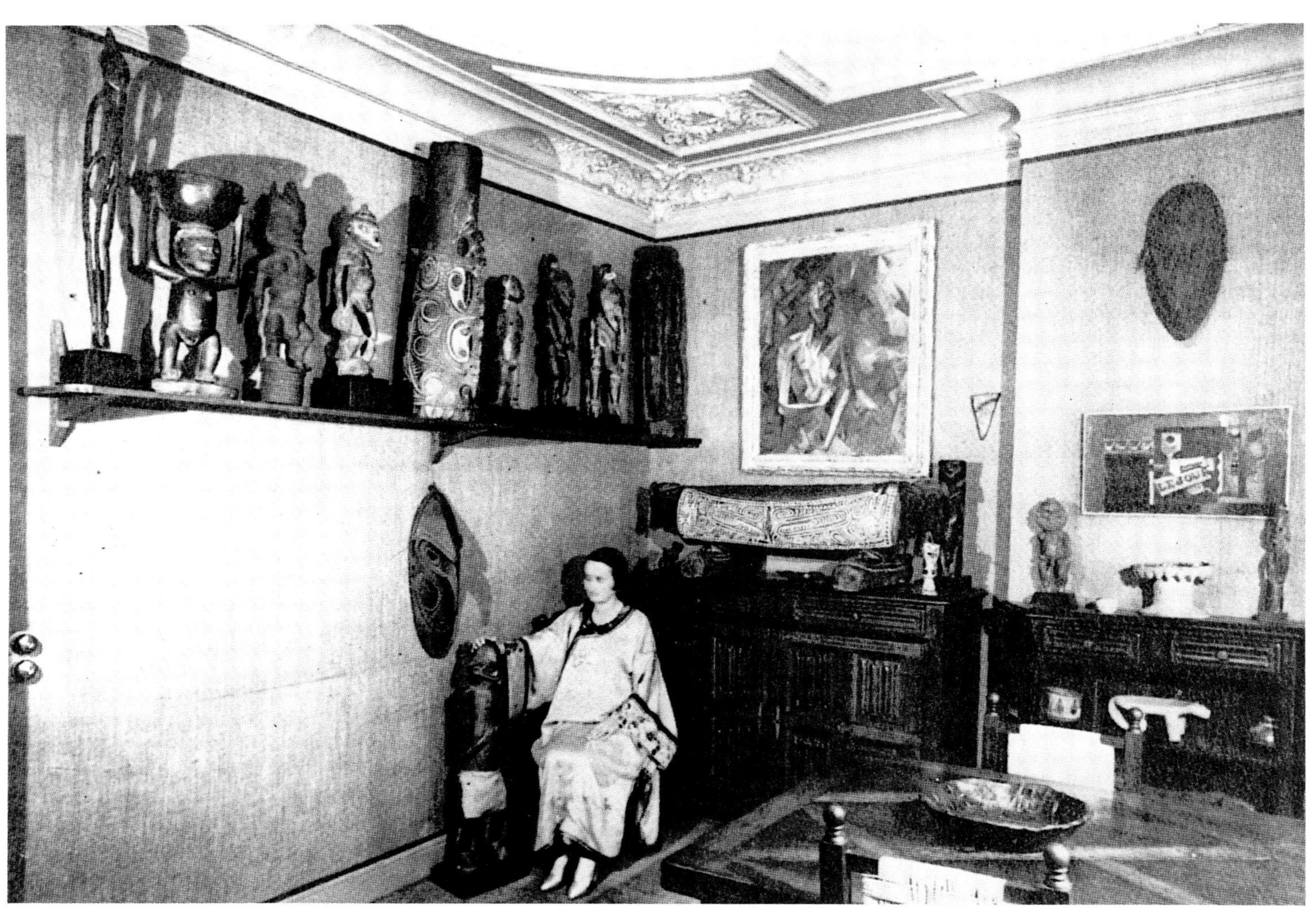

1 Mme Pierre Loeb in the family apartment in rue Desbordes-Valmore, Paris, in 1929

1 As explained in my introduction, we are here exclusively concerned with seats from sub-Saharan Africa produced during the last one hundred to one hundred and fifty years.
2 This sculptural quality is lacking in the European-influenced ceremonial chairs of the Asante and the chiefs' chairs of the Pende and Chokwe. As these merely represent African variants of the archetypal chair found in all cultures, they are not considered in the following discussion.
3 The fact that this concept is virtually unknown to their creators and users should not deter us from employing it. 'There are numerous societies', writes the art ethnologist Ingrid Kreide-Damani, 'that engage in trade without possessing a word for "commerce" and that worship higher beings without possessing a word for "religion".' (Kreide-Damani 1992, p. 62.)
4 Gilot 1964, cited in Rubin 1984, p. 335, note 8.

Sandro Bocola

Through Western Eyes

On the Aesthetic Dimension of African Seats

In this essay I propose to discuss the aesthetic of African seats from the point of view of the modern observer in the West.[1]

In spite of the astonishing variety of the examples presented here, it will suffice for the present to divide these into two main groups. The first embraces chairs and stools intended for everyday use by everyone in the community; and the second, those much rarer seats that have a ritual or political significance, and whose use is either limited to special occasions, such as birth, initiation, marriage or death, or reserved for the political and spiritual élite – kings, chiefs, priests, medicine men, midwives and honoured dignitaries. Among the best known examples of this second type are the bead-embroidered thrones from the grasslands of Cameroon (e. g. plate on p. 103), the caryatid stools that can be found throughout Africa, their seating surfaces supported by human or animal figures (fig. 2), and the chiefs' chairs of the Pende and Chokwe, decorated with figurative motifs (e. g. plate on p. 150). The ceremonial and ritual functions of these seats also find expression in their elaborate design. Their figurative representations, skilful decoration and magical accessories have an entirely symbolic significance; they stand for the powers and ideals to which the society owes its sense of cohesion. As symbols of religious or secular authority, the seats in this second group have much in common with the thrones of ecclesiastical or worldly rulers that we know from European history (fig. 3). As far as their shape is concerned, however, they can be compared neither with these nor with corresponding examples from the Ancient Far East or from Graeco-Roman Antiquity. Despite their elaborate design, the thrones of these high cultures remain pieces of seating furniture, whereas – with a few exceptions – their African relations may be understood as works of sculpture.[2] In this respect, therefore, they are comparable to the masks, the figures of ancestors and the ritual objects that we nowadays term 'African Art'.[3]

This concept is a recent one. Although Paris already possessed a substantial public collection of Oceanic and African tribal art before the turn of the century with the opening of the Musée d'ethnographie du Trocadéro (now the Musée de l'Homme) in 1882, the collection aroused purely ethnological interest until the beginning of the twentieth century. Its aesthetic qualities were not discovered until 1906, when Maurice Vlaminck, Henri Matisse, Georges Braque and André Lhote purchased their first African sculptures and showed them to their painter friends. These artists admired the qualities of 'l'art nègre' but they did not allow them to influence their own work. This was not the case with Picasso, who, on a visit to the Musée du Trocadéro in June 1907, suddenly recognized the expressive potential of this art and resolved to use it in his own painting. 'At that moment,' he recalled, 'I realized what painting was all about.'[4] The overpowering impression of this visit is reflected in his monumental painting *Les Demoiselles d'Avignon* (fig. 5), completed shortly afterwards. With this work, Picasso definitively broke with the mawkish Symbolism of his Blue and Rose Periods. The sentimentality and the melancholy pathos that pervade so much of his early work gave way to the immediacy, the expressive vehemence and the formal power that he had discovered in primitive art.

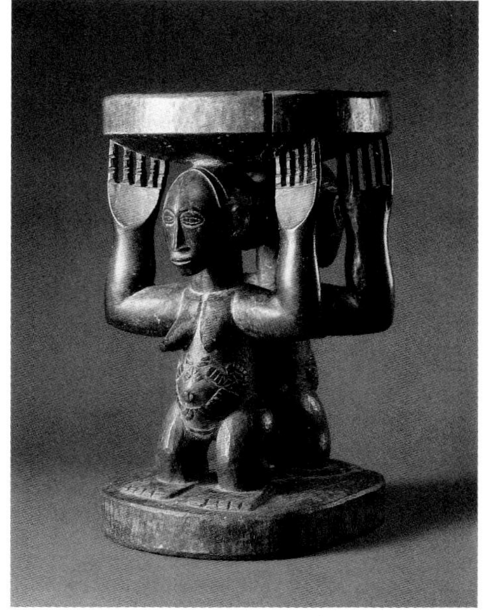

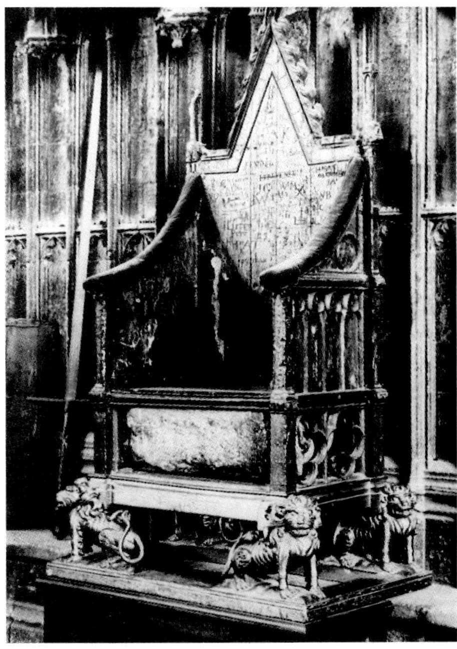

2 Caryatid stool of the Hemba, Zaire
Wood, height 53 cm; colour plate on p. 113

3 Coronation Chair of 1299 in Westminster Abbey, London
A secular throne that still retains its function: seated here, the English monarch receives the symbols of sovereignty.

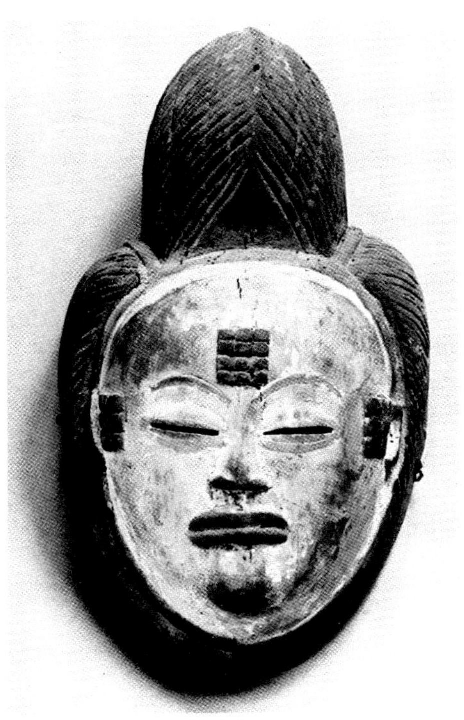

4 Mask
Shira-Punu (Gabon or People's Republic of Congo)
Wood, height 28 cm
Formerly in the collection of Pablo Picasso

Les Demoiselles d'Avignon not only produced a shock among the painters, writers, collectors and dealers who came to see it in Picasso's studio; it also aroused their interest in African tribal art and thereby made no small contribution to its dissemination. Both in exhibitions and in the press African tribal art was increasingly presented in connection with the work of the European avant-garde. This enthusiasm rapidly took hold in other countries too, notably in Germany, where the painters of *Die Brücke* and *Der Blaue Reiter* found extensive collections, and thus a rich visual stimulus, in the ethnography museums of Berlin, Dresden and Munich. These representatives of Modernism looked to primitive art in much the way that the Humanists of the fifteenth and sixteenth centuries had looked to the art of Classical Antiquity. African, Oceanic and Indian masks and sculptures, utensils, weapons, textiles and jewellery served painters and sculptors as sources of inspiration and as direct sculptural models. The Surrealists, with their debt to Symbolism, preferred the flowing, painterly art of Oceania, while artists preoccupied above all with form, such as the Cubists, the Constructivists and the Fauvists, were far more interested in the haptic qualities and the direct, simple and reduced creations of African sculpture.

In 1984 the splendid exhibition at the Museum of Modern Art in New York, *'Primitivism' in 20th Century Art*, showed the scale of this influence: works by Picasso, Brancusi, Lipchitz, Léger, Modigliani, Klee, Miró, Moore and many others were confronted with their primitive models and with their equivalents. William Rubin, the exhibition's curator, ascribed the formal correspondence between the art

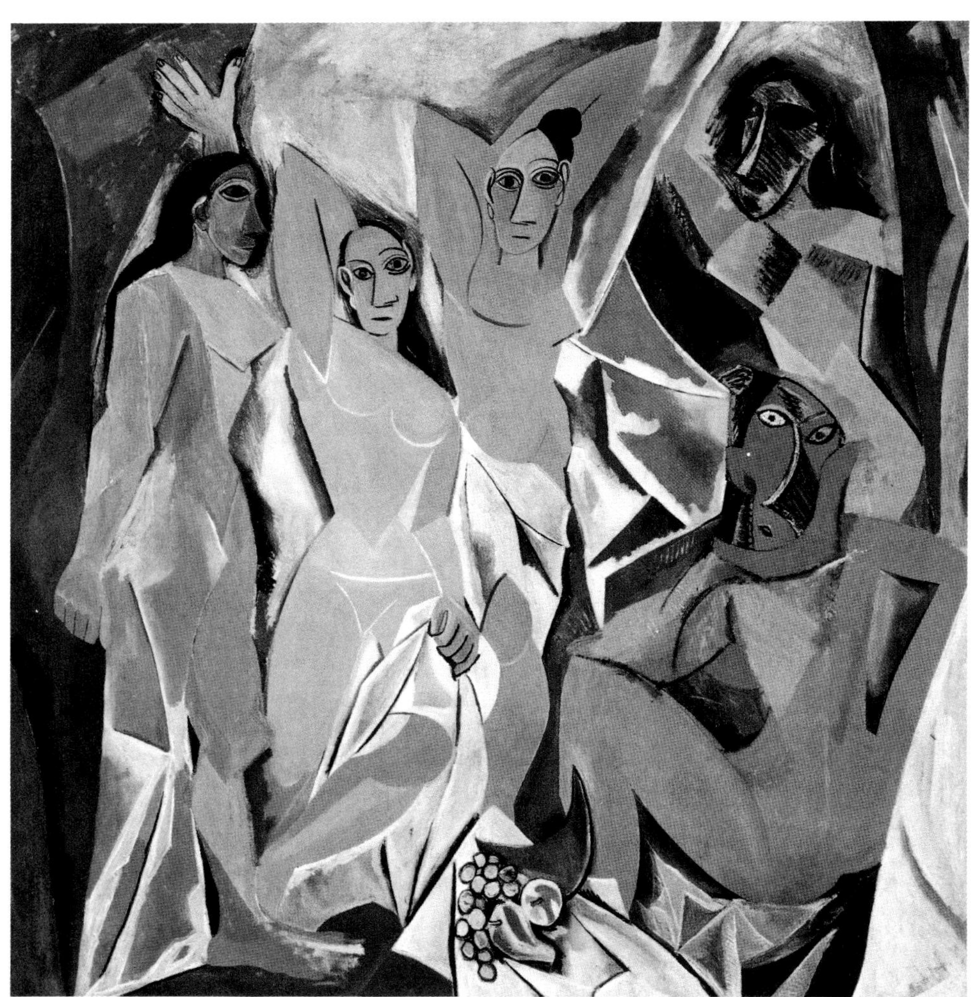

5 Pablo Picasso, *Les Demoiselles d'Avignon*, 1907, oil on canvas, 244 x 238 cm
The Museum of Modern Art, New York

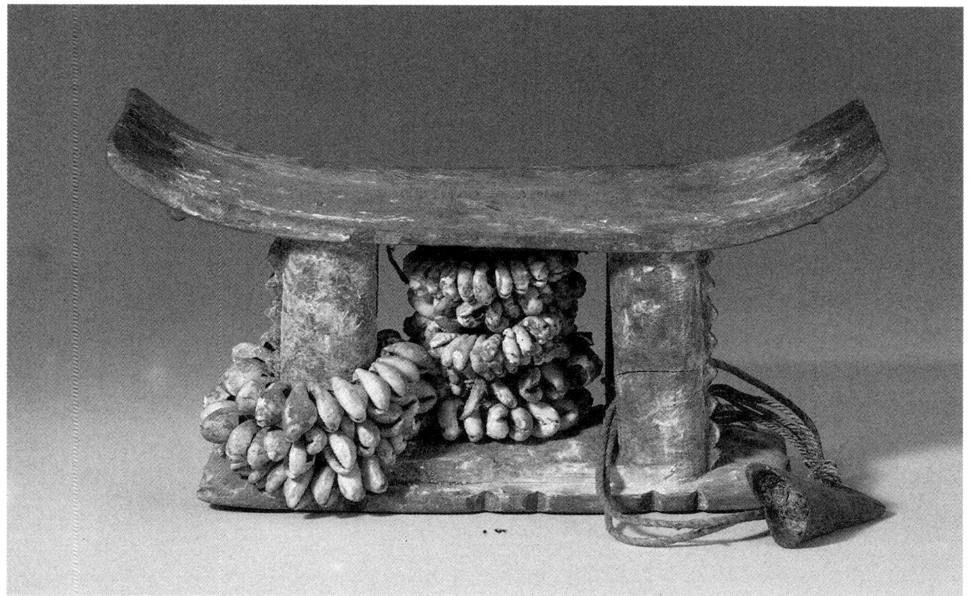

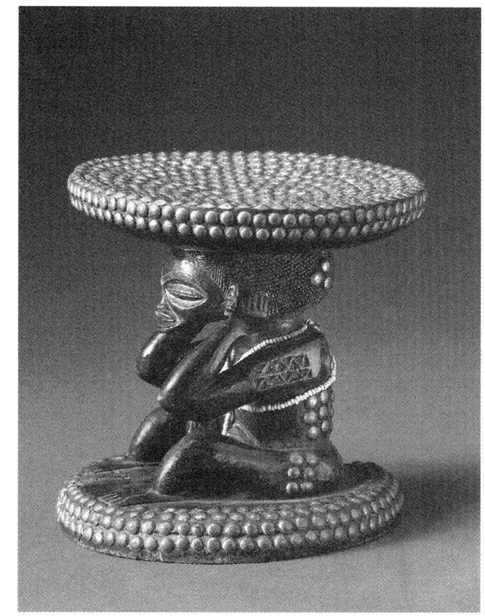

6 Stool with patina left by its use in sacrifices
Kuwe, Togo
Wood, cowrie shells, leather cord, horn, plant fibres, height 16.5 cm
Cat. 39

7 Caryatid stool
Chokwe, Zaire
Wood, brass tacks, glass beads, height 21.3 cm
Colour plate on p. 145

of Modernism and that of sub-Saharan Africa to the twentieth-century tendency towards a conceptual manner of representation. Relinquishing naturalistic reproduction and turning to a reduced graphic language, modern painters started to investigate forms of analogy of a type long familiar to Africans. Consequently, tribal art did not lead to any fundamental reorientation in modern painting; rather, it merely reinforced and sanctioned a development that was already under way.[5]

Equally important here was the authenticity and depth of the magical experience embodied in these aboriginal masks and idols: 'For me the [tribal] masks were not just sculptures,' Picasso told Malraux. 'They were magical objects . . . intercessors . . . against everything – against unknown, threatening spirits . . . . They were weapons – to keep people from being ruled by spirits, to help free themselves.'[6]

Tribal societies certainly recognize divinities, but not gods in the strict sense, that is to say divine beings removed from human society. 'The higher powers that man, whether threatened or protected, always feels surrounding and reassuring him are anything but removed. They live in man's immediate vicinity: in the nearest tree, in the nearest rock, in the lakes and rivers, in the souls of the dead and, in many cases, in the wooden figures carved for them. Each and every member of a tribe, each inhabitant of a village, is directly affected by their activity; and even if priests and medicine men act as intermediaries, they are not able to protect the individual from such influence. The directness and the immediacy of dealings with these spirits, their very familiarity and their constant presence all impinge, in a quite decisive manner, on the art through which they are encountered.'[7]

The art of sub-Saharan Africa serves primarily as a means of rendering life more secure; it is intended to protect humanity from the influence of spiritual powers that could threaten it. To this end, it must have a direct and palpable effect, that is to say it must itself be imbued with supernatural forces. The suggestive impression of something animated and alive that emanates not only from African objects of worship but also from the seats presented here is not easy to explain. Werner Schmalenbach attributes it, among other things, to the living power of the wood that can always be felt in African sculpture, even if the carver appears to have worked 'against the wood' by polishing, darkening or painting it.

In addition, the African carver often increases the magic power of his objects – be these masks, figures or items of everyday use – by adding to them alien elements

5 Rubin 1984, p. 59.
6 In Malraux 1937, cited in Rubin 1984, p. 255.
7 Schmalenbach 1988, pp. 14 ff. Werner Schmalenbach is one of the few historians of Western art to have seriously addressed the question of the aesthetic of African art. The following discussion is based on his arguments.

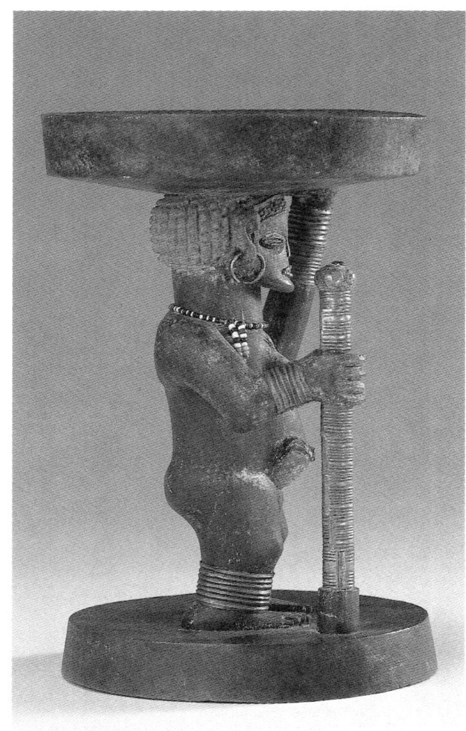

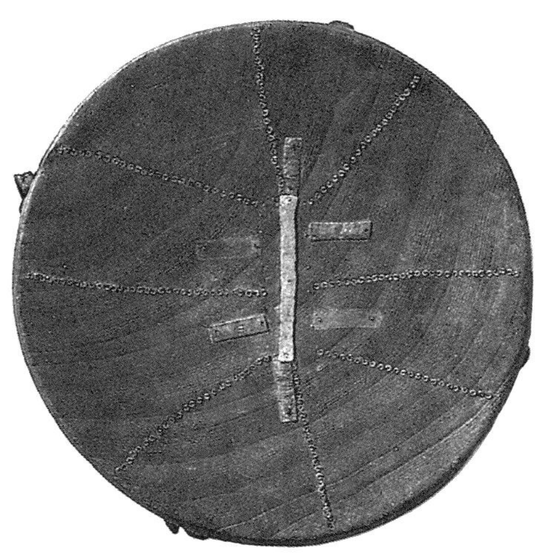

8 Caryatid stool
Chokwe, Zaire/Angola
Wood, brass tacks, copper wire, glass beads, height 31.5 cm
Colour plate on p. 146

9 Seating surface of a stool
Kamba, Kenya
Wood, copper, iron, leather, height 11.2 cm
Colour plate on p. 163

believed to be especially effective, such as teeth, hair, feathers, glass beads, pieces of mirror or metal and nails, or by rubbing oil, rust, paint, blood or other substances into their surfaces. The traces of such a process are strongly suggestive. They bear witness to the unquestioning belief in the power of supernatural beings and forces which may also take hold of the unprejudiced European observer. The horn and the cowrie shells strung on leather cord of our Kuwe stool (fig. 6), the brass tacks, the copper wire and the glass bead necklace of the two Chokwe caryatids (figs. 7, 8) and also the small copper disc and the metal intarsia of the Kamba stool (fig. 9) serve the requirements of worship and the quest for reinvigoration but also those of the display of secular and sacred power. Although the Western art lover may enjoy these magical accessories primarily from an aesthetic point of view, he is none the less susceptible to their spell and, by this means, is able to partake of a truly African feeling for life.

The conceptual form of representation and the magical aura of African objects do not, however, suffice to explain their unparalleled impact; for this is equally grounded in their formal structure. Its dominant characteristic here is an ambivalence between a state of rest and one of unrest, an exciting combination of the measured and the dynamic. Physical activity, that is to say the representation of animal or human figures in motion, is very rare in African art. Its figurative creations are distinguished by their frontality, the clear organization of their parts, an emphasis on the central axis and the almost always total symmetry. This fundamentally static character would appear to contradict their dynamism; but in fact it constitutes its precondition. 'If the figures in African art virtually always stand or sit as if at rest,' Schmalenbach observes, 'this is above all because their activity is not that of the human body.'[8] Their effectiveness depends on an inner store of energy. It is as if the body must keep still so that this energy may come into its own. It is not manifest through any continuous organic movement but finds expression in the confrontation of distinct volumes, surface patterns and body parts, and in the abrupt impact of one formal element on another.

This discontinuity and the rhythm that it inevitably sets up constitute a basic principle of African art – and one that has its equivalent in African music.[9] This basic principle emerges in especially distinct form in the caryatid stools of the Luba and the Songye: the markedly architectonic structure of their figures, as in the example opposite (figs. 10, 11), is emphasized by the disregard for a naturalistic proportion. The oversized, rounded head, the protruding and pointed rump and stomach, the large, stereometric feet and the short bent legs of this female figure combine to produce a rhythmic entity – full of tension, rich in contrasts and extremely dynamic – that finds its formal, as well as functional, resolution in the stool's seating surface. This powerful dynamism is taken up in the patterns of the tattoo scars and the extremely elaborate coiffure (fig. 10).

Like the art of the European Middle Ages, African art is a collective undertaking. Most of its creations present types of masks and figures that are defined by tradition. The formal concept of these basic types establishes a structure that provides the individual artist with support and orientation but severely restricts the scope for individual initiative. None the less, clear differences in aesthetic quality are to be detected: the expressive power and sensitivity of a few exceptional works reveal the enormous individual talent and the superior ability of their respective makers. The same is true of objects of everyday use in Africa.

In the case of the caryatid stools, thrones and ritual seats we have mentioned, the 'plastic' quality – the clarity and decisiveness in their formal construction – tends to be eclipsed by their spectacular appearance and is thus very often insufficiently appreciated by the inexperienced observer. Not so with the unpretentious stools intended for everyday use, in which I see the real 'discovery' and the subtle 'sen-

8 Schmalenbach 1988, p. 19.
9 Transformed into jazz, this had as far-reaching an influence on modern music as did African sculpture on the visual art of the West.

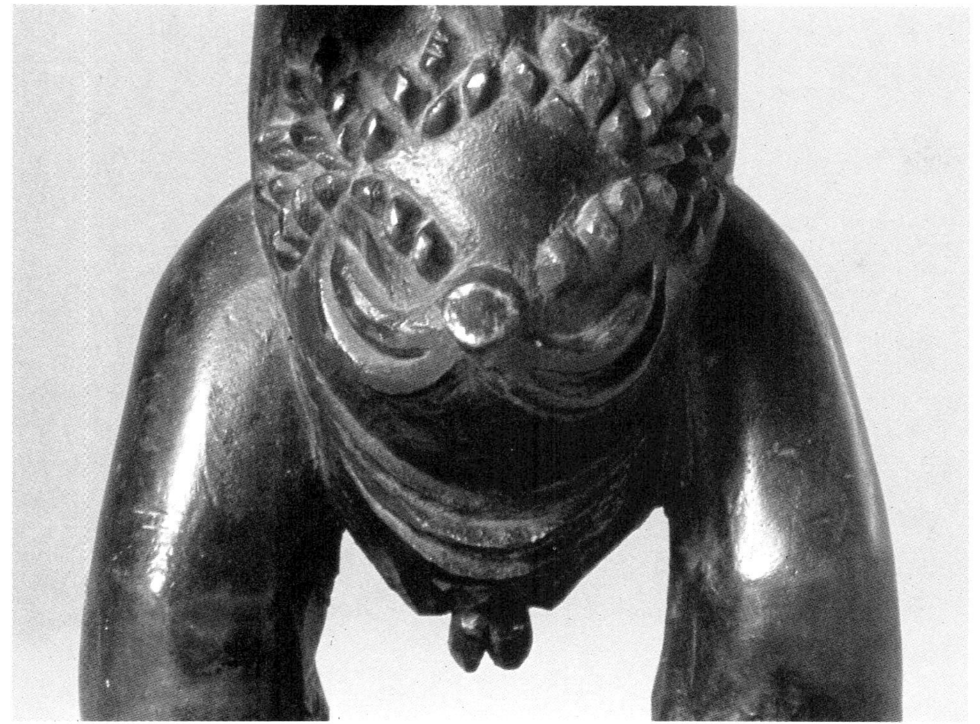

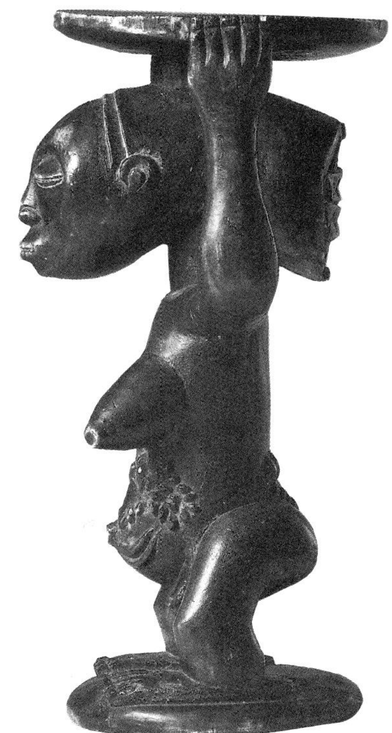

10, 11 Caryatid stool (with detail of frontal view)
Luba, Zaire
Wood, height 41.5 cm
Colour plate on p. 112

sation' of this exhibition. They are limited to an elementary form of support and their makers have withheld any decorative embellishment: the exciting tension of their equilibrium thus emerges all the more powerfully.

These stools, traditionally fixed in their shape, but varying with regions and peoples, are (like the caryatid seats) monoxylous, that is to say carved, in sculptural fashion, from a single block of wood. Their basic shape is either a cylinder or, more rarely, a cube (figs. 12–17). The enormous variation among the seat types evolved from these two basic shapes itself offers compelling evidence of the astonishing richness of invention to which African carvers can lay claim. And we have not even touched on such bold artefacts as the semi-reclining chairs unique to the Lobi and the Gurunsi (fig. 18).

If one compares any of these austerely worked seats with the minimalistic creations of modern furniture design (fig. 19), one is struck by obvious formal similarities but also by a series of fundamental differences. The African seats testify, without exception, to an all-embracing image of the self and the world, to a direct, sensual relationship with both the natural and the man-made environment that has long been lost to our own culture.

For one thing, there is the striking difference in height: African seats vary between 8 and 30 centimetres, European chairs between 48 and 50 centimetres. The former range corresponds to the squatting position widely adopted in Africa, thereby evoking a way of life that has its natural resting and working place on the ground. Secondly, one notes that, because of the way in which African seats are made (worked entirely by hand and dispensing with any mechanical assistance), no two examples are identical, not even when they belong to the same basic type. Departures from the norm at which the carver has aimed are unavoidable. The wood resists his creative intent, and this resistance is reflected in the multitude of small irregularities that bestow on each stool a subtle, individual character.

An additional factor to which these modest objects owe their innate 'living' character is the patina, which gives them a dark, silky sheen, especially notable on their slightly concave seating surfaces. These traces of years of loving use bear

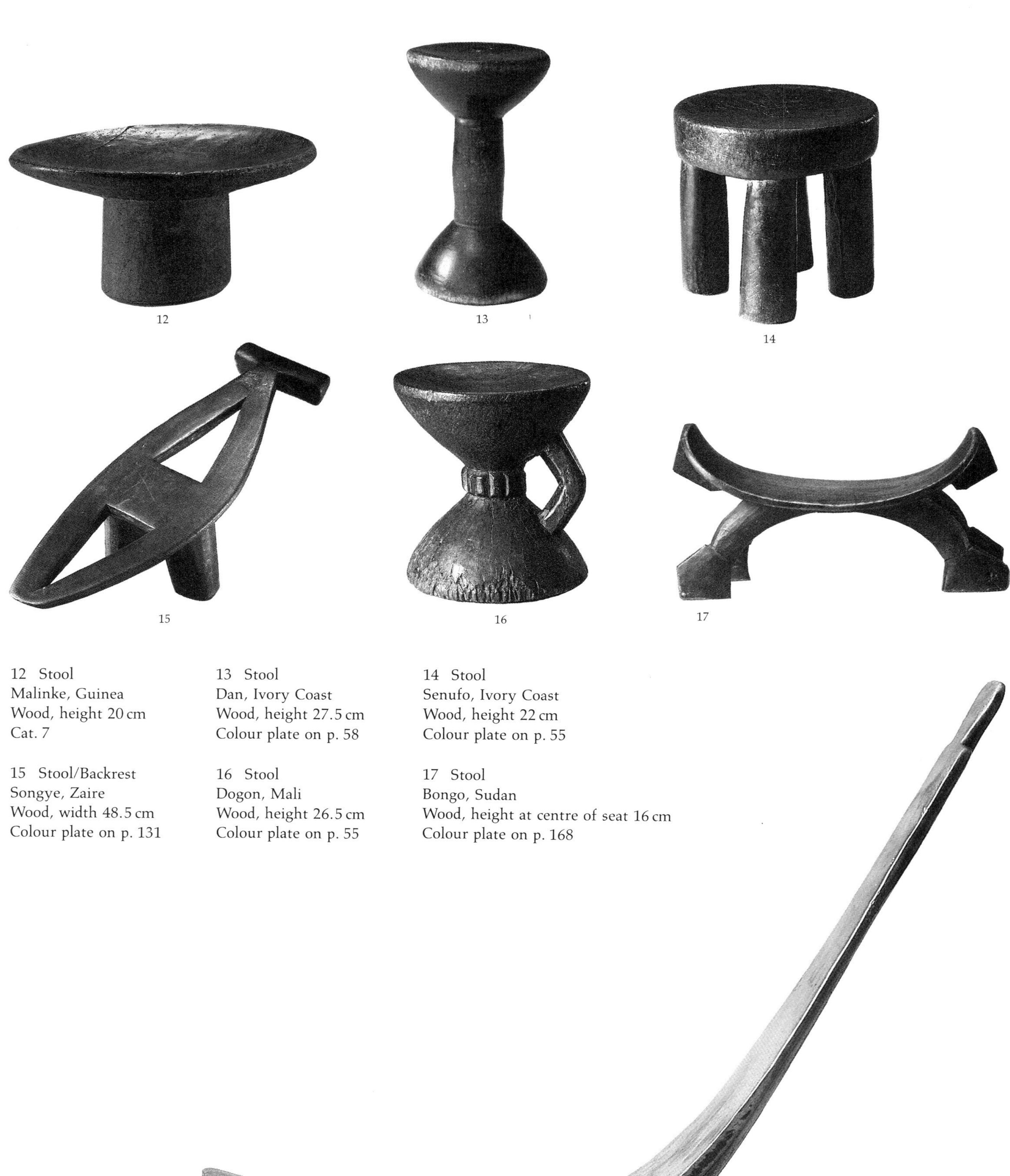

12 Stool
Malinke, Guinea
Wood, height 20 cm
Cat. 7

13 Stool
Dan, Ivory Coast
Wood, height 27.5 cm
Colour plate on p. 58

14 Stool
Senufo, Ivory Coast
Wood, height 22 cm
Colour plate on p. 55

15 Stool/Backrest
Songye, Zaire
Wood, width 48.5 cm
Colour plate on p. 131

16 Stool
Dogon, Mali
Wood, height 26.5 cm
Colour plate on p. 55

17 Stool
Bongo, Sudan
Wood, height at centre of seat 16 cm
Colour plate on p. 168

18 Semi-reclining chair
Lobi, Ivory Coast
Wood, max. height 59 cm
Colour plate on p. 54

witness not only to the sensual presence of our distant relatives – of the weight of their bodies and the power of their movements – but also help us to grasp the place that these objects occupied in their owners' minds and emotions.

In his essay (see pp. 31–7), Roy Sieber refers to the personal character of African household objects, which is especially marked in the case of seats. According to his account, an African would be shocked if anyone else – be it a member of the same family, a friend or a stranger – used his seat. In the context of European culture, such a relationship between an everyday object and its owner is only familiar from the pre-industrial period. The photograph of a pile of used Senufo stools, on sale in a shop in Korhogo (fig. 20), reveals that, in Africa too, this attitude has since become a thing of the past.

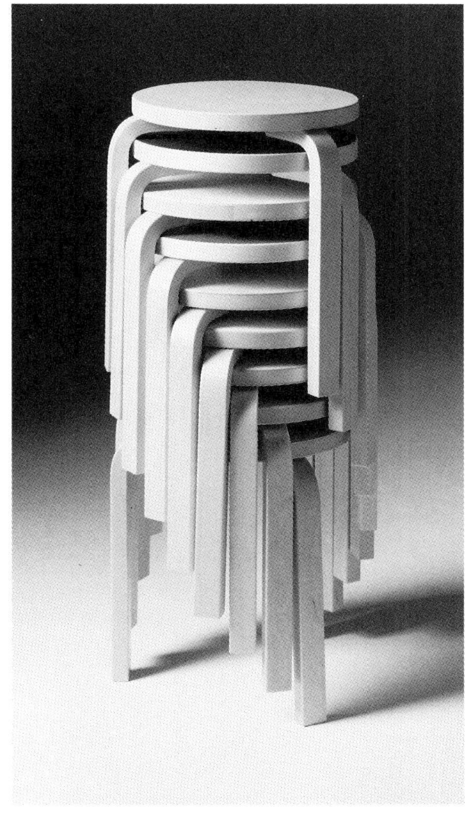

19 Alvar Aalto, Stackable stools, model 60, 1930–3, birchwood, seating surface covered with linoleum. (Photograph: artek, Helsinki)

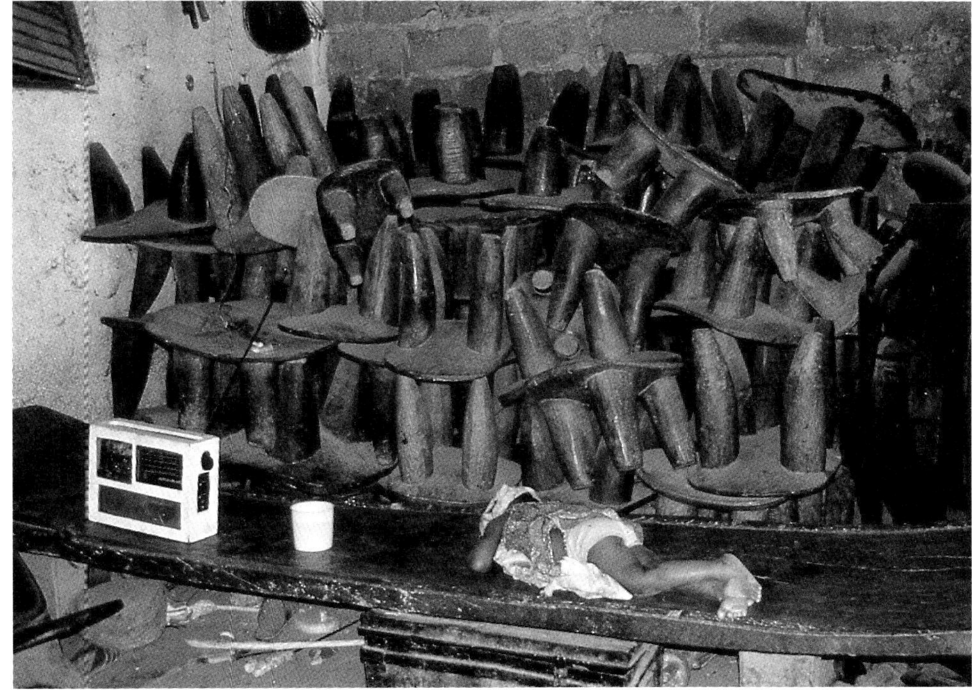

20 Shop in Korhogo, Ivory Coast, with used, traditional Senufo stools for sale to tourists. (Photograph: Jean Paul Barbier, 1990)

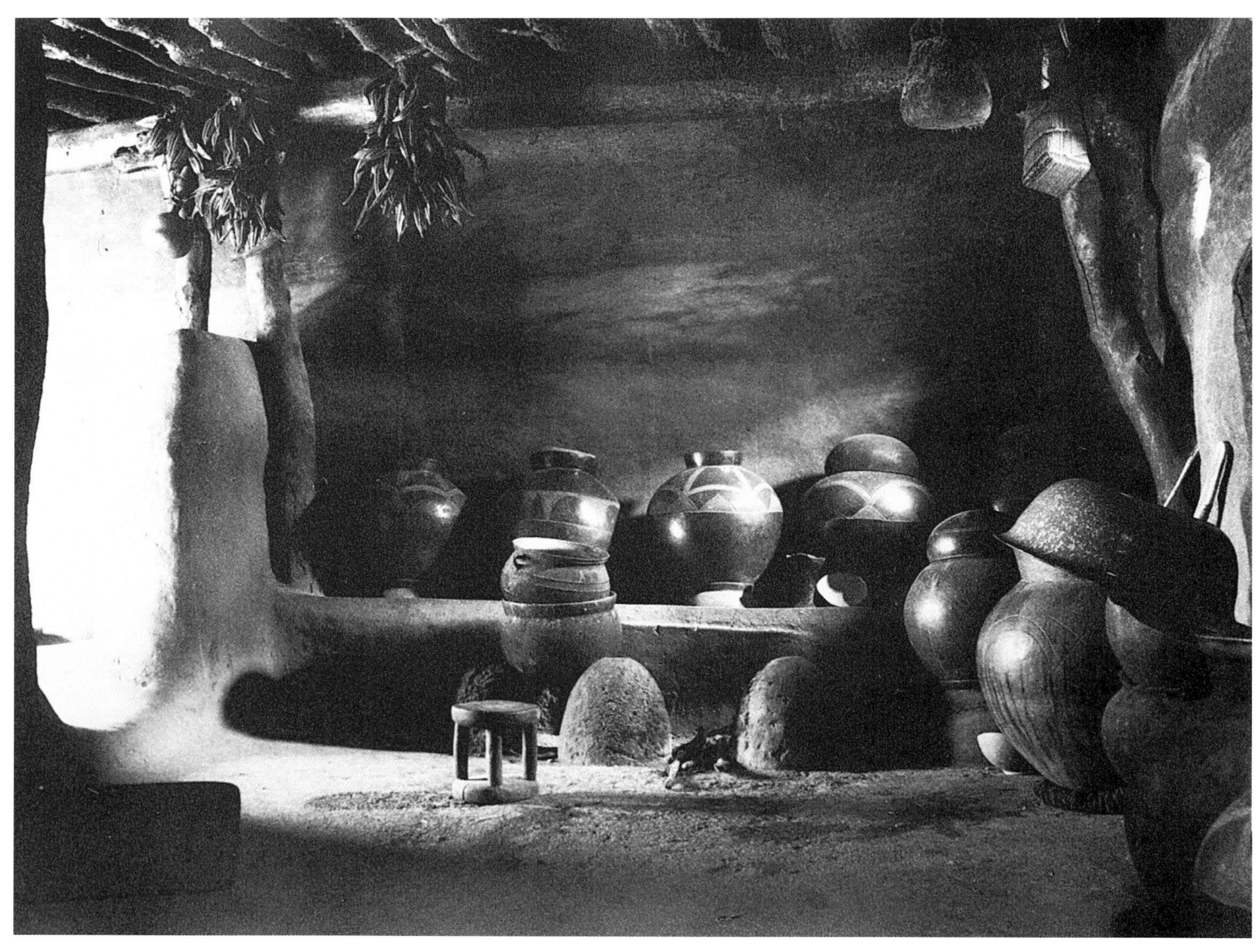

1 Cooking area in the room of a Lobi woman in Wourbia, Burkina Faso. The Lobi live in cool mud houses, with narrow doors and windows. The women, responsible for most of the housework, carry out their tasks while seated on small stools. (Photograph: Piet Meyer, 1980)

Lorenz Homberger and Piet Meyer

Concerning African Objects

Today our civilization is so rich in objects and furniture of every kind that we are usually no longer aware of what it is that distinguishes our surroundings. From the earliest times man used objects in order to make his domestic life easier. In many regions of the world – in those areas inhabited by so-called 'primitive' peoples – it has been considered important that these objects should be not only useful but also beautifully made. Those commissioning them frequently requested rich decoration so as to express their own high social standing; and in these cases the materials used – ivory, rare woods, imported items – were often invested with a sense of prestige. Special objects like these, though also those of extreme formal simplicity, were treasured by their owners and were regarded as important personal possessions. They were used with care, and attention was paid to the preservation of their original condition. If they were damaged, much time was spent in restoring them. For all their familiarity, their owners took great pleasure in them and derived from them a feeling of pride and prestige. In modern Western society, on the other hand, everyday objects are taken for granted, both because replacements are always available and because the functional and practical is usually rated above the aesthetic.

In African cultures it is not often easy to distinguish between domestic and specialized techniques of handicraft. Basket weaving and related activities, for example, might be taken for domestic skills. In reality, there are women who are specialists in this field and who largely work to commission. Comparable borderline cases are to be found among potters, smiths, woodcarvers and cloth weavers.

Because of the prestige that was seen to derive from these objects, some of them were used as dowries or exchanged, as signs of well-wishing, between dignitaries. Traditionally, personal objects such as pipes, stools, neck-rests and tools were either destroyed on their owner's death or – even though classed among profane, worldly objects – buried along with him.

There seems no likelihood that everyday objects of this sort will continue to be produced on a large scale. Contact with the modern world has brought cheap factory produce to even the remotest villages of the Dark Continent. Even in those regions where, in the past, a subtly decorated calabash would have been presented to the honoured guest, it is now the kitschy porcelain plate from Hong Kong that has become an object of prestige. The continuing production of objects made by local craftsmen now has to meet the demand established by all the dealers whose customers, principally tourists, look for souvenirs in the larger African cities. The neck-rests, weavers' bobbins and spoons they buy may come from Dakar or Mombasa, but also from street traders in Paris or New York. All these objects display signs of decadent mass-production and, although generally well made, they are essentially mere imitations without any of the aura or excitement of the real thing. For some time now a shockingly large proportion of African art production has consisted of fakes, sophisticated techniques being employed to evoke the impression of age and use. None the less, above all in rural regions, there persists a demand for everyday household objects made in the traditional manner – whether this be because a home-made cooking spoon is even cheaper than an aluminium ladle or

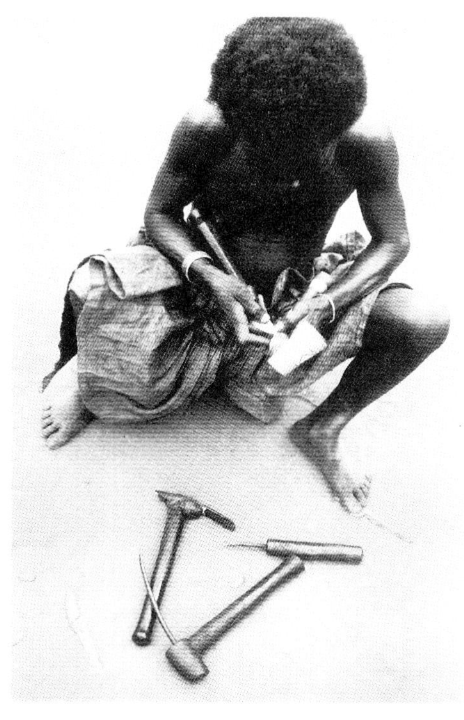

2 Carver of the Shobwa-Kuba with his tools, Zaire. African carvers produce even their finest work with relatively large and simply produced tools. (Photograph: Hans Himmelheber, 1938/9)

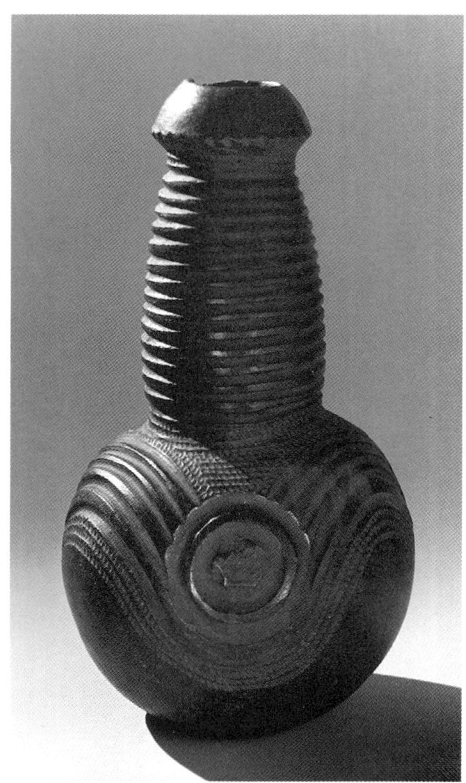

3 Vessel from the Boa region, Northern Zaire
Clay, height 23 cm
Museum Rietberg, Zurich

because certain medicines may only be cooked and stored in traditionally produced clay pots.

The old cosmos of African objects is impressive – even if we do not take into account here the masks and figures now all too familiar in the West: engraved ostrich eggs, combs with figurative decoration, dolls, toys, local forms of money, decorated pipe bowls and tobacco mortars, musical instruments, weapons, rods and maces used in dances and ceremonies, objects grouped in a special manner of magical significance, the instruments and paraphernalia of augury, basketwork and of course textiles, jewellery and various small art objects made of metal and ivory, and, as already mentioned, pottery. From a historiographical point of view, it is interesting that earlier researchers in Africa repeatedly described religious and magical objects such as masks, figures used in worship, and instruments used by soothsayers, yet hardly mentioned, and even more rarely published, objects of everyday use: forms of furniture for sleeping and sitting, looms and household utensils. In the following discussion we shall deal with a number of objects that are especially distinguished from the point of view of their design.

It is no coincidence that in his extensive *Ethnologie de la chambre à coucher*, Pascal Dibie included only a few examples from sub-Saharan Africa. As a rule the culture of the bedroom is not especially developed in this continent. Many Africans are happy simply to roll out what we would regard as a rather thin mat on their own smoothed out area of a floor covered with home-made cement, and to sleep there. We know of very few African 'beds' in our sense of this term, that is to say objects constructed specifically for the purpose of sleeping. Roy Sieber distinguishes three types of bed found south of the Sahara. The first is a couch carved out of a single block of wood (that is to say, monoxylous) – as a rule rectangular and the length of a man – that either lies like a box on the floor or is raised up on four legs. The second is a berth constructed out of wooden sticks, the spines of palm leaves and other bits and pieces. The third is a bed made out of dried mud and securely wedged between wall and floor.

Far more familiar to us is another piece of African furniture associated with sleeping – the neck-rest. Also known as the head-stool, neck-stool or headrest, this is usually made out of wood, more rarely out of ivory, pottery or stone. This item really comes into its own in cultures that place great stress on large and elaborate

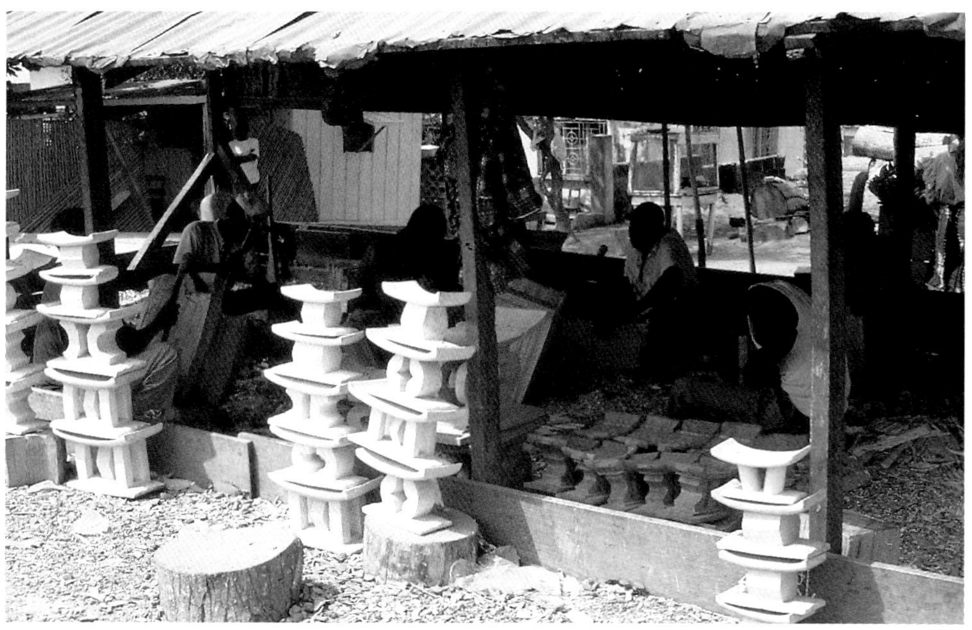

4 Carver's workshop in Ahwiaa, Ghana. The small upturned stools have yet to be stained and polished. They are intended for sale in the numerous souvenir shops located along the street. Nowadays most stools are produced to appeal to the taste of European and (Afro-) American tourists: that is to say, extremely richly carved and stained the colour of mahogany. (Photograph: Andrea Knecht Oti-Amoako, 1994)

coiffures intended to last for some time. The neck-rest is then used to raise the head from the ground so as to protect the coiffure. The traditional means of creating such coiffures, where this is still practised, takes half a day or more; and the finished product is intended to remain undisturbed for some time. (We shall leave aside the question of whether such coiffures follow the dictates of fashion or of religion or respond to socio-political considerations.) It is difficult for us to imagine how so hard an object as a neck-rest could be used at all: sleepers usually lie on their sides so that the support holds the head just below the ear, in effect between head and neck (fig. 7).

From the formal point of view, neck-rests are very varied. Throughout Africa they usually stand on one, two or three legs and are small and easily portable. Only a few have a human or animal figure (even fewer an object) serving as a caryatid to support the horizontal section with its head or hands or on the curve formed by its bent back. Naturally, it is these figurative neck-rests, such as the one of the Yaka in Zaire shown here (fig. 5), that are best known in the West; but most neck-rests are much more simply carved. Often, as a makeshift solution, they are made straight from the forked branch of a tree that already has the right shape to provide two or three legs and a supporting surface. In many cases neck-rests were used as seats during the day; and, if especially beautiful and finely carved, they often became a status symbol. A talented carver could ask a high price for a fine piece of work. In older cultures neck-rests were often buried along with their owners if these had been influential figures. The oldest surviving African examples (mostly made of alabaster and wood) come from Ancient Egypt.

Neck-rests are not, or rather were not, found throughout Africa. In the western regions, for example, they were very rare indeed; in Central Africa they were more common and were often equipped with caryatid figures of the sort we have mentioned. They were most commonly found, however, among the societies of East Africa, above all those of the semi-nomadic peoples of Uganda, Kenya and Somalia. Here, in cultures not very rich in terms of material possessions, neck-rests, as also stools, were seen as one of the most important status symbols for men (fig. 6).

We shall turn now to a small object that plays a part in the work-oriented world of the peoples of West Africa – the weaver's bobbin (fig. 11). When, in 1933, the German art ethnologist Hans Himmelheber asked why a West African small-gauge loom was decorated with an elaborately carved bobbin, he was told by a weaver of the Guro: 'It's impossible to live without these beautiful things.' Fifty years later we received the same answer. We shall not here attempt, once again, to justify the use of such artistic objects by reference to religion or magic. Both weavers and sculptors insist repeatedly that decorated bobbins are displayed in this way on account of their beauty. As is frequently the case with African works of art, we find in the case of the weaver's bobbins a wide variety of style and quality. They range from naïvely carved forms to the most refined motifs, from plain, almost abstractly simplified heads to those that are rendered in realistic detail, not to mention the many gradations between such extremes. The work of different hands can also be distinguished, although the result is often so similar that it is hard to believe one is not looking at deliberate copies.

From the realm of African eating culture, to which many beautiful objects belong (bowls, cups, drinking horns, decorated calabashes and – very important – the broad range of ever-varying and bewilderingly shaped pottery), we will single out one small item – the wooden spoon. From the earliest times the spoon has served man as an important instrument for the preparation and consumption of food. It was principally required to transfer hot food, in the form of thin or thick liquids, from one container to another. Astonishingly, the use of spoons was only very rarely recorded by ethnographers, and this is the more surprising if we consider that the

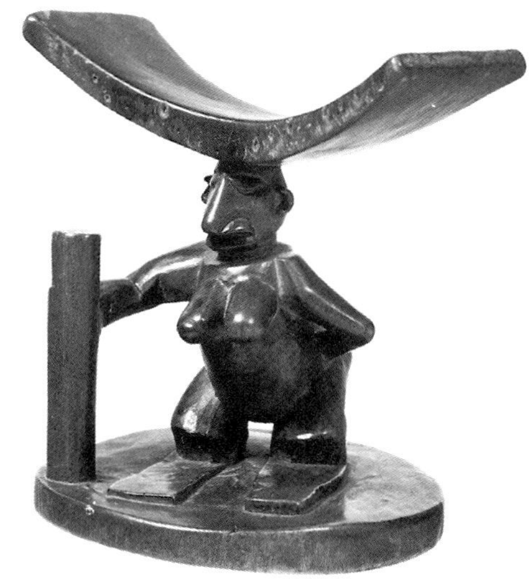

5 Neck-rest
Workshop of the Yaka region, Zaire
Wood, height 19.5 cm
Museum Rietberg, Zurich

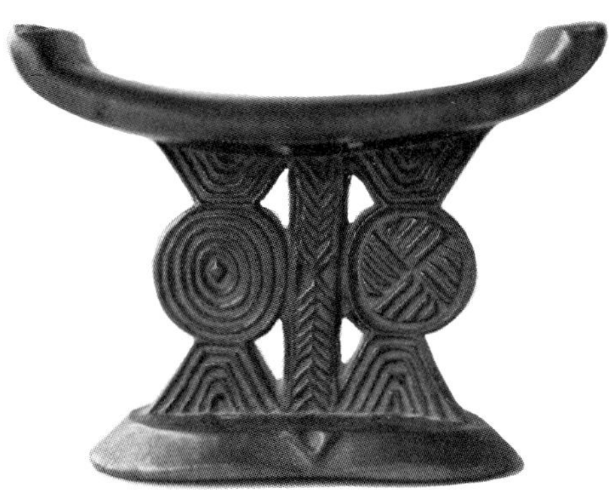

6 Neck-rest
Workshop of the Shona region, Zimbabwe
Wood, height 18 cm
Private collection

7 A neck-rest in use, Samburu region, Kenya. (Photograph: Katherine C. White, 1978)

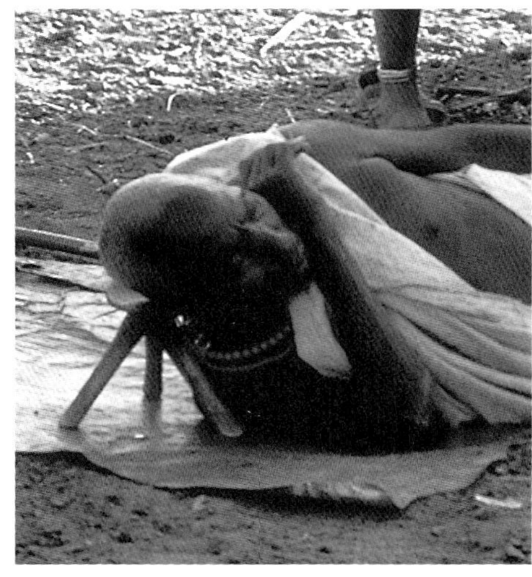

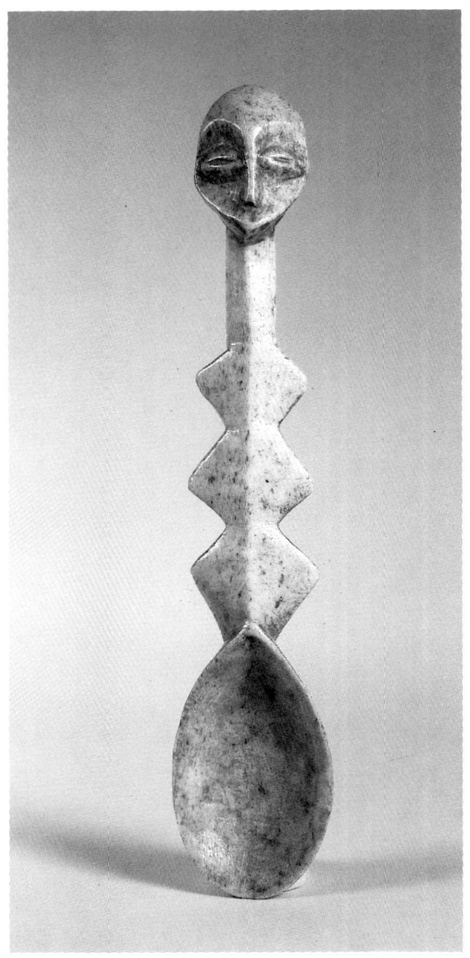

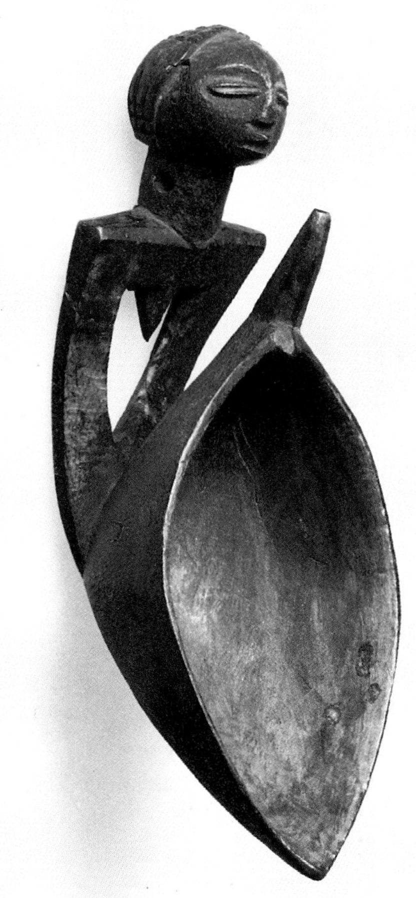

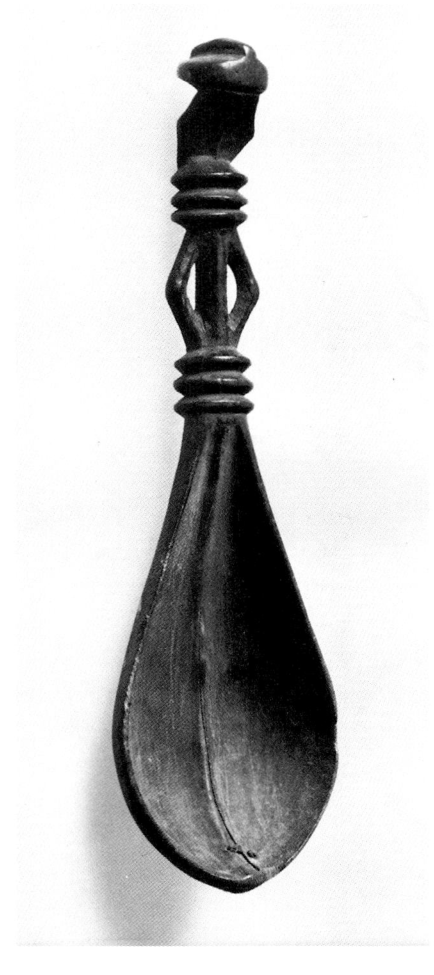

8 Spoon
Workshop of the Lega region, Zaire
Ivory, height 25.4 cm
Private collection

9 Spoon
Workshop of the Tabwa region, Zaire
Wood, height 24 cm
Museum für Völkerkunde, Berlin

10 Spoon
Workshop of the Lega region, Zaire
Wood, height 24.2 cm
Museum für Völkerkunde, Berlin

spoon had already appeared in the pre-colonial period in many parts of West and Central Africa. In some regions it was removed from its original functional significance as a utensil for making and consuming meals and – as in the case of the Dan in Liberia – offered for sale by art dealers as a 'ritual object'. Alternatively, as with certain spoons from Gabon, it took on a new role as an object of prestige and display. We know of some African spoons that are small and delicately formed; but there are also large ladles that are plain but very inspired in their carving. As in the case of the weaver's bobbin, we find that these simple utensils can be transformed, in the hands of a master, into works of art that meet the highest aesthetic criteria. In the case of spoons, their makers have broken with established formal limitations regardless of these objects' practical or ritual significance (figs. 8–10). From out of the tension between intended function and the desire for artistic freedom there has emerged a wide range of forms.

Tables – understood as raised planar supports resting on legs – did not exist in traditional societies south of the Sahara. We in the West eat at tables, work at tables and meet each other – whether at home or in cafés or in conferences – at tables. In sub-Saharan Africa, on the other hand, people sat or squatted on the ground in order to eat, or they sat on small chairs or stools. It is true that meeting places within a house or a village were distinguished in some way; but they were not marked by the presence of tables. And what of chairs, stools and smaller supports? These were to be found in a thousand different shapes and variations, and were predominantly made of wood, much more rarely of stone and ivory. The simplest were the very basic supports made, for example, from the forked branch of a tree which already had a suitable shape (fig. 14; cats. 94 and 95). These objects, manufactured with the least effort, often have for us the charm of an 'objet trouvé'. Better known in the West are the many stools that are more refined and delicate in their workmanship. Such simple forms of seating, it is true, provide support for neither the back nor the arms; but they are made in accordance with a very precisely fixed aesthetic canon. Its interpretation differs, however, from region to region, so that the origin of individual items is easy to identify.

The basic form of the stool is circular or, more rarely, square. The stool may be made out of a single piece of wood (monoxylous) or – rather more rarely – assembled from several parts. The seating surface may be supported by one or several legs or it may be part of a continuously solid body that rests directly on the ground. It goes without saying that stools, individually produced and worked by hand, may be produced with greater or lesser care.

The small, light wooden stools used, or formerly used, by the various semi-nomadic cattle-breeders of East Africa are sometimes real works of sculpture. Their form is extremely, almost puristically, reduced. Through years of domestic use, these objects have developed a wonderful, gleaming, deep brown patina, highly valued by collectors in the West. In many of the societies in which these stools originated their use was reserved for the older men; and these, when out and about, often carried their stools around with them, attached by a cord (fig. 13).

A third type of stool is the so-called 'caryatid stool', with its seat surface borne by a figure. This figure can be human or animal, and its burden may be carried on its head, on its back or on its hands. The seats of caryatid stools are generally higher than in the types of stool we have so far discussed; yet they too generally have neither back nor arm supports. Such stools, of extremely fine workmanship, used to be especially common in Zaire and Angola, that is to say in a region where powerful kingdoms flourished (cats. 127–138). Rich or privileged individuals favoured the use of an iconography of power in the decoration of such items.

Are chairs in the European sense to be found at all in traditional African societies? They are, but they have occurred only very rarely and have then been reserved for tribal headsmen, notabilities, princes and kings. Such stools had an unambiguous political function: they signalled the power of those who often had the unique right to use them. They have been, in effect, thrones. Many of these African thrones count as early examples of what more recent literature has termed 'contact

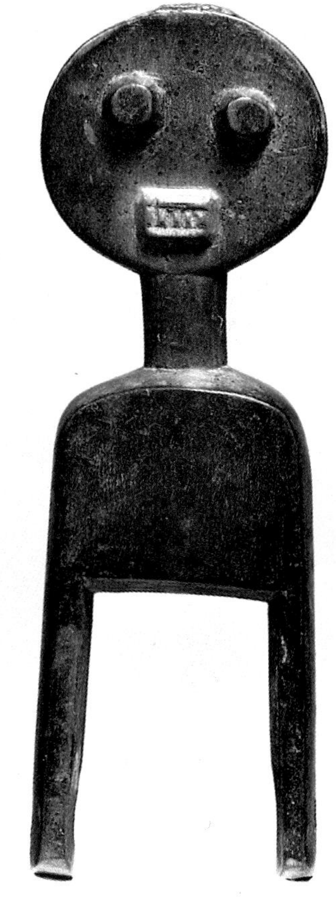

11 Weaver's bobbin
Workshop of the Asante region, Ghana
Wood, height 17 cm
Musem Rietberg, Zurich

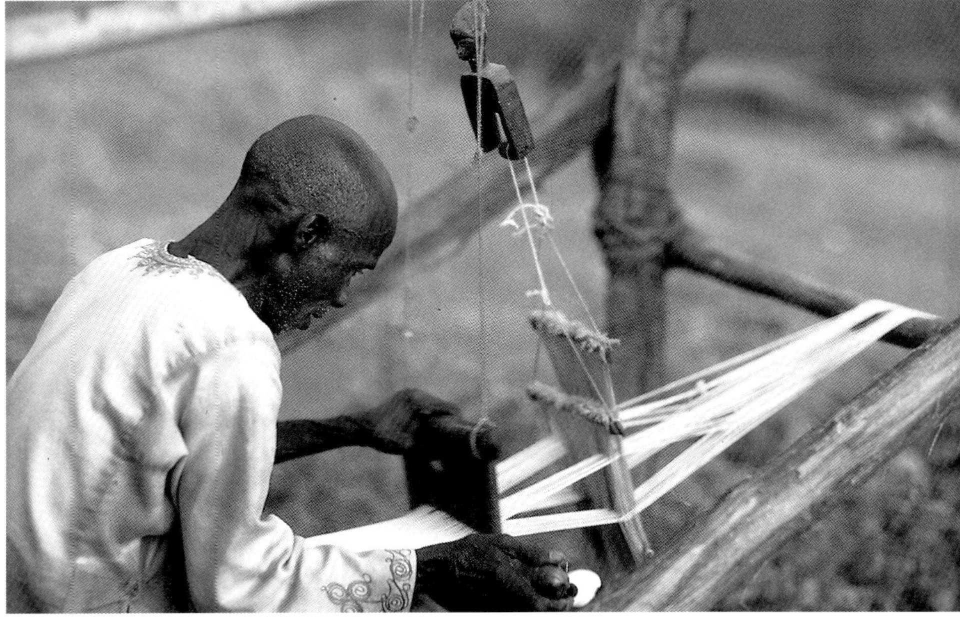

12 Guro weaver in Brodufla, Ivory Cast. Clearly visible at the upper edge of the illustration is the small bobbin through which runs the string that is attached to the two shuttles. (Photograph: Lorenz Homberger, 1983)

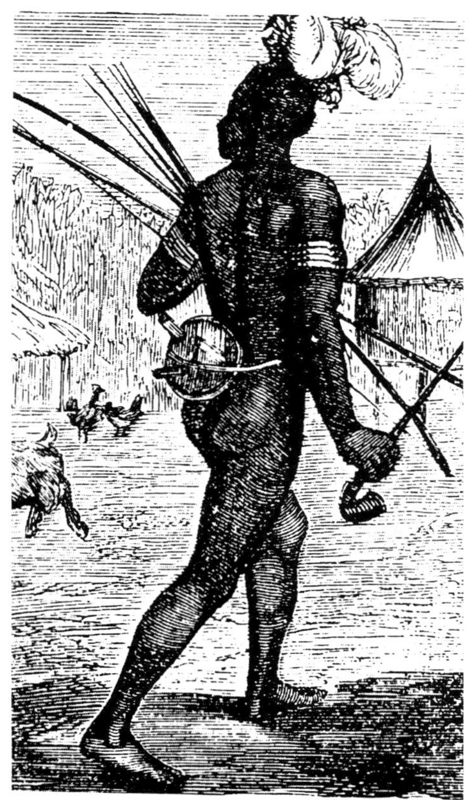

13 In this engraving of 1871 by the Reverend J. G. Wood, a man of the Bari from the Sudan is shown carrying about with him his three-legged stool, as well as his weapons and his pipe. In East Africa one finds relatively few sacred art objects; but this region offers a wealth of splendidly designed everyday objects.

art' – an art evolving from the contact between Africa and Western civilization. In the context of our present concerns, the best known examples are probably the prestige chairs of the Pende and Chokwe in Zaire and Angola, carved with elaborate figural embellishments (fig. 15; photograph on p. 151; cats. 114–121). In the seventeenth century the Chokwe encountered the European chairs that Portuguese merchants brought with them to West Africa. They copied these, but transformed the European models through the application of their own formal vocabulary to the original designs. The result was an entirely new and independent sculptural creation which was then fully integrated into Chokwe culture and passed down through the generations.

In addition to the political significance we have already mentioned in connection with African stools and chairs, these items could also have important psychological and religious connotations. Among the Asante in Ghana, for example, a stool was not simply an object to be used by anyone at any time. It was the absolutely personal possession of its owner and regarded as the seat of his soul. For this reason, the owner, when not using his stool, would always lay it on its side, so that no one – neither man nor spirit – might use it and thus pollute it (figs. on pp. 31, 74; cat. 35). This belief in the animation of the seat went so far that, after a king's death, his principal stool would be kept in a royal ancestral shrine and ritually honoured as ancestor statues were honoured elsewhere in Africa (fig. 4, on p. 33). The Asante, moreover, still possess a Golden Stool that is seen as the collective soul of the Asante people. No one may sit on it, not even the king. It was introduced by Osei Tutu, the first king of the Asante, as the central and highest symbol of kingship (fig. on p. 31).

14 A pygmy of the Efé in Zaire, smoking as he lounges on a semi-reclining chair made from a tree root. The simplest forms of seating are carved from a piece of wood that already possesses a suitable shape, for example a forked branch. In such cases the natural form is hardly altered by the maker's intervention. (Photograph: Paul Schebesta, 1930 or 1934/5)

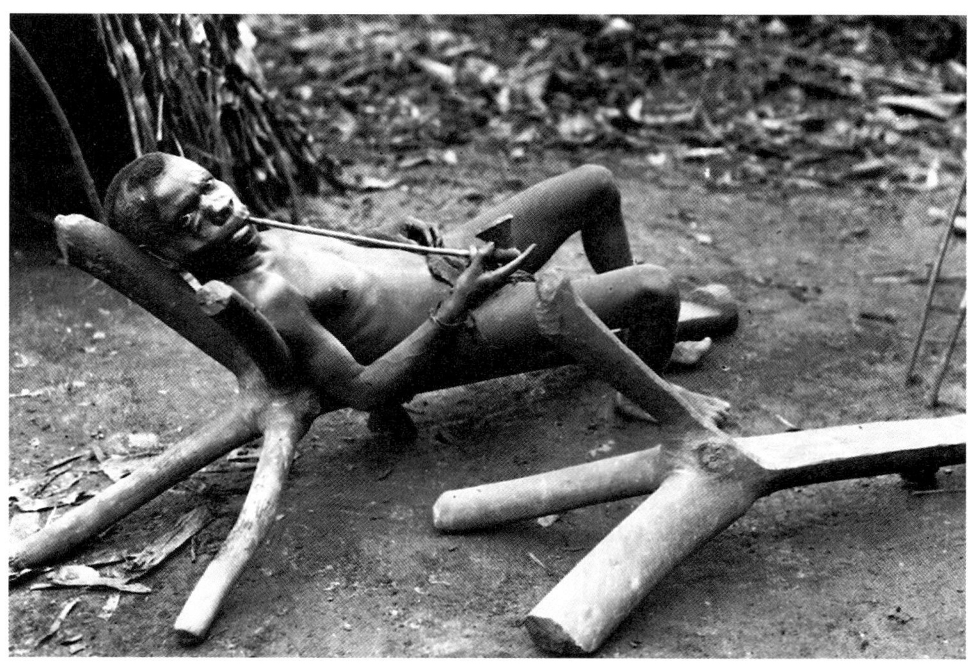

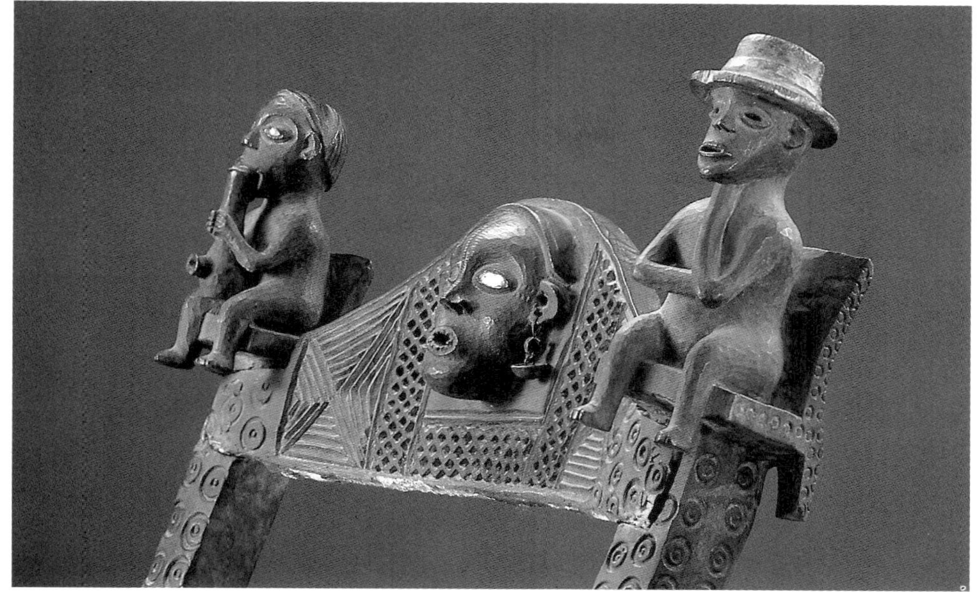

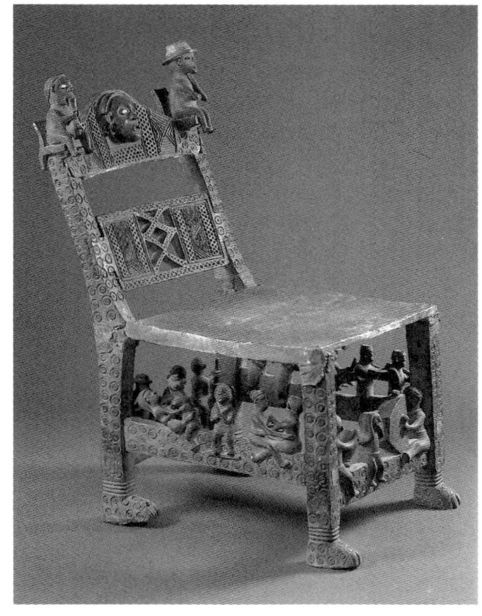

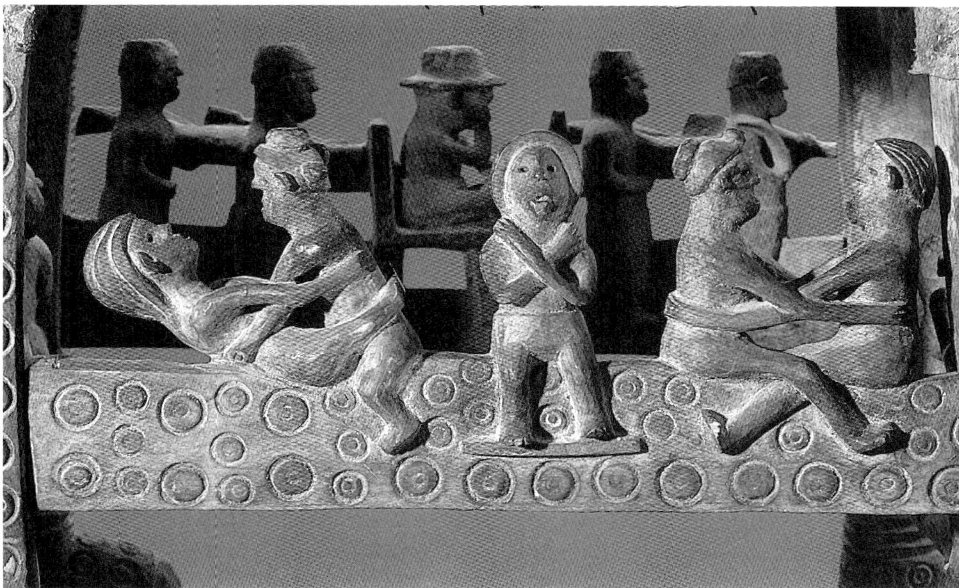

15–17 Chair of the Pende (with details), Zaire
Museum Rietberg, Zurich
Chiefs' chairs of this type are imitations of European armchairs of the sixteenth and seventeenth centuries. Their decorations, however, adhere to traditional local motifs from everyday life or from history, religion and mythology; cf. cat. 114.

Literature (for details see pp. 197–9):

Himmelheber 1935 (cf. pp. 42–3 of the present volume); Sieber 1972; Picton/Mack 1979; Sieber 1980; Fischer/Homberger 1985; Dibie 1987; Vogel 1988; Falgayrettes 1989; Fischer/Himmelheber, in Homberger 1990; Homberger 1990; Siroto, in Homberger 1990; Ravenhill 1992.

This essay is a slightly altered version of a text first appearing in: Claudette Sèze (ed.): *Confort moderne: Une novelle culture du bien-être*, Série sciences en société, no. 10, Paris, 1994

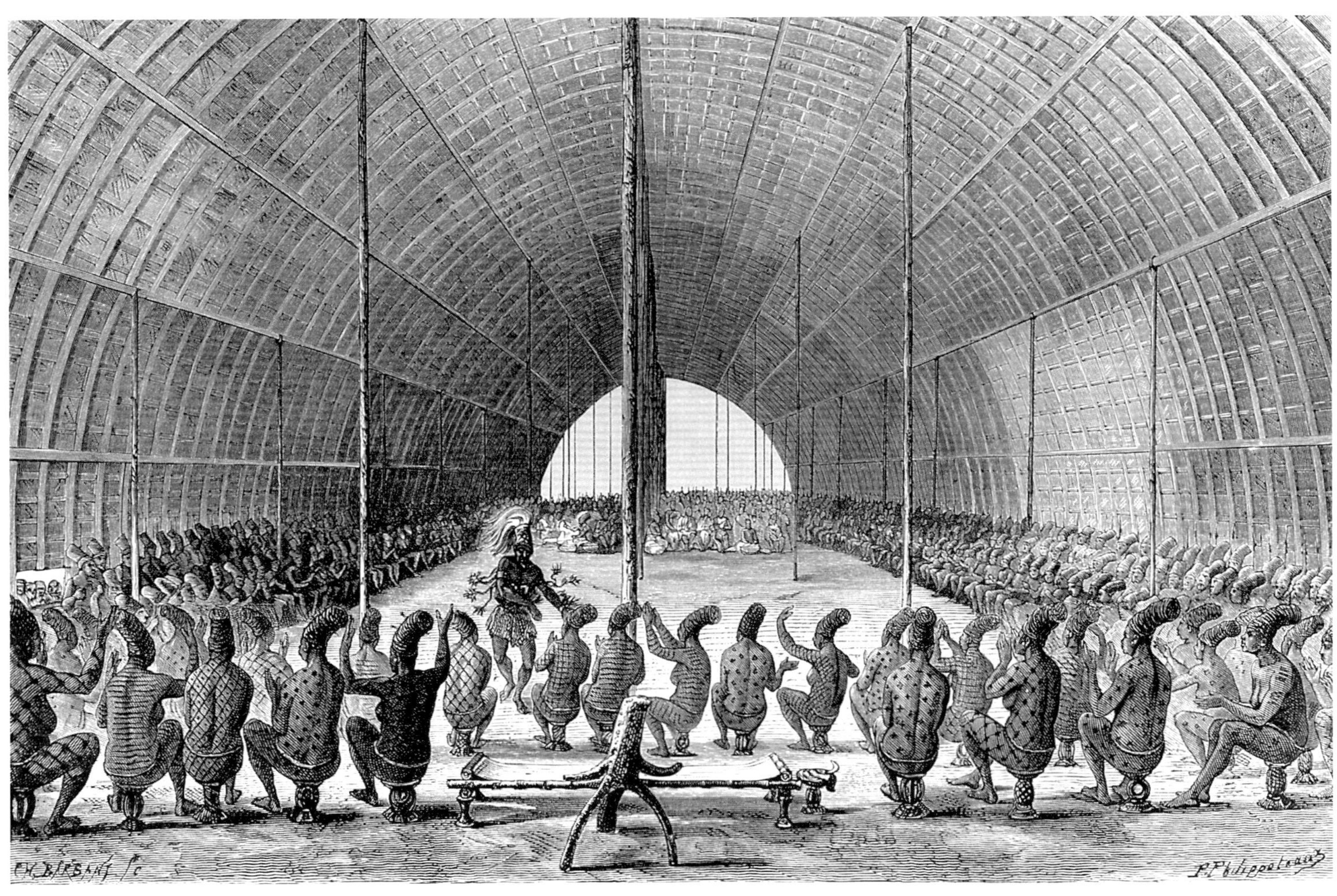

1 King Munsa of the Mangbetu 'in full dress', dancing for his wives, who are shown seated on stools. The king's throne in the foreground combines a typical bed form with a tripod backrest; cf. plate on p. 129. A similar scene was recorded in 1913 by the photographer Herbert Lang; cf. fig. on p. 110. The kings of the Mangbetu might have as many as two hundred wives. On the wives' body painting, cf. fig. on p. 126. (Woodcut from Schweinfurth 1873, vol ii, frontis.)

Roy Sieber

African Furniture between Tradition and Colonization

Societies in Africa, as in all other parts of the world, have always been in a state of flux. The study of change is, of course, what constitutes history. From the written and oral histories of kingdoms and empires, of peoples and places, the flow of change in the form of objects can often be reconstructed. This is as true of everyday utensils as it is of masks, figures, ceramics, architecture, kingly regalia or ordinary dress. Unfortunately, unlike much of the history of the world, we know far too little of the specifics of change for Africa. As a result, recorded changes in recent times loom larger, and seem more drastic and more rapid, than changes in what we quite inadequately call 'traditional societies'. Too often, we know only the end of an undocumented series of historical changes, an end recorded when foreign visitors reported their observations. The accounts of outsiders, writing in Arabic or in a European language, have provided us with a baseline that is in fact remarkably recent At times correctly, but more often with no justification, we project this information back into the past so that the cultures and objects we are considering seem timeless and unchanging.

An assumption of the constancy of forms may at times be supported by archaeological or historical evidence. In his essay, Ezio Bassani gives an account of the earliest known seating furniture in African societies. In the following remarks, I shall concentrate on examples from the more recent past, and discuss briefly their uses and meanings.

Some pieces of furniture that Westerners might naturally assume to be intended for general use – that is to say, to be used freely by the members of the family or by friends – are in Africa considered to be extremely personal. In many cases an African would be shocked if anyone else – family member, friend or stranger – should use his seat. In fact, among some Akan peoples, in particular the Asante, a stool was not only considered a highly personal item; it was also believed to house the soul of the owner. When unoccupied the stool would be tipped on its side so that no alien force could occupy it and thus contaminate the owner's soul. The stool of a chief was of particular importance, not only because it was the repository of his soul, but because the chief was considered to be a divine king, and one aspect of his divinity was the belief that the well-being of his kingdom directly reflected the well-being of his soul. The king's soul had thus to be protected from spiritual contamination in order to ensure the prosperity of the kingdom. After the death of a king, his stool was preserved in an ancestral shrine, both to commemorate the deceased and to house his soul. The stool thus functioned much as ancestor figures did in other cultures. Among the Asante the ultimate and consummate form of the stool was the Golden Stool. Invented by Osei Tutu, the first Asantehene, it was believed to house the collective soul of the Asante peoples and thereby to become the overarching symbol of the Asante, a symbol superior to the blackened (i. e. sanctified) stools of the kings and chiefs of lesser kingdoms (fig. 2). In this way, through the successive levels of meaning that may be attached to it, a utilitarian object might attain a role far removed from that of 'ordinary' furniture. Indeed, one of the principal characteristics of the Golden Stool is that no one, not even the

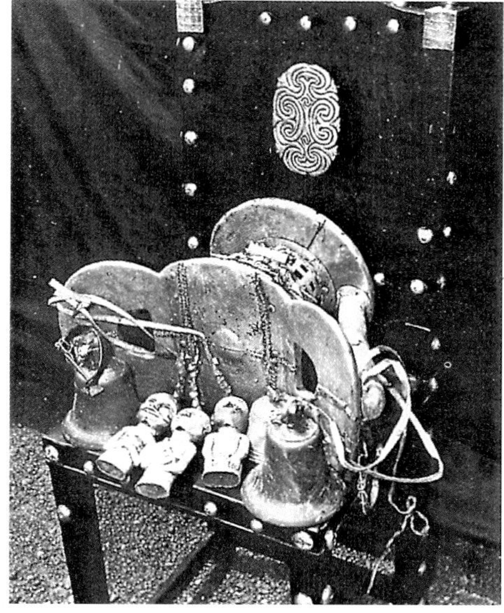

2 The Golden Stool, identified with the soul of the Asante nation, on a *hwedom* chair. The Golden Stool is a symbol of unity and is regarded as the common heritage of all the Asante. No one may ever sit on it, and it may only rarely appear in public and never touch the ground. For this reason it is laid on its own chair or on an animal skin. (Photograph: Ghana Information Service, 1964)

Note: Parts of this essay were first published in Roy Sieber, *African Furniture and Household Objects*, 1980.

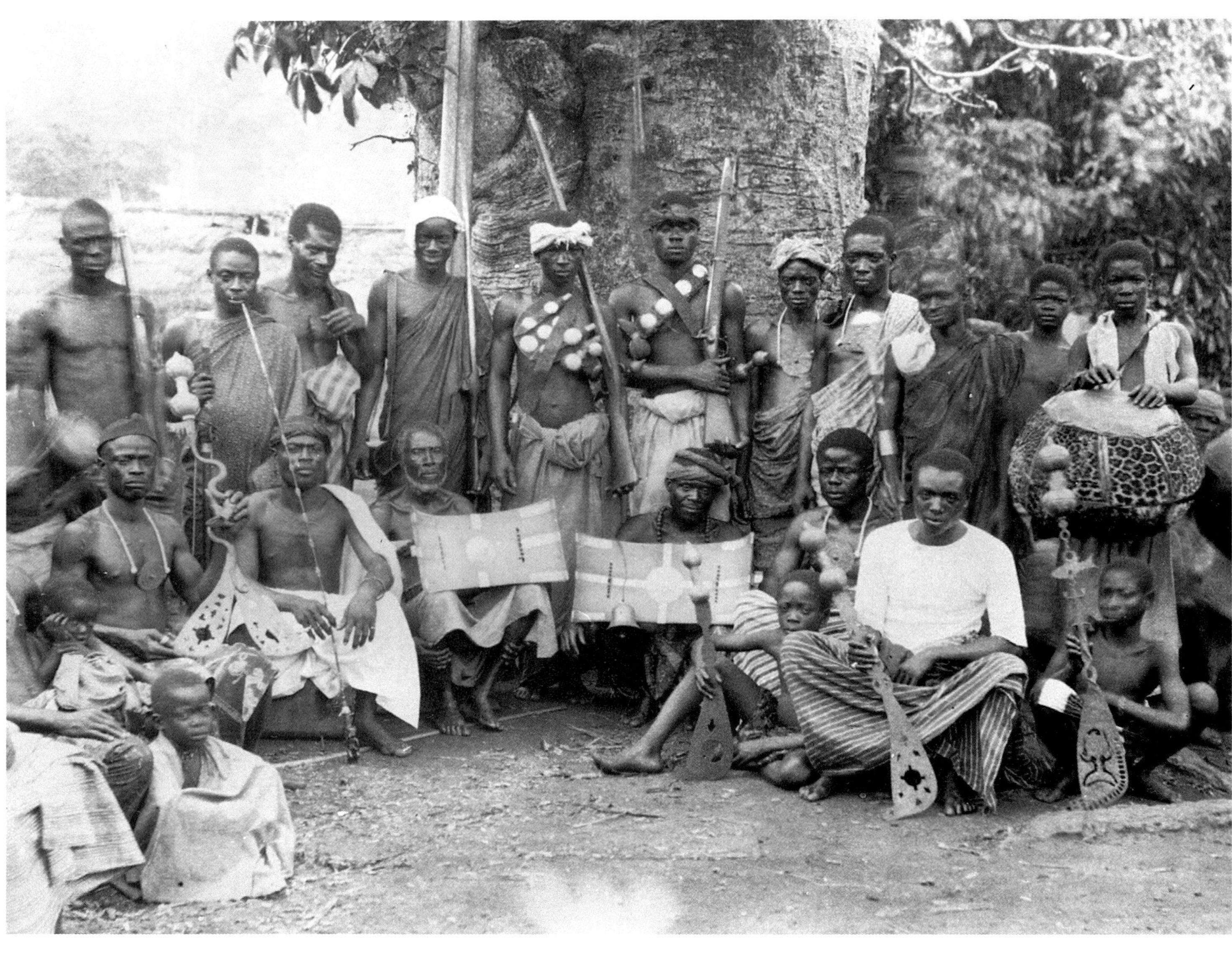

3 A king's courtiers presenting his insignia: in this case they display stools with silver mounts (from the Kwahu region, Ghana, perhaps from Obomeng). Alongside their purely practical purpose, stools also had a spiritual significance: they were regarded as the seat of their owner's soul. A king's stool was, moreover, identified with his political position and understood as a symbol of the unity of the nation. (Photograph: Fritz Ramseyer, 1896)

Asantehene himself, can sit on it. Mundane use has here been completely superseded by symbolic meaning.

Stools are associated with leadership not only among the Asante but among the Bunyoro of Uganda, the Rwanda, the Luba and the Kuba, among others. In addition there are tantalizing references to royal stools from Mali, made of terracotta, that may date from the seventeenth century; and there is even a twelfth-century reference to a thirty-pound gold nugget attached to the royal throne of the Kingdom of Ghana in the western Sudan.

Archaeological evidence, early reports and more recent descriptions have established that stools play an important role in leadership regalia. It must be assumed that there were more mundane forms of seating (made out of leaves, or consisting of mats, wooden billets or tripods) and more ordinary stools but that these were not considered worthy of note. Almost any object can come to signify status and it is reasonable to suppose that the well-tended stool might have been treasured by the owner and been recognized by his or her peers not only as private and personal, but as an object of prestige, an indicator of the status of the owner.

Stools vary a good deal. They may be simple, but ingenious adaptations of natural, branch-like forms that serve as stools or as backrests (plate on p. 129; see also fig. 1), or more elaborately carved tip-stools that double as stool or backrest (plates on pp. 130 and 131). They may be constructed, as are some beds, out of stacked palm-leaf ribs in the manner of a log cabin, or out of pieces of bark, curved into cylindrical form and attached to tops and bases made from wooden discs.

A great number of stools are monoxylous – that is to say, carved from a single block of wood. Such stools fall into two categories: one predominantly cubic in form and the other cylindrical. Examples of the first type have a deeply curved seat and appear rectangular when viewed from above. They are found in three regions of West Africa: firstly, in the Arquipélago dos Bijagós, off the coast of Guinea-Bissau (plate on p. 68); secondly, among the Akan of the Ivory Coast and Ghana (plates on pp. 78–82) as far as the old kingdom of Dahomey; and thirdly, on the Cameroon coast, near the modern city of Duala (plate on p. 83). If there are historical ties to account for this unconnected distribution, they are not clear. Particularly tantalizing is the resemblance of the Golden Stool of the Asante to the style found among the Bidjogo.

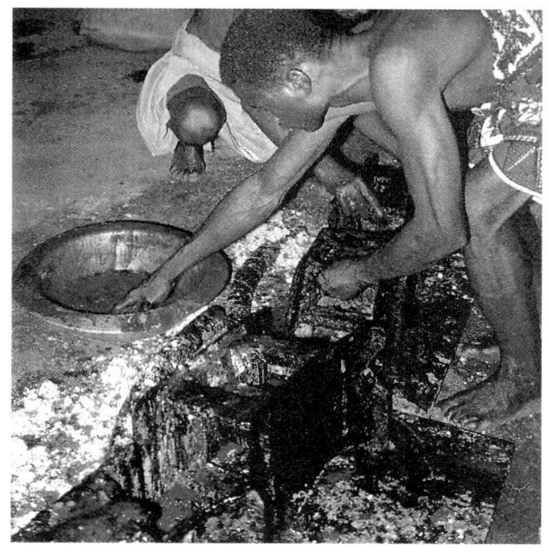

4 During the celebration of harvest, sacrifices are made to the sacred stools of the deceased chiefs of the Akan.
(Photograph: Monique Barbier-Mueller, 1988)

Stools of cylindrical form may range from a simple spool or reel shape to quite elaborate examples. Complex geometric forms may occur, as in the two- or three-tiered Igbo examples. Caryatid stools, with human or animal figures supporting the seating surface, are found in many parts of the subcontinent. Those from south-east Zaire are particularly well-known (plates on pp. 112–21, 124, 125). Leon Kochnitzky suggests that this form may be an artistic embodiment of a 'kingly prerogative to sit on a living throne, on the back of a slave'.[1] Old prints (fig. 5) and photographs – such as the photograph of the Kuba king (fig. on p. 108)[2] – clearly establish that this practice existed. However, the usual form of the carved caryatid stool, that of a standing or squatting figure supporting the seat on its head and raised arms, does not echo the pose of the slave-as-seat, who kneels to support the sitter on his or her back.

The earliest reference to stools in European reports seems to be that of the Portuguese Azambuja, who in 1481 received permission from the Africans to build the first trading fortress on the Gold Coast. This fortress, Elmina, was to remain a major entrepôt for nearly four hundred years. Barbot, whose account seems to derive from a journal kept by Azambuja (now lost), offers the following descrip-

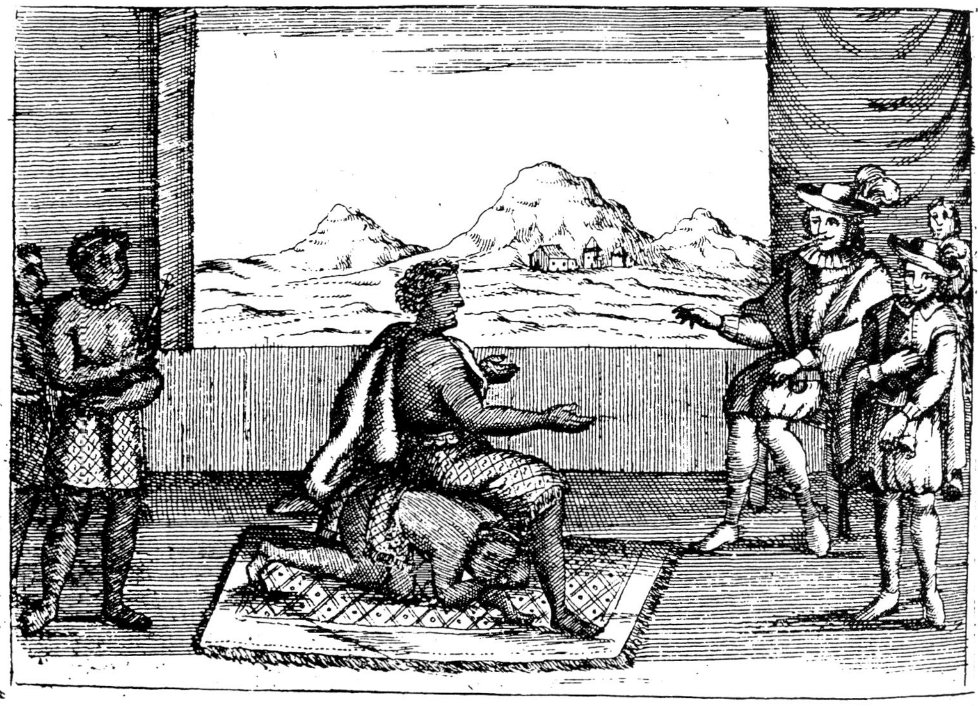

5 Queen Zingha of Matamba, sister of the reigning king of Ndongo (in the region of modern Angola), was one of the outstanding African figures of the sixteenth century. She was regarded as an extremely skilful negotiator and fought vehemently and successfully against the new colonial powers. She is here shown seated on a slave receiving the Portuguese governor in Luanda. (Engraving from Cavazzi 1687)

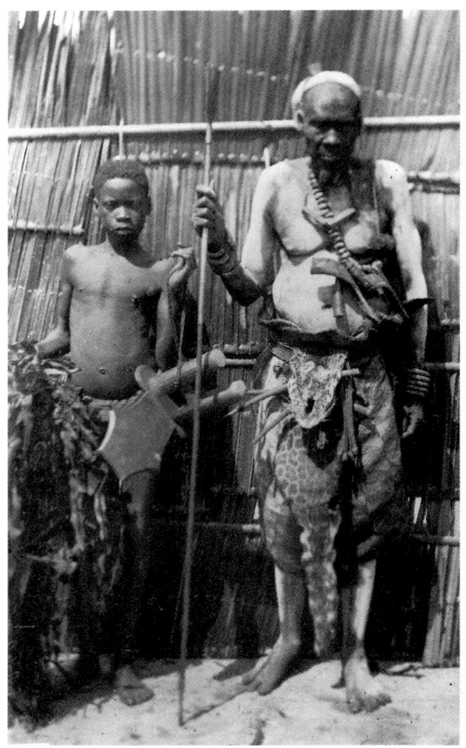

6 Chief Kokokoko Lusukia of the Yongo Booli, Mbole, Zaire. The young man carries the chief's seat, in this case a tip-stool (cf. plates on pp. 130, 131). (Photograph: S. Molin, 1926)

tion: 'After mass, Azambuja was inform'd of the coming of Casamanse [the local chief], and having rang'd his men in order, sate down in an elbow chair, having on a gold brocade waistcoat, and a gold collar set with jewels, all his followers clad in silk, making a lane before him, that the black prince might admire his grandeur. Casamanse, on his part, was not wanting to show his state, which appear'd by a great number of arm'd Blacks, with a mighty noise of trumpets, horns, tinkling bells, and other instruments, all together making a hideous noise. The principal Blacks were dress'd after their own manner, as they are to this day, . . . and follow'd, each of them, by two pages, one of them carrying a buckler, and the other, a little round stool, their heads and beards adorn'd with gold, after their fashion.'[3]

We know of other descriptions of royal seats. Before 1500 there is a reference to an ivory chair for the King of Kongo;[4] and in 1702, Nyendael noted that at Benin the King sat 'on an Ivory Couch under a Canopy of Indian Silk.'[5] In the mid-sixteenth century Towrson described a chair from near the Pra River in the Gold Coast. His account is similar to that of Azambuja, and in turn is nearly matched by R. Austin Freeman's late nineteenth-century description from Adanse, also in The Gold Coast: 'As soon as the king had advanced to us and shaken our hands his stool-bearer set down his stool, upon which he forthwith seated himself; and the chiefs who accompanied him, having had their stools set down for them, took their seat in like manner.

'This is another custom that strikes the stranger rather oddly, . . . When a chief or better-class native visits another he is invariably accompanied by his stool-bearer, who carries the stool or chair upon which his master is accustomed to sit [fig. 6]. For even the best and most elaborate of West African households are quite simple in their arrangements and do not include a supply of furniture sufficient for the accommodation of visitors. Hence the stool-bearer is a regular constituent of all kinds of native processions.

'The stools of the king and chiefs having thus been placed in a semicircle in front of us, their owners took their seats, and the numerous attendants seated themselves on the ground, with the exception of those whose duties required them to stand, such as the umbrella-bearers and the sword-bearers; then the palaver began.'[6]

Although the stool as known in sub-Saharan Africa may have been of African inspiration and development, there is one form of seat that has been markedly influenced from outside: the European-style chair. As noted above, the Portuguese Azambuja introduced the 'elbow chair' to the Gold Coast as early as 1481. This type of chair was quickly recognized by Africans as signifying prestige and power. As a result early descriptions of West Africa soon abounded with references to European chairs. Barbot and the Sieur d'Elbee refer to 'Damask Elbow-Chairs' presented by Europeans to the King of Ardrah (an area corresponding to that of the modern border between Nigeria and Benin) in 1670; Brüe mentions a velvet-covered armchair in 1701; Atkins refers to chairs on the Gold Coast (modern Ghana) in 1721; and LeBat speaks of velvet-covered armchairs in Senegambia in 1728. All of these are recorded in Astley, who, quoting a report by Marchais of 1725, offers what might be considered a typical description of a throne presented as a royal gift. 'His Throne was a large gilt Arm-Chair, on the Back of which were the Arms of France, which shewed it was a Present from that Nation. He was seated on a Velvet Cushion, richly laced with Gold, having another of the same at his Feet.'[7]

Dalzel took 'a very handsome sedan chair, and a chamber organ' as gifts to the King of Dahomey in 1743.[8] The king, he reports, had at least two chairs, both covered in crimson velvet and embellished with gilt carving or a gold fringe.[9] Finally, in 1844, T. B. Freeman describes how the King of Dahomey received him 'seated on an European chair, covered with cloth, and before him was placed a small European table. . . .'[10]

1 Kochnitzky 1948, p. 30.
2 Torday and Joyce 1910, fig. 35.
3 Barbot 1732, pp. 161–2.
4 Astley 1745–7, vol. i, p. 20.
5 Bosman 1721, p. 474.
6 R. A. Freeman 1898, pp. 59–60.
7 Astley 1745–7, vol. iii, p. 45.
8 Dalzel 1793, p. 126.
9 Dalzel 1793, pp. 126, 134.
10 T. B. Freeman 1844, p. 260.

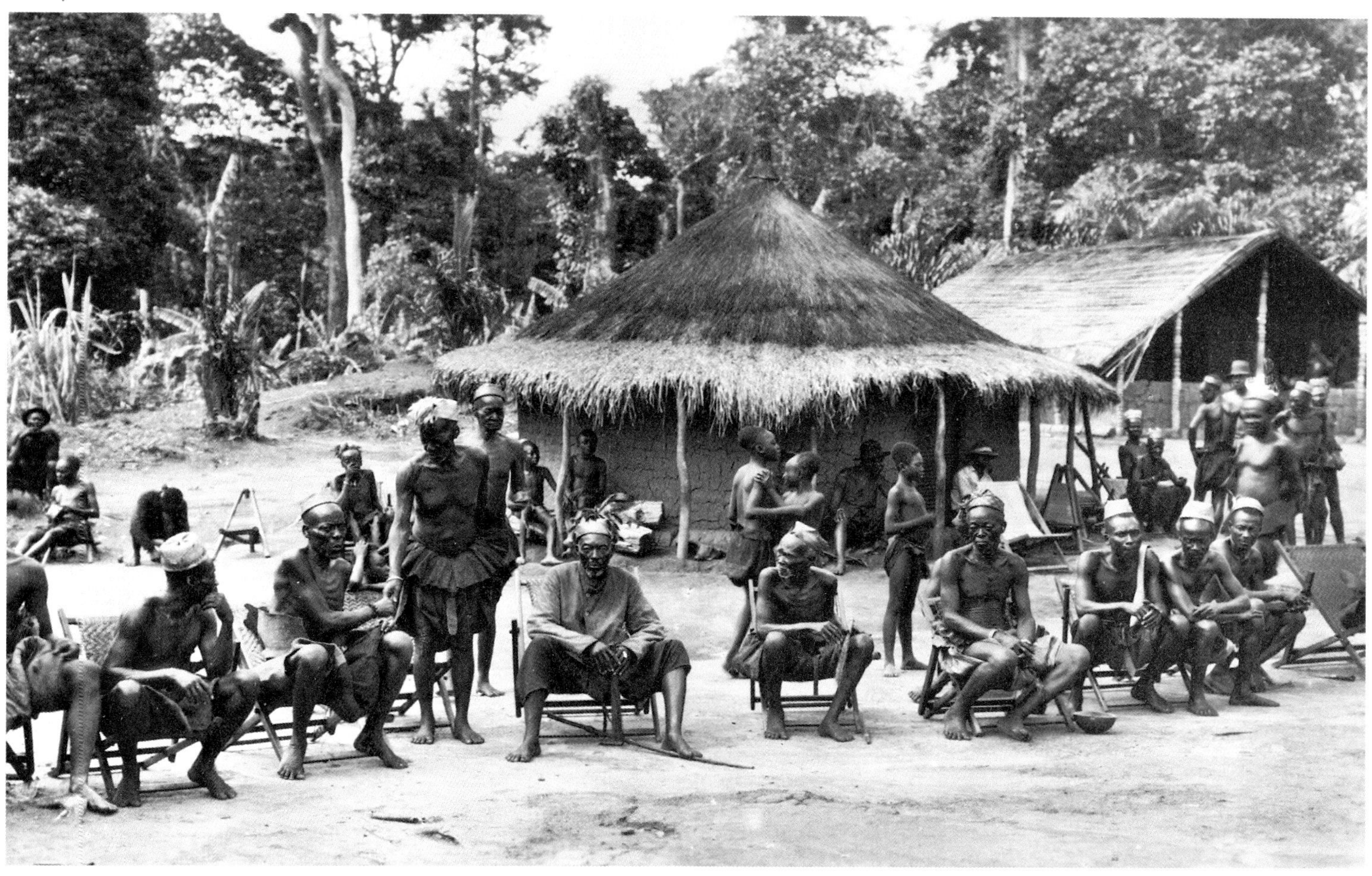

7 Mangbetu elders seated in cane sling chairs, Zaire, the design based on that of the European deck-chair. The great skill in cane work, evident in the backs of the chairs seen here, astonished European travellers in Africa; cf. cat. 97.
(Photograph: Casimir d'Ostoja Zagourski, 1926)

Other forms of European furniture also found their way to the West African coast: bedsteads, canopies, mirrors, pewter and brass basins, tables and 'Turkey' carpets. Yet it is the European chair that seems to have had the strongest impact, to judge from the number of copies and variations that exist. Although the copies are rarely slavish imitations, in most cases the shape of the original is self-evident. Among the copies are Asante chairs of three types. The first type is a copy of a European chair folding chair: it is delightfully called a 'praying mantis' (*akonkromfi* in Twi) and makes its appearance on joyful occasions (plate on p. 77). The second type, the *hwedom*, frequently has high arms and a straight back. It is painted black and is often decorated with silver ornaments (shown in fig. 2, as a support for the Golden Stool, and in the photograph of the Omanhene on p. 74). The third type, the *asipim*, occurs in two sizes; one is of a size that in Europe we would consider 'normal' and the other looks as if it had been made for a child, but may have been a size found on board ships at the time (plate on p. 76). *Asipim* chairs are without arms, have a slightly sloping back and are usually richly decorated with brass nails, knobs and finials. All three types have leather seats and backs, are occasionally decorated with sheet metal and reflect European prototypes dating from the fifteenth to the seventeenth centuries. Similarly, the so-called chiefs' chairs from Angola and southern Zaire, made by the Chokwe and related groups, derive from European, probably Portuguese, prototypes (plates on pp. 150–5).

Other forms that seem to be derived from European prototypes are found in the Cameroon grasslands and among the Tabwa and Nyamwezi (plates on pp. 91, 140, 158). Nor can one exclude the so-called grandfather chairs of the Ivory Coast and Liberia (plates on pp. 70–3) or the stools with backs found among the Ngala of

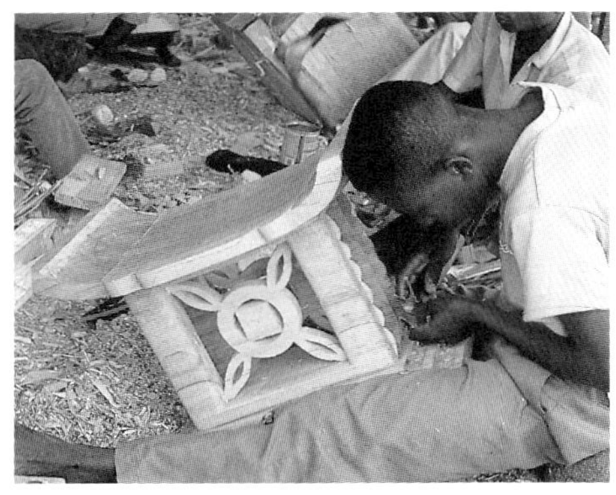

8 A carver at work in Ahwiaa, Ghana. Although predominantly intended for sale to tourists, the stools are usually carved in traditional patterns. In the Asante region, around the capital Kumasi, the residence of the king, individual villages have traditionally specialized in a particular type of handicraft. The village of Ahwiaa is nowadays especially notable for its many shops devoted exclusively to selling wood carvings to tourists.
(Photograph: Andrea Knecht Oti-Amoako, 1994)

Zaire. In all these instances a very African characteristic emerges: the copies are not mechanical reproductions, but are elaborated or modified to meet local aesthetic and/or symbolic requirements.

With the introduction of carpentry workshops, first by missionaries and later by colonial administrators, the copying becomes more mechanical and repetitive. Thus, in the British colonies of the Gold Coast and Nigeria, there evolved a furniture style that stressed simplicity of form, strength and ease of manufacture. To my knowledge no one has seriously studied the development and spread of what might be termed 'African mission style'. In English-speaking Africa this style became ubiquitous. Found in all government-issue housing, it also became the style for chiefs' houses and was the form adopted by a growing African élite.

In the June 1938 issue of the journal *Nigeria*, there is a photograph showing cane chairs being made in Calabar. The caption notes that 'cane work is one of the crafts taught at the Elementary Training Centre, Uyo.' Similar workshops for cane chairs existed in Cameroon (fig. 9). Among the local élite in British, French, Belgian and Portuguese colonies, furniture styles – either in the form of imports or as locally made copies – clearly reflected the styles popular in Europe. Lower down the economic scale, Africans have tended to continue using a mixture of older, more local styles and simple carpentry forms.

With the coming of independence, however, many African societies reevaluated their traditions and emphasized older forms. The Ghanaians, for example, particularly the Akan, revived the use of traditional types of stool. Although these had never been totally abandoned, the Ghanaians' newly invigorated sense of their heritage encouraged them to revive the use of both traditional dress and personal stools.

Finally, the inventiveness of the African craftsman cannot be dismissed without a further observation. In 1971, I photographed a workshop in Nigeria which was producing quite marvellous barbers' chairs out of scrap metal from lorries (fig. 10).

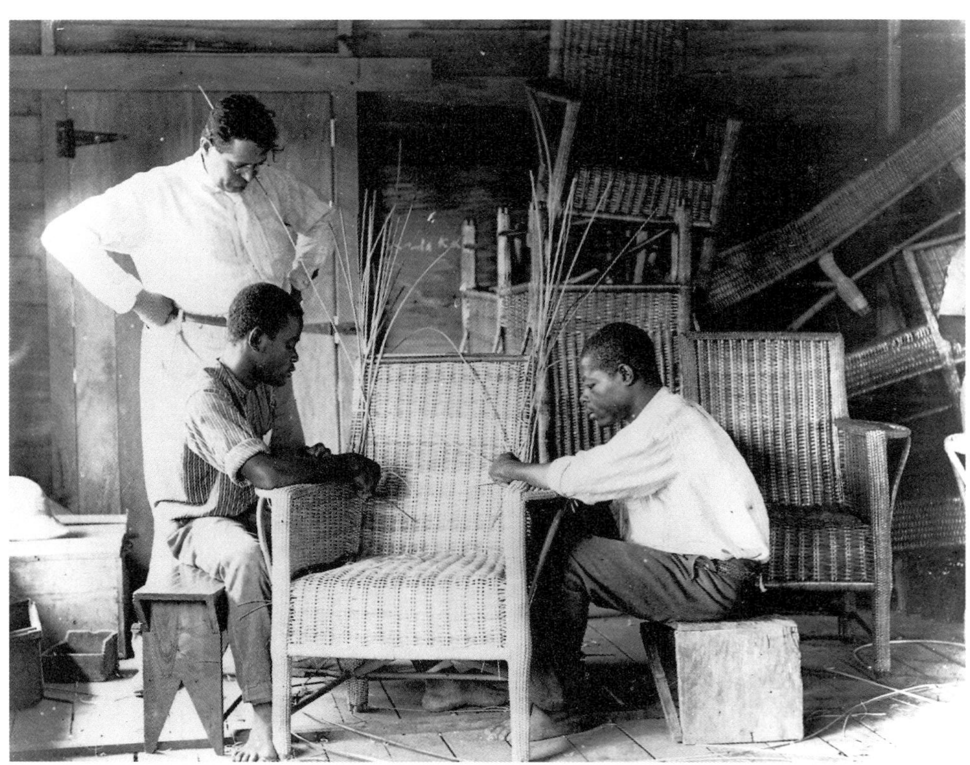

9 The workshop of a Presbyterian mission in southern Cameroon, in which cane-work items, for example chairs, were produced following European models.
(Unknown photographer, *c.* 1910)

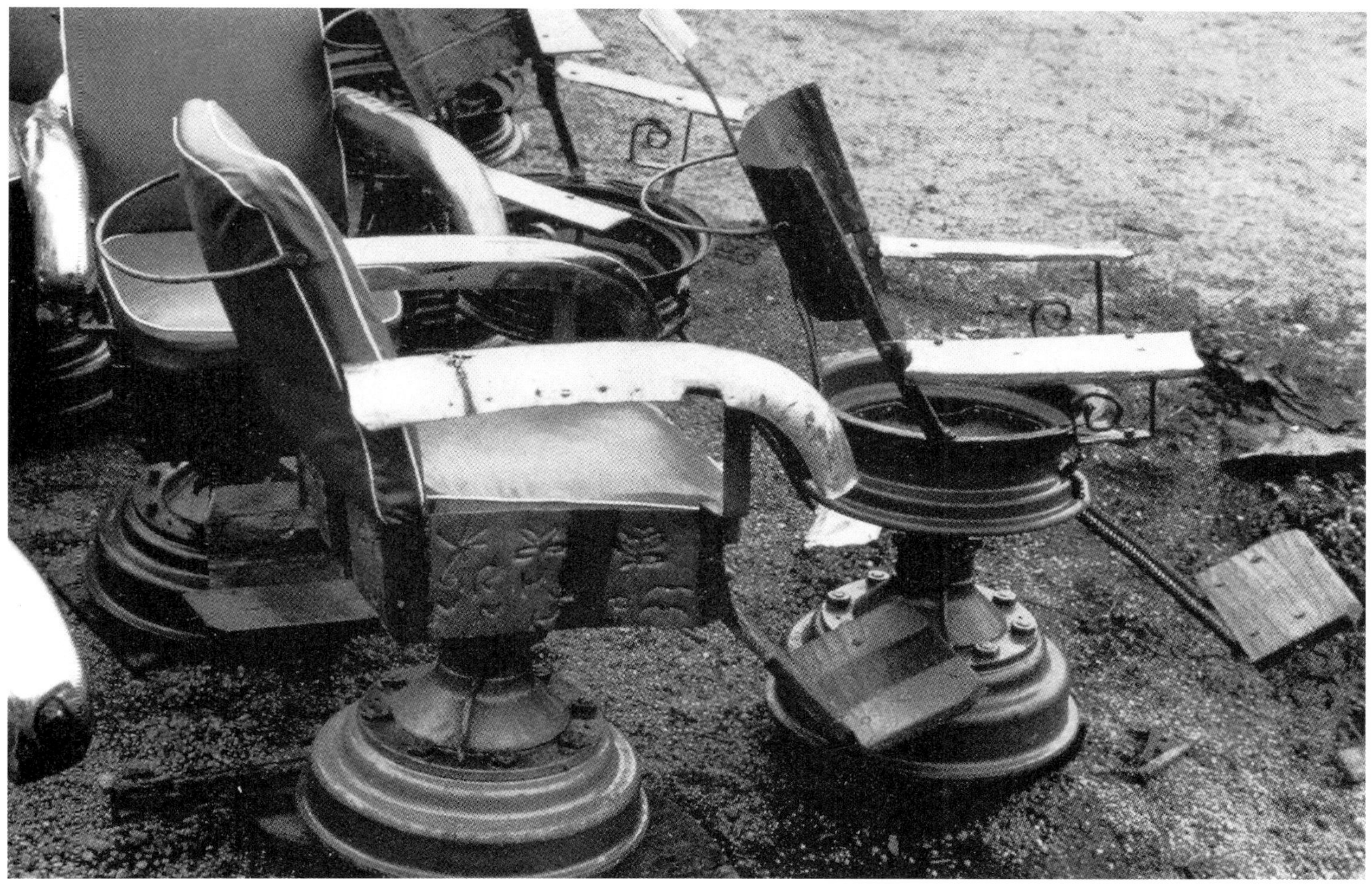

No discussion of African seats could be considered complete without an acknowledgement of the high degree of skill and inventiveness that have played such a major part in the development of all forms of African seating furniture. Whether the source was a modified tree branch, or a log cut horizontally or vertically to create the basic stage of a cylindrical or rectangular stool, whether the styles were traditional or were modified versions of, or copied from, foreign models, the quality, the skill and the ingenuity of the craftsmen have made the work of each generation admired and sought after.

10 Recycling and improvisation in modern Africa: barbers' chairs made out of scrap metal from lorries, plastic cloth, iron rods for reinforced concrete, and paint. Oshogbo, Nigeria.
(Photograph: Roy Sieber, 1971)

Ezio Bassani

Early Evidence of African Seats

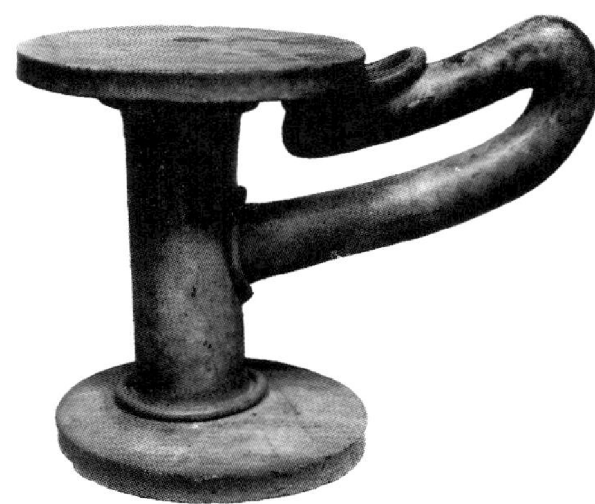

1 Seat
Yoruba artist, 11th to 15th centuries, Ife, Nigeria
Quartz, height 54 cm
Museum of Mankind, London

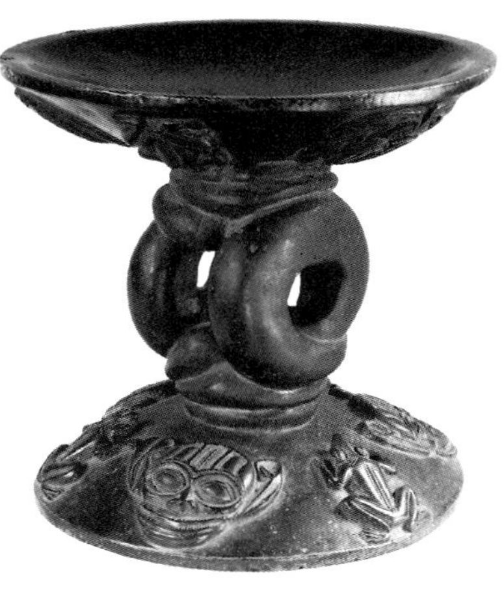

2 Seat
Edo artist, 18th century, Benin, Nigeria
Bronze, height 39 cm
Museum für Völkerkunde, Berlin

Stools and chairs, both as objects of everyday use and as symbols of status and power within society, are a traditional part of the culture of furniture in sub-Saharan Africa. Over the centuries the most varied forms of seating have evolved among the peoples of this region.

The greater part of the early specimens, mostly made of wood, have been lost. However, we have both direct and indirect evidence of their existence, mainly in West Africa. The oldest and most numerous evidence has so far come from the area corresponding to modern Nigeria. The quartz chairs of the eleventh to fifteenth centuries from Ife, the holy city of the Yoruba, are works of the greatest elegance and are distinguished by their purity of form. They are composed of circular discs linked by a central pillar and a looped handle. The only undamaged example we know is in the Museum of Mankind in London (fig. 1). In the museum at Ife there are several fragments of circular seats made of quartz and granite, a slightly damaged example made of soft stone, and a rectangular, four-legged seat made of granite that is both solid and refined in character. In addition, Frank Willett mentions fragments of a seat, unique in form, made of soft stone and with two looped handles, that is probably from a later period.

The shape of the circular quartz seats is thought to derive from that of the large circular wooden chests that were used both as containers for ritual objects and as seats. The loop appears to be a stylized representation of the strap that attached the lid to the body of the container. This hypothesis is borne out by the evidence of fragments of a large-scale terracotta statue, in the classical Ife style, found at Iwinrin Grove. This shows a figure seated on a cylindrical seat very similar to the quartz examples. The seat indicated in this sculpture was, however, in all probability made of wood, and its surface decorated with incised patterns and with metal strips and glass studs. The sculpted figure's feet rest on a rectangular footstool with four rounded legs, with ornamental motifs recalling those of the seat itself (fig. 4).[1]

In the National Museum in Lagos there is a brass sculpture dating from the twelfth to fifteenth centuries (fig. 3): it combines a circular seating surface that is almost an exact copy of the one in quartz, and a bowl with the body of a queen (signalled as such by her crown and sceptre) twined around it.[2] According to Bernard and William Fagg, this small work of art is evidence that the quartz seats are of the same period as the classical works of brass and terracotta.

Until recently, thrones used as containers for regalia were still in use in the Igala region. They were constructed from large cylindrical chests with sides made of bark, a wooden base and lid, and two identical wooden footrests.[3] Correspondences of form and function between these seats and the early Ife thrones also indirectly confirm the theories of the Fagg brothers.

The Bini artists designed elaborate and very varied bronze seats notable for their combination of imagination and elegance. In the case of two very attractive examples with circular bases and a central column (sixteenth to seventeenth centuries), the seating surface consists of two flat, interlocking catfish (fig. 5), the catfish being a royal symbol. The sinuous lines and the suitably austere decoration indicate an

1 B. and W. Fagg 1960; Willett 1960, plates iv–v; Willett 1967, pp. 82–4, plates 76–79; Allison 1968, figs. 7–9; Drewal 1989, fig. 51–52. Drewel assumes that 'looped "handles" such as that emerging from the central column may have been inspired by an elephant's trunk.' On the technique used here, see also Underwood 1949, pp. 4–5.

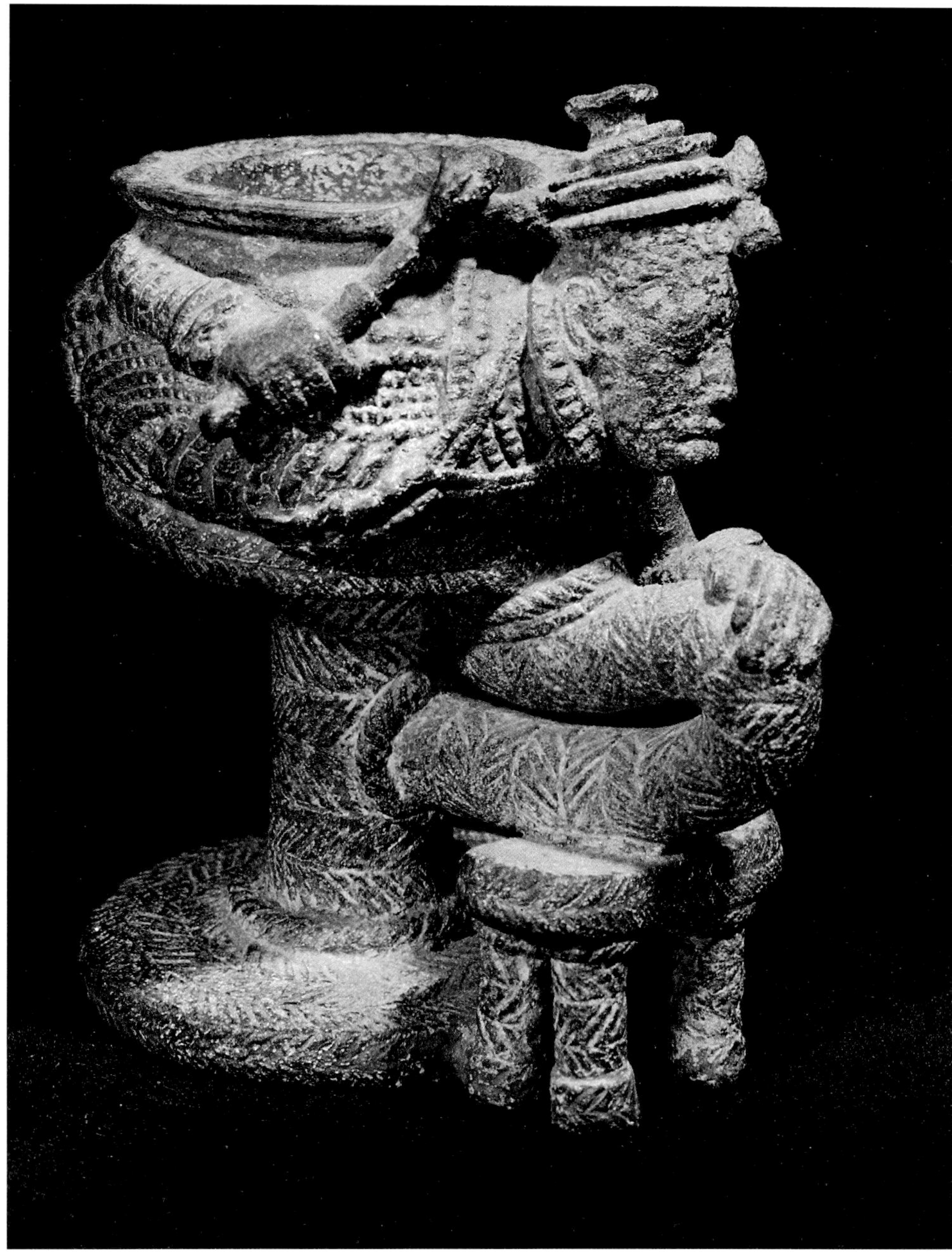

3 Vessel resting on a seat
Yoruba artist, 12th to 15th centuries, Ife, Nigeria
Brass, height 12.4 cm
National Museum, Lagos
(Photograph: André and Ursula Held)

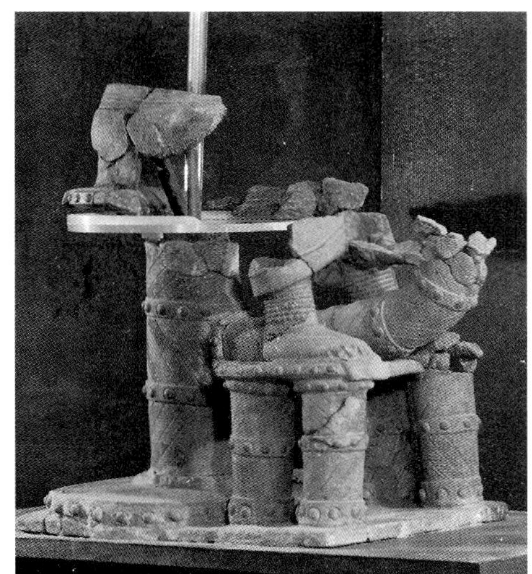

4 Fragments of a terracotta figure seated on a chair
Yoruba artist of the classical period, Ife, Nigeria.
(Photograph: Frank Willett, 1964)

attempt to achieve fluidity of form. One of these seats is in the National Museum in Lagos, the other is in the Museum of Mankind in London.[4]

Two bronze seats (probably from the mid-eighteenth century), now in the Museum für Völkerkunde in Berlin, have a more complex structure (fig. 2). Two intertwined snakes link the seating surface with the base, which is itself decorated in low relief with mask-like faces of monkeys, with animals, with symbolic figures and with both ritual and everyday objects.[5]

There are a few further examples, made of wood; but their execution does not have such elegance. Their design was certainly inspired by that of a metal prototype.[6]

Circular wooden seats with ornamental copper strips were also used in the Igbo Ukwu region in what is now south-eastern Nigeria, even earlier than in Ife and Benin. In one location, known as Igbo Richard, Thurstan Shaw discovered the remains of a circular wooden seat, decorated with spiral-shaped copper studs, in the

2 B. and W. Fagg 1960, plate K (d); Willett 1960, plate vi; Eyo and Willett 1980, no. 46; Drewal 1989, fig. 44.
3 A throne made out of bark was published in B. and W. Fagg 1960, fig. 3; another in Sieber 1980, p. 138. The vessel of yet another, now in the Horniman Museum in London, is made of carved wood instead of bark.
4 Dark 1960, plate 40; Eyo and Willett 1980, no. 88.
5 Luschan 1919, plates 813–823; W. Fagg 1963, fig. 26; Dark 1973, plate 65, fig. 153.
6 Luschan 1919, fig. 824; B. and W. Fagg 1960, fig. 2; Dark 1960, plate 20; Kaplan 1981, plate 57.

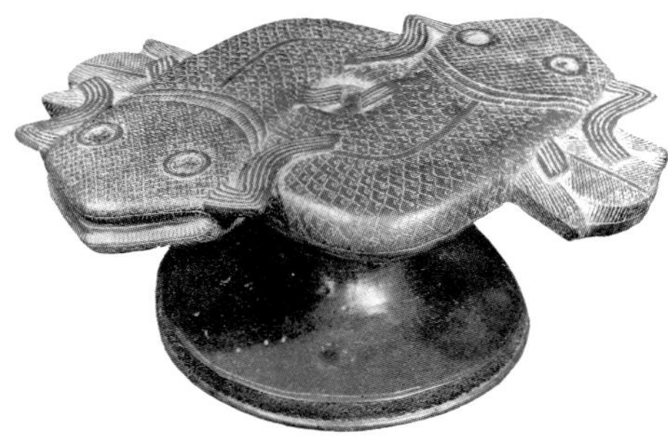

5 Seat
Edo artist, Benin, Nigeria
Bronze, height 34 cm
National Museum, Lagos
(Photograph: André and Ursula Held)

burial chamber of an important figure (identifiable as such through the presence of precious bronze objects). By means of radio-carbon dating, the seat was shown to date from about the tenth century.[7] No undamaged example of this type has ever been found, however; its exact form when complete is thus not known.

The form of many of the African seats reserved for notabilities in the Nok and Esie cultures of what is now Nigeria is known through sculptures showing seated figures (fig. 6). The name Nok derives from a location on the Jos plateau, where, in 1943, a terracotta sculpture was discovered. The dating and localization of the Nok culture have since been repeatedly expanded through the further findings of scholars (the maximum temporal extent being 500 BC to AD 1000).[8] On many fragments subsequently found in this area one can detect figures seated on small stools of very simple form, consisting of an upper inverted truncated cone resting on a lower upright one. It is presumed that the original stools thus recorded were made of wood and so have not survived.[9]

The artists of the Esie culture carved about a thousand remarkably large figures from soft stone. These, presumed to date from the twelfth to fifteenth centuries, are now kept in the sacred wood of Esie in the Yoruba region of Igbomina. Male and female figures are shown poised, in a dignified manner, on circular seats which have a central column connecting the base with the usually smooth surface. Only in a few cases is the border of the seat decorated and the connecting column given a spiral form.[10]

Through figures cut from soft stone (*nomoli*) and the ivories carved by the Sapi for the Portuguese in the fifteenth to sixteenth centuries, we also know of the triangular backed three-legged chairs of this people, the original inhabitants of what is now Sierra Leone. The astounding similarity to specimens still in use today in

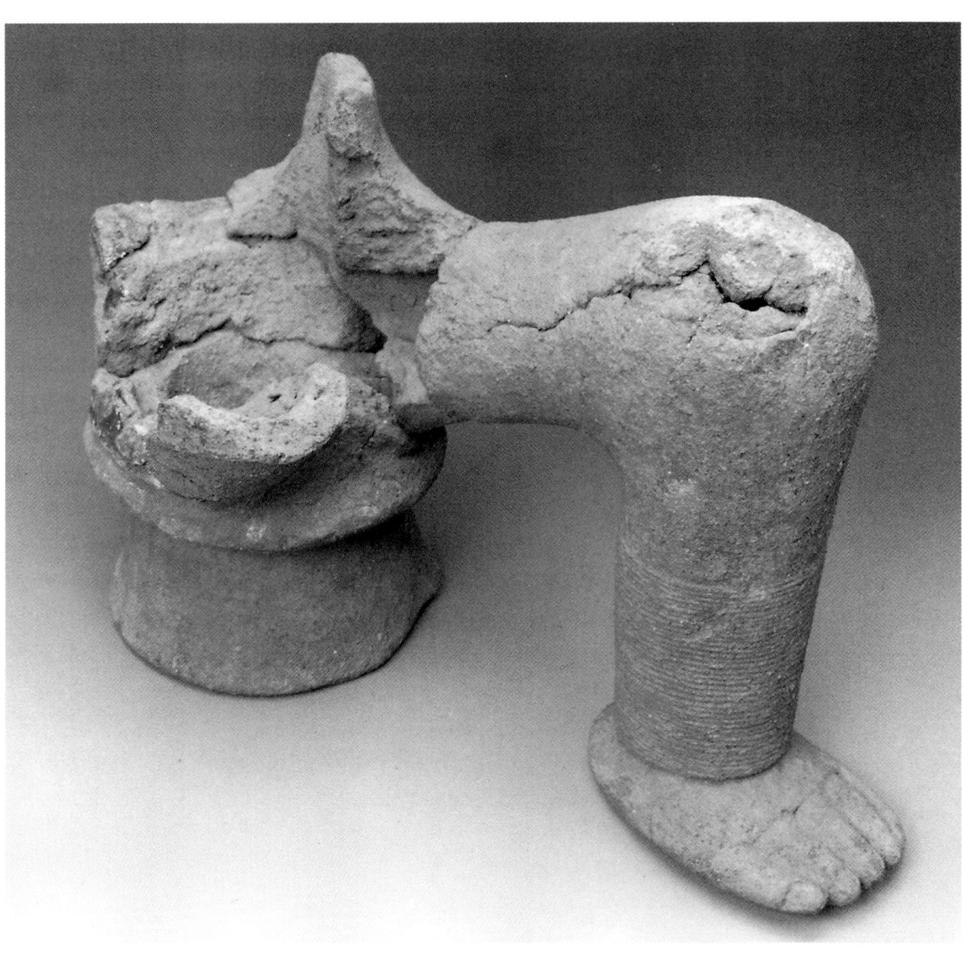

6 Fragments of a sculpture of a seated man
Artist of the Nok culture, 11th century, from Katsina Ala, Nigeria
Terracotta, height 28 cm
National Museum, Jos
(Photograph: Denis Rouvre, R. M. N., Paris)

7 Shaw 1970, vol. i, p. 260. See also the record of the burial chamber in the watercolour by C. Sassoon in Eyo and Willett 1980, fig. 5.
8 B. Fagg 1977, passim.
9 *Vallées du Niger* 1993, no. 198. Willett (1967, p. 115) hypothesizes that the seat may have been an 'upturned mortar'. See also Willett 1967, fig. 20, and Willett 1986, figs. 3, 5.
10 Allison 1968, plates 15–16, 20, 22–26; Stevens 1978; Eyo and Willett 1980, nos. 98 ff.; Pemberton 1989, pp. 77–89, fig. 79, pp. 82–9.
11 Sieber 1980, pp. 134–5; Bassani and Fagg 1988, p. 62, figs. 36–38, 74; Tagliaferri 1989, figs. 27–28.
12 Cole and Ross 1977, pp. 134–6, figs. 291, 293–297; McLeod 1981, pp. 112–18.
13 Hair 1992, vol. ii, fig. 47.
14 Bassani 1987.
15 Cf. Bastin 1982, nos. 111, 114, 116, 119, 122, 124, 135.
16 Heintze 1989, pp. 36–7.

this region confirms the accuracy of the early representations. Both the chair on which the *nomoli* figure sits (Monzino Collection) and the seat on the cover of an ivory salt-cellar (Seattle Art Museum) may, for example, be compared with the later chair in the Museum für Völkerkunde in Munich (figs. 7, 8 and 9).[11]

As far as a I am aware, no representations of seats have occurred among the numerous terracotta figures that have been found in the inland delta of the River Niger in what is now Mali and in the north of Ghana.

The stool with a typical rectangular concave seating surface, made out of a single tree trunk, has an important place in the society of the Asante in what is now Ghana. Each stool is seen as the seat of its owner's soul. It is said that, during a large gathering of the Asante chiefs in Kumasi towards the end of the seventeenth century, a golden seat (the 'Golden Stool', of uncertain form) fell out of the sky into the lap of Osei Tutu, thus sanctioning the foundation of a united Asante kingdom. Osei Tutu was then appointed supreme leader; and the high priest Okomfo Anokye declared that this stool contained the soul of the Asante nation. According to Cole and Ross, the rectangular stool type may have been introduced at this time in order to mark the change in the political situation.[12]

Asante stools of this type are not known from before the early nineteenth century; but a drawing (certainly made from life) in Jean Barbot's manuscript of 1679 offers indisputable evidence of both their existence and their form.[13] The similarity with more recent examples is so great as to leave no room for doubt.

An earlier record, however, is that of Giovanni Antonio Cavazzi, who spent seventeen years as a Capuchin missionary in what is now Congo and Angola. He was certainly the first European to make sketches on the spot of aspects of African culture.[14] He left us thirty-three coloured drawings incorporating realistic details; these form part of volume A of the manuscript known as *Manoscritti Araldi* (1665).

In four of these drawings (nos. 2, 7, 20 and 26) both circular and rectangular seats are seen. In drawing no. 7, which shows the mythical smith-king of Ndongo-Angola making weapons and other utensils in his forge, we can make out three wooden seats. The two circular ones are decorated with minute geometrical motifs that recall the decoration on some of the works of art – mainly tools and ceremonial staffs – more recently produced by the Chokwe.[15]

The rectangular seat, which in drawings nos. 7 and 20 serves as support for the royal crown, has become in drawing no. 26 the throne from which Queen Zinga dispenses justice. In my view, the pattern on the side of this throne (a pattern also frequently occurring on cloth) is characteristic of the culture of the Congo. According to Heintze, however, this pattern could also be associated with other peoples living in what is now Angola, in particular the Ambundu.[16]

Although no similar chairs, even later ones, have been discovered in the Congo-Angola region (in contrast to the situation with almost all the other objects illustrated in the *Manoscritti Araldi*), Cavazzi's drawings remain of great interest for us. They are still our only source of early information on the form and function of such objects in this part of Africa.

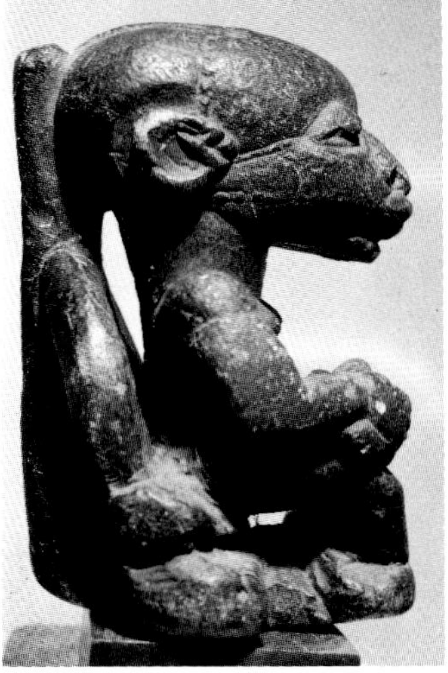

7 Seated figure
Sapi artist, 15th to 16th centuries, Sierra Leone
Soft stone, height 23 cm
Monzino Collection

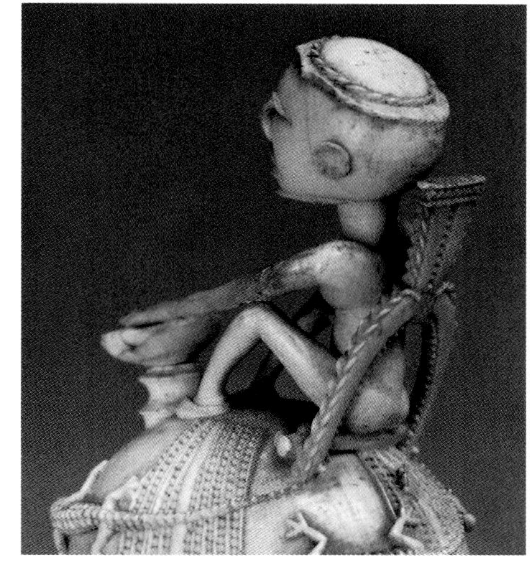

8 Sapi-Portuguese salt-cellar
Sapi artist, 15th to 16th centuries, Sierra Leone
Ivory, height 20.7 cm
The Seattle Art Museum, Seattle

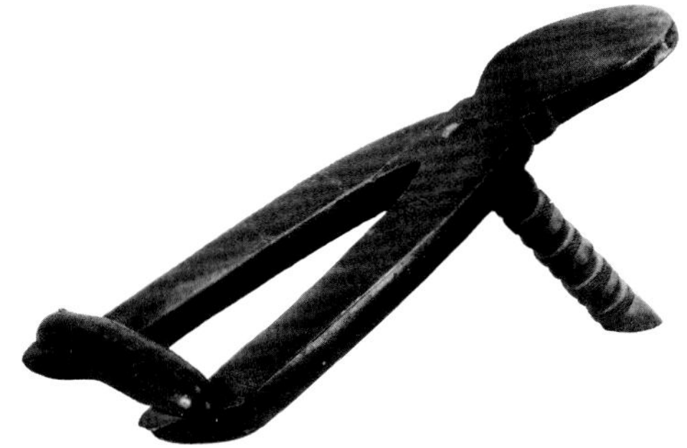

9 Three-legged seat of the Toma, Liberia, early 20th century
Wood, iron nails (support carved later), height 41 cm
Staatliches Museum für Völkerkunde, Munich

Hans Himmelheber

The Small Grandfather Chairs of the Gere

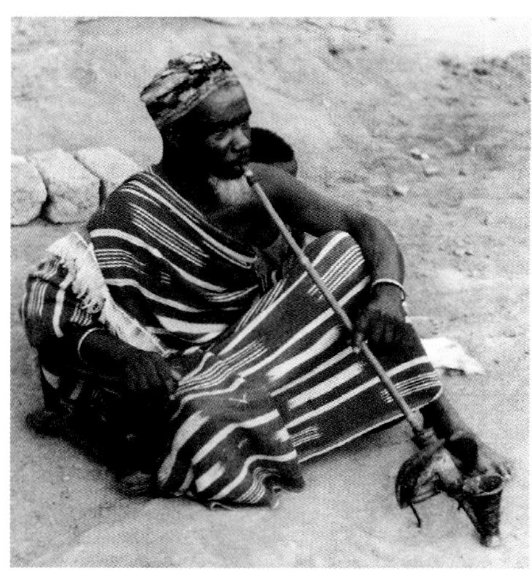

1 The small chairs belong to the old men of the village. They sit on them during the day and use them as headrests at night. (Photograph: Hans Himmelheber, 1956)

This essay was first published in *Baessler-Archiv*, Neue Folge, vol. XIII (1965), pp. 539–44. It is here reproduced with kind permission of the Baessler-Archiv, Museum für Völkerkunde, Staatliche Museen zu Berlin, Preußischer Kulturbesitz.

Among the peoples of the central and western Ivory Coast, the Baule, the Guro, the Gere and the Dan, there is to be found a type of small, low chair that, in essence, resembles a European chair. It has four legs, a rectangular seat and a back, and it is made up of eight parts (plates on p. 73): the seating surface; two wooden slats, into which the seating surface is fitted sideways; two front legs, inserted into the front of these slats; two back legs, drawn up through the slats to form supports for the back; and the curved back itself, into which the two supports are in turn inserted.

These small chairs are always deep brown – with age, soot and sweat. Among the Baule and the Guro each of the two ends of the back are often decorated with a prettily carved human head (plate on p. 71). The legs usually have a very simple outline.

Among the Gere these chairs (*gba*) are especially small (sometimes only 25 centimetres wide) and, in particular, conspicuously low: the seating surface between 8 and 10 centimetres, and the backrest 30 centimetres, above the ground. The backrest is simply a branch bent into the required shape and is left without any decoration. Among the Gere, however, the rear border of the seating surface is always decorated with an incised pattern. On occasion one also sees a small chair that has a seat and legs but no back. The Gere recognize this as an older form. Backs were probably introduced only after the encounter with European chairs. The small Gere chairs are made by the same carvers who make masks – the *qui ya zre*.

My attention was drawn to these small chairs as used by the Gere in 1956, when I was carrying out research on one of their subgroups, the Wobe. On the outskirts of the village eleven girls were performing a dance in which each one supported herself on one of these small chairs, banging it on the ground in time to the song she was singing. The dance itself, accordingly, was performed in a stooped position. The girls' faces and breasts were painted white, in each case with a different pattern, and their hair was plaited into elaborate coiffures (fig. 2).

These girls were undergoing circumcision, a rite carried out in camps established each January and February – the height of the dry season – not far from each Gere village. In front of any such camp there is always a small, empty open space, where the girls' mothers and younger siblings, and sometimes also young boys, may stay; the boys are not, of course, allowed into the camp itself. The girls, however, are not forbidden to appear outside the camp, and they are always willing to perform this chair dance in this open space – a dance learnt, and eagerly practised, in every circumcision camp.

The small chairs belong to the old men of the village. They sit on them or they lie on their sides with one arm over the backrest. The old worthy shown here (fig. 1), with his small white pointed beard and his blue and white robe, is resting in this manner, with the chair placed on a goatskin, while he smokes his metre-long pipe with its elaborately cast metal bowl. 'He then thinks', I was told by the chief of the village of Geso, 'about everything that he wants to consider.' At night, however, the chair serves as a headrest, and it is for this reason that it is so low.

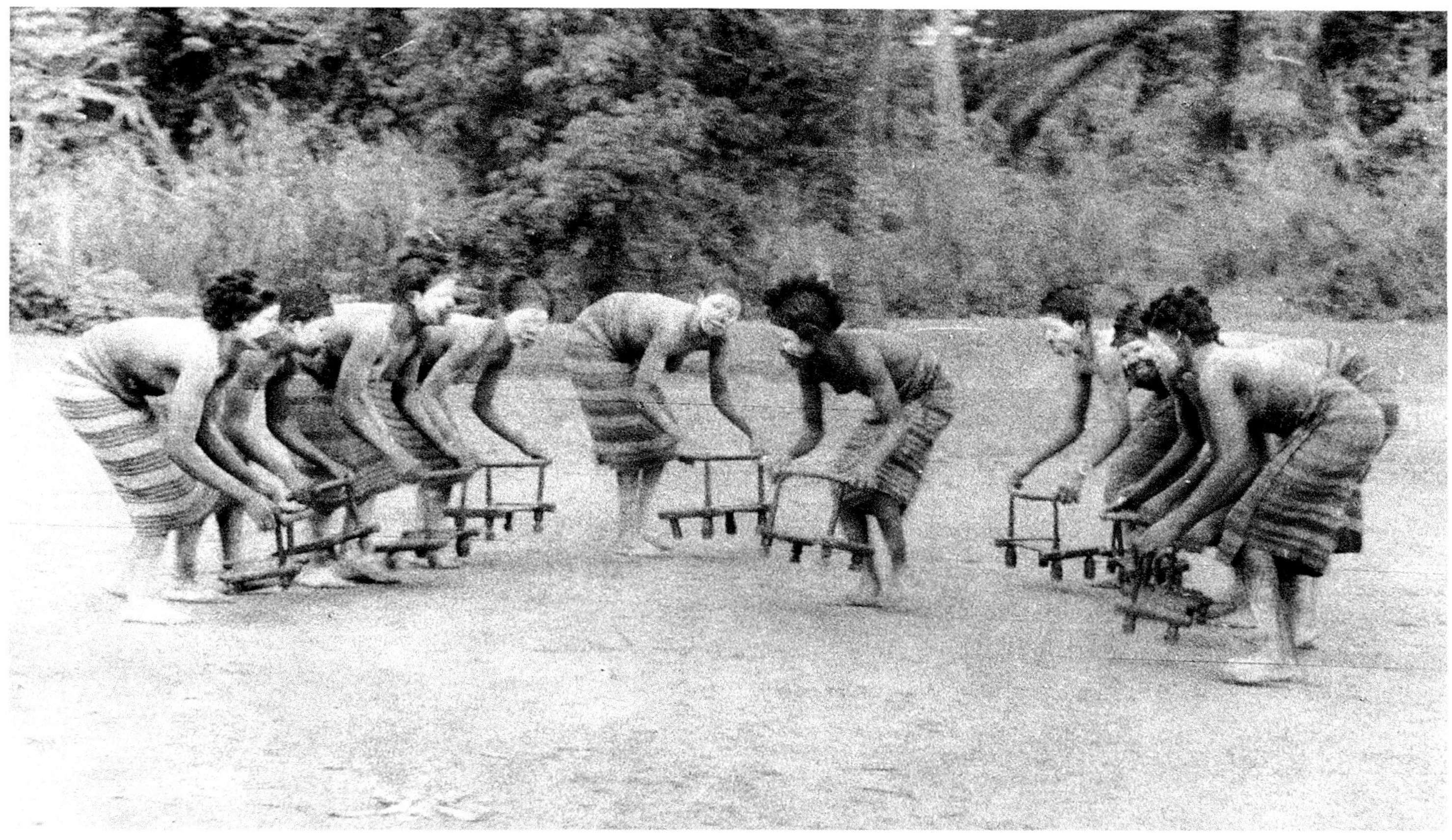

2 Girls performing a dance in which they support themselves on the small chairs, banging them on the ground in a corresponding rhythm. (Photograph: Hans Himmelheber, 1956)

When it is time for a girl to be circumcised, she goes to her grandfather and asks him to lend her his chair for the duration of the circumcision camp. It is very sad if a girl cannot get a chair, for then everyone will be able to tell that she is a poor orphan with no family to support her.

According to my informant, the girls need the chairs in the camp 'because, when they are there, they are not allowed to sit down when speaking to visitors outside the camp, lest their loincloths gape open. They may only kneel, and they kneel on the chairs.' We should, however, bear in mind that the Gere only recently adopted the use of cotton cloth from the Guro. More to the point may be the fact that sitting is painful for the girls while the circumcision wound is still fresh. The custom may also relate to the fear of the influence of evil spirits and thus the desire to avoid exposing the wound and the female sexual organs. There is, of course, the firm conviction that evil spirits lie in waiting to prey on people, especially during any transitional phase of life, where they are like butterflies sliding out of a chrysalis and still helpless and unprotected. For this reason no circumcision camp is without its specially assigned exorcists.

It is clear, then, that these small chairs are an element of Gere culture that especially preoccupies the Gere imagination. There are, accordingly, sayings which symbolically incorporate these chairs. One may, for example, say; '*gba bo guli*' (a little chair in one's own courtyard). This signifies: in a debate it is often the case that each one is right from his own point of view (or, each one has his own little chair in his own courtyard), and one can cease to be in the right if one insists too much on one's own point of view (or on one's own seat).

3 A small chair of the Dan, comparable to those of the Gere, Ivory Coast; cf. cat. 14.

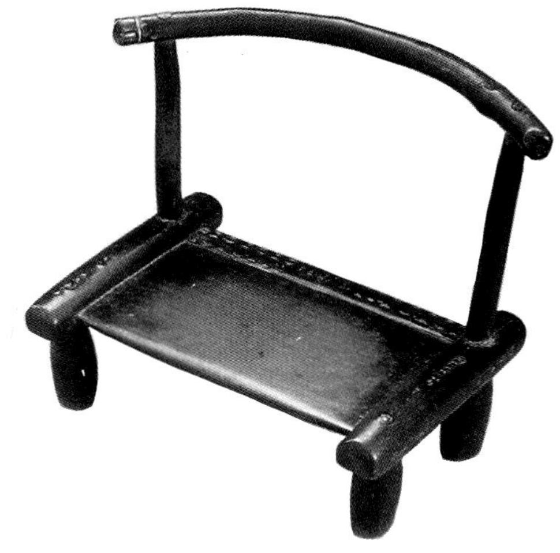

Asante Stools

Drawing on a flexible canon of basic types, the Asante of Ghana have evolved a wide variety of stools, to which many different meanings are assigned. Here, sayings play an important role. Each Asante king was keen to put his name to a stool with a new design. We offer here a selection from the large range of forms found among Asante stools. (Information provided by Prof. E. Ablade Glover, University of Science and Technology, Kumasi.)

1 Owo Foforo Adobe Dwa
The snake climbs up the palm tree. The impossible should be attempted.

2 Srane Dwa
The moon stool is for both men and women.

3 Sakyi Dua Koro Dwa
This stool is only to be used by priestesses and priests during ceremonies.

4 Esono Dwa
The elephant stool may only be used by the Asantehene.

5 Mmarima Dwa
Only the male head of the family may sit on this stool.

6 Mframadan Dwa

7 Nnama Dwa
The poor man's 'tuppence stool'. It is simply carved and originally cost tuppence.

8 Kotoko Dwa
The porcupine stool. The porcupine is a symbol of the Asante nation: if one is killed, there are hundreds following. It embodies the notion of readiness to defend one's nation.

9 Nsebe Dwa
The amulet stool.

10 Mmom Dwa
A stool for chiefs of the second degree.

11 Ahema Dwa
This stool for the queen mother has features in common with the porcupine stool (no. 8). We may presume this is to show how close the queen mother and the Asantehene are, both politically and socially.

12 Nkonta Dwa
Stool for the principal stool-bearer.

13 Obi-Te-Obi-So Dwa
One man sits on another's stool. This stool is used only by the highest kings on festive occasions.

14 Nyansapow Dwa
The wisdom knot stool. Only a wise man can untie the wisdom knot.

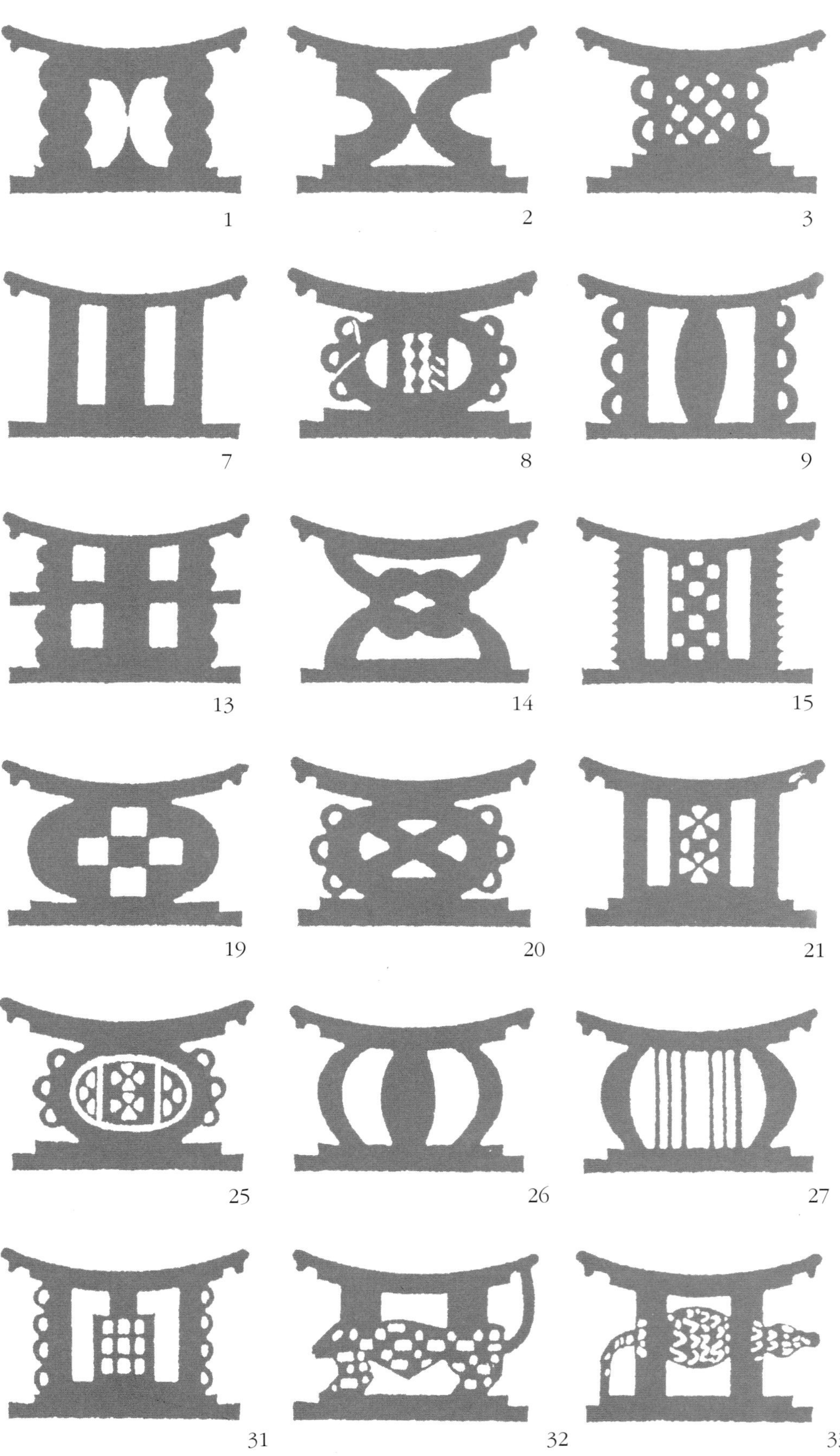

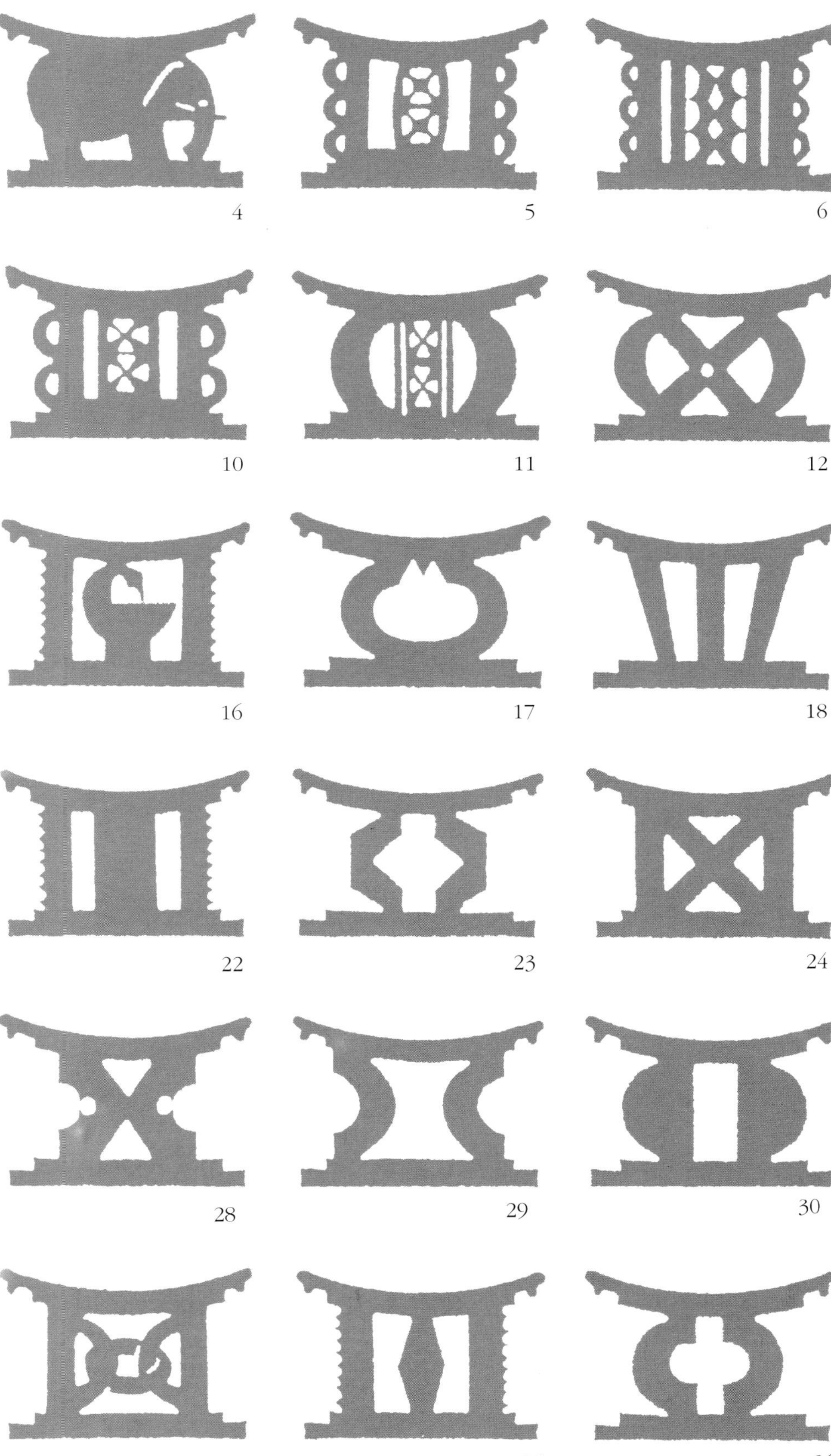

15 Mma Dwa
Womens' stool. Traditionally, a man gives his wife a stool when they marry.

16 Sankofa Dwa
The stool with the backward looking sankofa bird signifies: learn from the past.

17 Krado Dwa
The stool in the shape of a padlock is used by chiefs and the king's spokesmen.

18 Owuo Atwere Dwa
Stool in the form of a ladder, signifying: each man must climb the ladder of death.

19 Damedame Dwa
Chequer-board stool. The symbolism probably testifies to European influence as there is no draughts tradition in Africa.

20 Mmaremu Dwa
The cross stool. This stool belongs exclusively to the Asantehene. Others may sit on it only with his permission.

21 Me Fa Asa Dwa
This stool was exclusively for use by women.

22 Ahema Dwa
A queen mother's stool.

23 Wenchihene Dwa

24 Juasohene Dwa

25 Kontonkoriwi Mpemu Dwa

26 Adinkra Dwa

27 Atuduro Kwadom Dwa

28 Kumawuhene Dwa

29 Ede Nka Anum Dwa
Sweetness in the mouth is transitory: there are bad times as well as good.

30 Adontinhene Dwa

31 Pantu Dwa
Stool in the shape of a gin bottle.

32 Osebo Dwa
The leopard stool symbolizes the power and influence of the Asantehene, and is reserved for him alone.

33 Ademkyem Dwa
The stool with the crocodile holding a fish in its mouth is used by priests for the shrine.

34 Brakante Dwa
Stool of King Brakante of Akyem. The motif echoes that of the wisdom knot stool (no. 14).

35 Agonahene Dwa

36 Mamponghene Dwa
Stool of the Mamponghene, who represents the Asantehene during the latter's absence.

Map of African Peoples

Listed below are the peoples whose seats are considered in this volume

1 Bidjogo
2 Baga
3 Guerze
4 Malinke
5 Toma
6 Dan
7 Gere/We
8 Senufo
9 Lobi
10 Bambara
11 Dogon
12 Gurunsi
13 Guro
14 Baule
15 Yohure
16 Asante
17 Kuwe
18 Nago
19 Yoruba
20 Nupe
21 Mumuye
22 Bamileke
23 Baham
24 Bamum
25 Babanki
26 Kom
27 Tikar
28 Oku
29 Duala
30 Kota
31 Ngombe
32 Jonga
33 Kuba
34 Mabinza
35 Meje
36 Mangbetu
37 Zande
38 Pende
39 Chokwe
40 Lwena
41 Imbangala
42 Lega
43 Kusu
44 Hemba
45 Luba
46 Songye
47 Bongo
48 Galla
49 Gurage
50 Tabwa
51 Nyamwezi
52 Hehe
53 Zaramo
54 Safwa
55 Kamba
56 Maasai
57 Makonde
58 Shona
59 Thonga

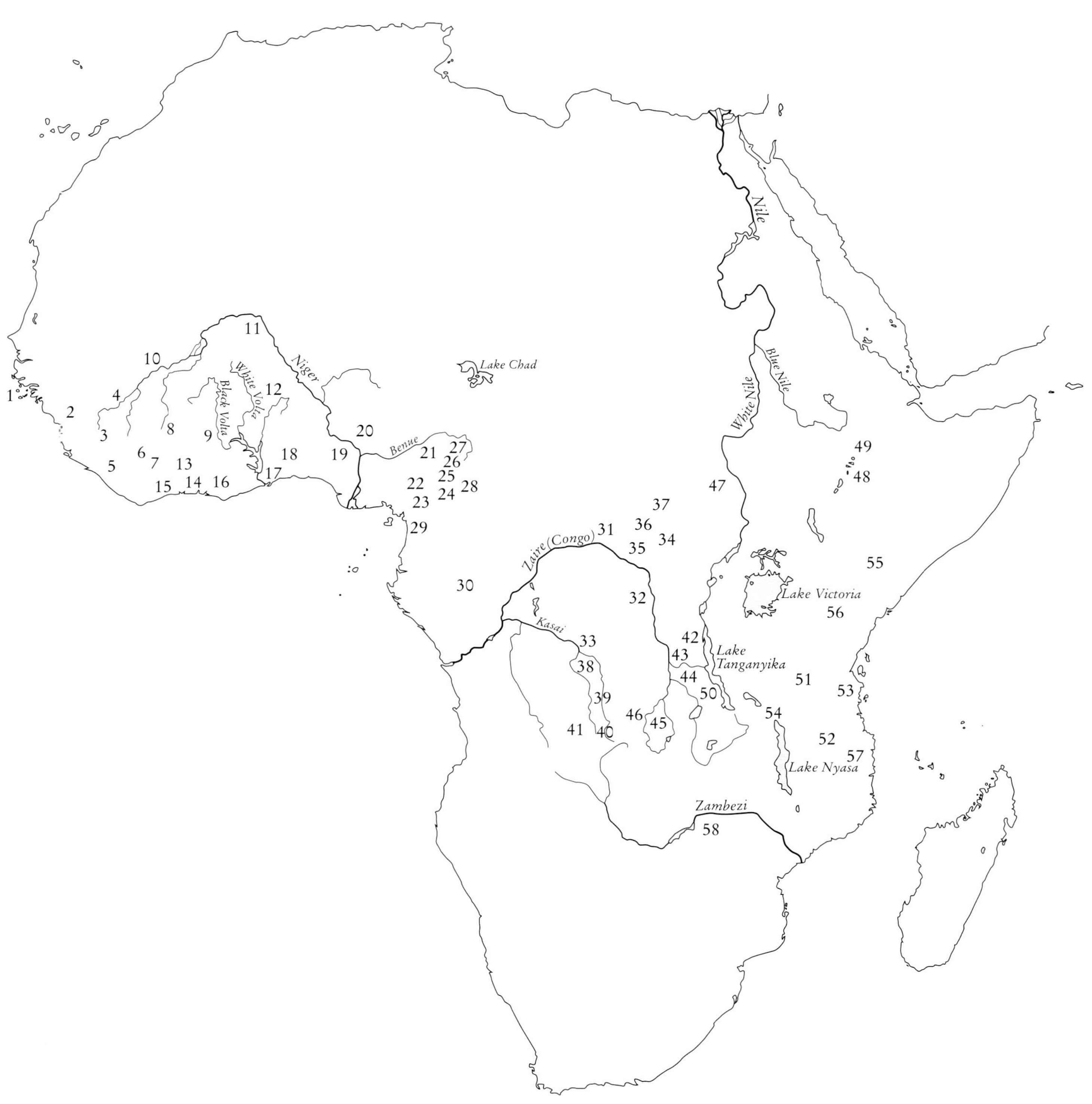
Nile
Blue Nile
White Nile
Lake Chad
Niger
White Volta
Black Volta
Benue
Zaire (Congo)
Kasai
Lake Victoria
Lake Tanganyika
Lake Nyasa
Zambezi
1
2
3
4
5
6
7
8
9
10
11
12
13
14
15
16
17
18
19
20
21
22
23
24
25
26
27
28
29
30
31
32
33
34
35
36
37
38
39
40
41
42
43
44
45
46
47
48
49
50
51
52
53
54
55
56
57
58

Political Map of Africa

Showing the modern states embracing the areas of origin of the seats considered in this volume

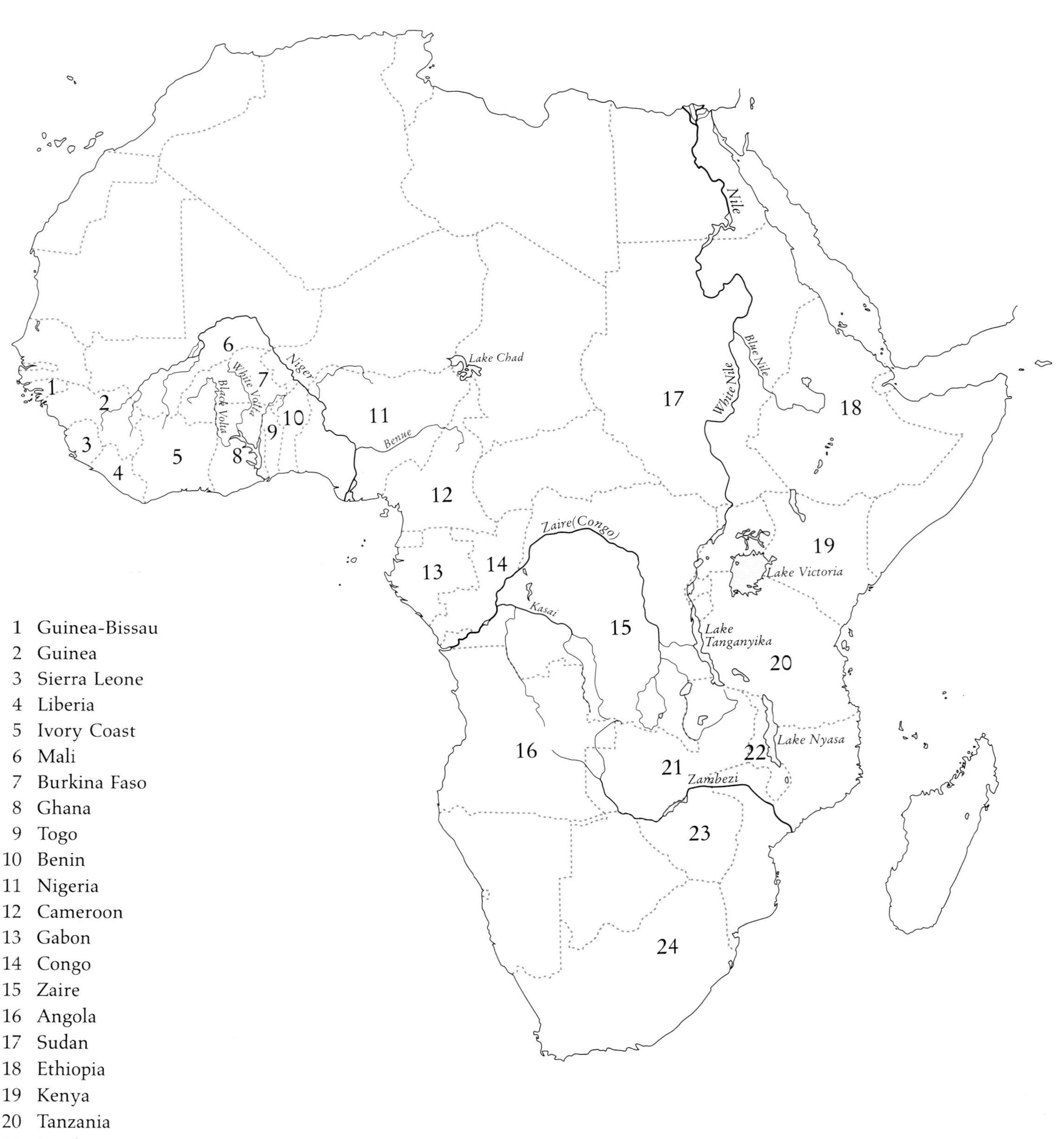

1 Guinea-Bissau
2 Guinea
3 Sierra Leone
4 Liberia
5 Ivory Coast
6 Mali
7 Burkina Faso
8 Ghana
9 Togo
10 Benin
11 Nigeria
12 Cameroon
13 Gabon
14 Congo
15 Zaire
16 Angola
17 Sudan
18 Ethiopia
19 Kenya
20 Tanzania
21 Zambia
22 Malawi
23 Zimbabwe
24 South Africa

Plates

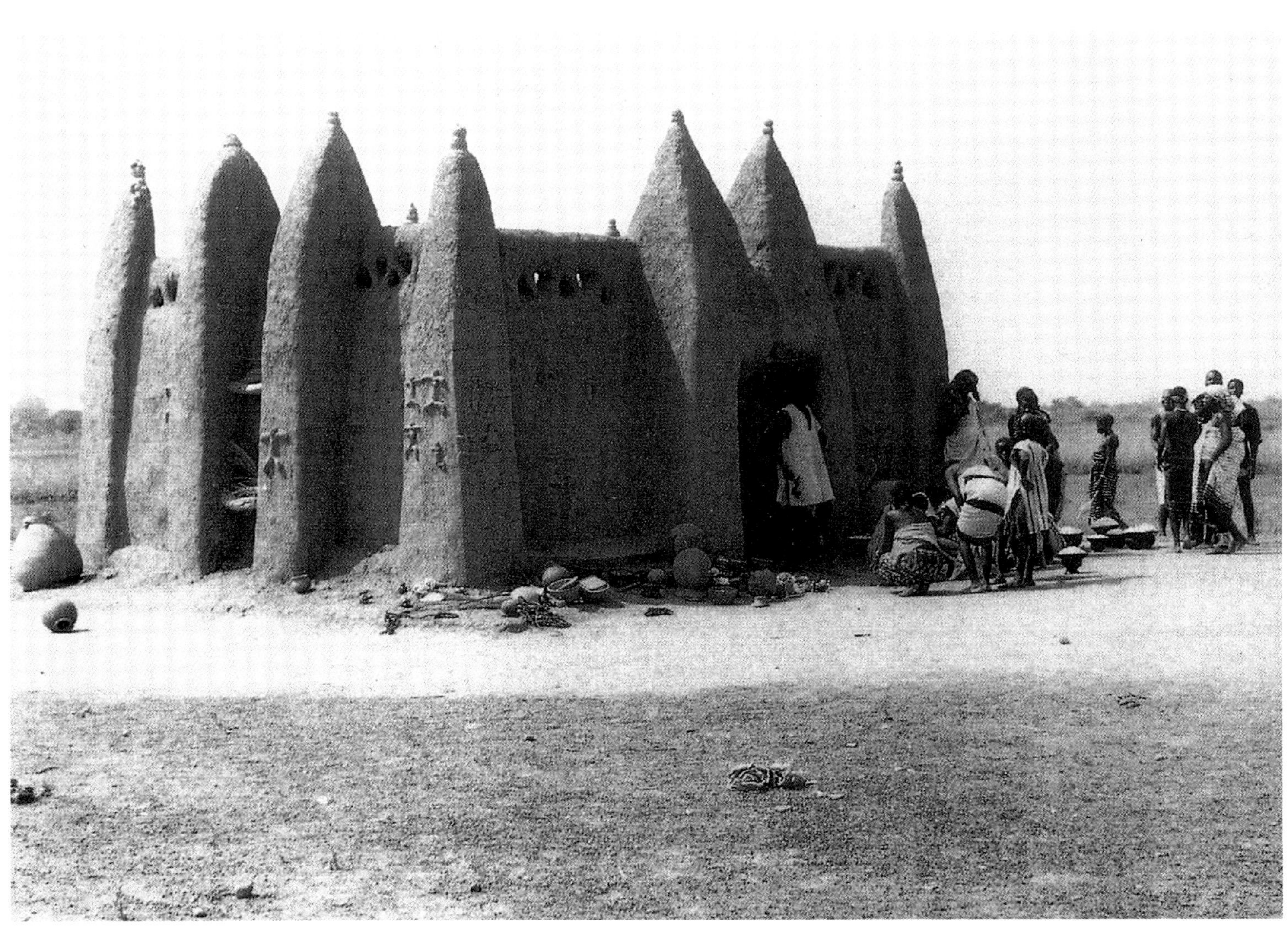

A temple dedicated to the Massa, a spirit worshipped by the followers of a syncretistic religious movement that evolved in the 1950s. This building, located in the north-eastern Senufo region, is in a style typical of the mud architecture of the Sudanese savannah. (Photograph: Hans Himmelheber, 1952)

Sudanese Savannah and the Coast of Guinea

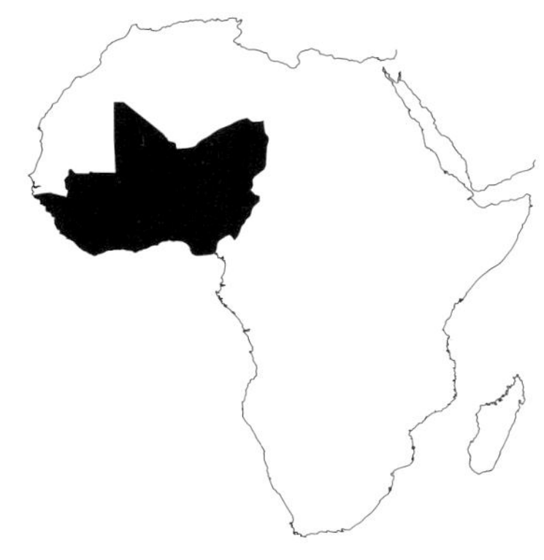

The Sudan – the Arabic term for 'land of the blacks' – extends right across the northern part of Africa, from west to east, embracing land at the edge of the desert, savannah and those tropical coastal regions where the rainforest has been almost completely destroyed by man over the last four centuries. From its source in western Sudan, the River Niger first winds its way to the north-east, into the desert regions. There, deep within the continent, it temporarily takes the form of an inland delta. Then, changing its course on the plateau of the legendary city of Timbuktu, it flows east and then south-east. After another three thousand kilometres, having widened into a much more powerful river, it meets the Atlantic in southern Nigeria, in the region of the Ijo. Many peoples – above all those living in what is now Mali, Burkina Faso and Nigeria – depend on the river for their fundamental needs.

The western Sudan has had a turbulent history. Traces have been found here of human cultures that could already lay claim to great artistic achievements thousands of years ago: prehistoric rock drawings in the Ahaggar Mountains, a range in the middle of the Sahara, not only hint at a culture of hunters and herdsmen, but also testify to the presence of a flora and fauna of the sort associated with rich woodland, in what is now the world's largest region of desert. When Carthage and Rome were in their heyday, there was still constant activity along both trade and communication routes between the Sahara and the Mediterranean.

The terracotta art works of the Nok culture were discovered near Jos in Nigeria: technical analysis has shown them to date from between the fifth century BC and the second century AD (fig. 6 on p, 40). From the point of view of cultural history, the most significant influence on this part of Africa came from the great kingdoms of Ghana (Shongai) and Mali, established, respectively, in the seventh and the thirteenth centuries. The impact of both on the science and economy of that period in turn marked the history of the Arab Mediterranean and thus the greater part of the Mediterranean region.

In the tenth century, in what is now Nigeria, the kings of Ife were sufficiently strong to establish an empire with a strict hierarchical structure. They also employed artists at their courts – above all bronze casters and ivory carvers, and certainly also sculptors who worked in wood (though traces of the work of this last group have not been found by archaeologists). These artists created works of consummate realism. Ife was at last defeated by its warlike neighbours, who were initially based in the classical city of Benin, capital of the kingdom of that name. These then established a trading empire in what is now south-western Nigeria, which endured from the fourteenth to the nineteenth century. Here bronze casting continued to flourish. While we now know a good deal about the bronze casters of Benin, the bronzes of the so-called Igbo-Ukwu culture, found along the lower reaches of the River Niger and datable to the eleventh and twelfth centuries, have yet to be more thoroughly researched.

Relatively few of the peoples of West Africa that have come to our notice on account of the works of art they produced can be associated with a feudal system. Most of the objects of everyday use presented in this exhibition – sometimes elaborately decorated but often plain and captivating on account of their form – emerged from rural societies. Most of the carvers who produced traditional figures were principally engaged in working the land as settled crop farmers. Their worship of the soil, variously detectable in funeral ceremonies and the commemoration of

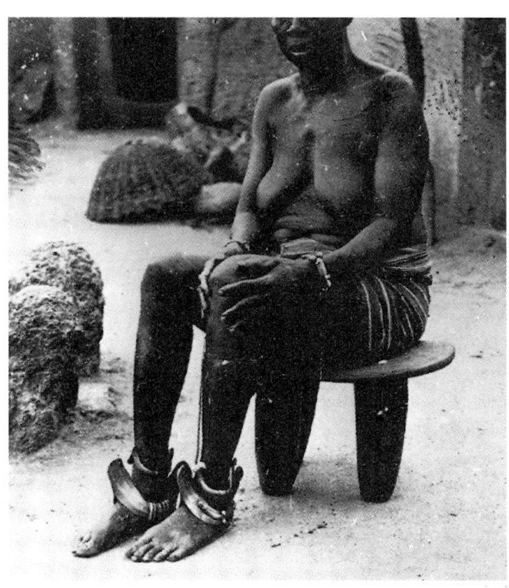

A woman sitting on a stool of the type still in use in the Senufo region. African women carry out a great many of their household tasks in a seated position. These Senufo stools are heavy and very stable. They are therefore also suitable for use as laundry tables when clothing is washed in the river; cf. cat. 24. (Photograph: Aubert de la Rue, before 1940)

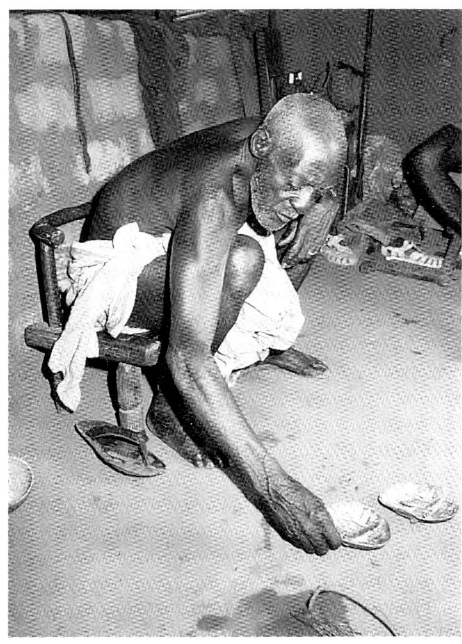

A diviner in Bogopenfla, Ivory Coast. The old man is sitting on a stool typical of those used by the Guro. (Photograph: Lorenz Homberger)

their ancestors, is closely bound up with a cult of masks and with rituals of veneration both for and through the figural assisting spirits of the household shrines. Masks representing human beings, spirits or animals played an integral part in important religious and social events, rites of passage (birth, initiation into secret societies, death etc.) and fertility rituals (at times of sowing and harvest).

Western Sudan is readily associated with traditionally produced stools that are simple and yet fascinating in terms of their design. Aesthetically appealing seats of this kind are part of everyday life for women, men and children. Among the Malinke and the Dan there are fine examples of stools with a circular seating surface, while circular and oval seats with two or four legs are above all to be found among the Senufo (Ivory Coast, Burkina Faso, Mali), the We (Liberia and Ivory Coast) and the Guerze (Guinea) (plates on pp. 55–8, 61). In the first group, the legs merge into a single solid base forming an almost exact reflection of the upper part of the seat. Many of these seats have four solid legs that hardly taper at all.

The seats produced by the Bidjogo workshops in Guinea-Bissau are often decorated with caryatid figures and have a U-shaped surface (plate on p. 68). The circular stools of this region have an expansive plate-shaped seating surface with three or more legs carved in the form of figures (cat. 2). The Yoruba, settled in Nigeria and Benin, have also produced magnificent carved stools with supports often in the form of women carrying children. According to specialists, these thrones are not used for sitting, but rather as a support for pots of medicine in household shrines. On many of these Yoruba stools one finds traces of blood or the encrusted remains of sacrifices (plates on pp. 62, 64–5).

Stools of an emphatic solidity that is generally offset by an elegantly sweeping shape are produced by the Dogon (Mali) and the Baule (Ivory Coast). The first, as a rule, have relief-like carvings and take the form of a rider's mount, with the addition of a horse's head and tail. Those of the Baule region have handles carved at the sides (plate on p. 67; cats. 31–34). Among the Mumuye, who live in south-western Nigeria, both head and tail are added to the opposite sides of plain stools, thus increasing their similarity to an animal (cat. 58).

In the region of the Lobi and the Gurunsi (Burkina Faso) we find seats that are unusually elegant in design, with the surface generally resting on three short, sturdy legs (plates on pp. 54, 59). These stools, always made from a single block of wood, are easily carried on the shoulder, their formal beauty notwithstanding. Here, functionality and sheer strength of design merge in an inspired manner.

The small chairs of the We (Gere), on the other hand, are usually assembled with legs, seat and back made from several separate pieces of wood. The very simple basic shape, presumed to have originated among peoples living on the southern Ivory Coast and in Liberia (who possibly adapted a European model), was later imitated by their neighbours – the Dan, the Guro, the Baule, the Malinke and the Senufo (plates on pp. 71–3; cats. 14–21; photograph on p. 70). The adapted forms found among the Malinke and the Senufo, moreover, have a virtually 'baroque' character, with legs and even backs cut in the form of figures; both this and their large scale reveal strong European influence.

As was the case with the Nigerian dynasties, the royal courts of the Akan peoples, who live in Ghana (the former Gold Coast) and along the Ivory Coast, employed sculptors and goldsmiths. These were responsible for the magnificent furnishing of the palaces, for royal jewellery and for the insignia of prestige. At the court of the Asantehene (the Asante king) the highest symbol of royal power was the Golden Stool (fig. 2 on p. 31). According to oral tradition, this throne (of pure gold) fell out of the sky and landed at the feet of Osei Tutu, who became the first Asante king. Since then this stool has been worshipped as a symbol of supernatural power and displayed to subjects on important holidays as a guarantee of the unity of the nation

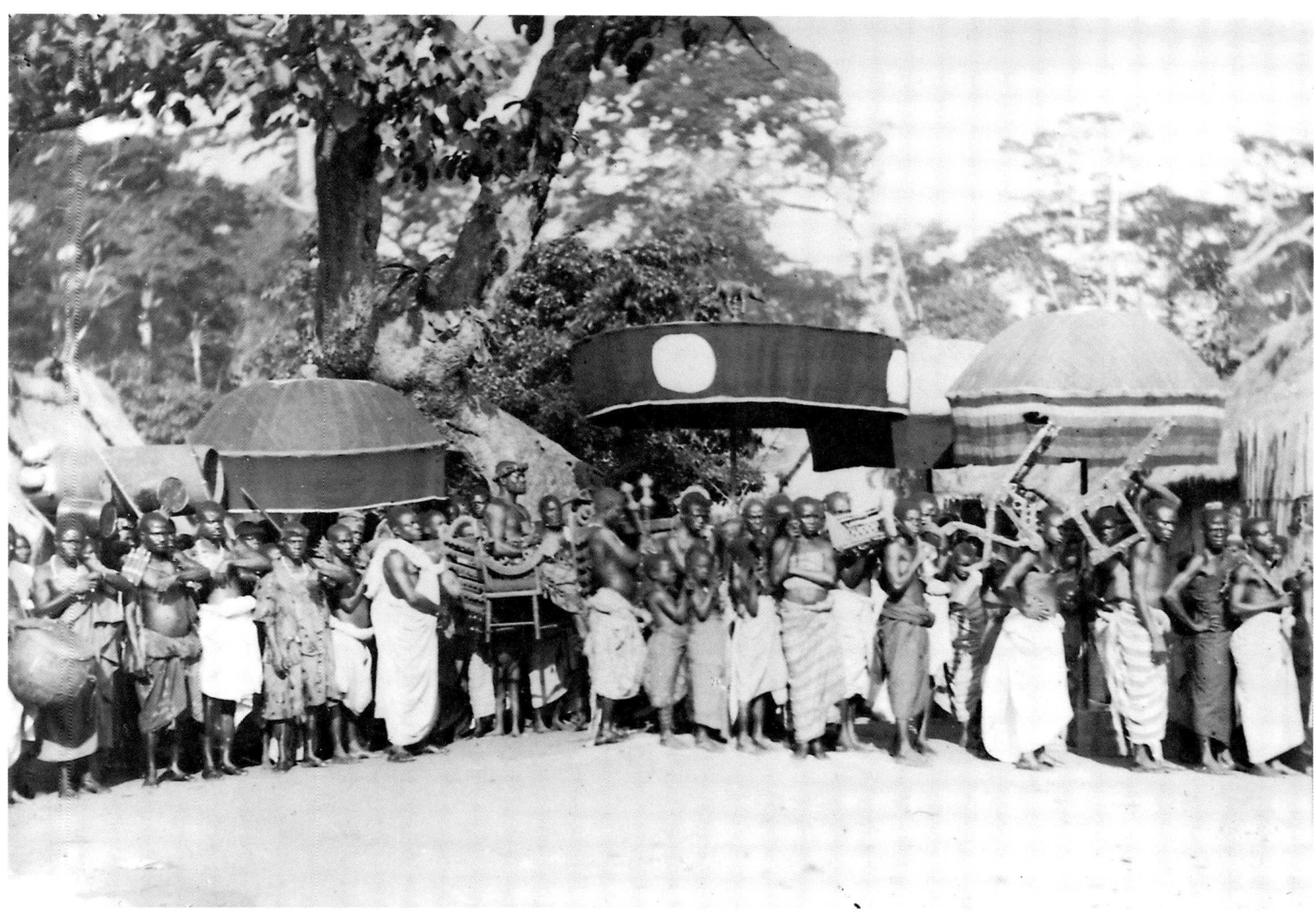

and the divine authority of the king. No mortal may sit on the Golden Stool. Today many superior personages among the Asante possess seats of this sort; and anyone who is an aristocrat of some significance within the courtly hierarchy inherits his own 'throne' from his father or uncle. These precious seats, with their unmistakable, softly curving T-bar form, the elongated oval of their upper surface, and their frequent covering of gold or silver leaf, are among the most important symbols of status, dignity and power in the Akan kingdoms (plates on pp. 75, 78, 79, 82; photograph on p. 74).

In addition to these traditional stools, Asante princes and notabilities also used chair-like thrones called *asipim*, their seats and backs often decorated with sheet metal and brass nails (plate on p. 76). The even more decoratively carved *akonkromfi*, which have further ornamentation added to their arms and can also be carried as a form of sedan chair, are already illustrated in very early engravings, thus establishing the existence of this type prior to the arrival of Europeans (plate on p. 77; cats. 50–52). Many of these brass-mounted chairs have a number of striking formal similarities to the golden throne of the Egyptian Tutankhamun, which was made in about 1358 BC. While this does not justify the attempt to evolve a new 'Nile Valley Thesis', the claim that 'European' styles became established in African tradition only after the arrival of the Portuguese does need to be considered more carefully.

Lorenz Homberger

A tribal prince in Kwahu, Ghana, perhaps the headman of Abetifi, with his court in a festive procession. Tokens of his exalted rank, for example particular stools and chairs, are also carried in the procession. This is characteristic of a strictly structured society with a markedly ceremonial form of art. Works of art are displayed on important public occasions in order to distinguish a prince and his court from their subordinates. (Photograph: F. Ramseyer, *c.* 1888–96)

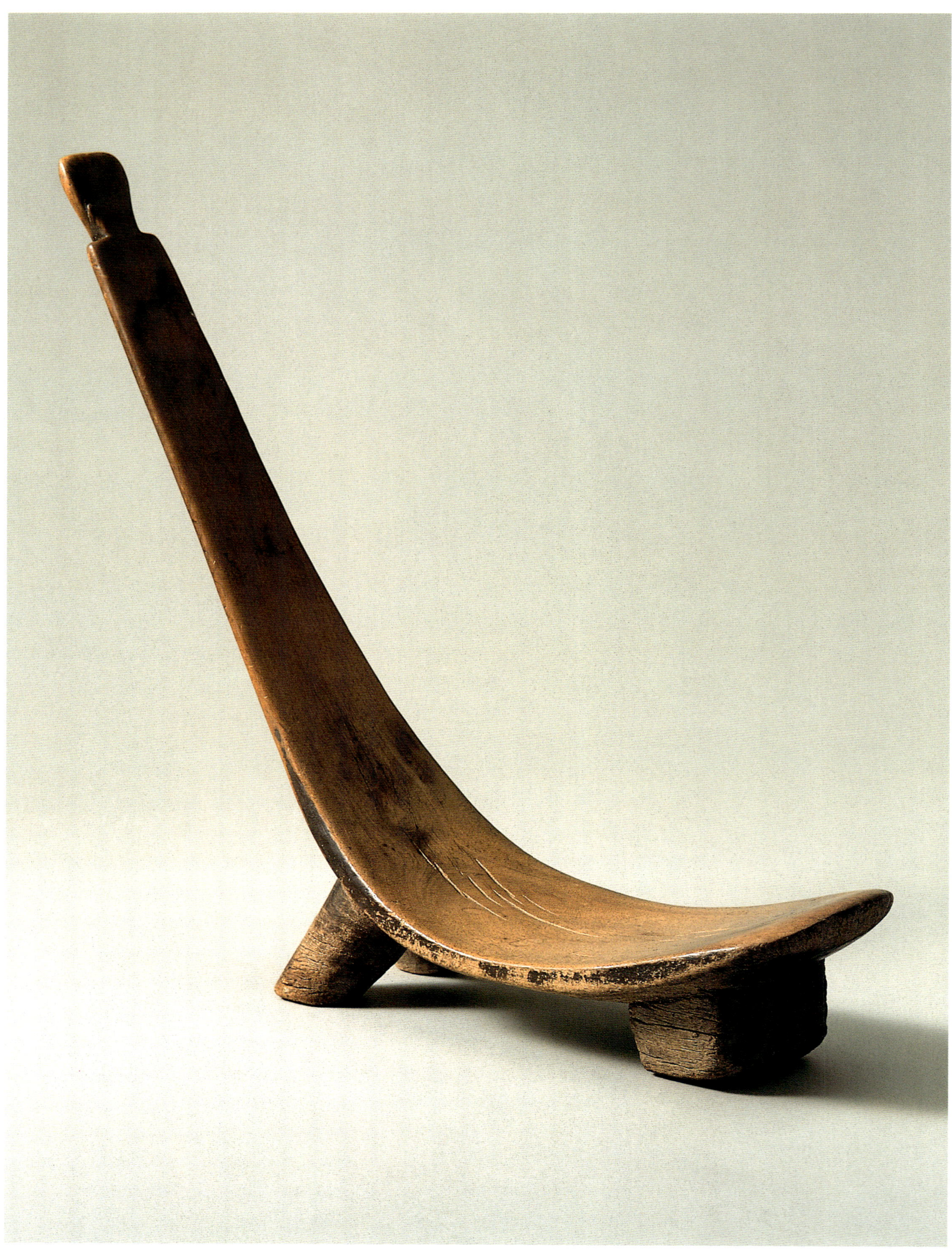

 Semi-reclining chair of the Lobi, Ivory Coast, height 59 cm Cat. 26

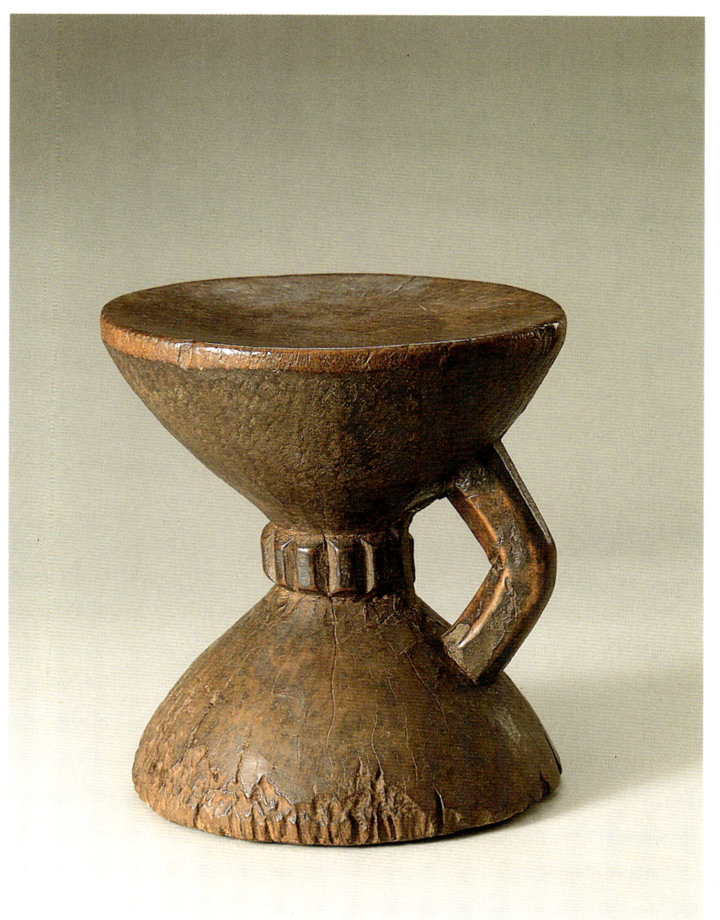

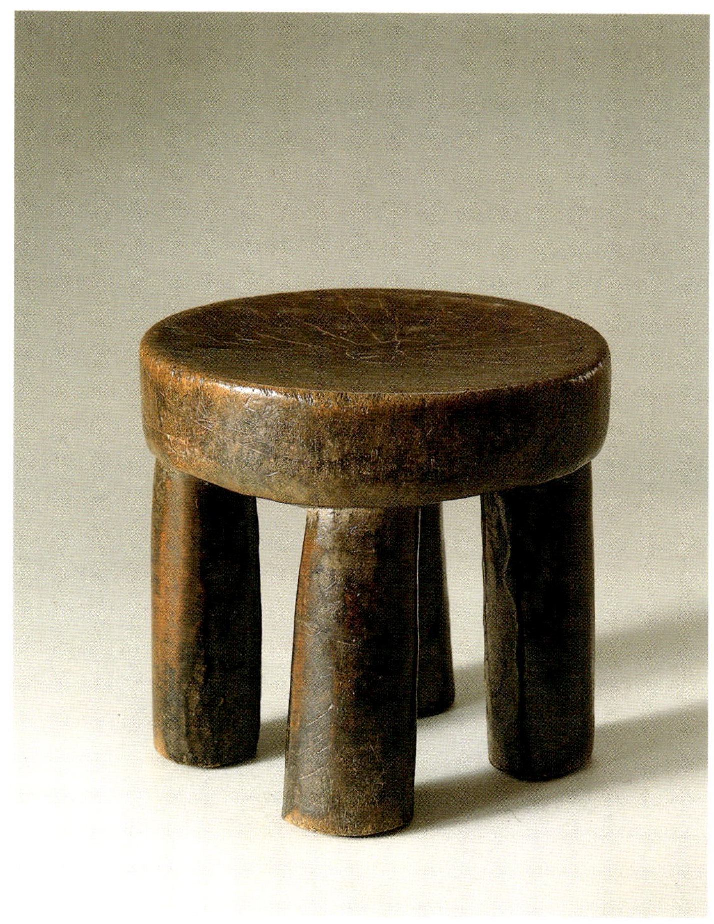

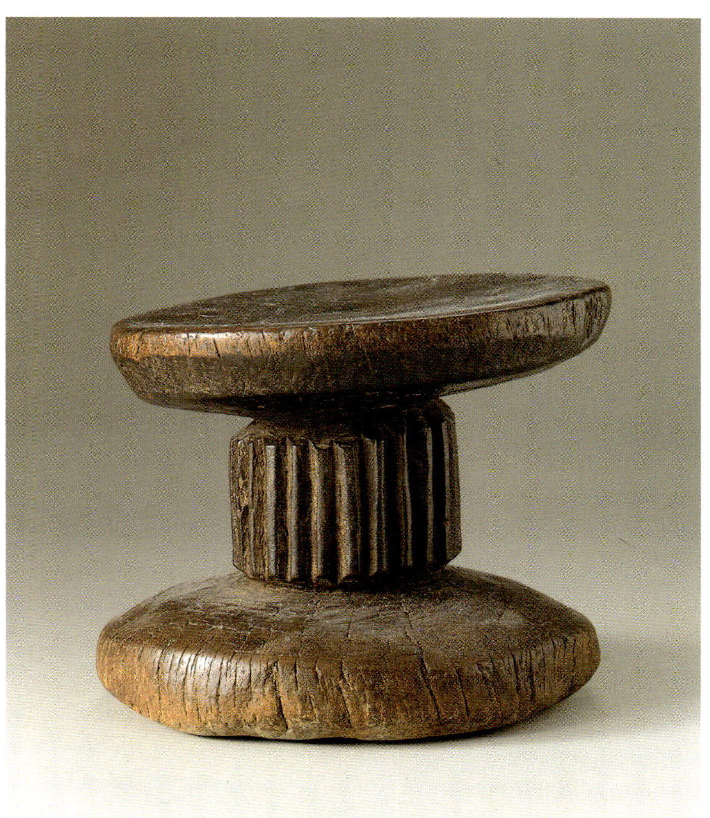

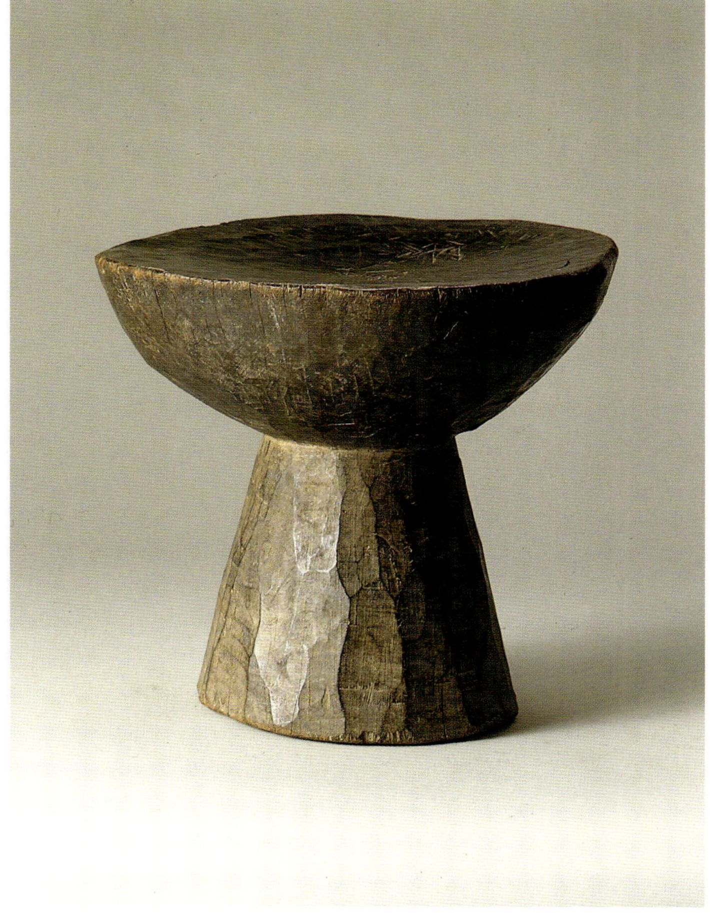

Top: Stools of the Dogon, Mali, and of the Senufo, Ivory Coast, height 26.5 cm and 22 cm   Cats. 12, 22
Bottom: Stools of the Malinke, Guinea, height 21 cm and 30 cm   Cats. 9, 8

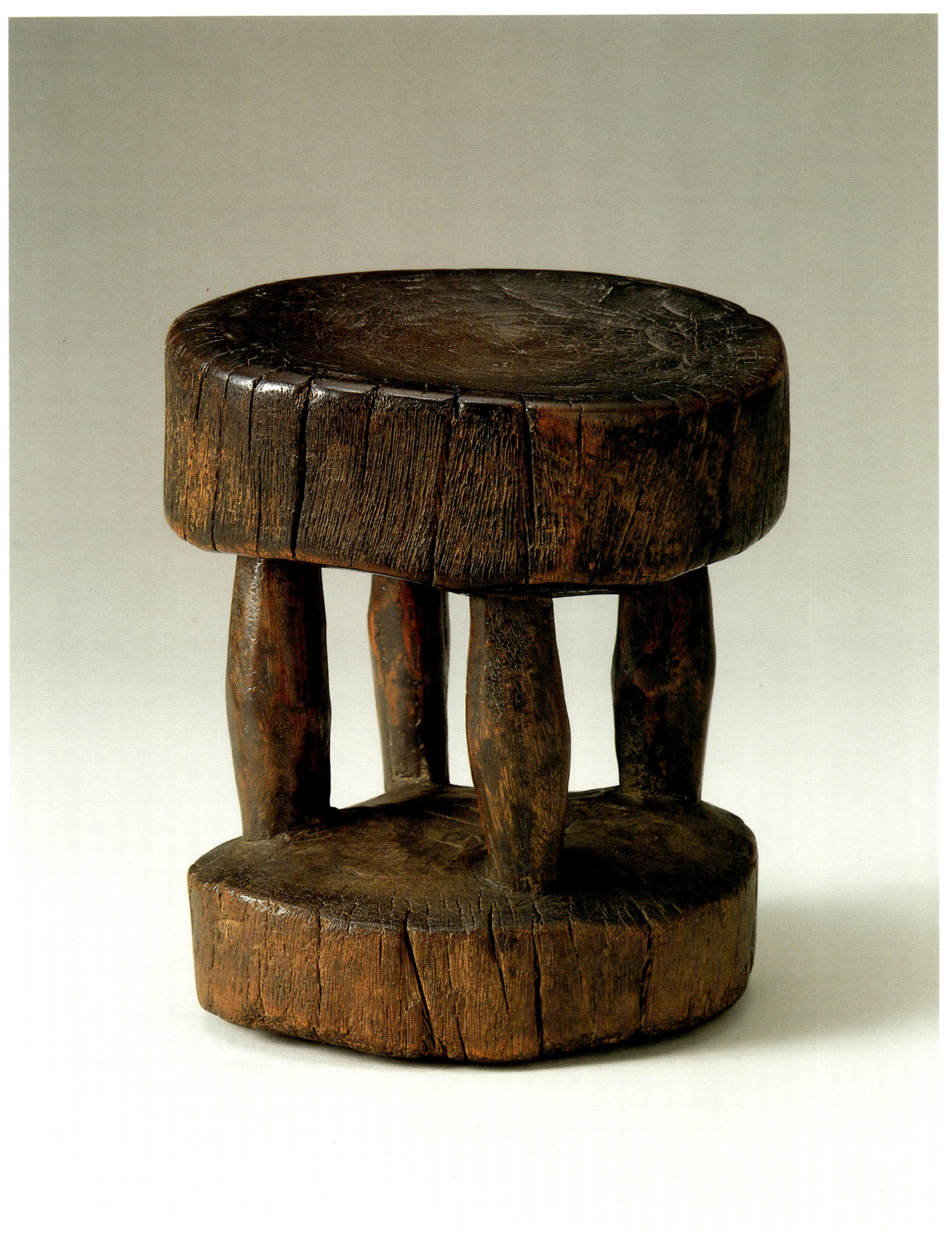

Stool from Guinea, height 27.2 cm Cat. 3

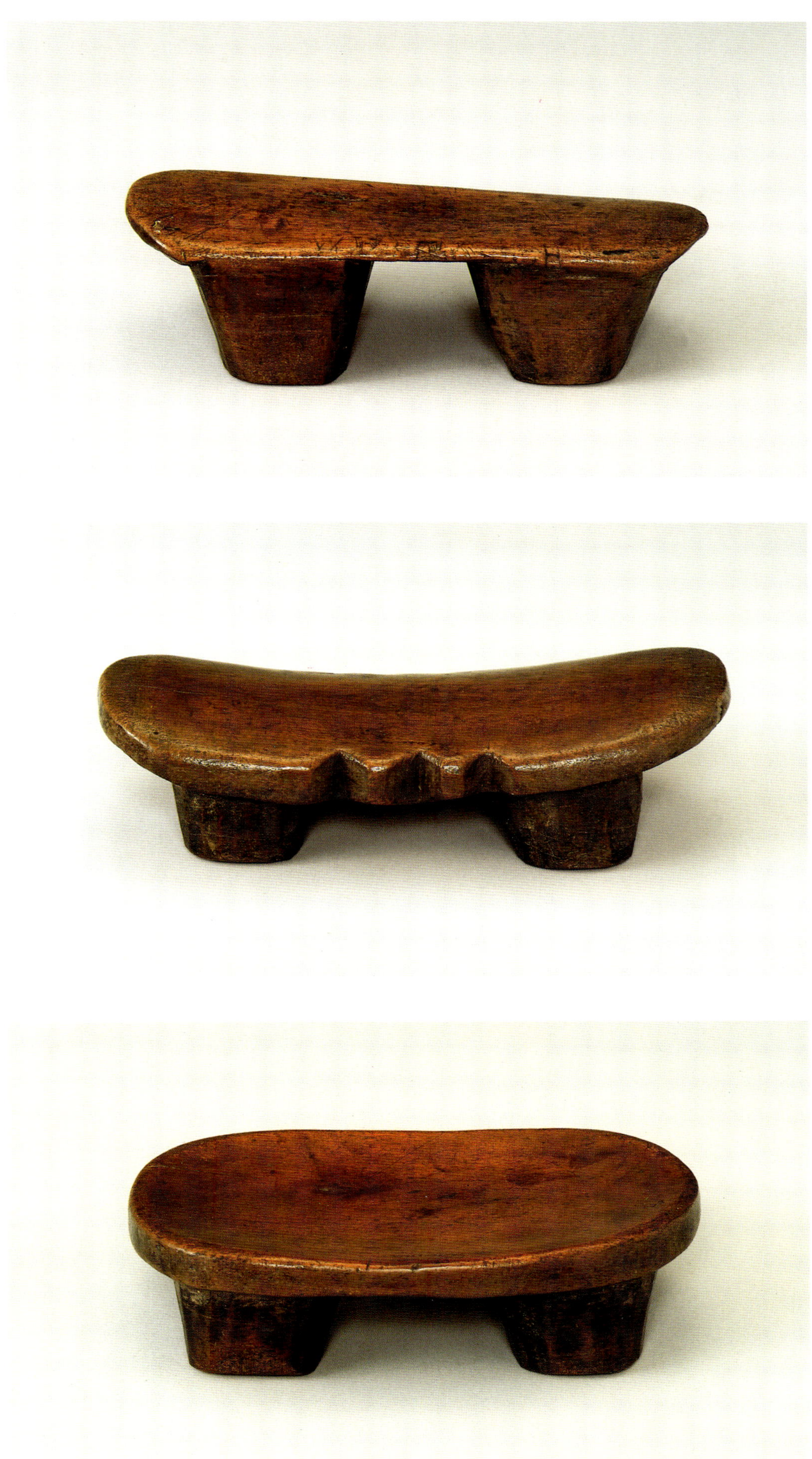

Stools of the Guerze, height 6.8. cm, 8 cm and 7 cm Cats. 4, 6, 5

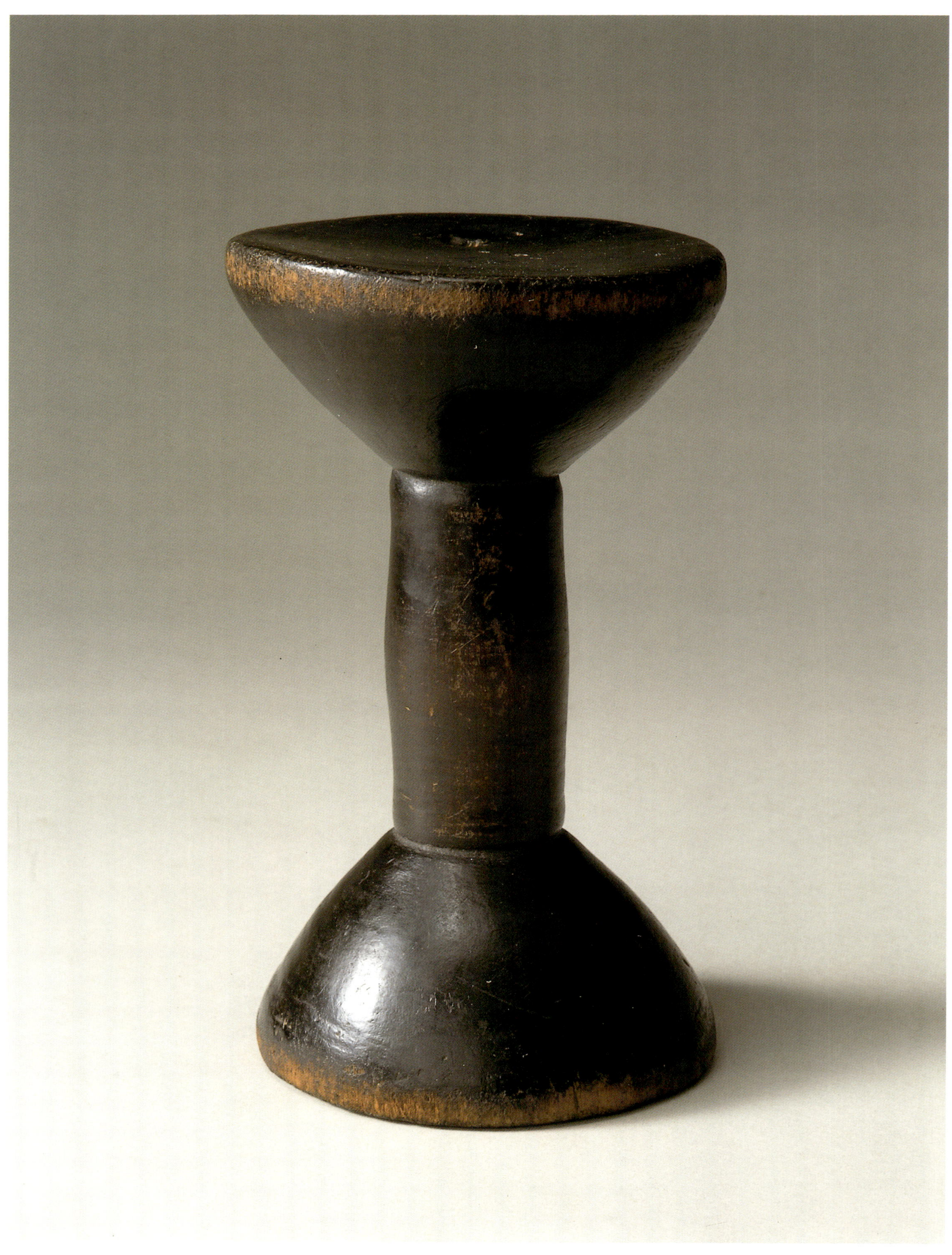

Stool of the Dan (Yacuba), Ivory Coast, height 27.5 cm Cat. 11

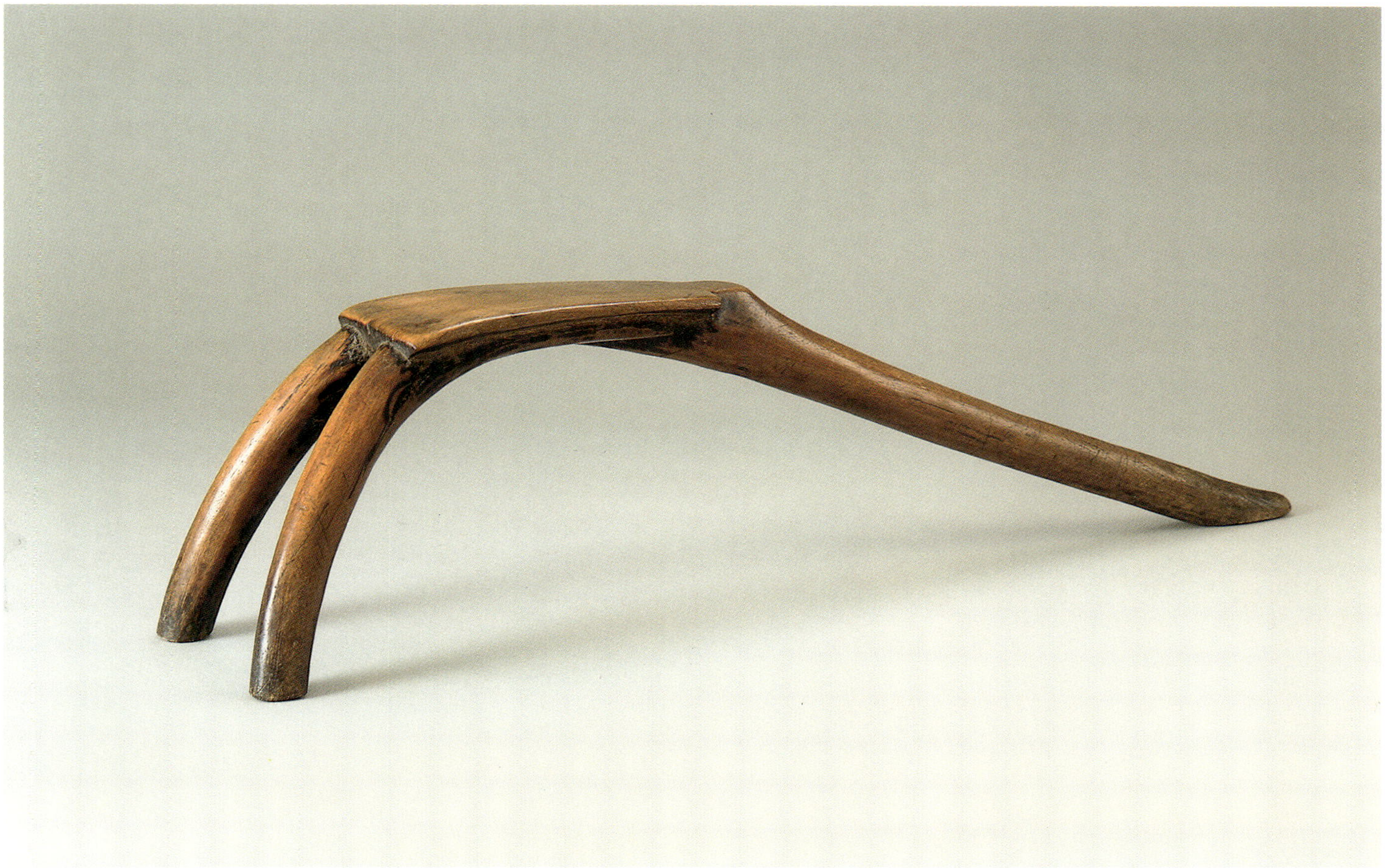

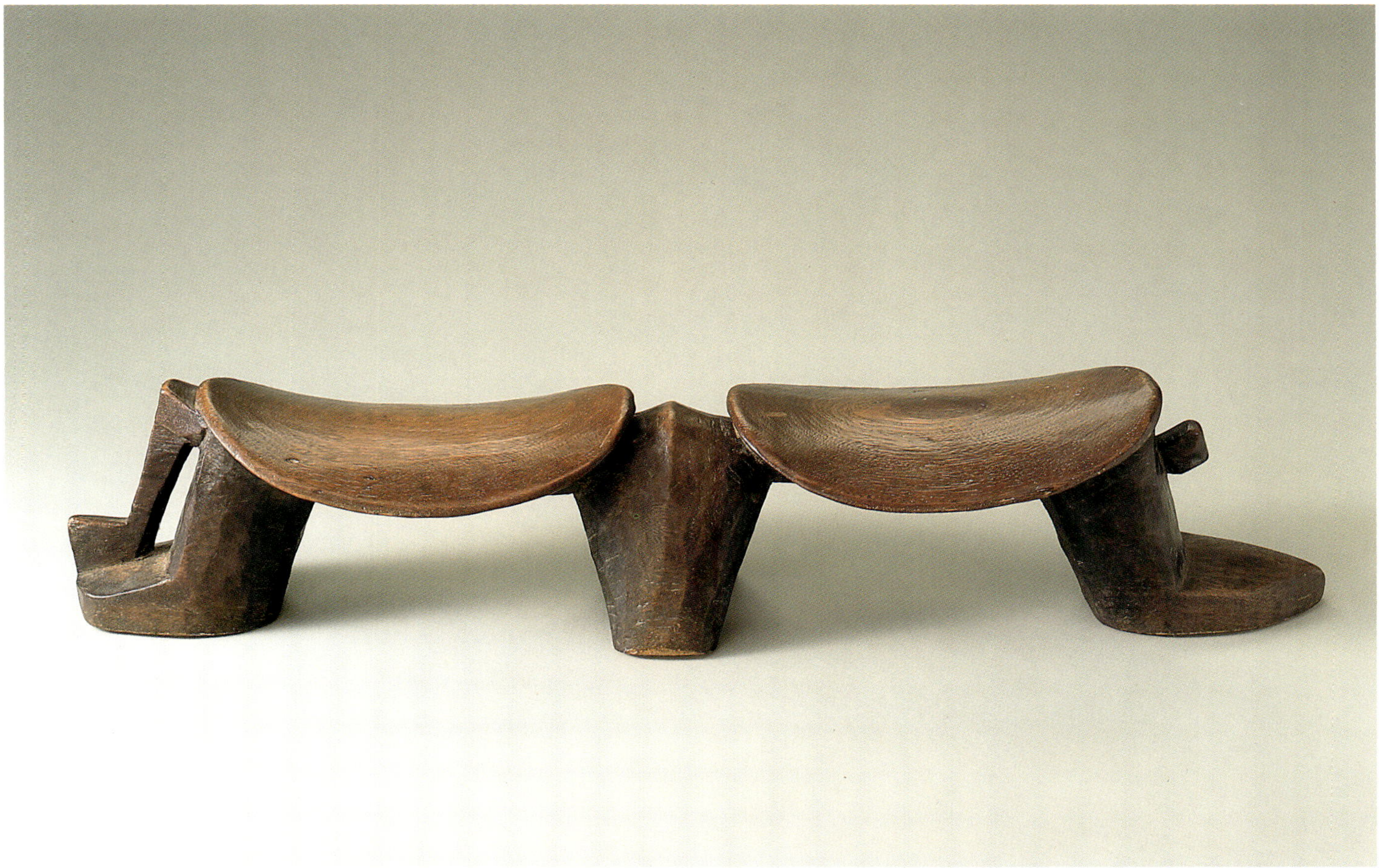

Stool of the Lobi, Ivory Coast, height 19 cm Cat. 25
Double stool of the Gurunsi, Burkina Faso, height 20.3 cm Cat. 27

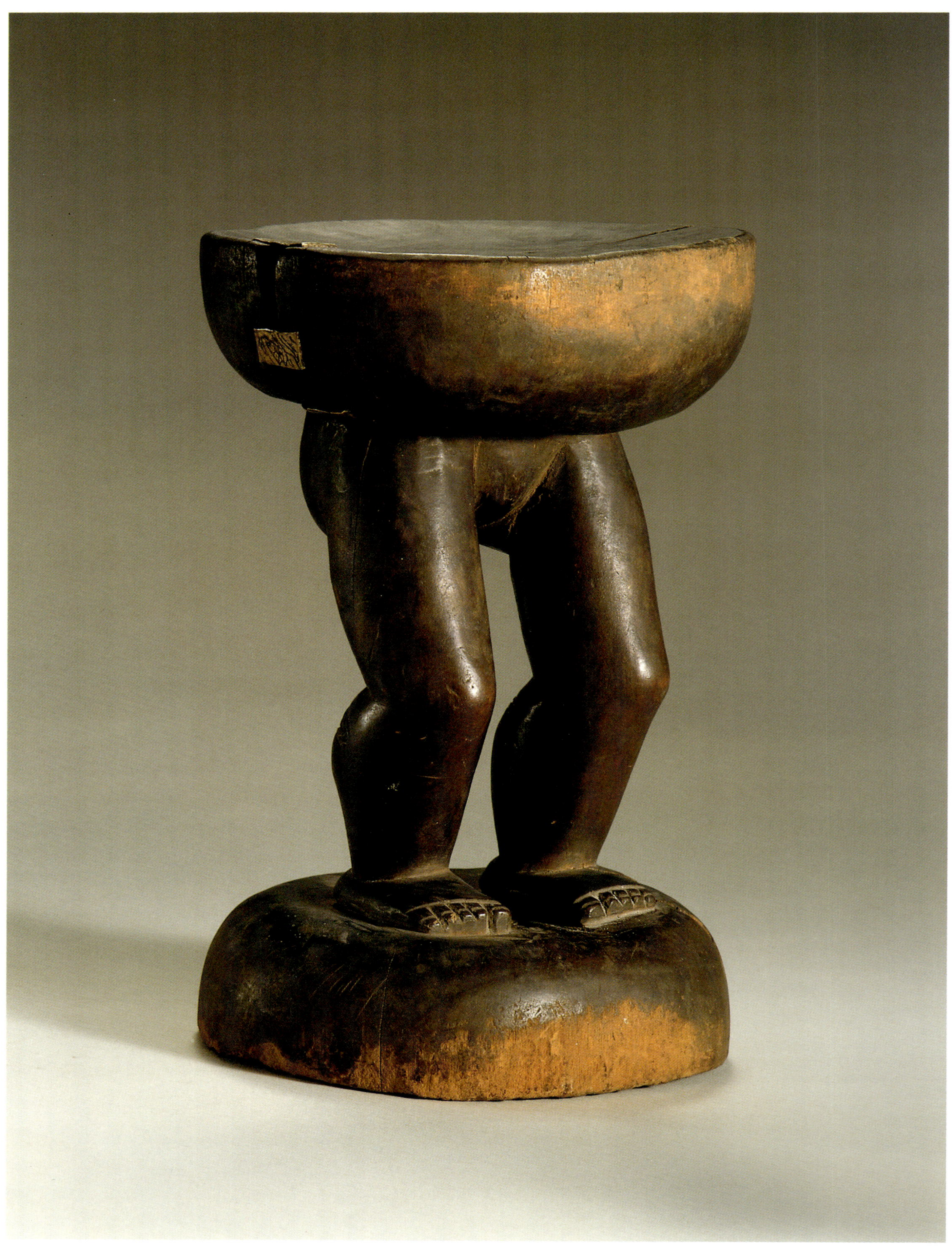

Stool of the Dan, Ivory Coast, height 30 cm Cat. 28

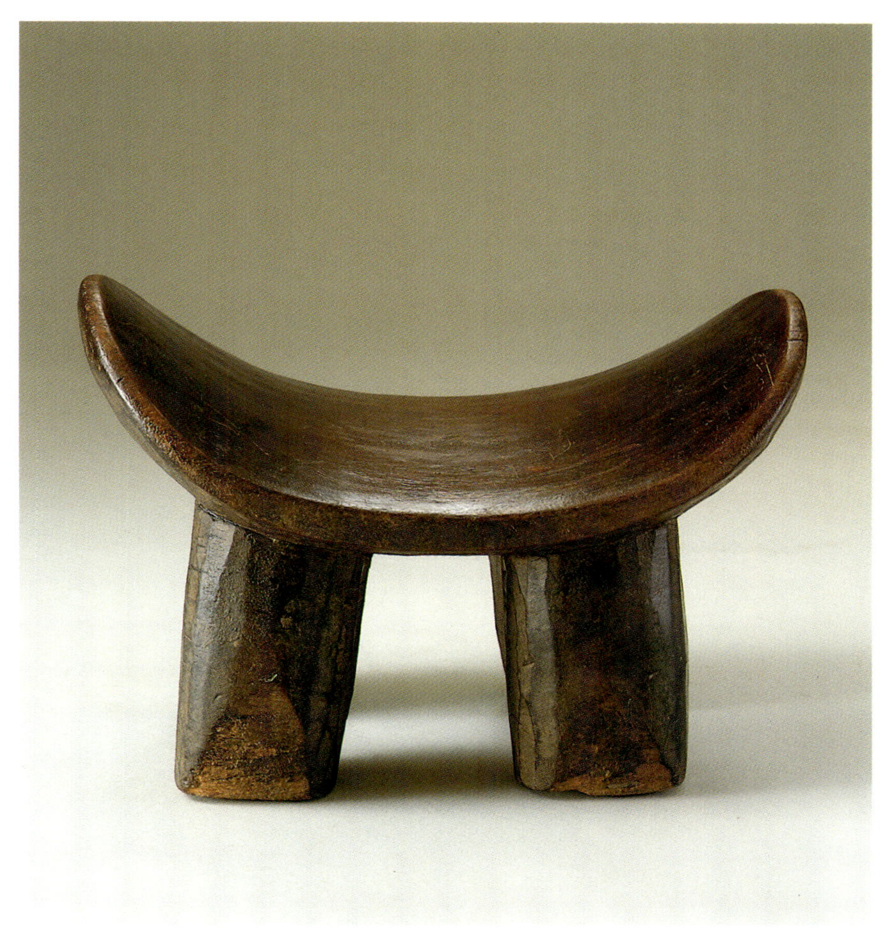

Stool of the Senufo, Ivory Coast, height 22 cm Cat. 23

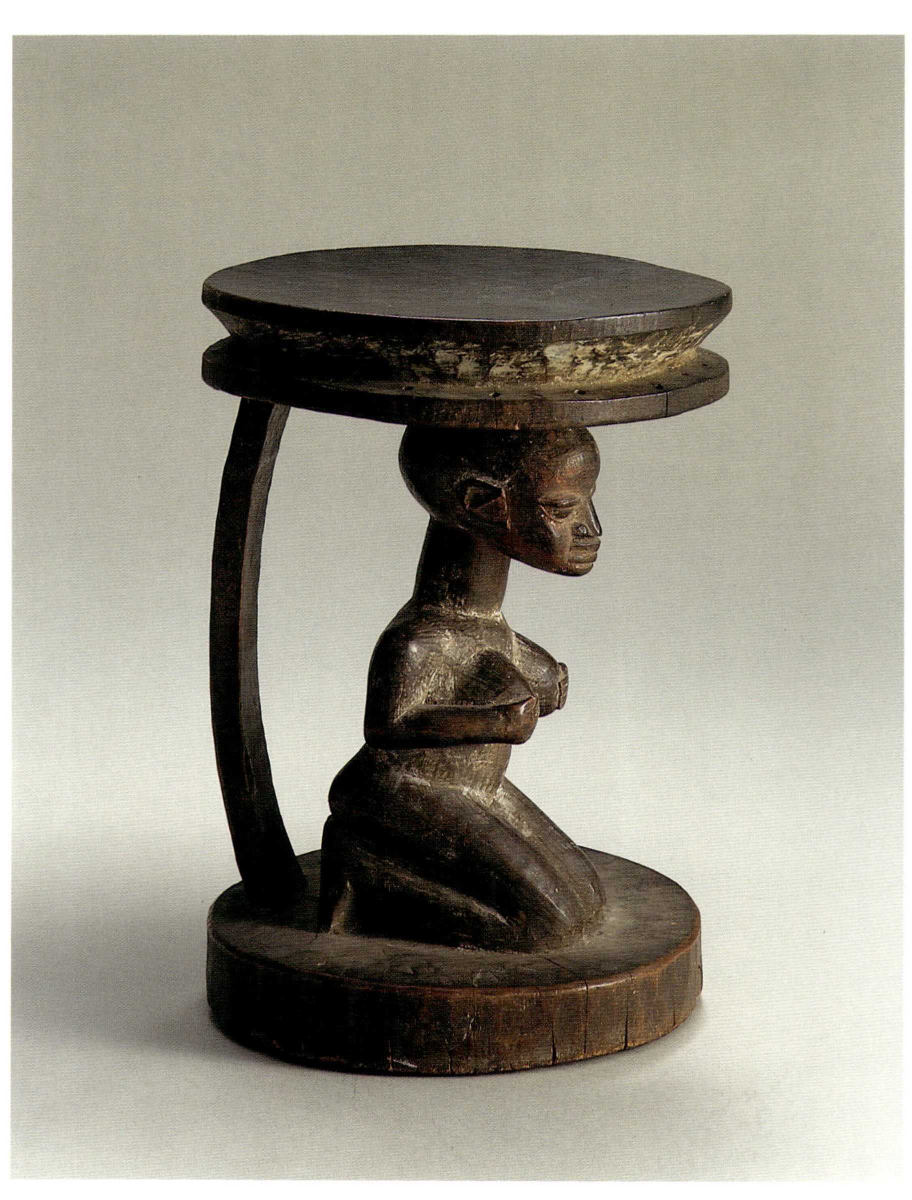

Caryatid stool of the Yoruba, Nigeria, height 32 cm Cat. 55

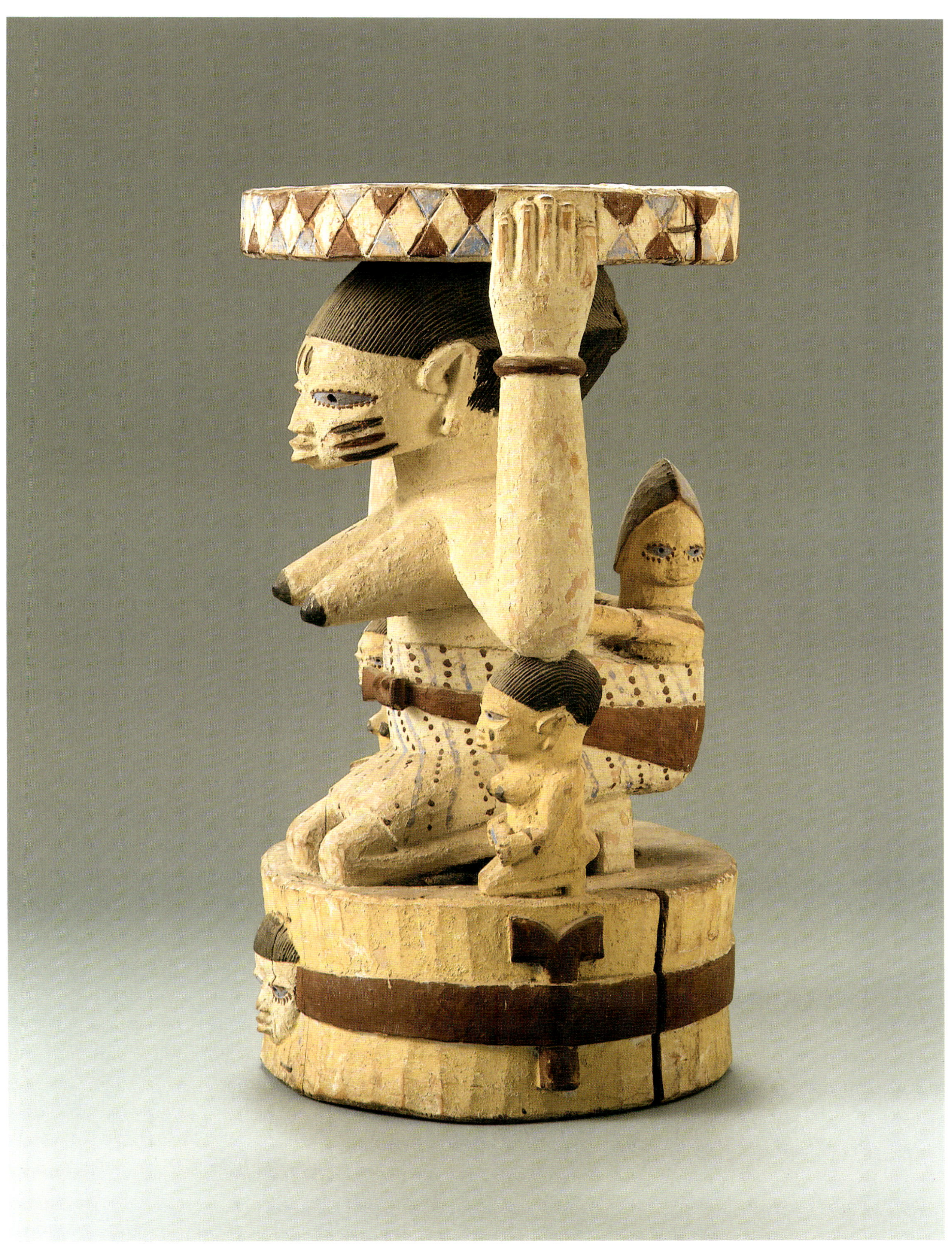

Caryatid stool of the Nago, Benin, height 60 cm Cat. 54

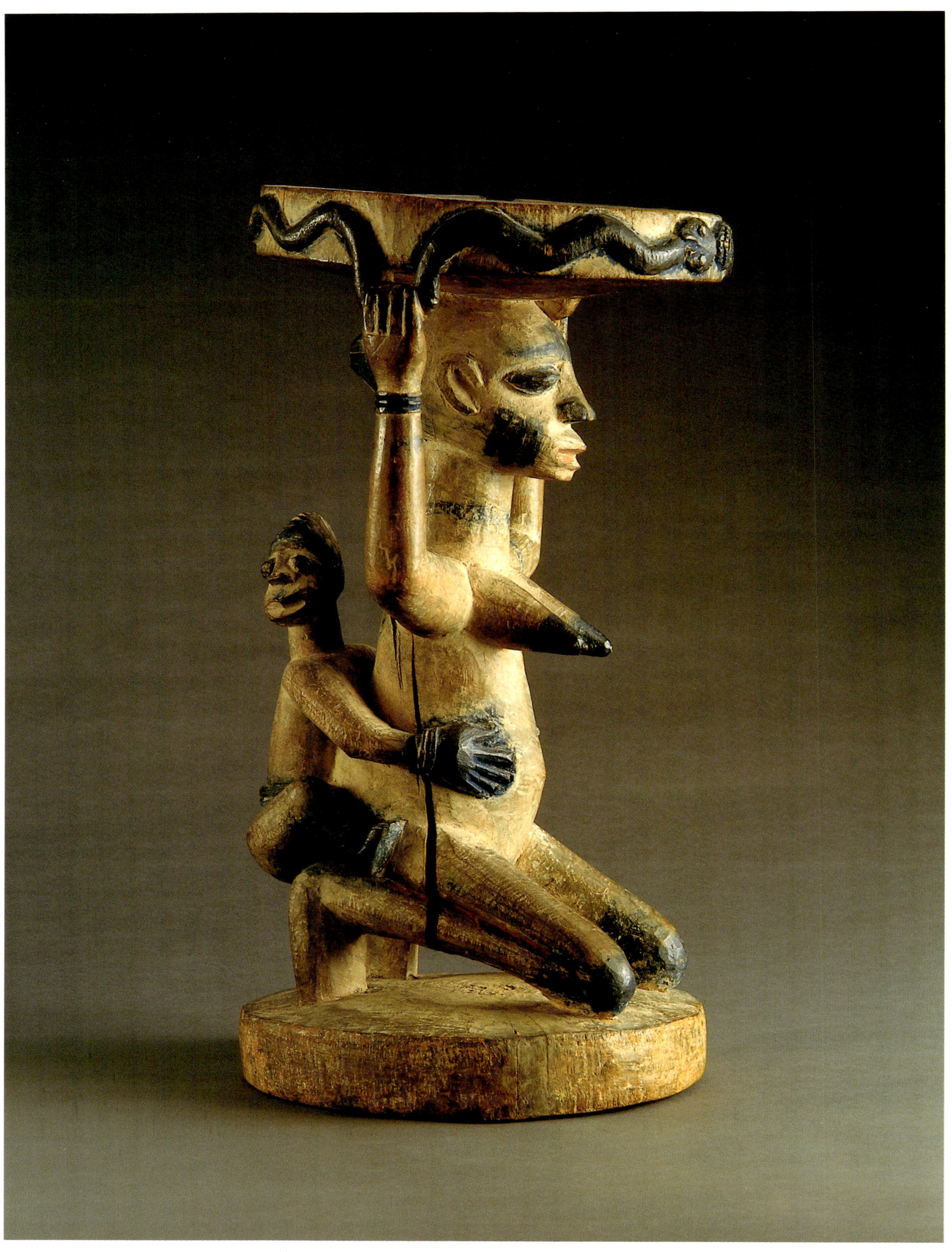

Caryatid stool of the Yoruba (?), Benin, height 52 cm   Cat. 53

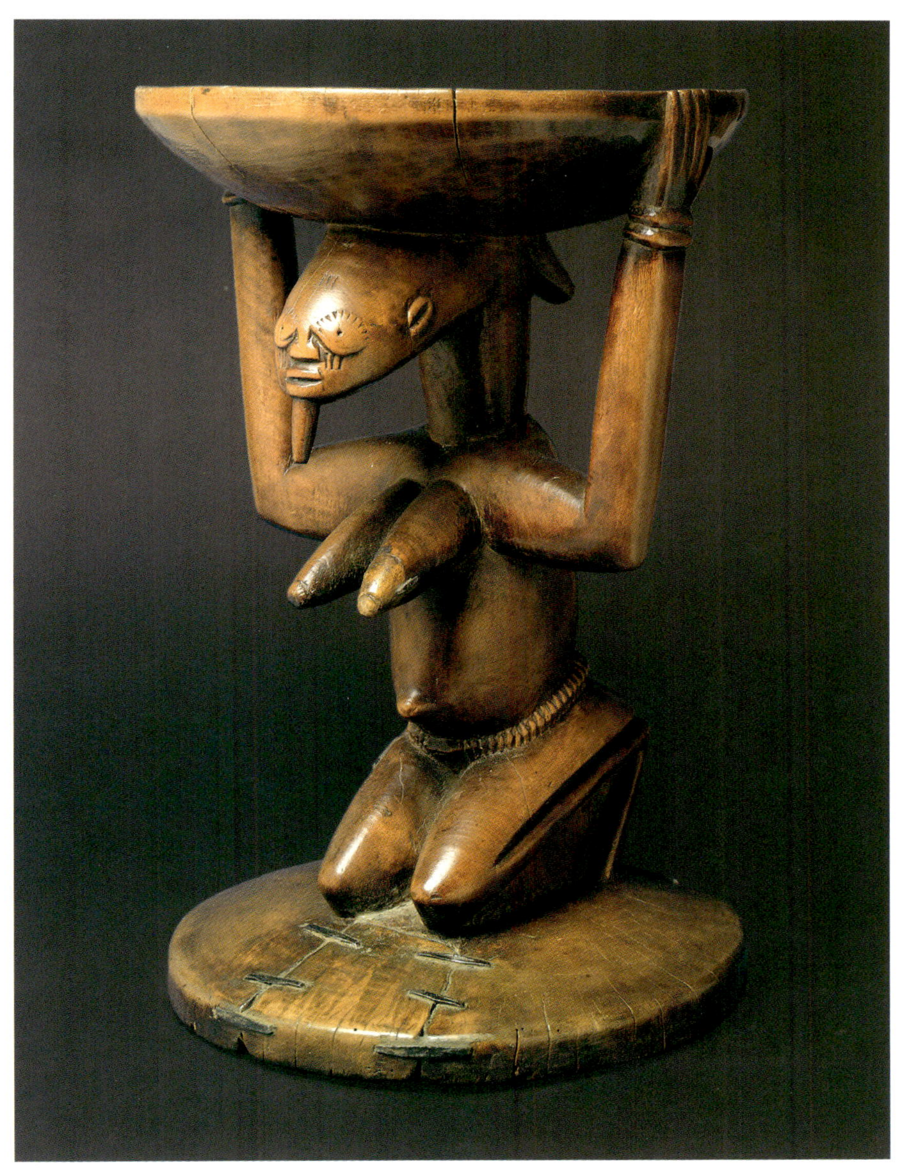

Photograph: Jeffrey Hammer, Los Angeles

Caryatid stool of the Yoruba, Nigeria, height 46.7 cm Cat. 56

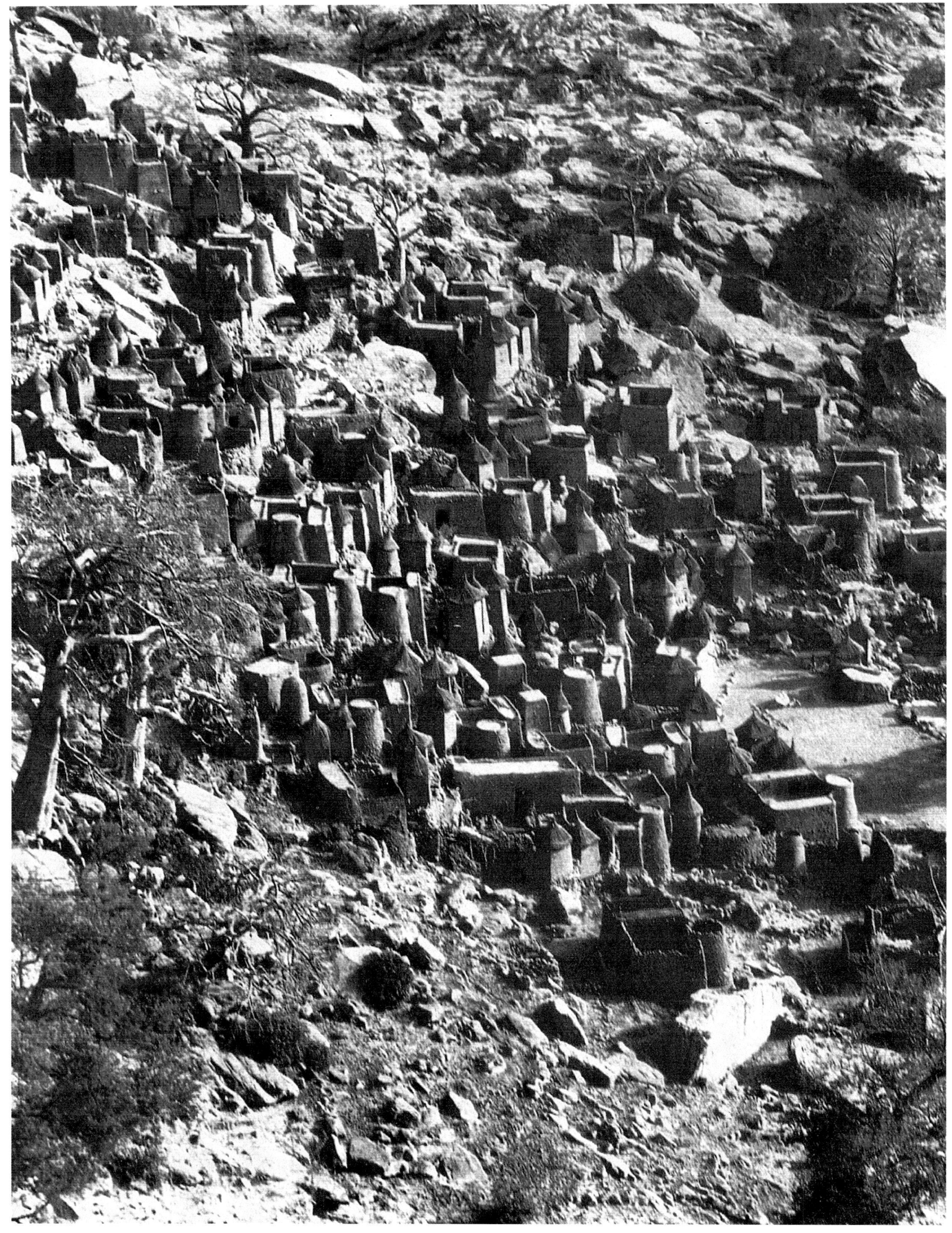

Photograph: René Gardi, 1973

View of a Dogon village

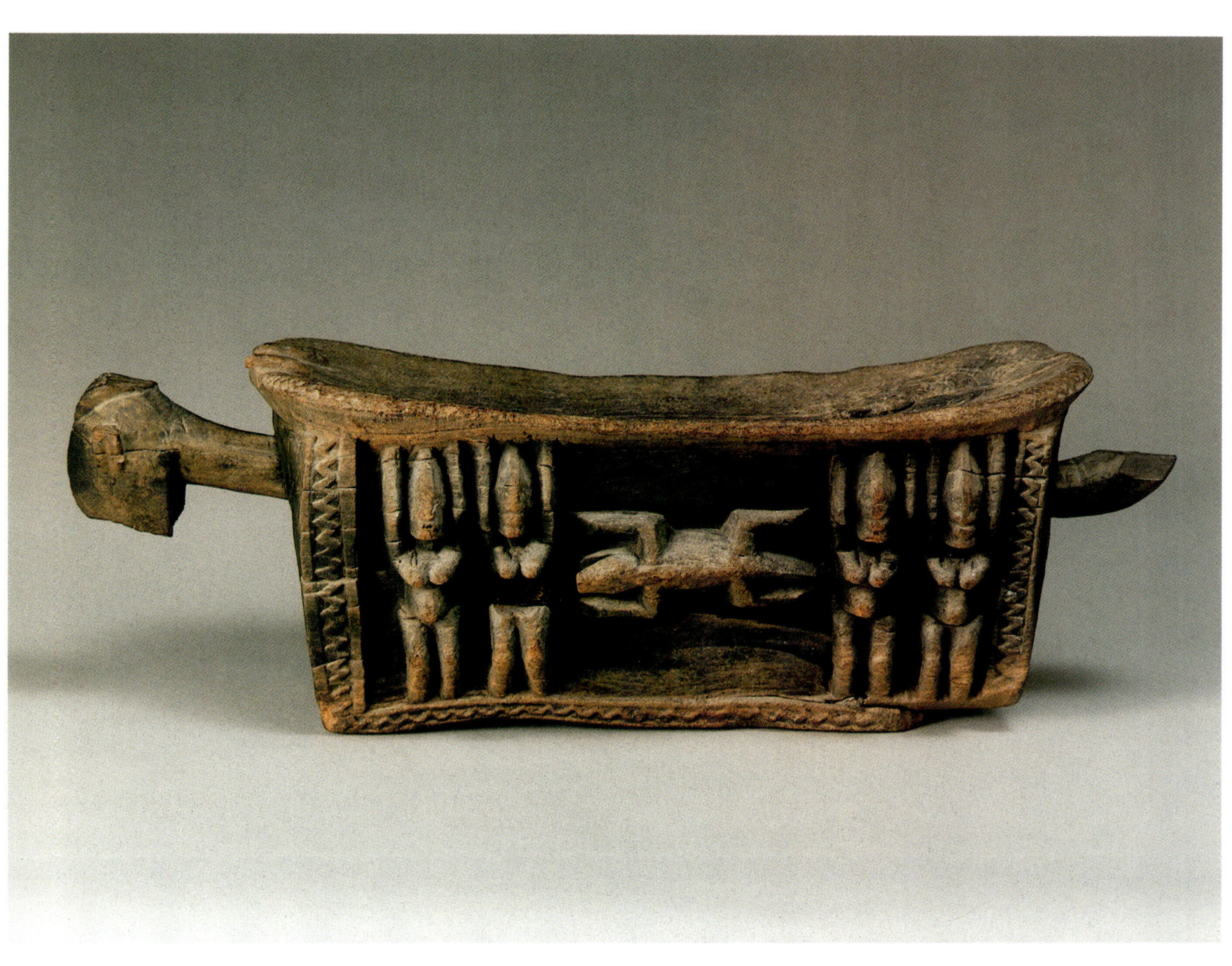

Ritual seat of the Dogon, Mali, width 67 cm Cat. 31

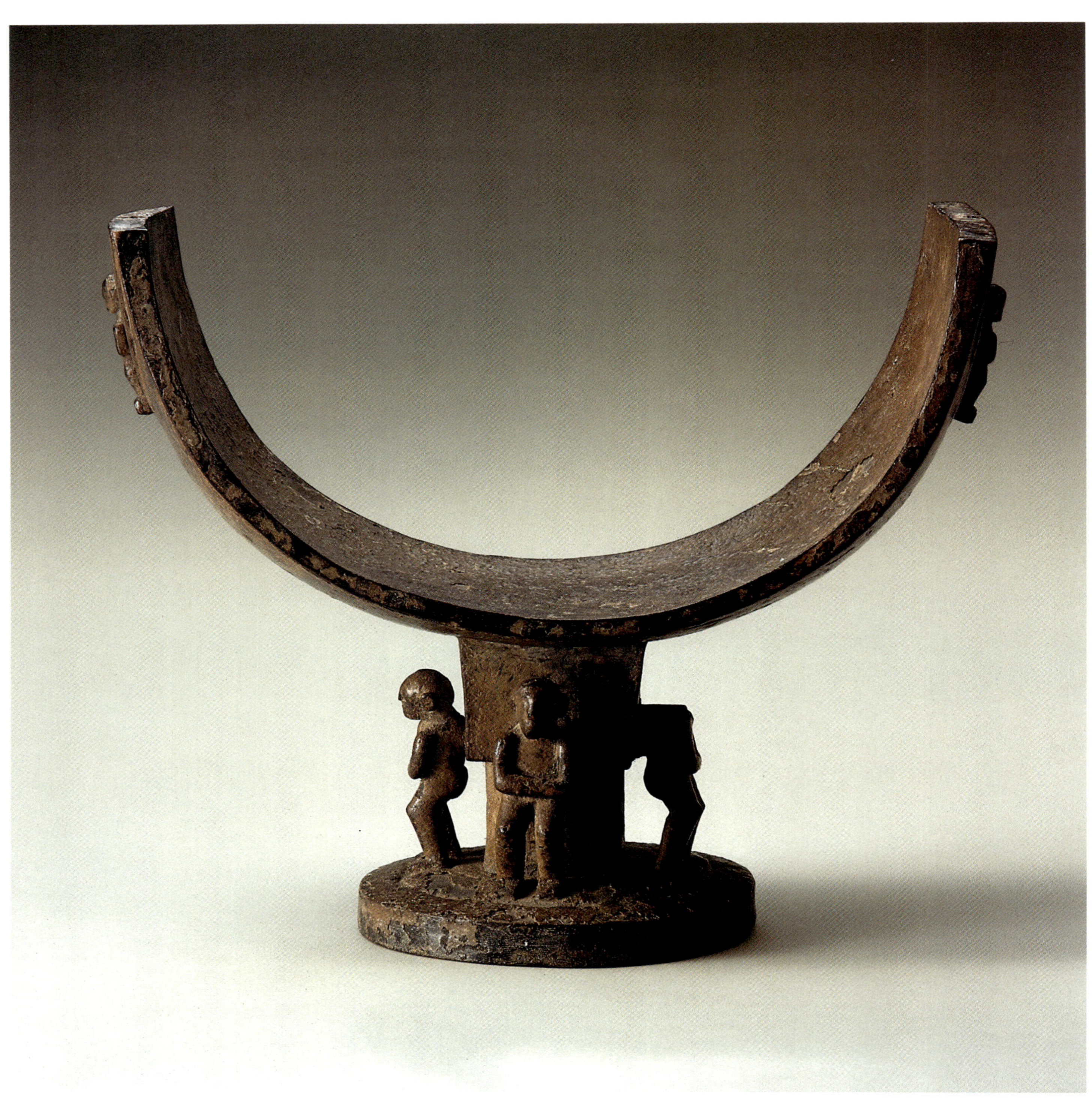

King's stool of the Bidjogo, Guinea-Bissau, height 39.5 cm Cat. 1

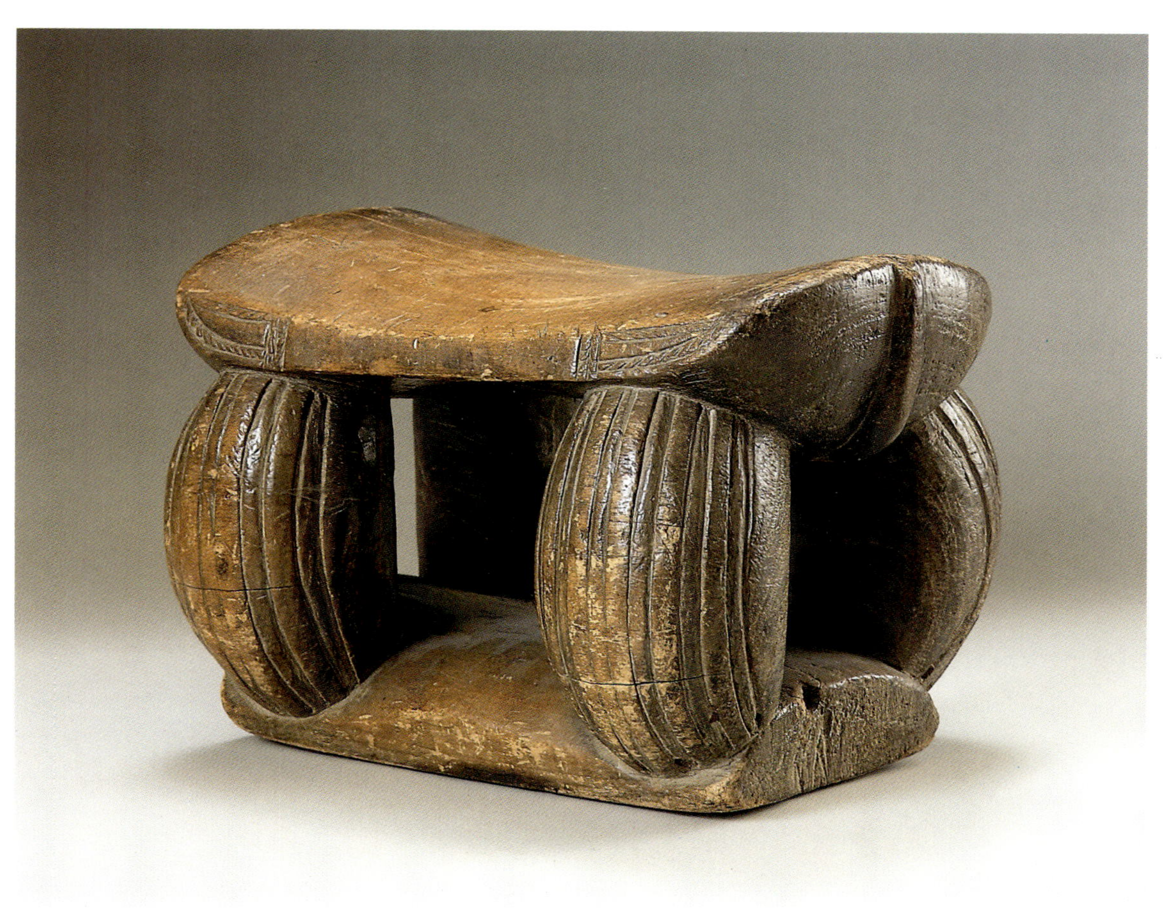

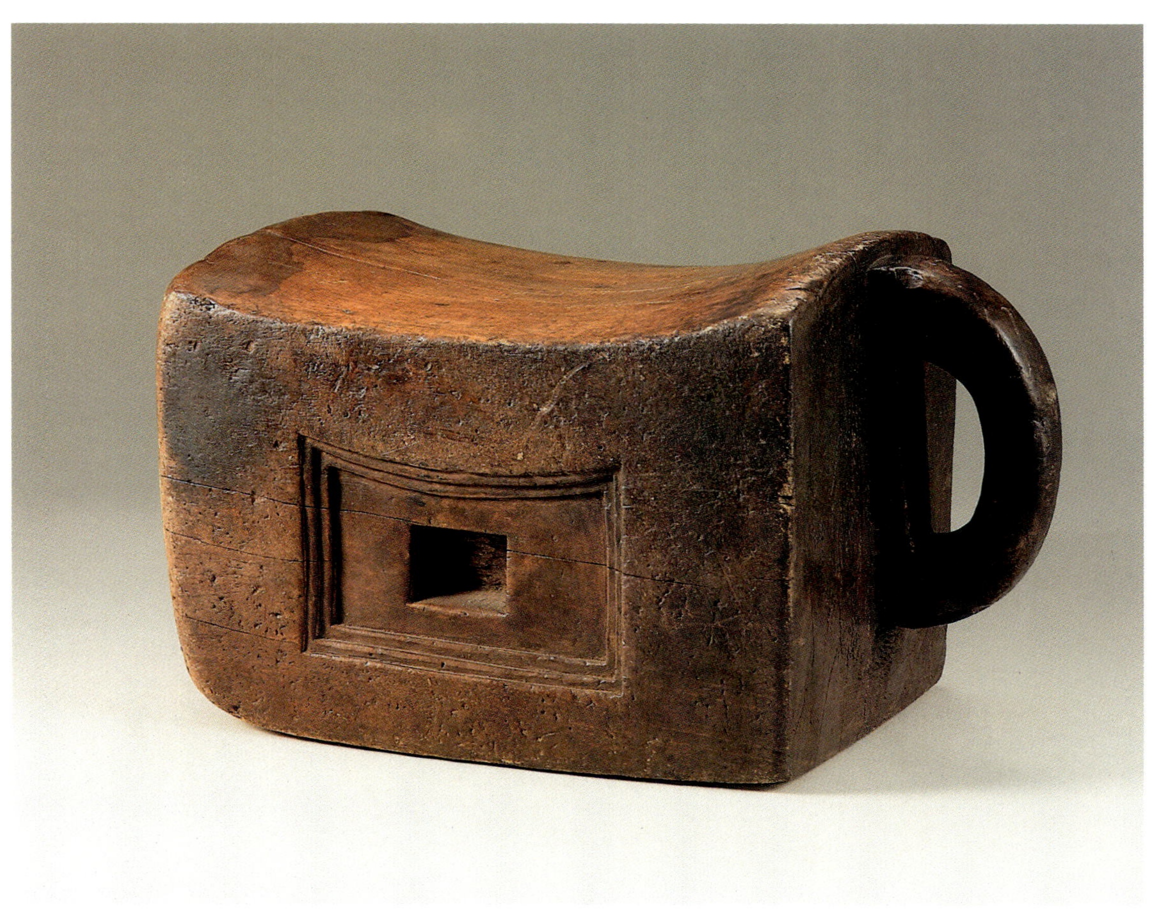

Stool of the Gere/We, Liberia, width 45 cm Cat. 13
Stool of the Baule, Ivory Coast, width 42 cm Cat. 34

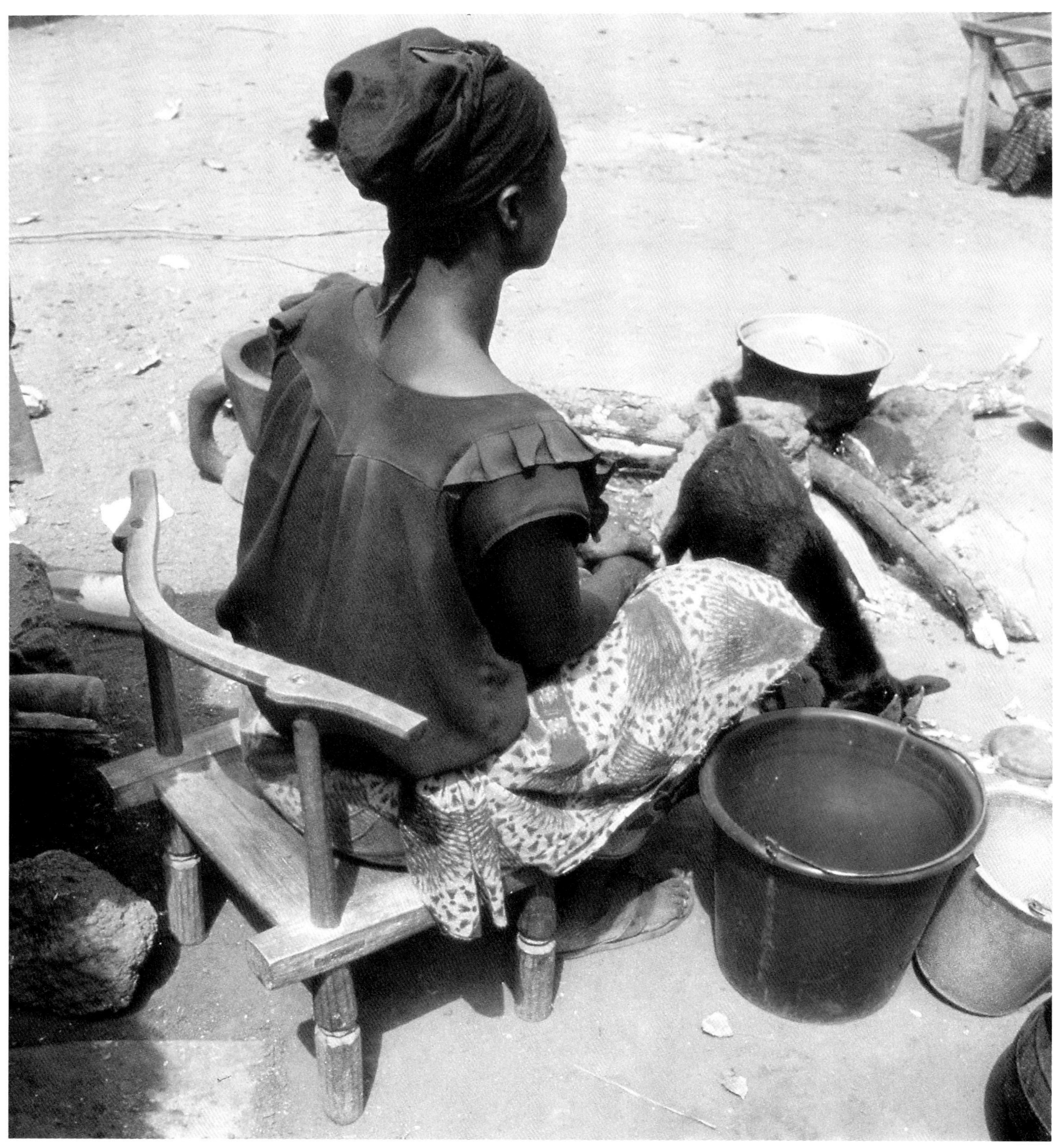

Photograph: Jean Paul Barbier, 1988

A woman of the Baule sitting on her small multi-part chair
in the village of Ngata Dolikro, Ivory Coast

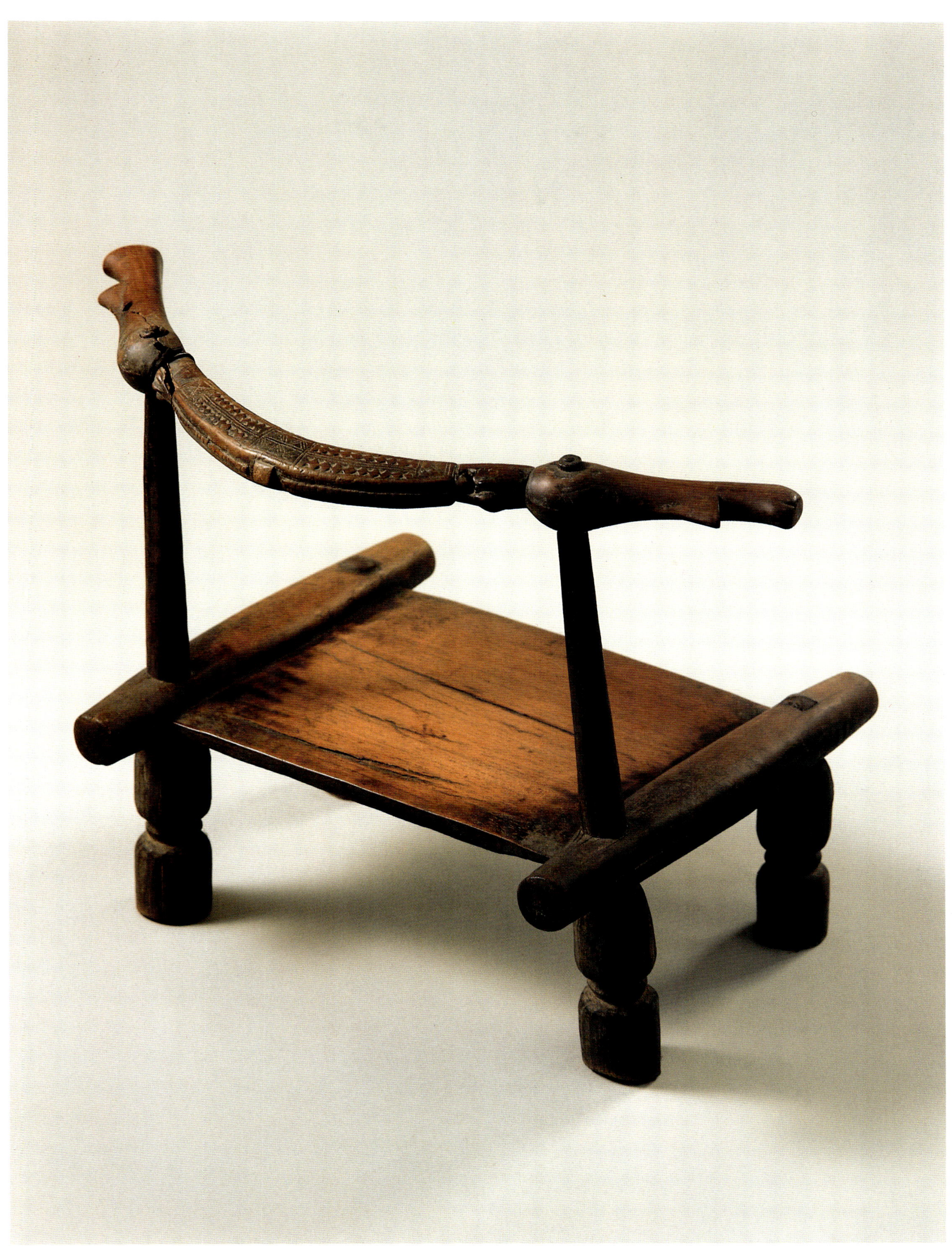

Chair of the Guro, Ivory Coast, height 53 cm Cat. 17

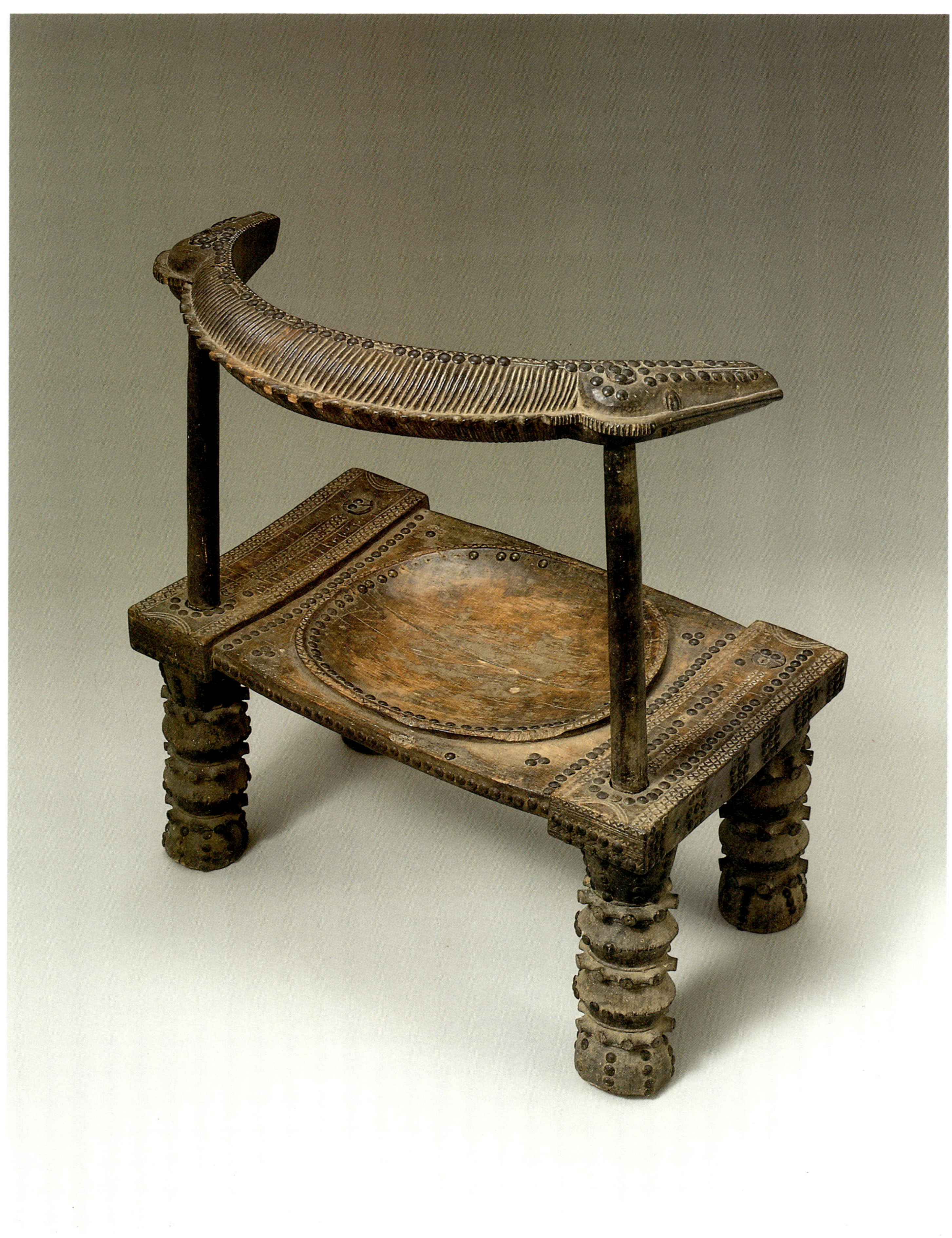

 Chair of the Baule, Ivory Coast, height 61.5 cm Cat. 18

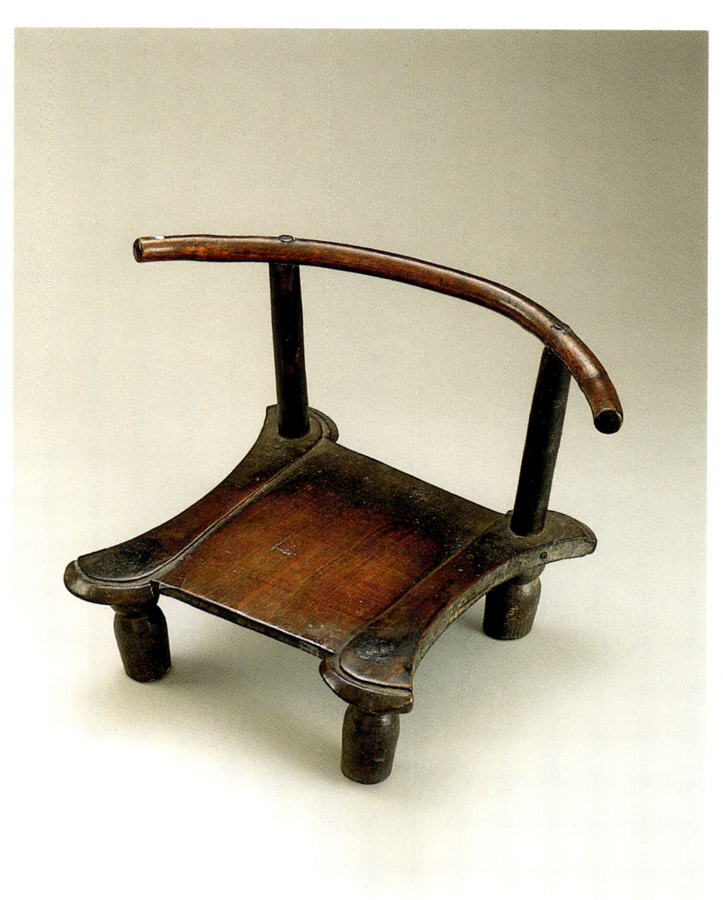

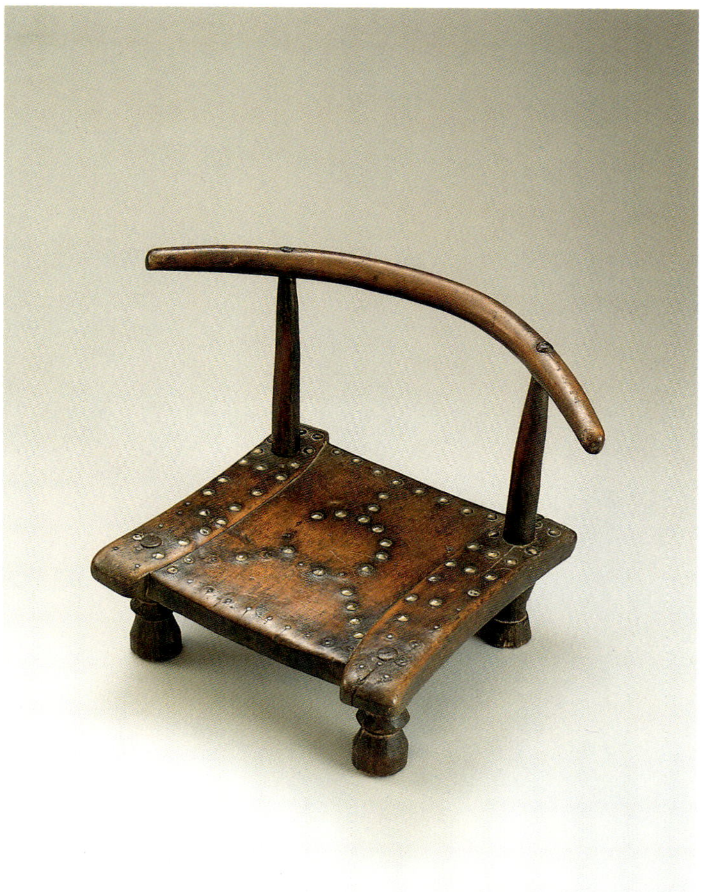

Chairs of the Dan, Ivory Coast, height 31 cm and 30 cm Cats. 16, 15

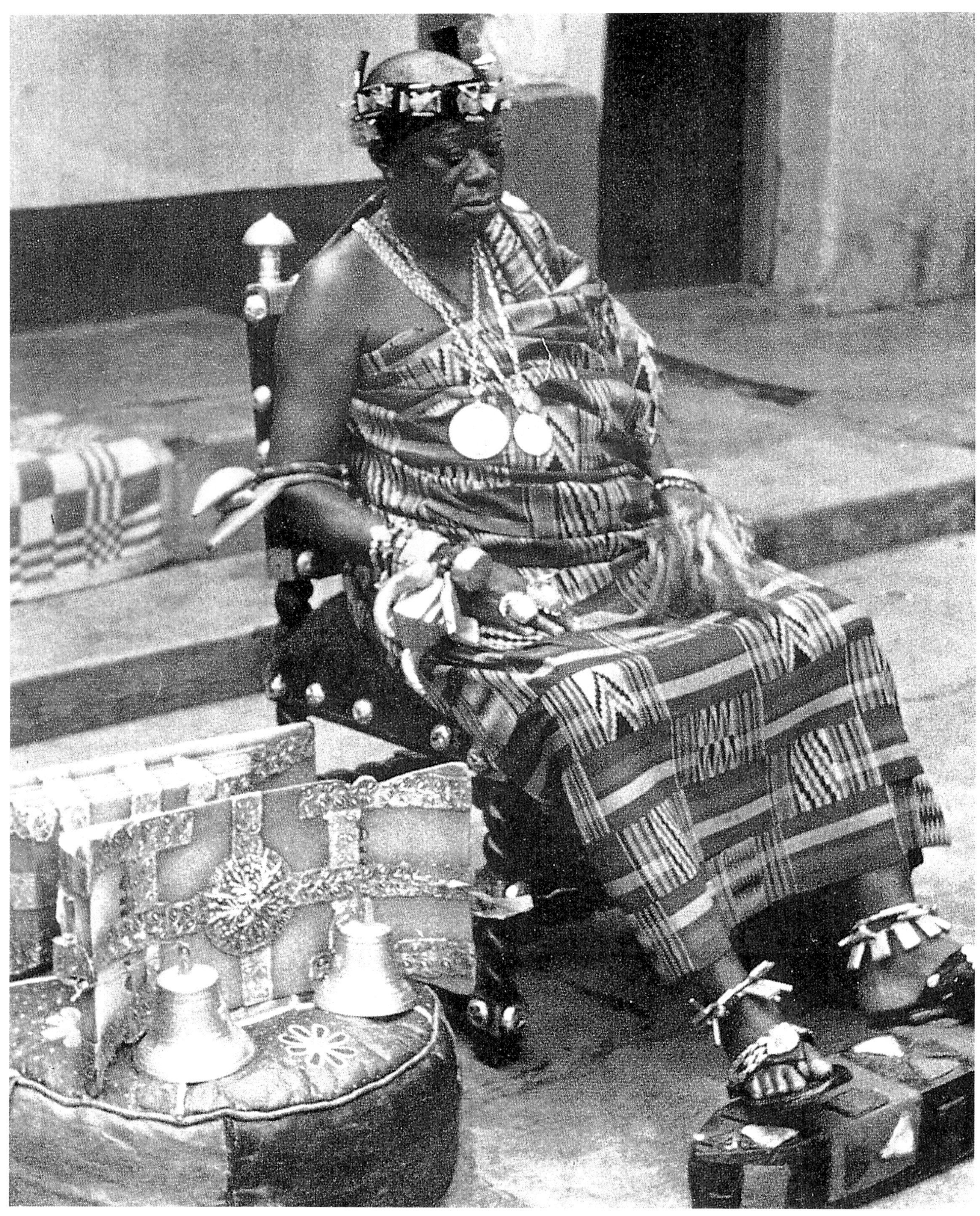

Photograph: Malcolm D. McLeod, 1970

The Omanhene (king) of Asumegya, Ghana, seated on a *hwedom* chair. Alongside him, tipped on its side, is his personal silver-mounted stool.

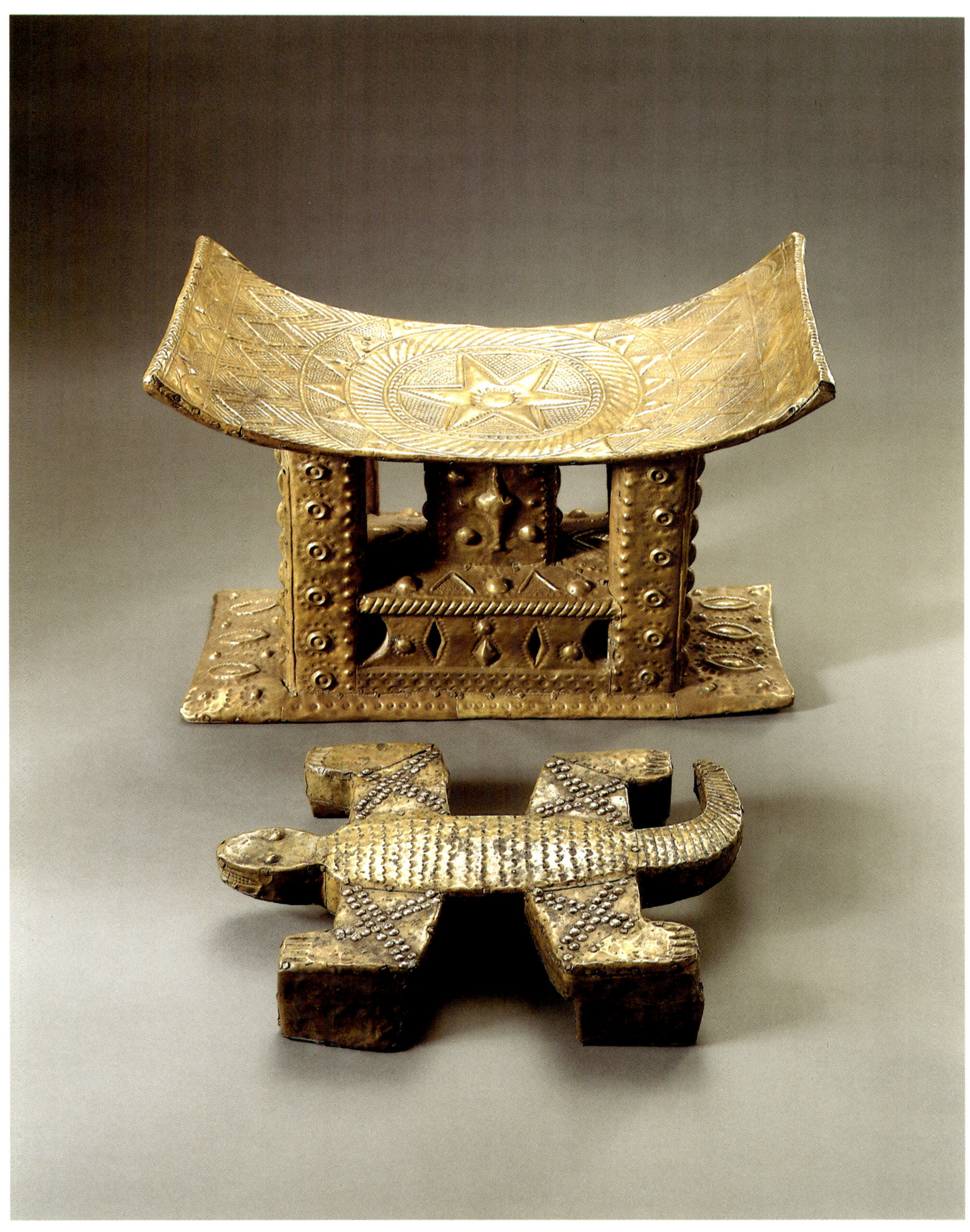

Stool and footrest of the Asante, Ghana, height 46 cm and 9 cm   Cat. 37

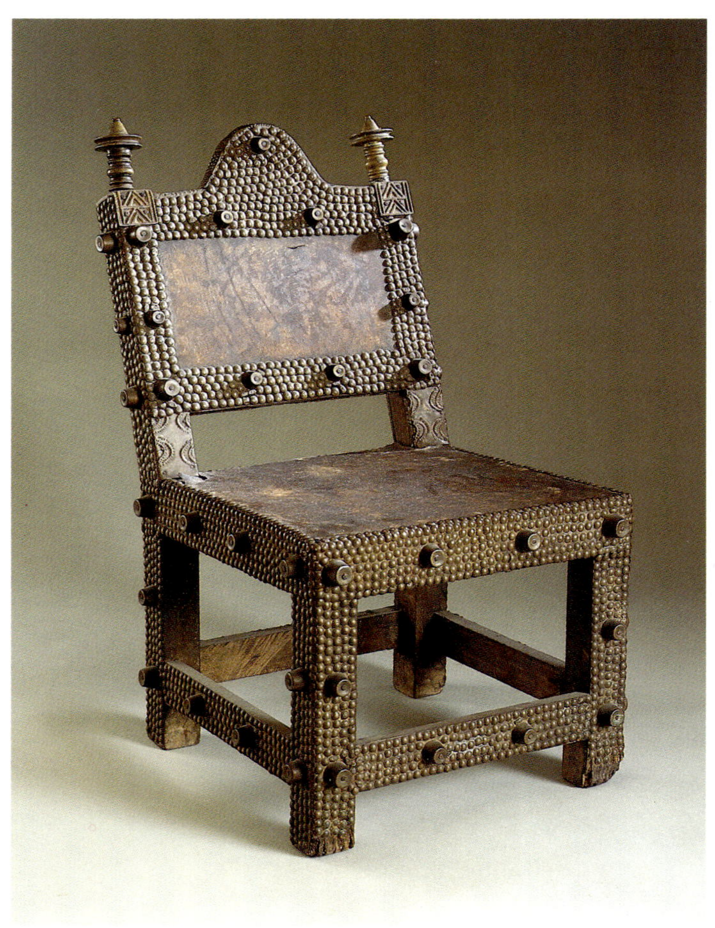

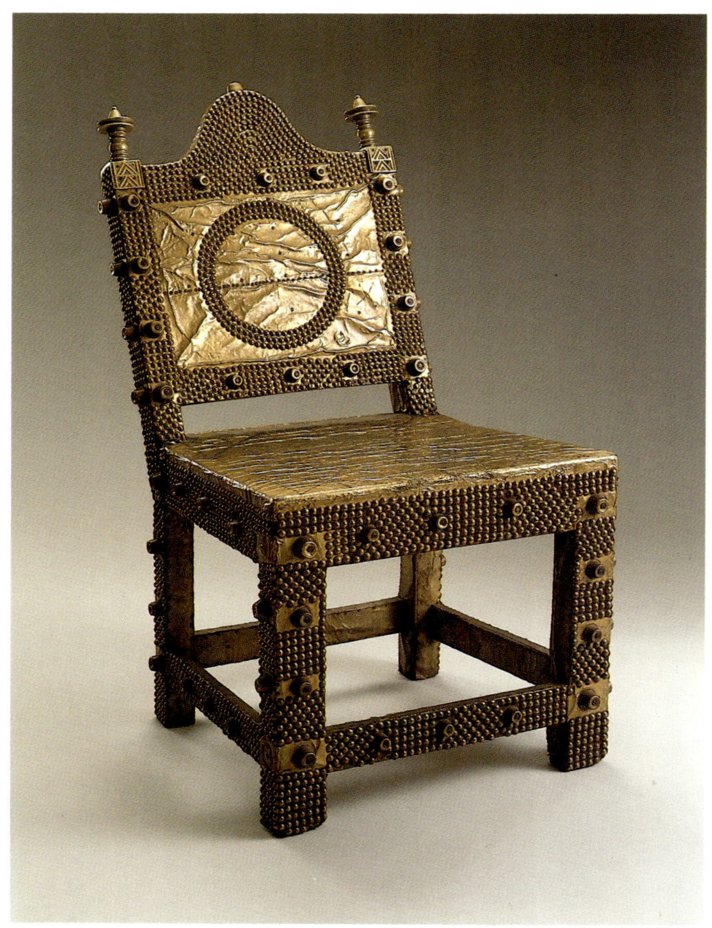

Chairs of the Asante, Ghana, height 68 cm and 88 cm Cats. 47, 49

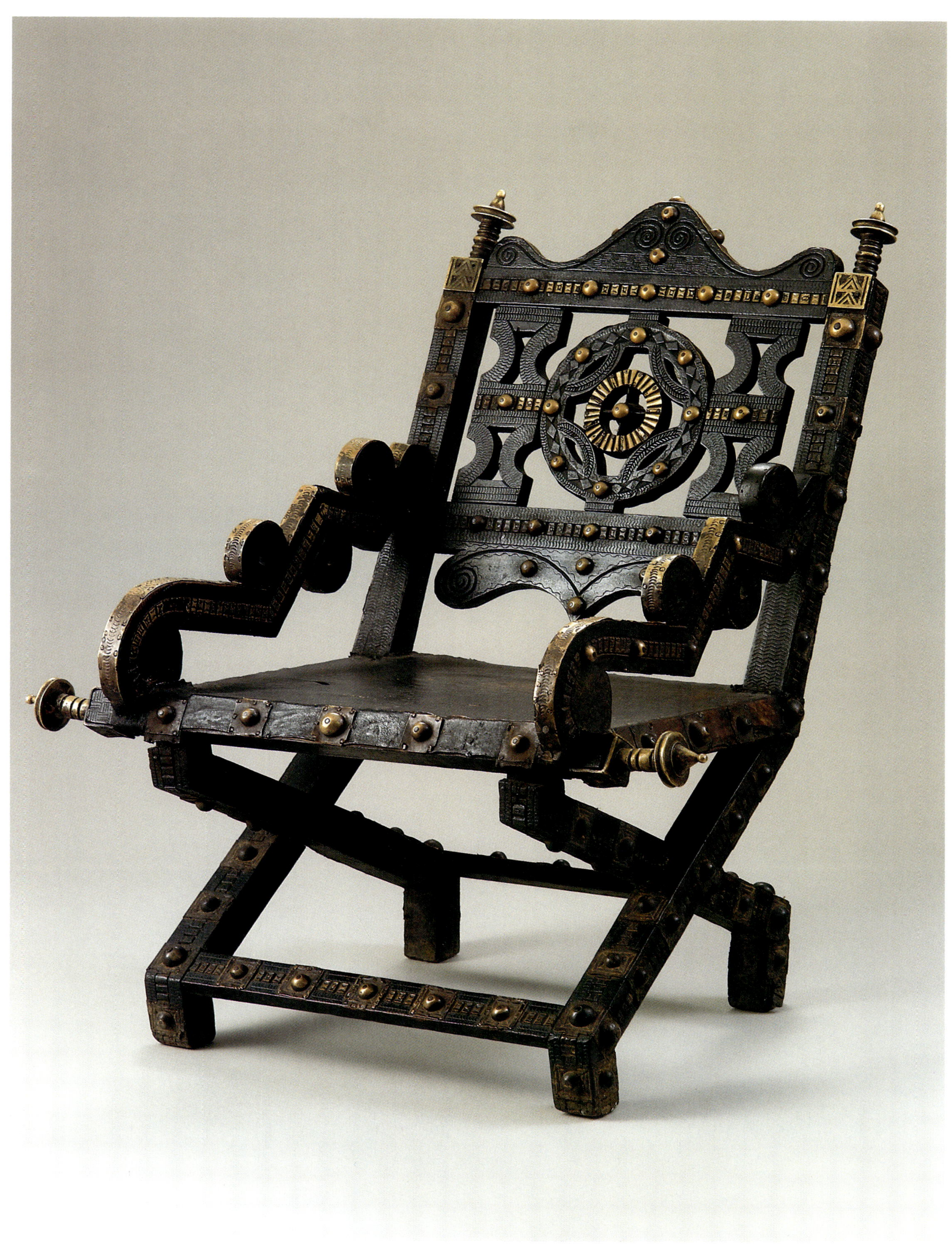

Chair of the Asante, Ghana, height 87 cm Cat. 51

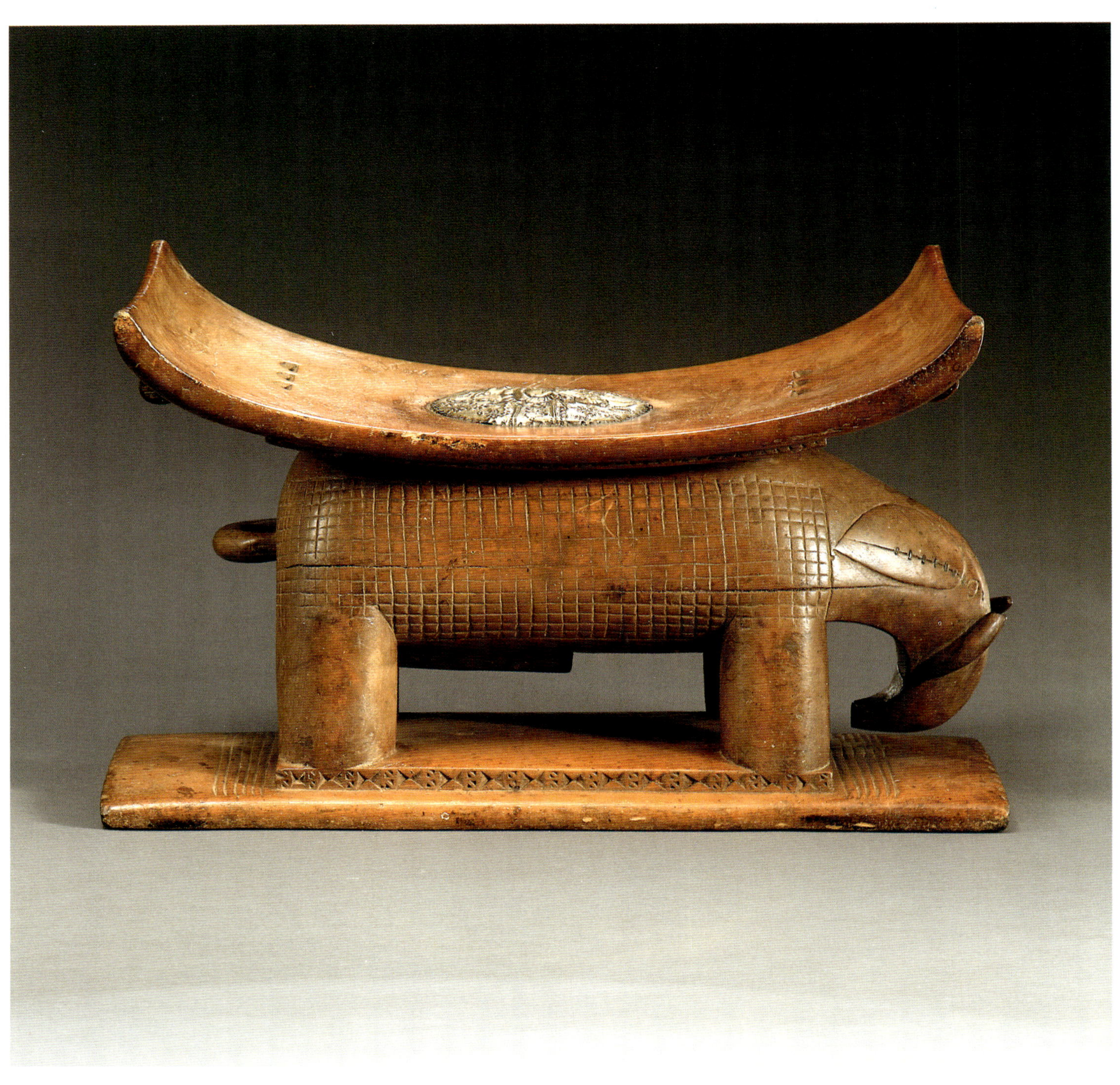

Stool with an elephant of the Asante, Ghana, height 32.9 cm Cat. 43

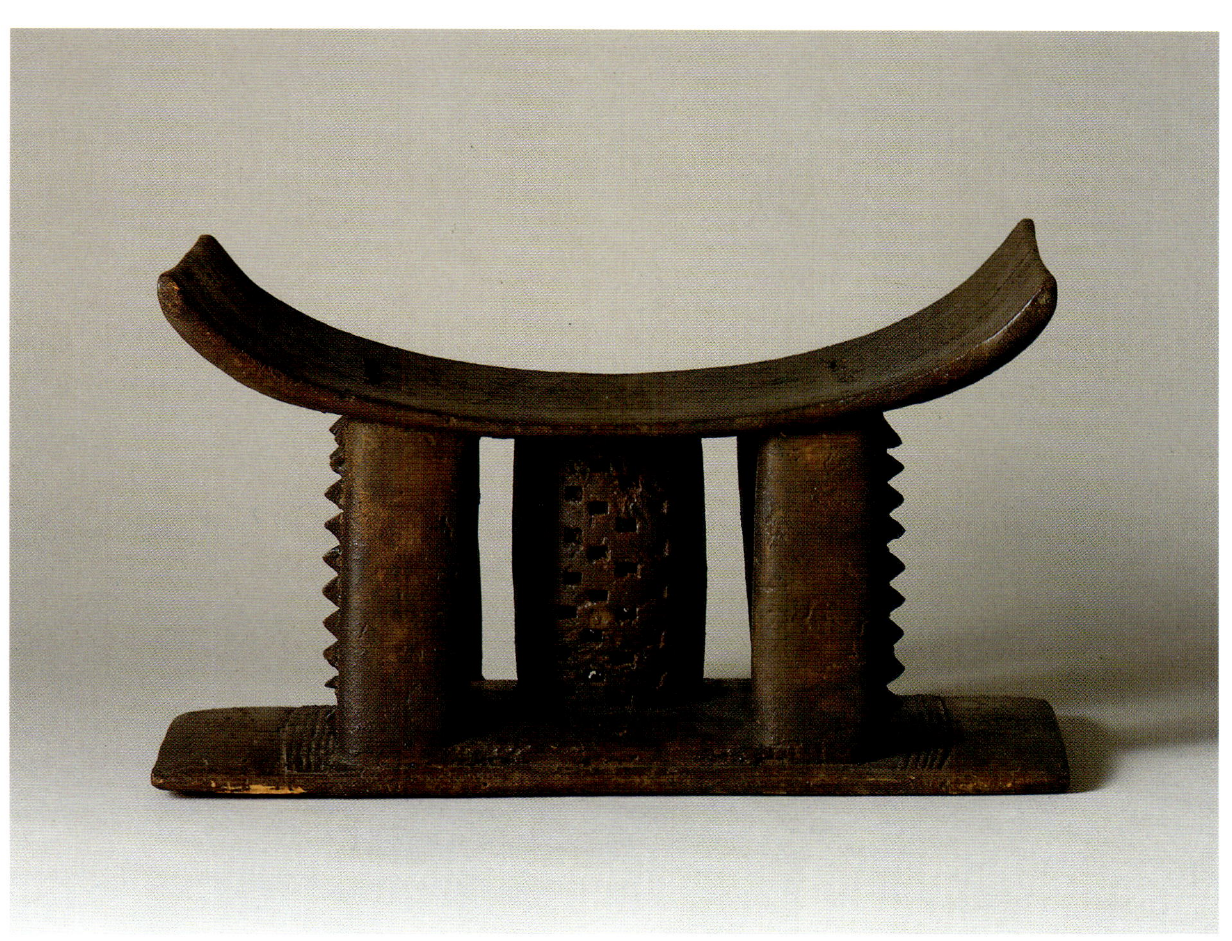

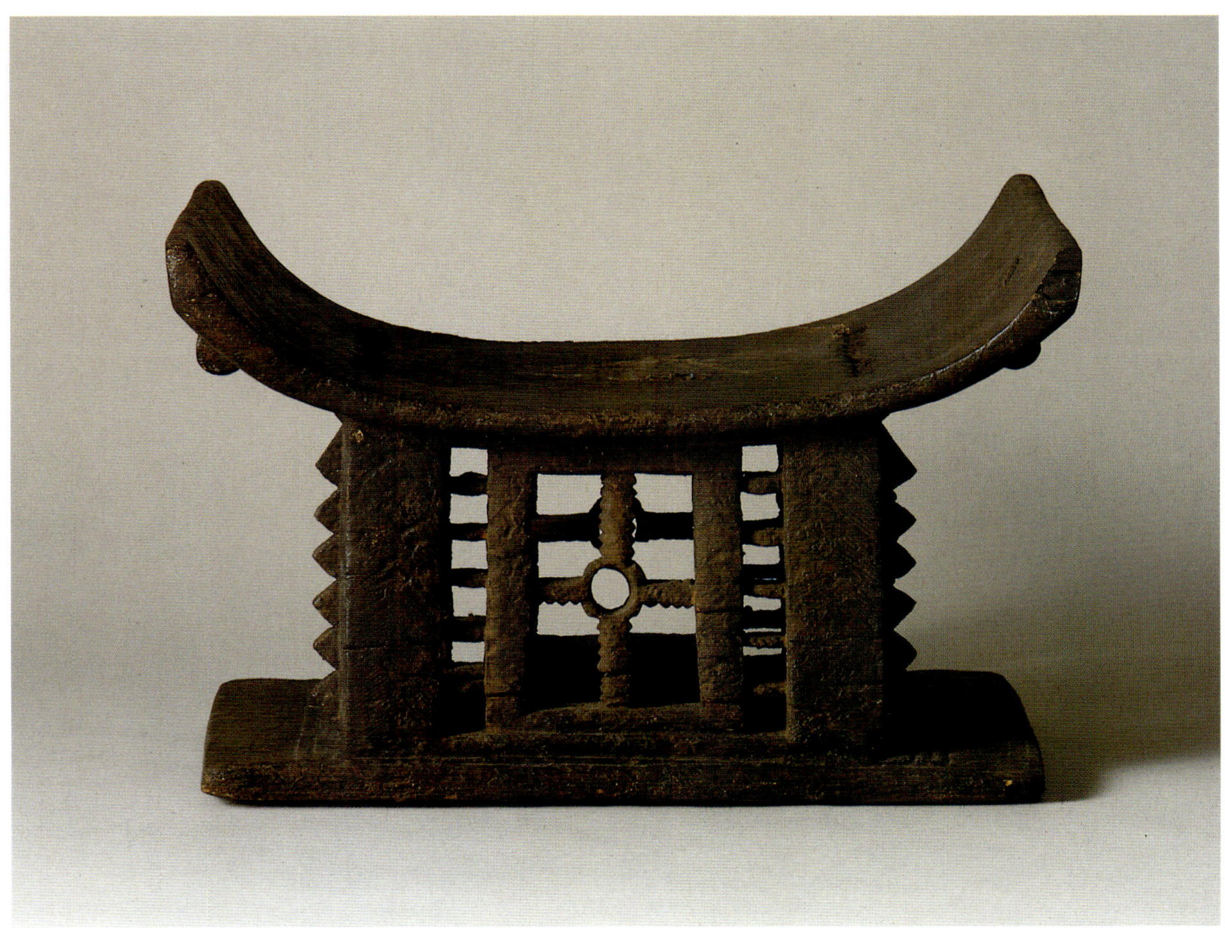

Stools of the Asante, Ghana, height 27.5 cm and 27.5 cm Cats. 36, 35

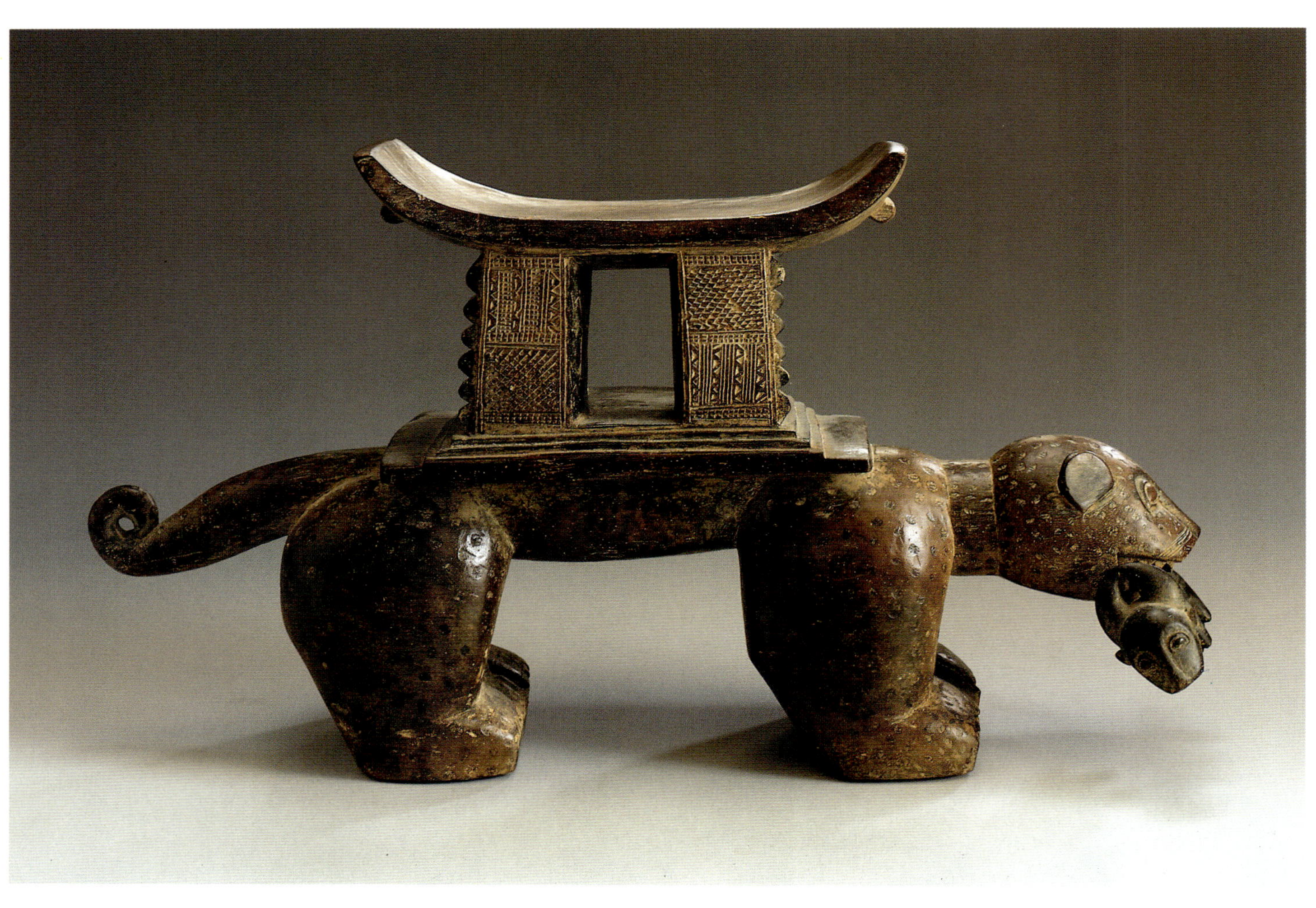

Stool of the Baule, Ivory Coast, width 73.5 cm Cat. 45

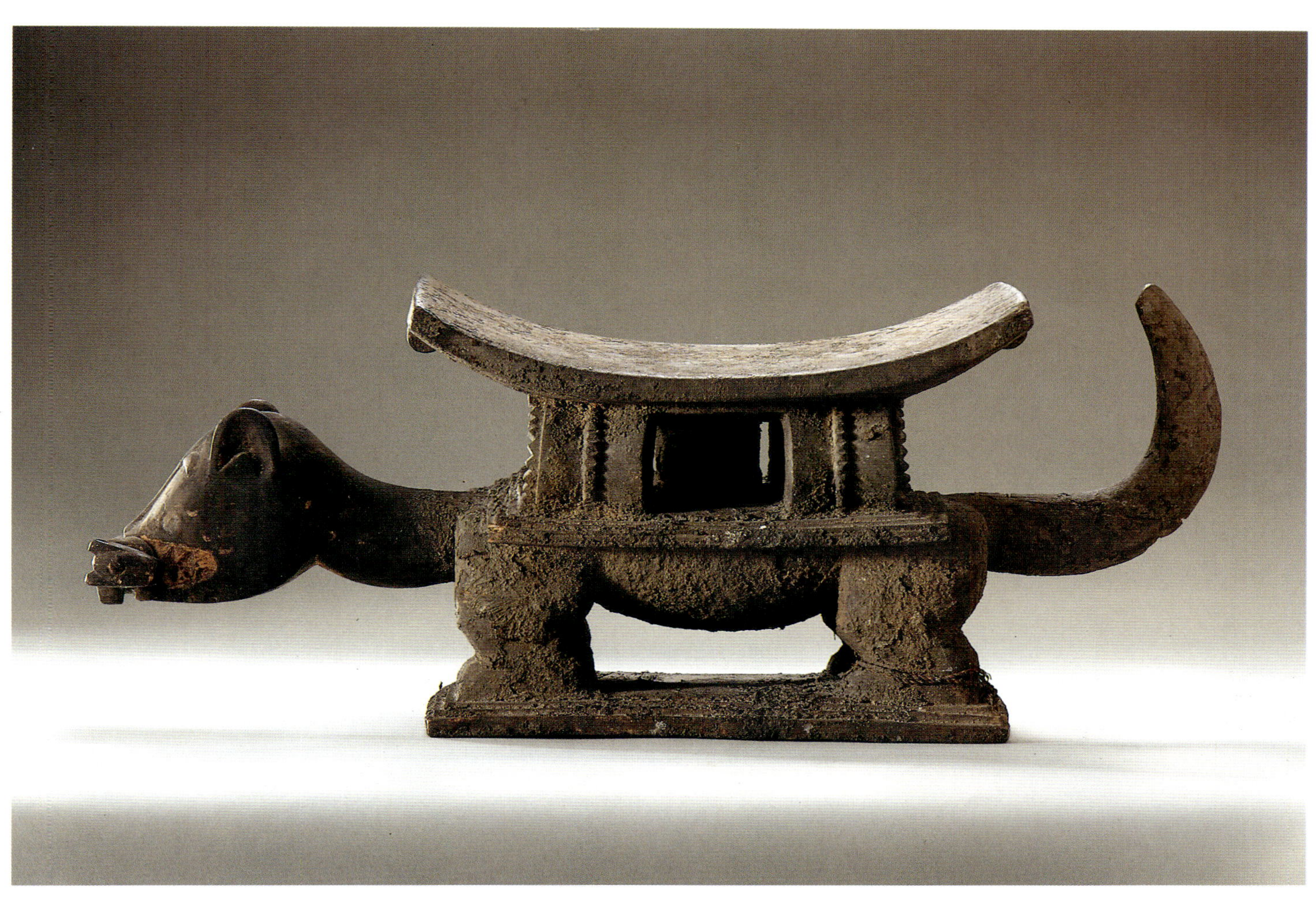

Stool of the Baule, Ivory Coast, width 63 cm   Cat. 44

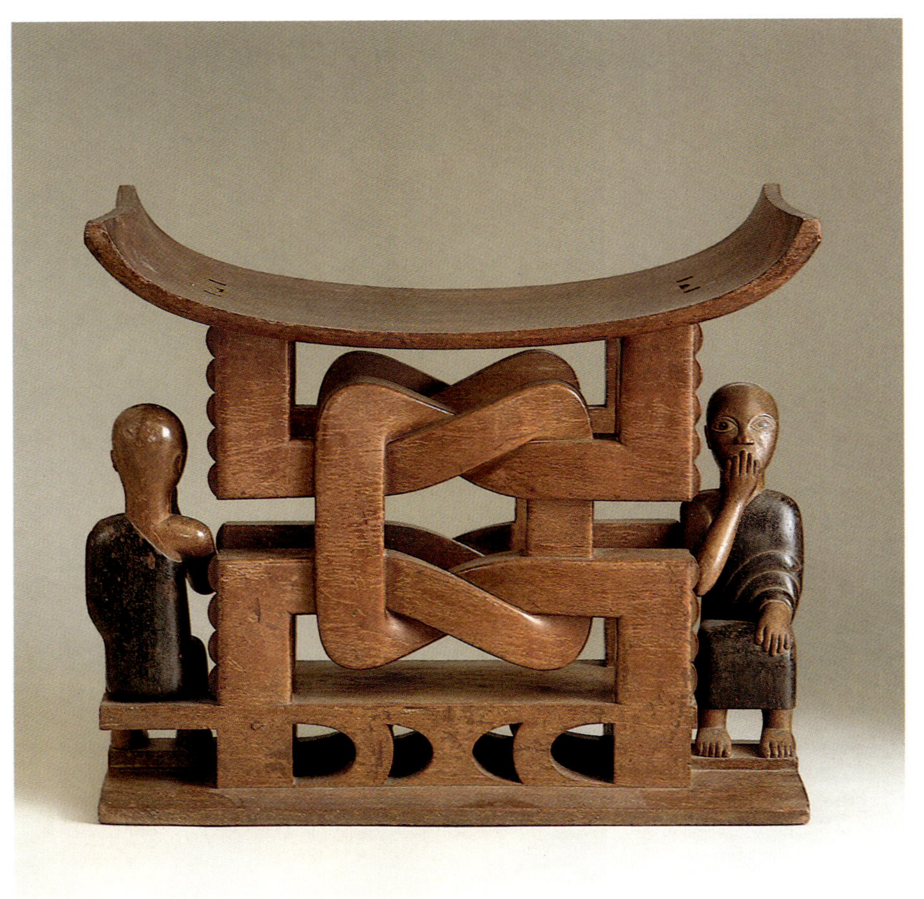

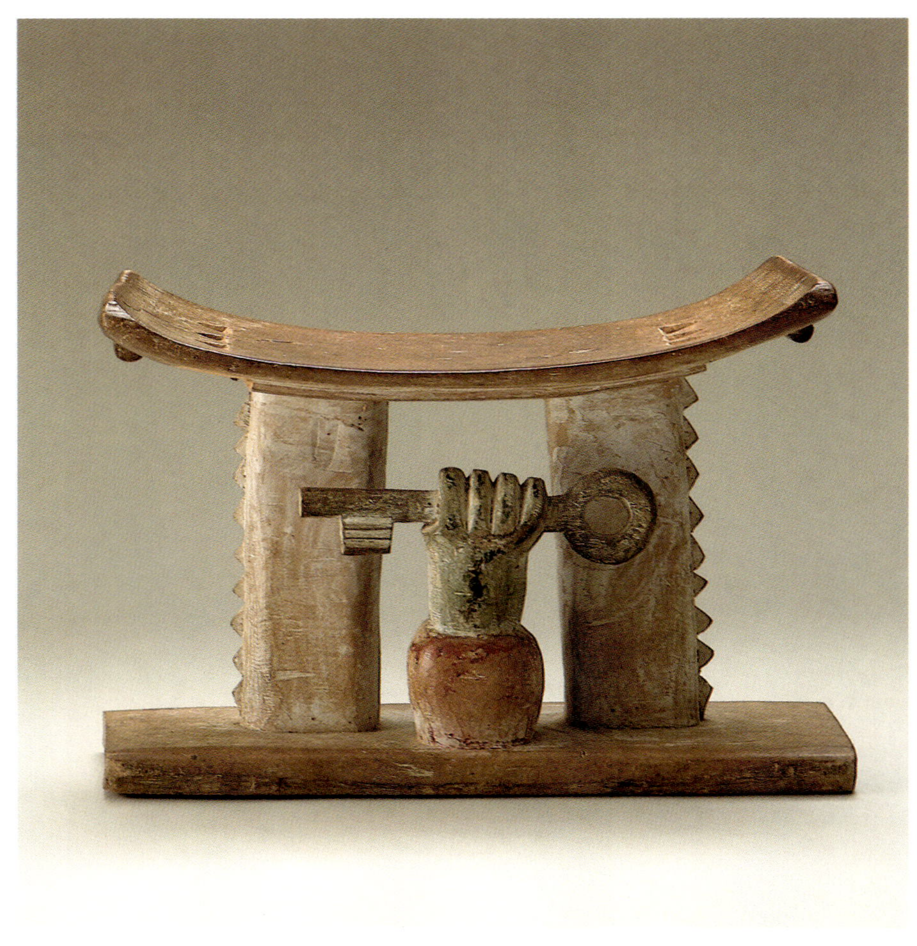

Stools of the Asante, Ghana, height 53.5 cm and 32 cm Cats. 40, 41

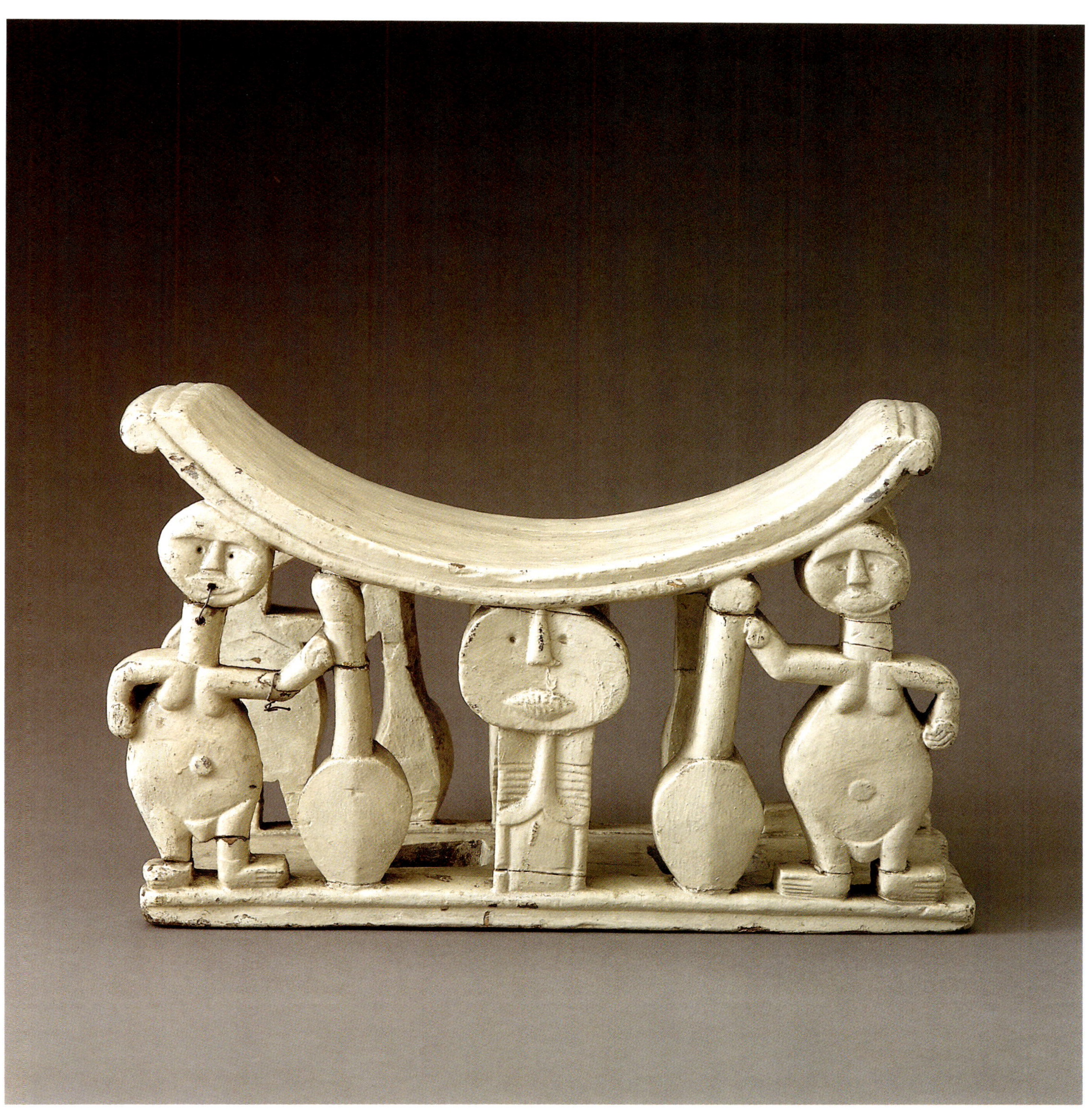

Stool of the Duala, Cameroon, height 30 cm Cat. 80

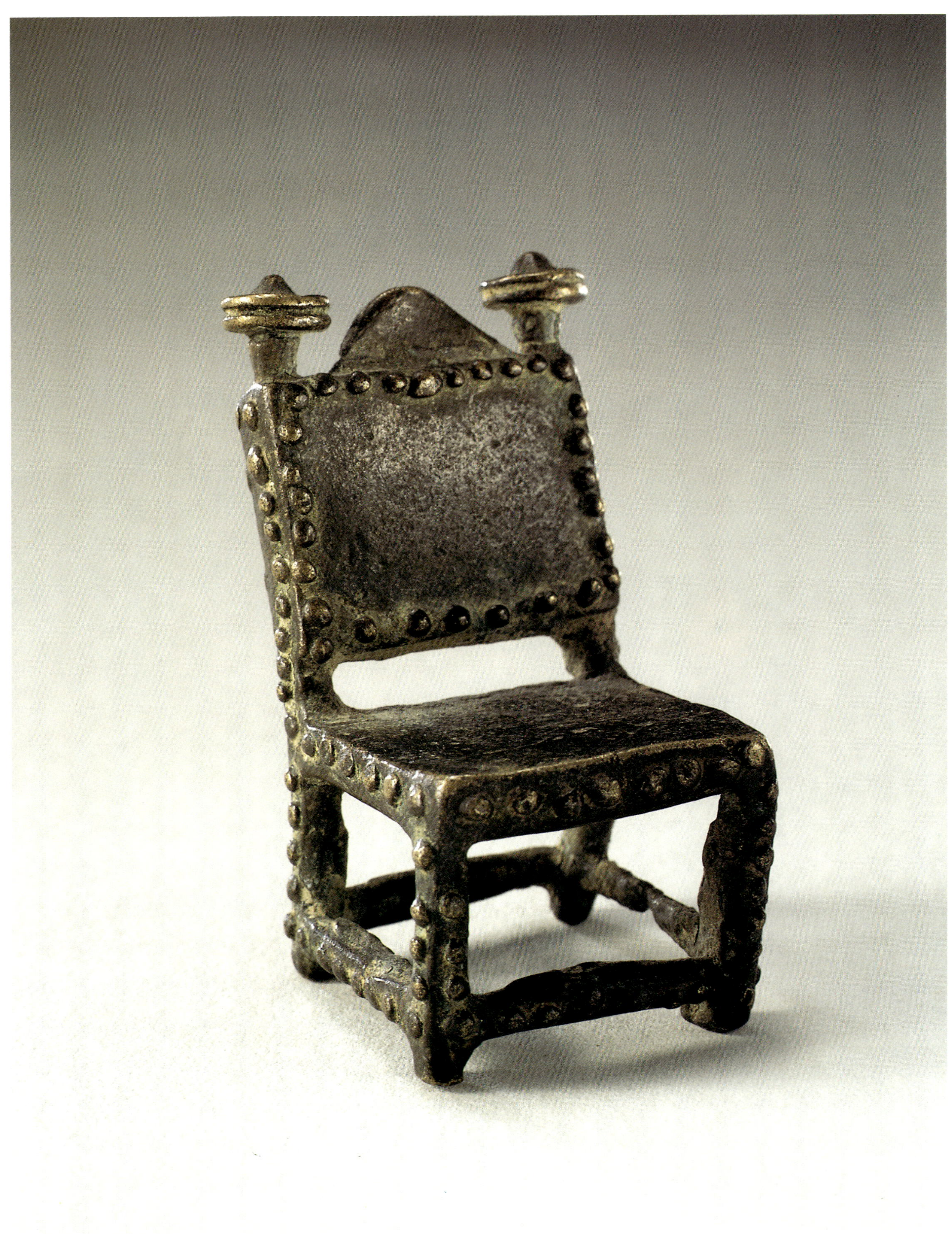

Goldweight, Asante, Ghana, height 4.4. cm Cat. 168

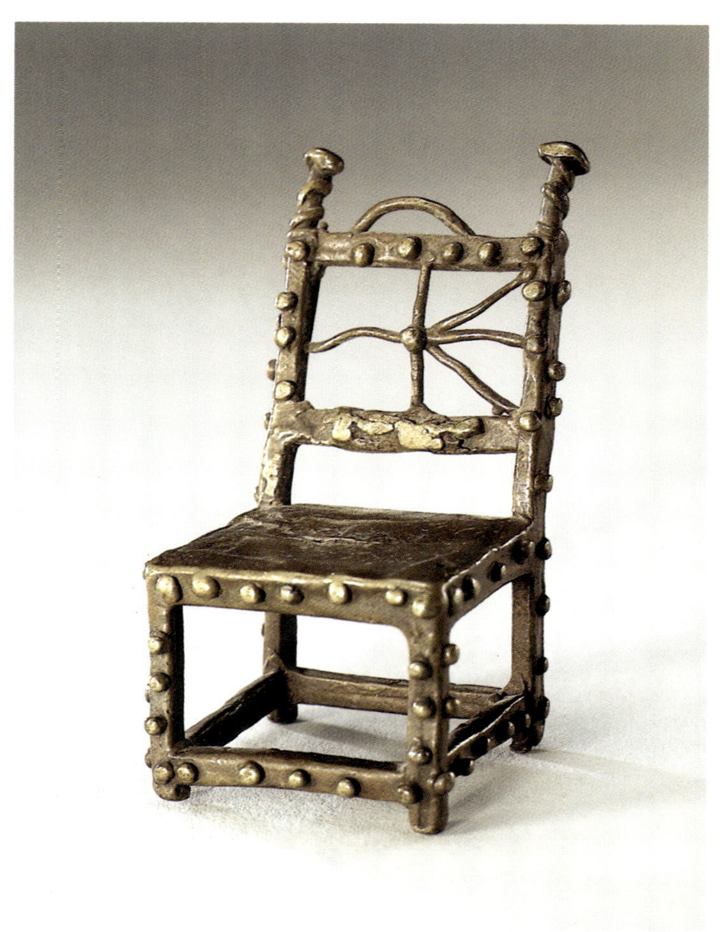
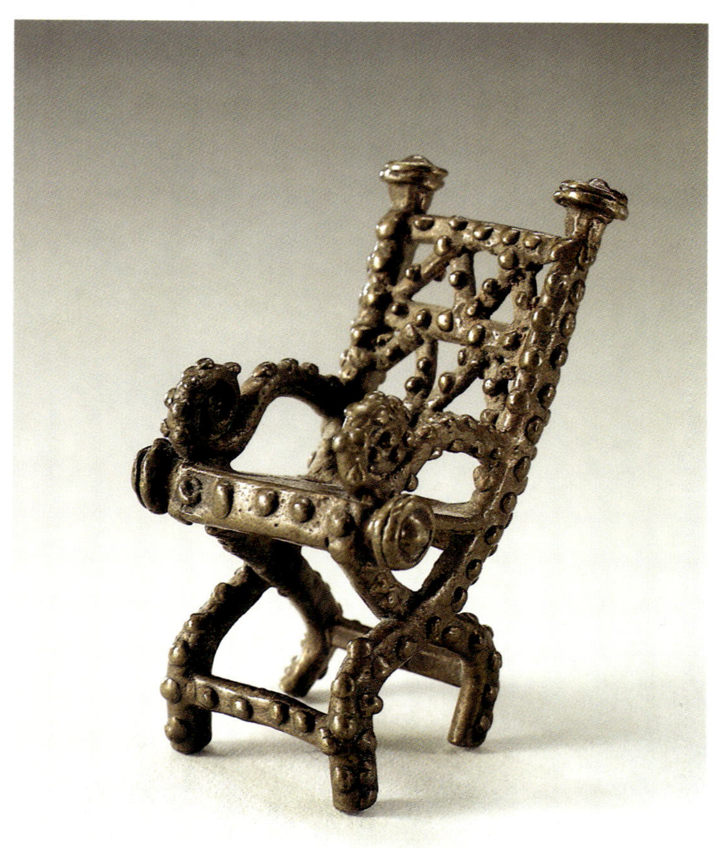
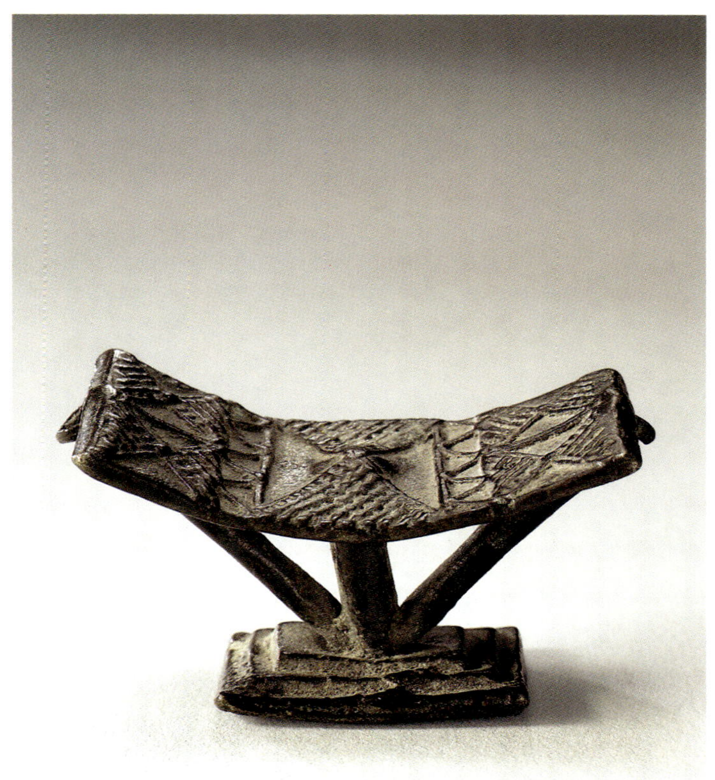
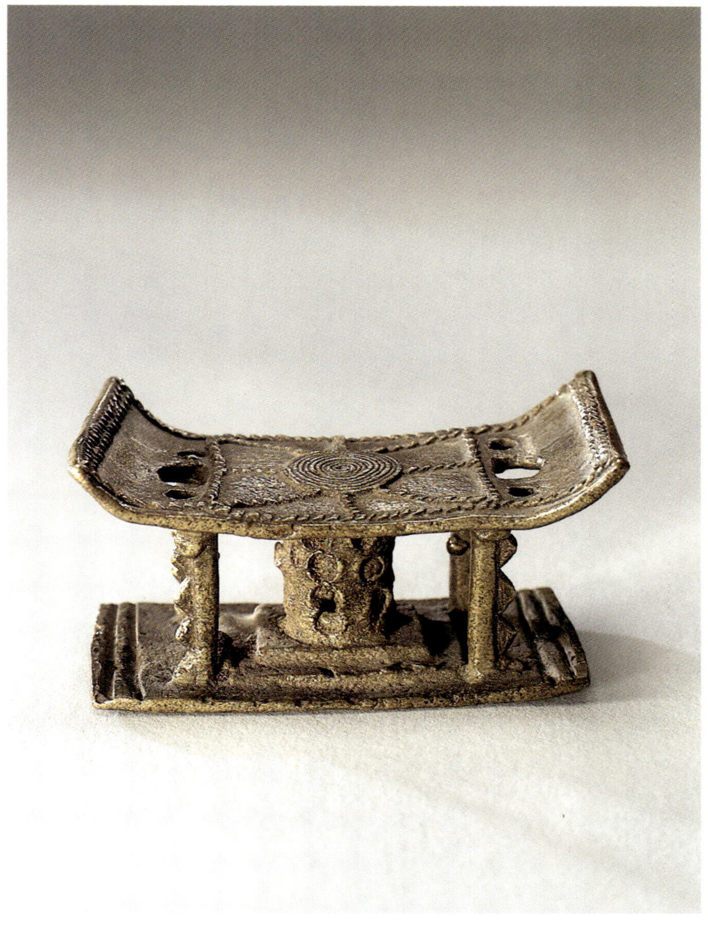

Goldweights, Asante, Ghana, height 6.4 cm, 4.4 cm, 3.2 cm and 2.7 cm Cats. 169, 172, 162 and 163

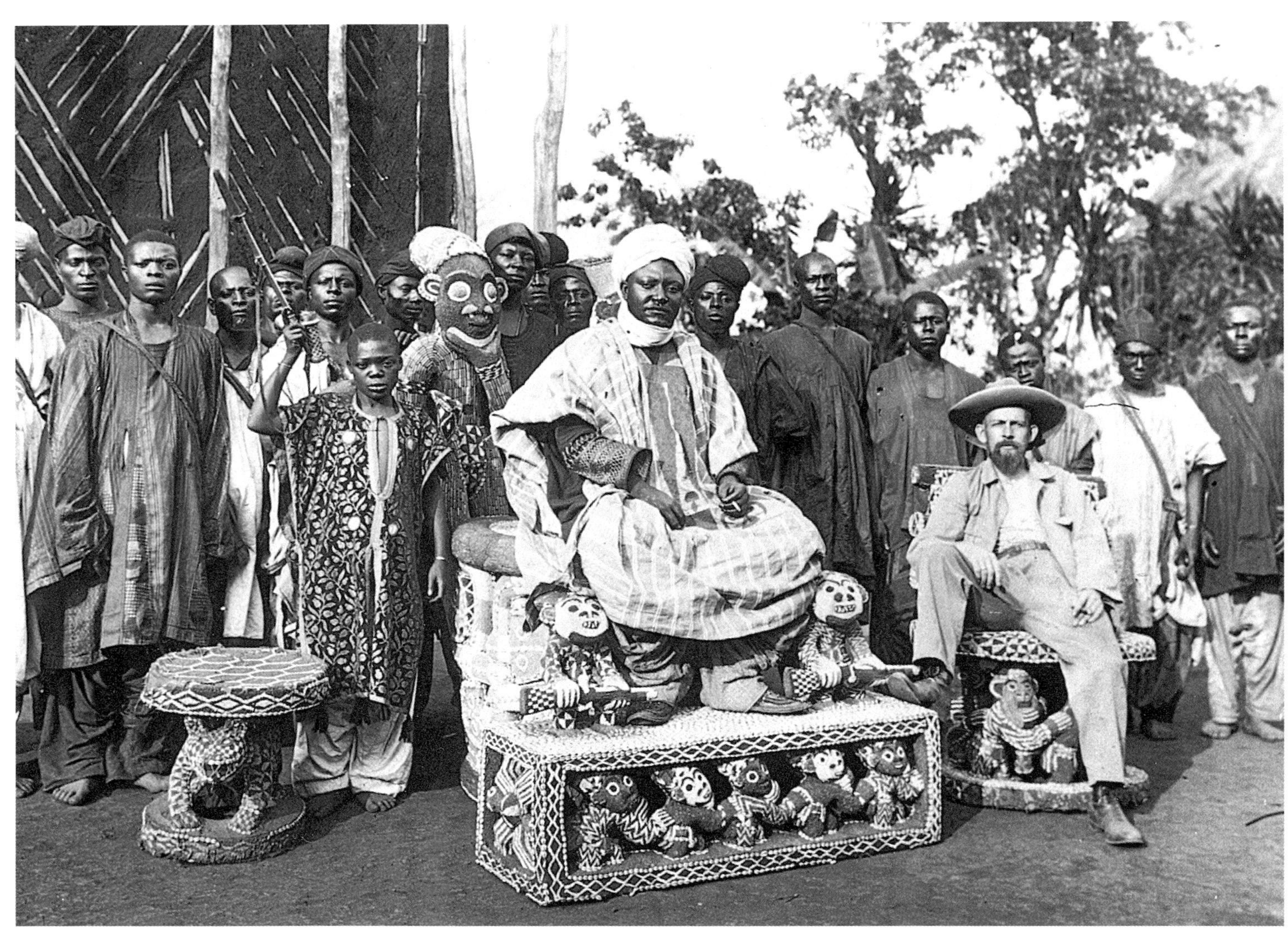

King Njoya with the merchant Rudolf Oldenburg, who carelessly rests his foot on the footrest of the royal throne. This is a disrespectful gesture not justified even by the friendship that existed between the two men. Foumban, Cameroon grasslands; cf. cats. 73, 74, 75, 76 and plates on pp. 90, 91, 102. (Photograph: Helene Oldenburg, *c.* 1912)

Cameroon

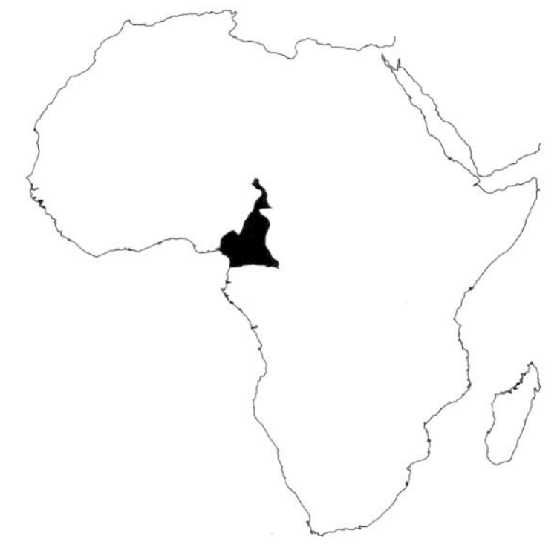

Cameroon, which counts as part of western Central Africa, has a number of very distinct centres of art production on account of its cultural and religious diversity. In the north, the Fulani herdsmen, famed for their warlike conquests, constitute the most important group of peoples. The dominance of Islam is evident even here, in a handicraft tradition oriented towards jewellery, leather-work (e. g. delicately decorated reins and ornamentally worked saddles) and the production of textiles. To the east of the Benue river various peoples, for example the Mambila or the Jukun, earn their living as settled crop farmers. Their religion, centred on the veneration of the soil and of their ancestors, is manifest in their figurative art – as in the case of many other settled peoples, and in contrast to those that have been Islamized. Among these peoples living on the border between Nigeria and Cameroon one finds, alongside objects of religiously and socially determined ritual, utensils of masterly design, such as spoons, clay pots, calabashes and stools.

The coastal region of Cameroon, the old port city of Duala and the hinterland offer clear evidence of early contact with Europe. This is reflected in the design of the prows of ships, which incorporate animal motifs. Both in form and colouring, these prows recall those of Portuguese fishing boats. The seats found here are striking for their formal affinity with examples from much further west along the same coast: the thrones of the Akan region and of the *fon* in the Republic of Benin (plate on p. 83; cats. 79–80).

The most significant art forms in Cameroon are to be found, however, in the south-west of the country. Nestled in a fertile, hilly landscape, numerous small kingdoms arose in past centuries. Their court sculptors could lay claim to outstanding achievements in the area of figurative art: as well as statues and masks, one finds a wealth of reliefs, figural door frames, drums, food bowls, tobacco pipes and other tokens of rank. This region also produces the most splendid thrones – works that have always occupied a prominent place in the realm of African art.

The art and architecture of this region reflect a social structure imbued with notions of courtly prestige; sadly, only a few of the traditional palaces have been preserved (see photographs on pp. 89 and 94). Thanks to earlier photographic documentation, we are able to establish some idea of the splendour and beauty to be found in these royal houses (their inhabitants having already established trading contacts with European merchants before 1900). Many of the most beautiful display thrones are recorded in this way (photographs on pp. 86–7, 96).

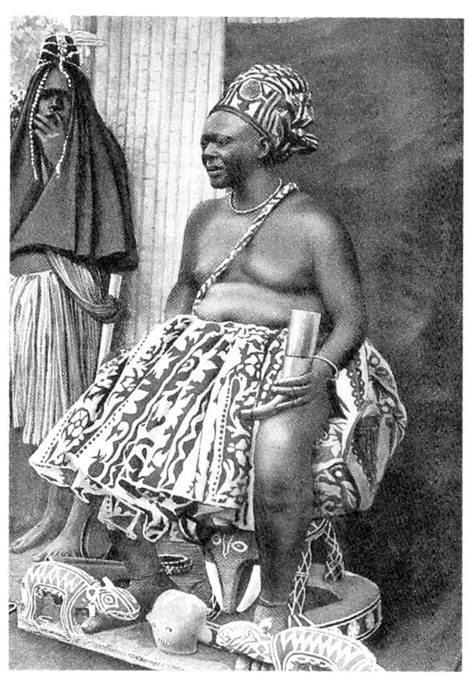

The *fon* Kana I of Bafou-Fondong, Cameroon, seated on a bead-embroidered stool with its support in the form of an elephant; the footstool is in the form of two leopards. Elephants and leopards are royal symbols. (Photograph: Eberhard, 1911)

Beyond the royal courts too there is to be found an astonishing variety of figurative art: masks for the members of secret societies, decorated bowls made of wood and terracotta for soothsayers, pipes, jewellery and small figures that serve to protect their owners against illness and black magic. Household utensils, bowls and stools are also of a high standard, though plain and of functional design – they are certainly less bombastic than the display seats made for the royal courts. None the less, even in the decoration of everyday furniture, one finds representations of animals that play a role in mythology. In the perforated supporting area of some seats (that allows them to be easily picked up and carried) there are motifs based on spiders, buffaloes, hares, snakes and leopards (plates on pp. 93, 102, 105–6).

Especially dignified in character are the large figural thrones of the royal palaces that were often worked from a single block of wood. The size and shape of each of these truly majestic objects always correspond to the hierarchical position of each

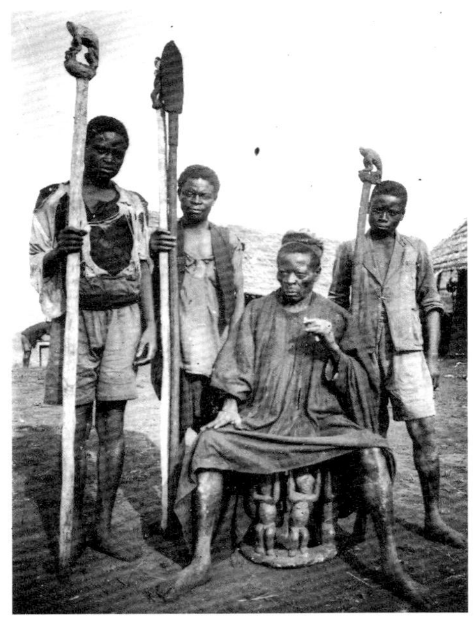

The carver Kwayep of Bawok with his assistants, who hold staffs with carved tops; Bamana, Cameroon. (Photograph: F. Christol, 1925)

The king of Bali, Cameroon, waiting to receive the Göhring brothers in 1905. Fonyonga II is seated on a bead-embroidered caryatid stool with its support in the form of an elephant. To the right there stands another such throne equipped with two figures. (Photograph: M. Göhring, 1905)

member of the king's family and of the nobility. The king's right to rule is derived from his nomination by a direct ancestor, but it also depends on the recognition of the secret society, whose influence on the monarch is already apparent through the assembly rooms provided for it in the palace. Each ruler usually has his own display throne made. This will be decorated with various symbols of power: leopards, elephants, snakes or portraits of dead princes will support the seat or back, the whole often reaching a height of some two metres (photograph on p. 96; plates on pp. 97 and 99). Many of these thrones are not intended for use as seats but rather for the display of royal power (plates on pp. 100 and 101). In the kingdom of Bekom the thrones are said to have served exclusively as supports for calabashes containing the jaws and other bones of deceased kings. These were publicly displayed during important ceremonies of commemoration (photograph on p. 96).

The aura of these magnificent thrones is often further increased through a great deal of paintwork and, even more often, through the application of a mosaic-like decoration using thousands of coloured glass beads (plates on pp. 90–1, 97, 100–3). The significance of such decoration can only be appreciated if one is aware of the extraordinary value of these glass beads – a value derived from the need to import them from distant places. Most of the thrones decorated in this manner were, accordingly, for use only by kings and courtiers. Even today, in various kingdoms, these thrones are still used in important ceremonies. Many of them (cf. plates on pp. 100 and 101; cat. 71) were never intended as seats but rather to acknowledge the memory of deceased kings or their wives or mothers. At funeral ceremonies, they were openly displayed in the square in front of the palace.

Lorenz Homberger

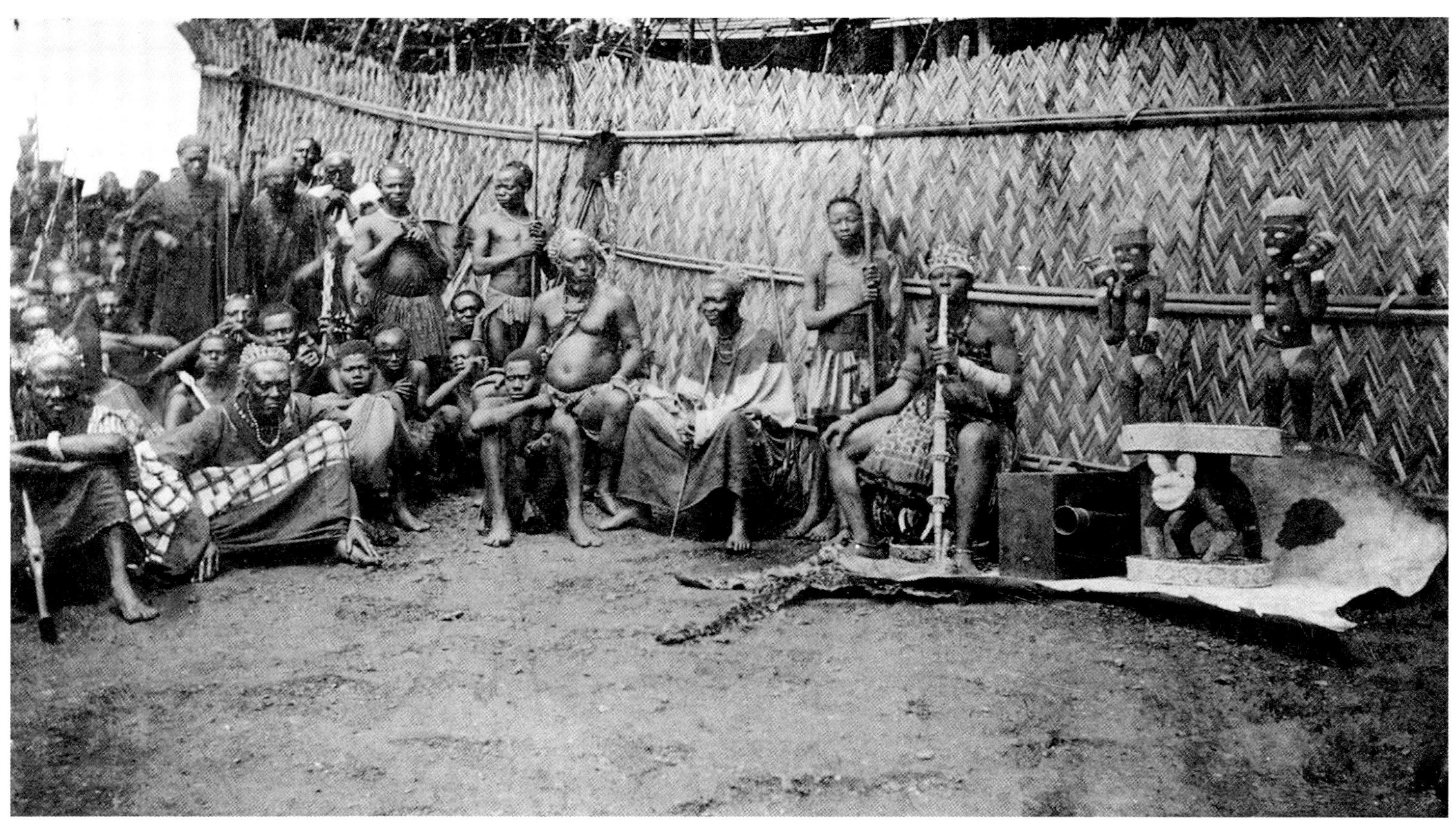

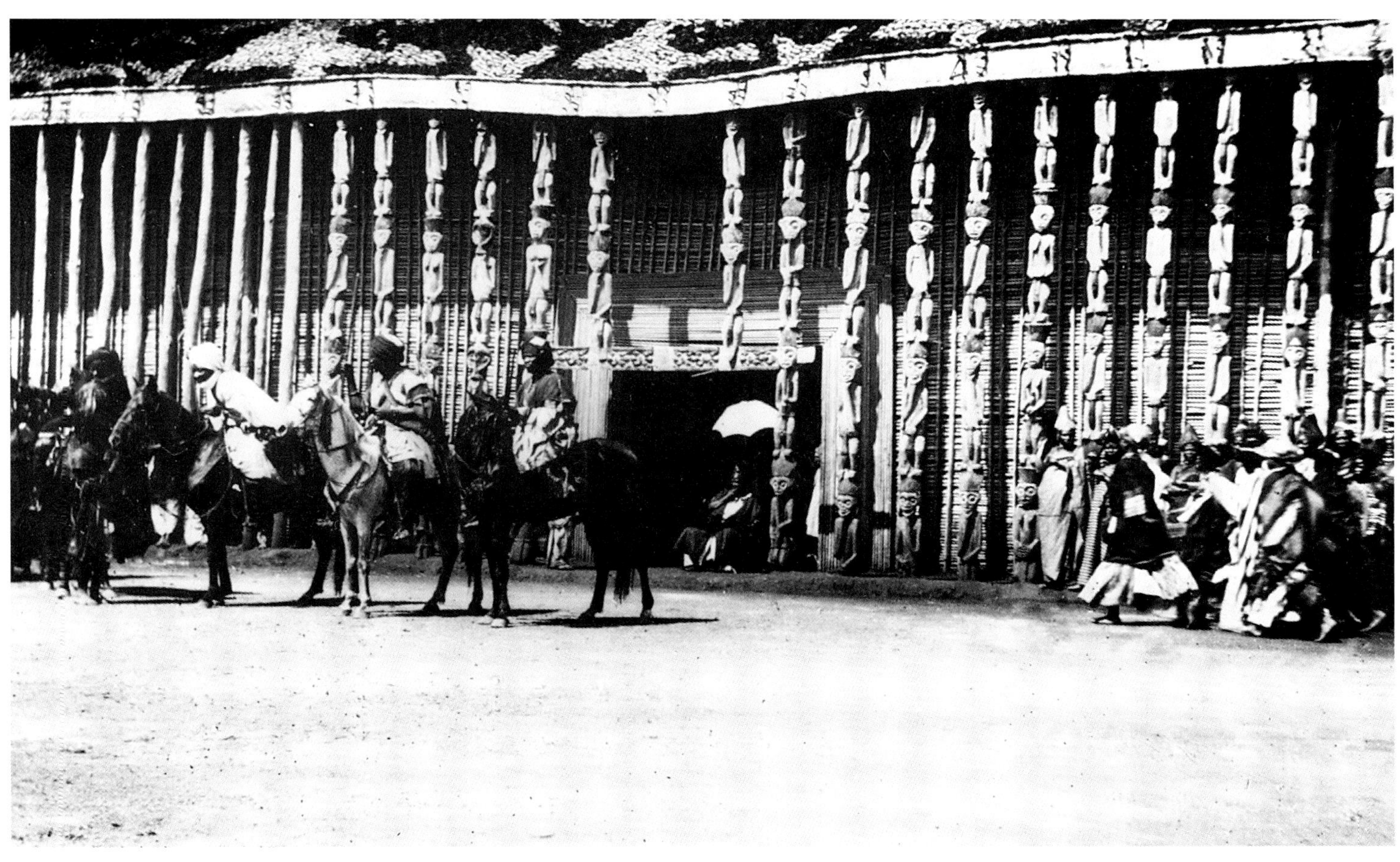

A parade in front of the old palace in Foumban, Cameroon. The royal palaces of the Cameroon grasslands were technical masterpieces. They were built with the wood of the raffia palm and with mud. The principal entrances and roof supports of important buildings were richly carved with human and animal figures. (Photograph: Anna Rein-Wuhrmann, *c.* 1911–15)

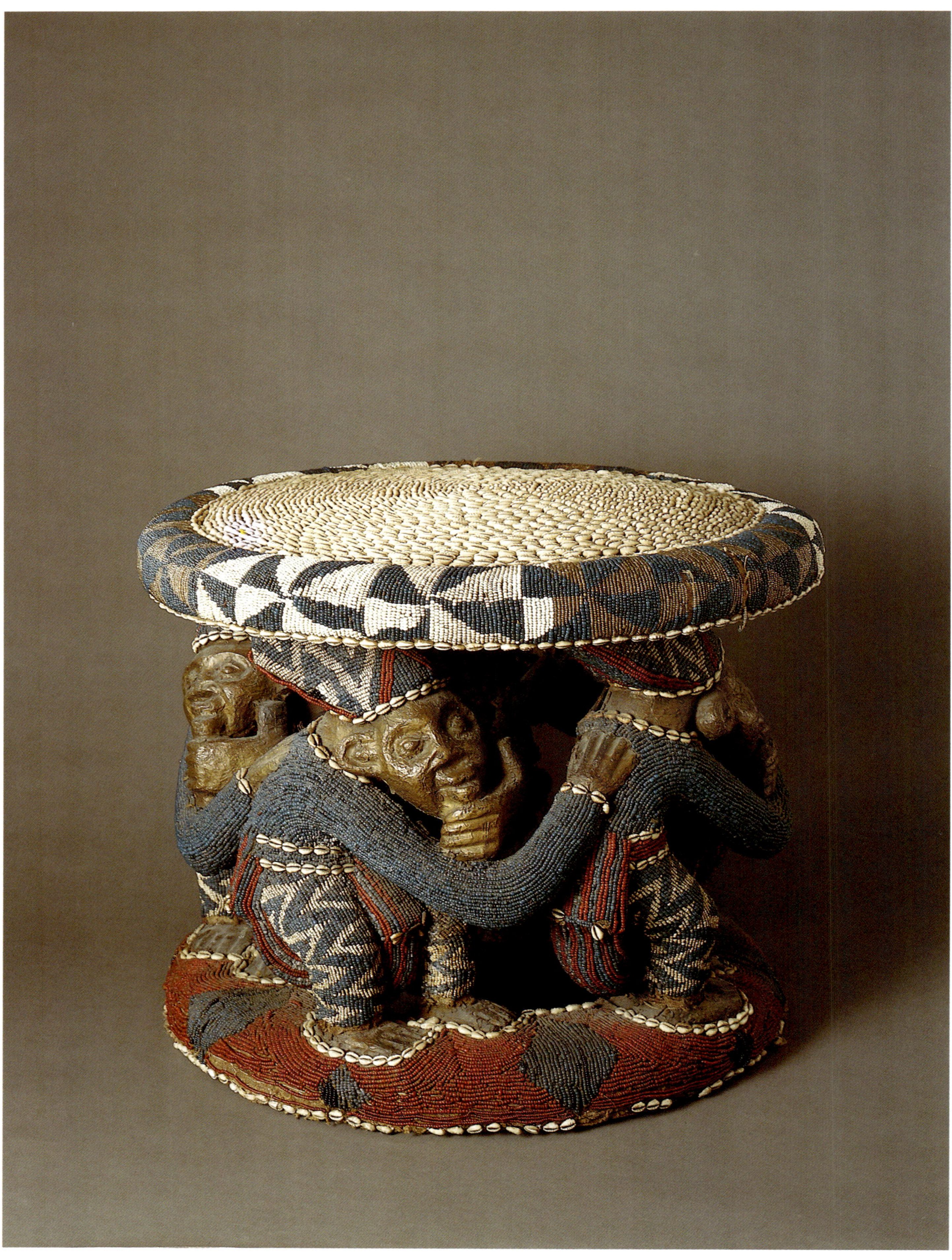

King's stool of the Bamum, Cameroon, height 57 cm Cat. 75

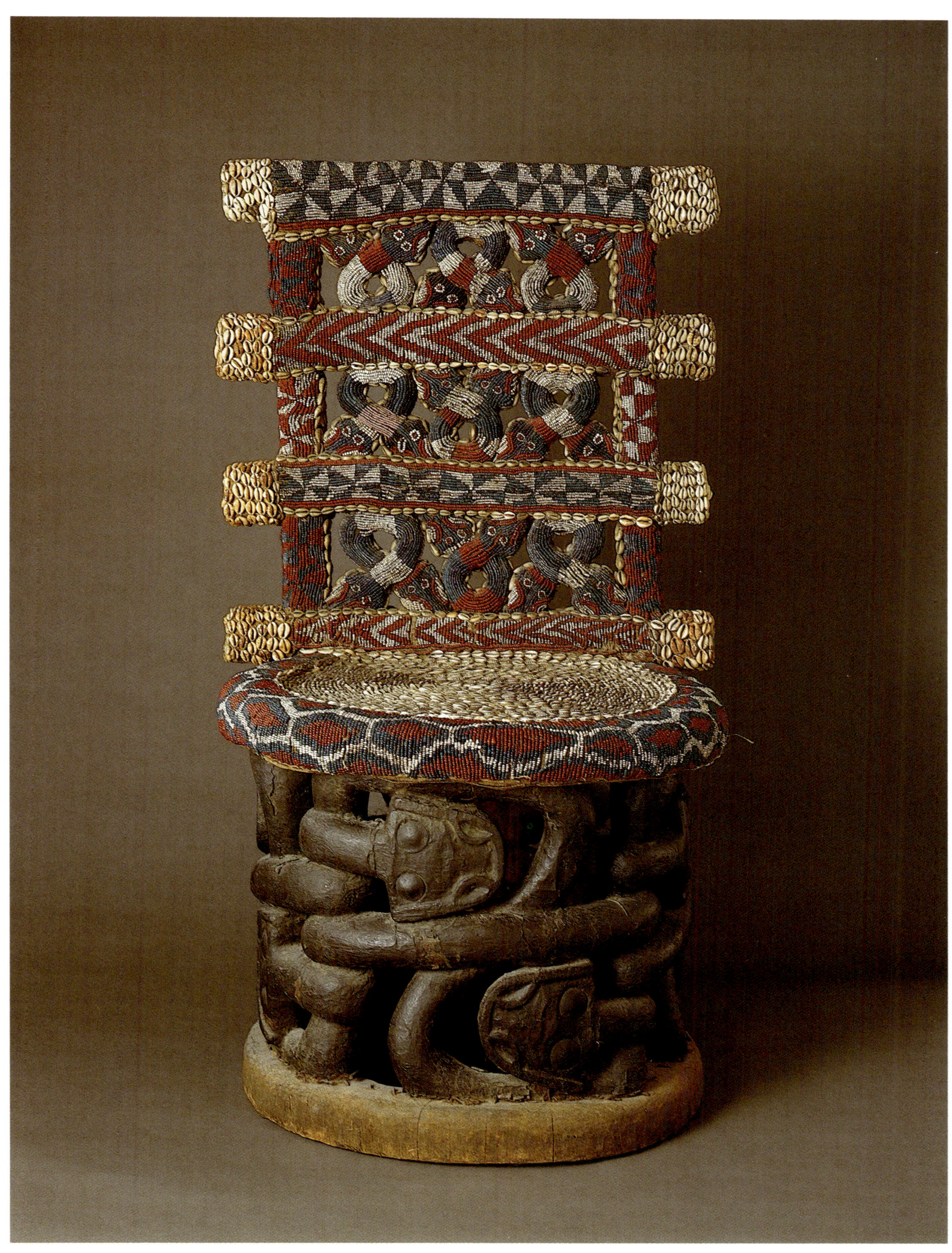

Chair of the Bamum, Cameroon, height 119 cm Cat. 76

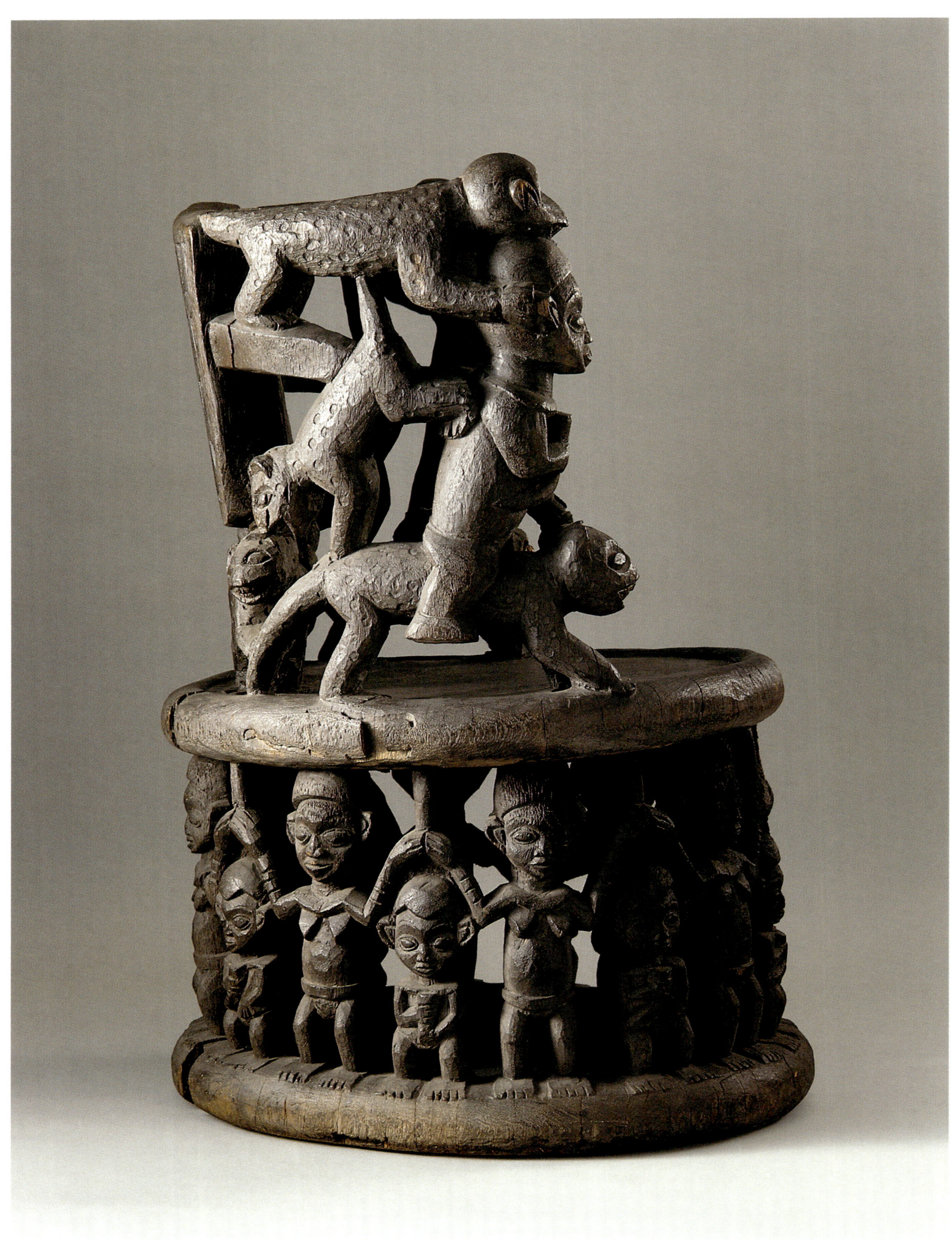

 Chair of the Babanki, Cameroon, height 89 cm Cat. 65

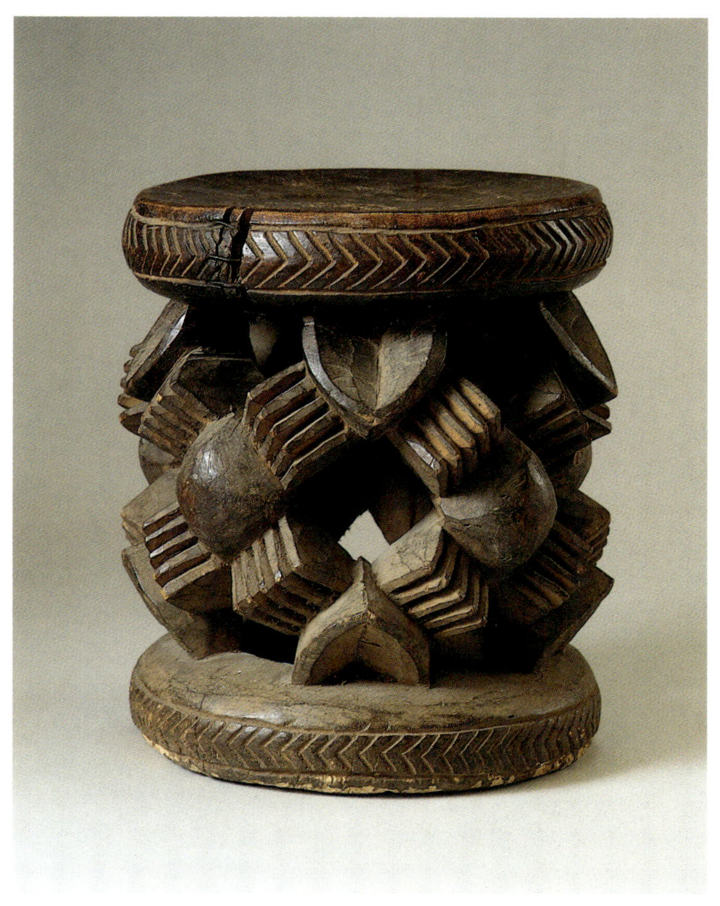

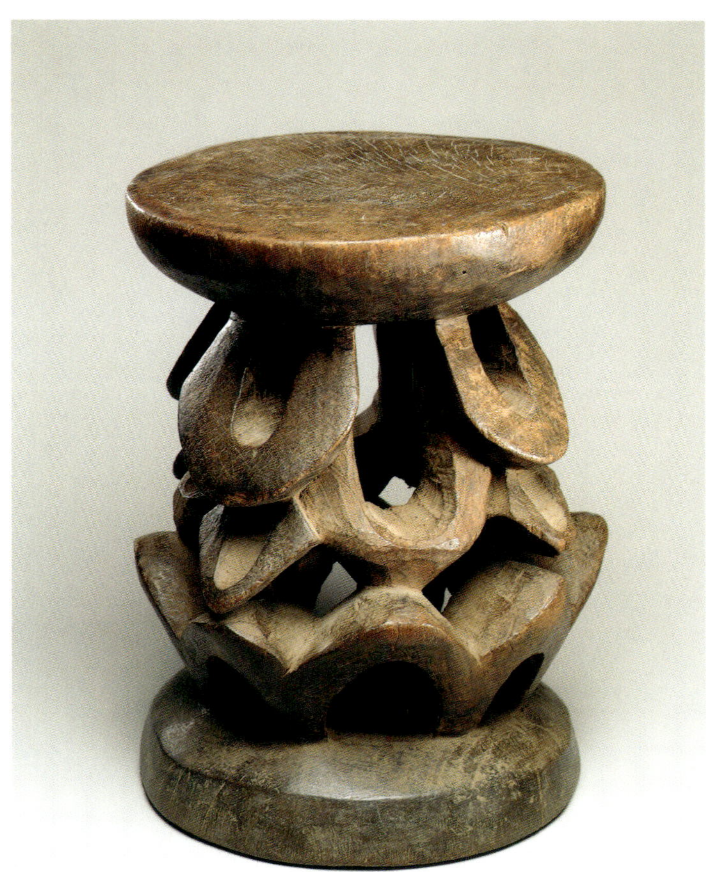

Photograph: Pierre-Alain Ferrazzini, Geneva

Stool of the Bamileke, Cameroon, height 37 cm Cat. 59
Stool from Cameroon, height 30 cm Cat. 61

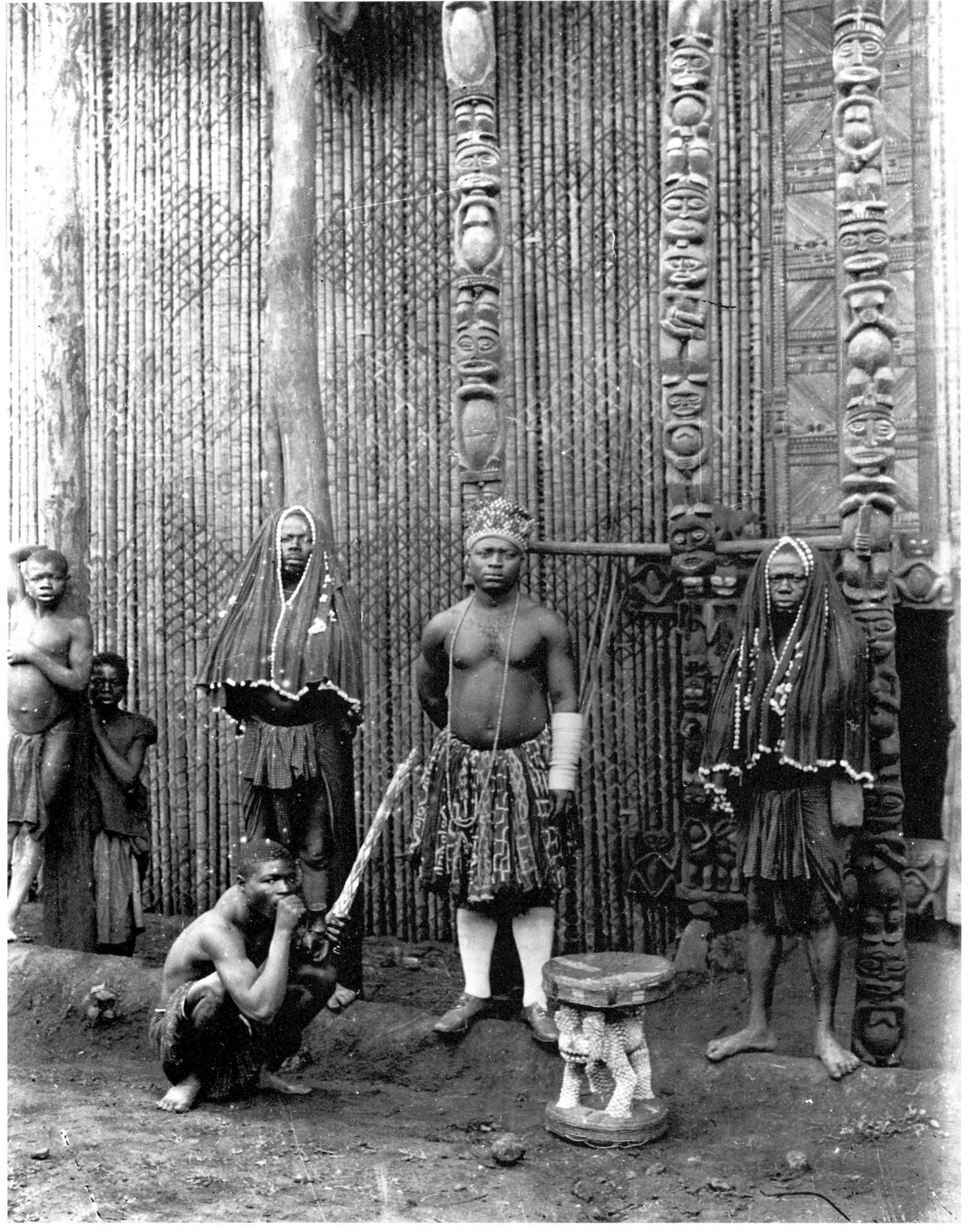

Photograph: F. Christol, 1925

The *fon* Kamga II of Bandjoun, Cameroon, after his enthronement

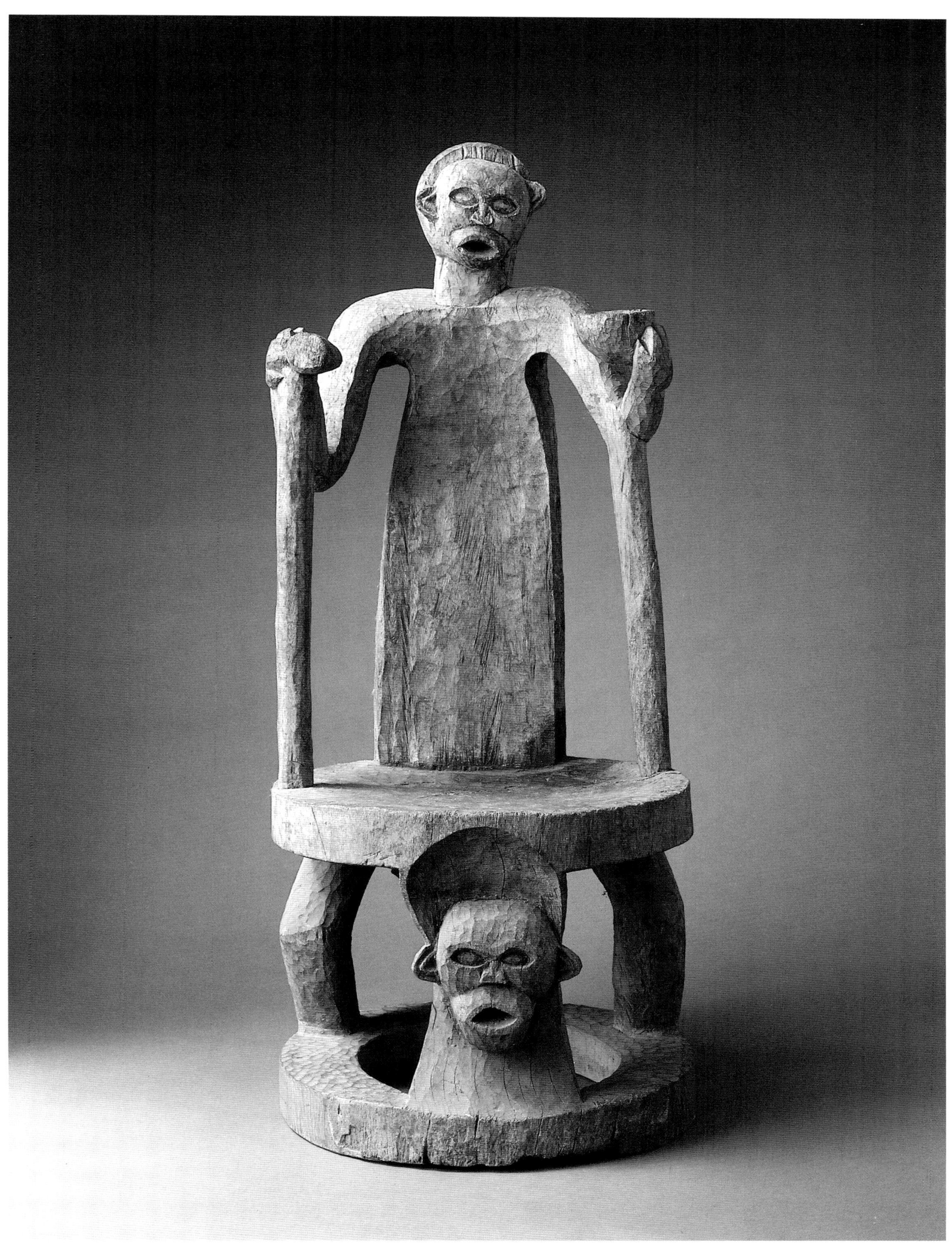

Chair from the Cameroon grasslands, height 120 cm Cat. 69

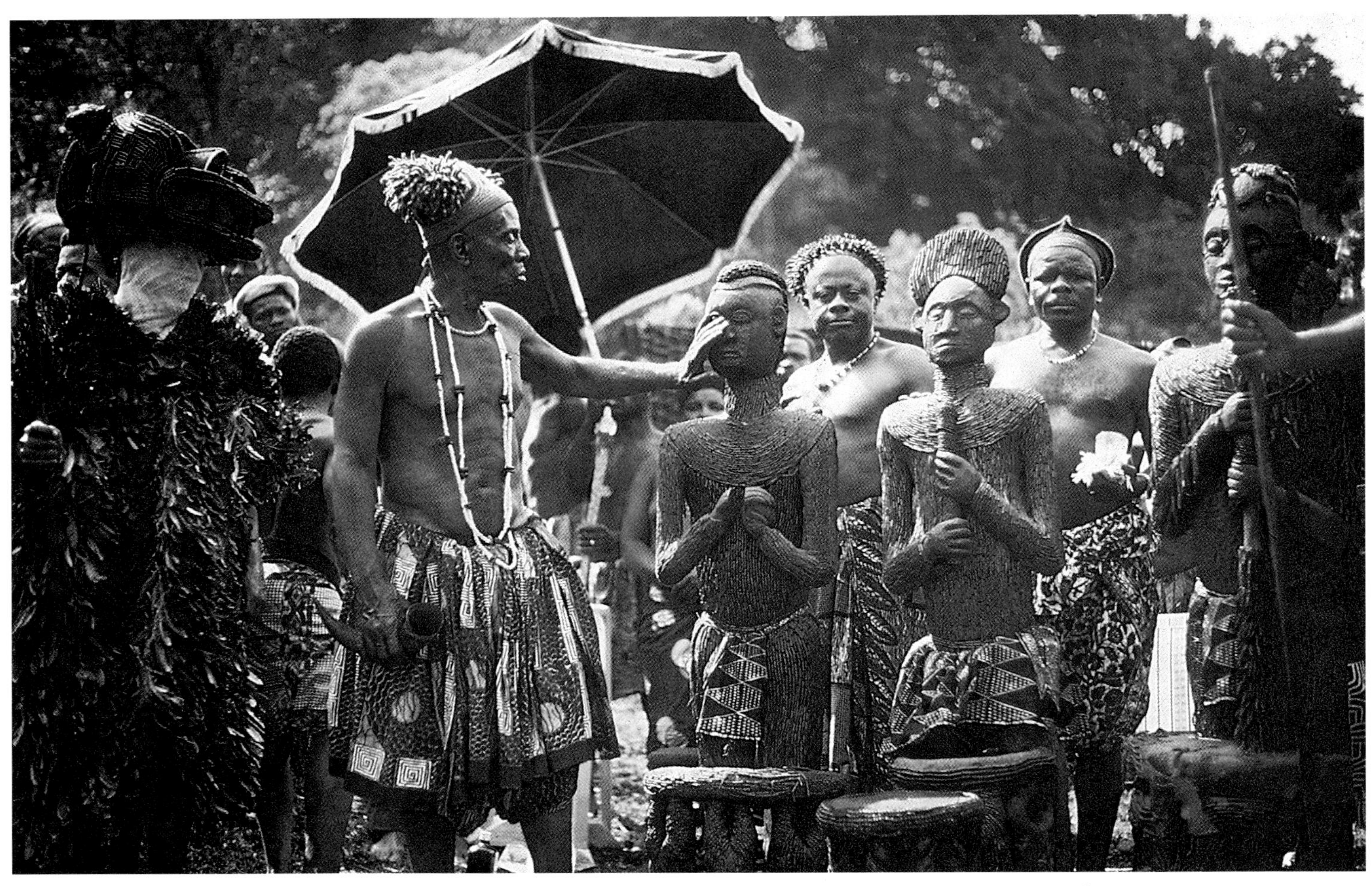

Photograph: Hans-Joachim Koloß, 1976

Enthronement ceremony for Jinabo II, the new king of Bekom, January 1976. The king approaches the royal figures that represent, respectively, the king's first consort, the king himself (Afo-A-Kom) and the queen mother. These figures are said to date from the time of the first king of Bekom and are seen as symbols of the kingdom. Stolen in the late 1960s, they were not returned to Cameroon until 1974; cf. cats. 77, 78 and plates on pp. 97, 99.

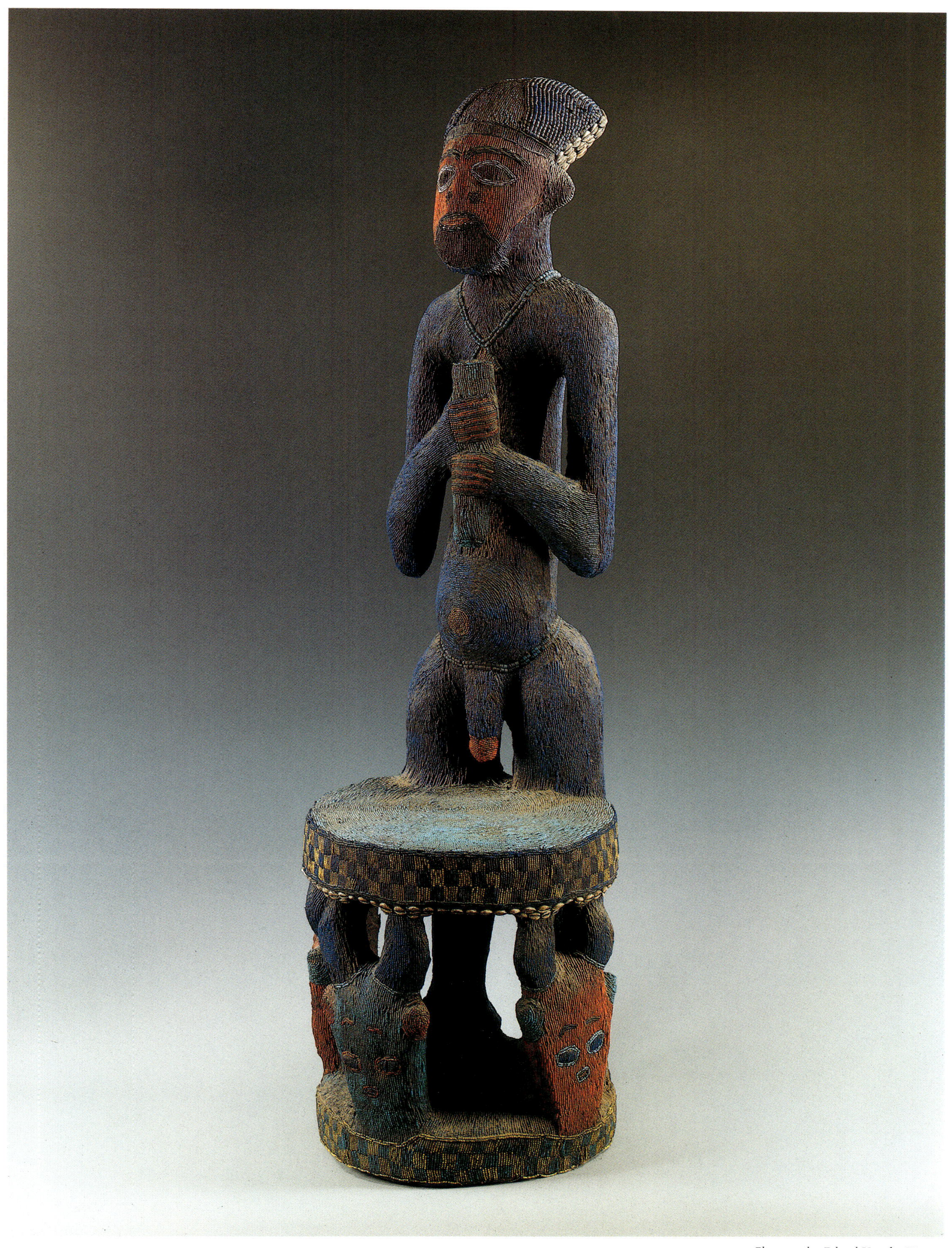

Photograph: Erhard Vessely, Vienna

King's chair of the Bamum, Cameroon, height 175 cm Cat. 77

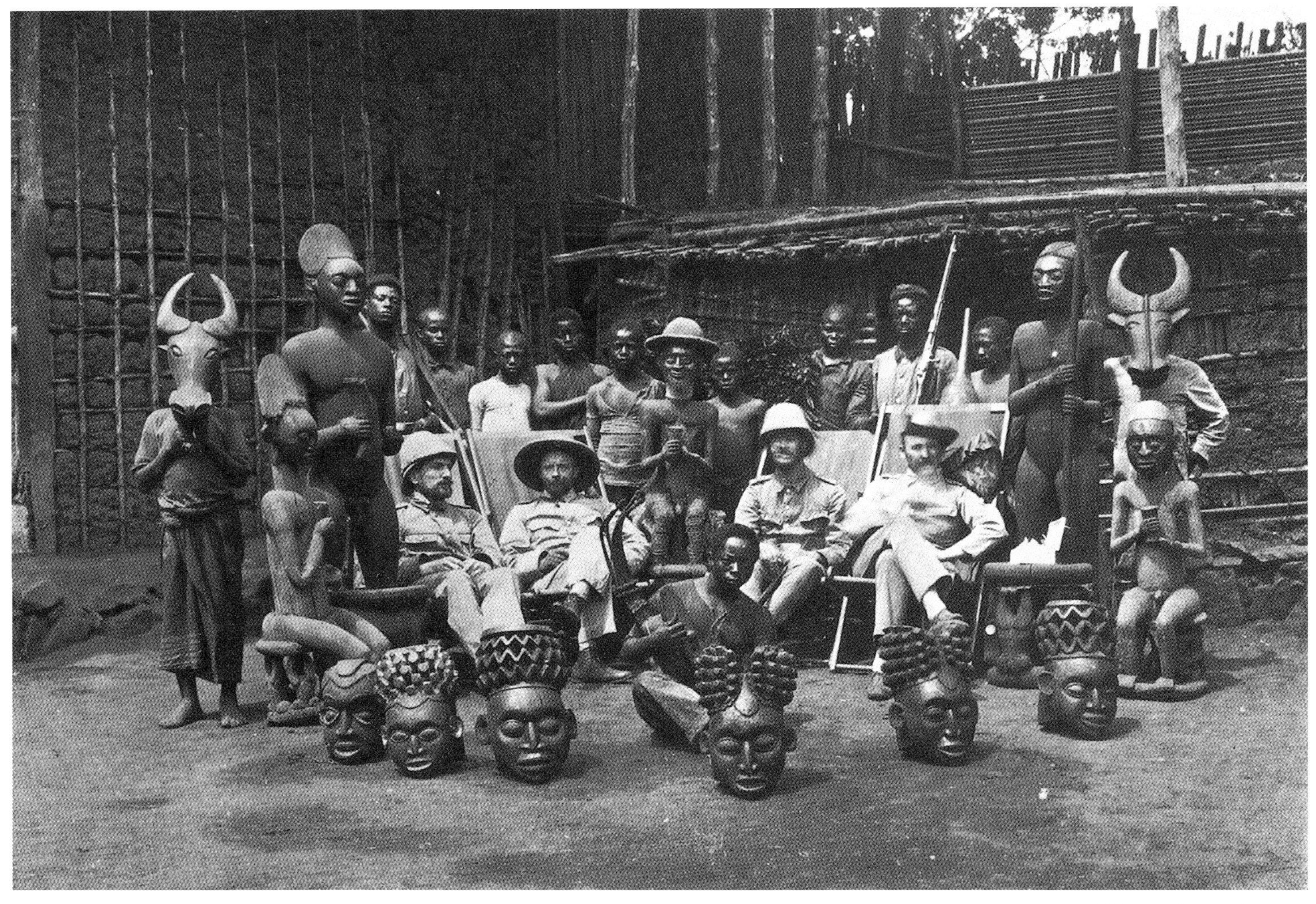

Unknown photographer, 1905

Members of the German colonial forces after the conquest of the kingdom of Kom, seated in front of the royal palace in Laikom, Cameroon. The objects lined up beside them are now in the Museum für Völkerkunde, Berlin (see also plate opposite).

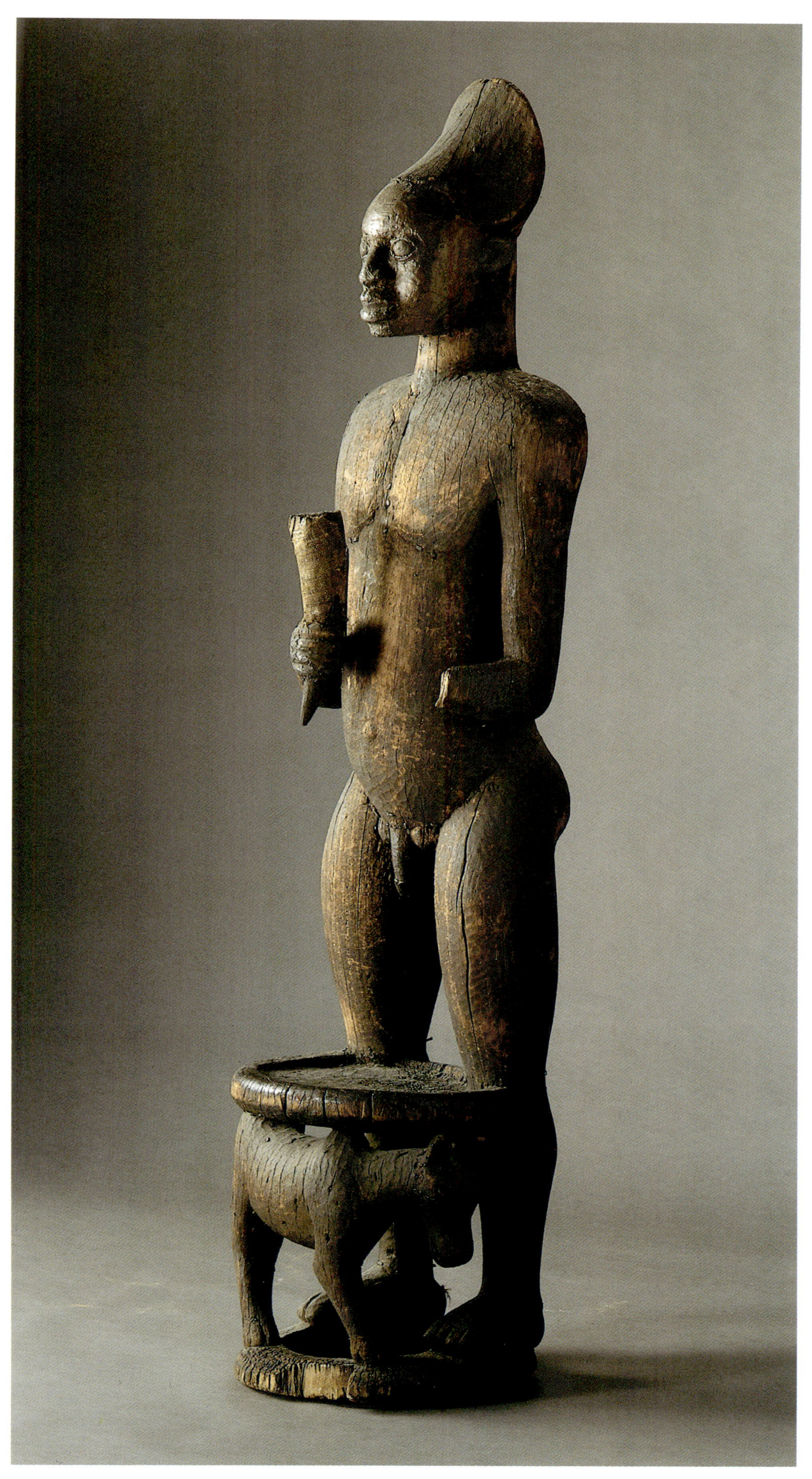

Chair with standing male figure of the Kom, Cameroon,
height 190 cm Cat. 78

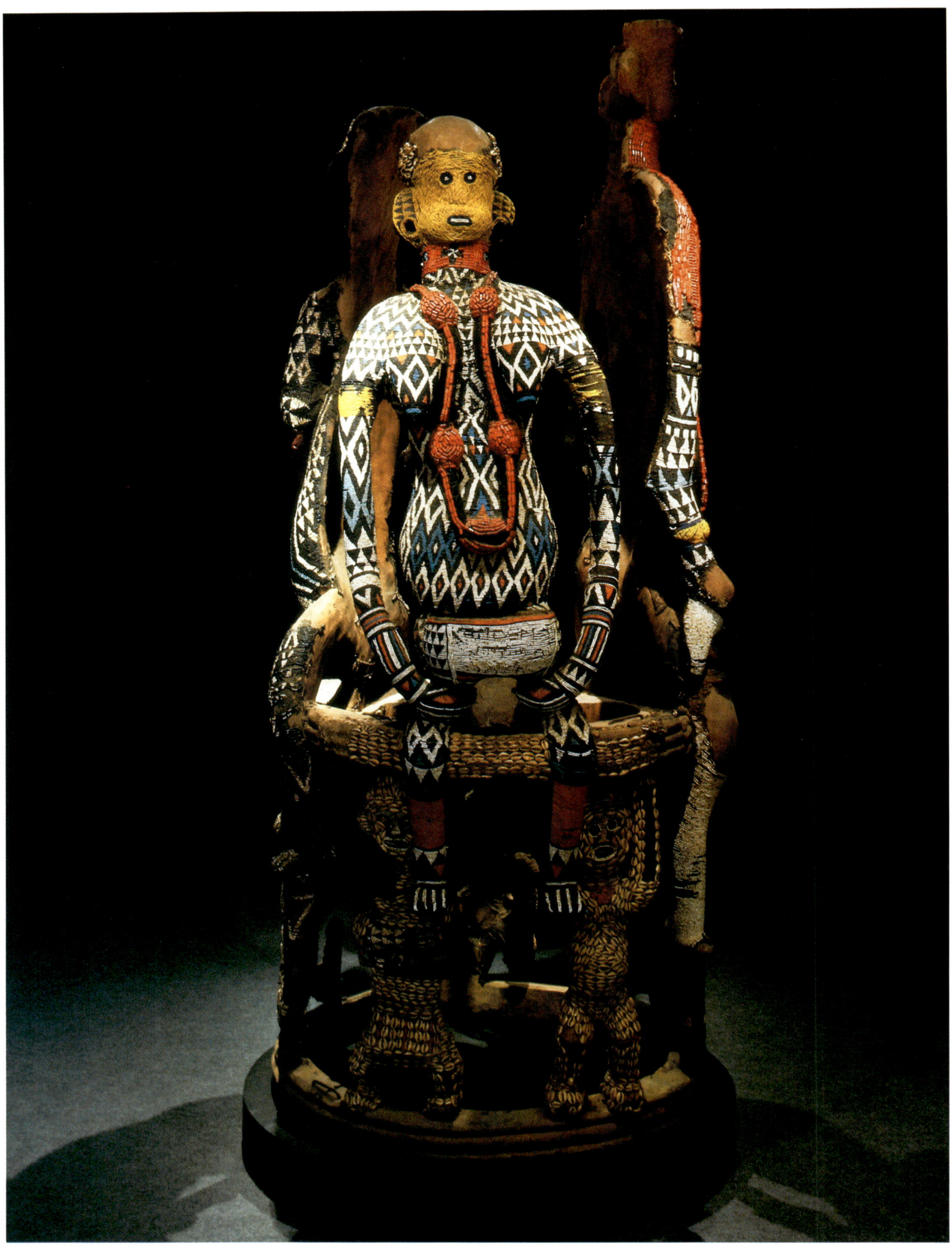

Photograph: Luc Hautecœur, Paris

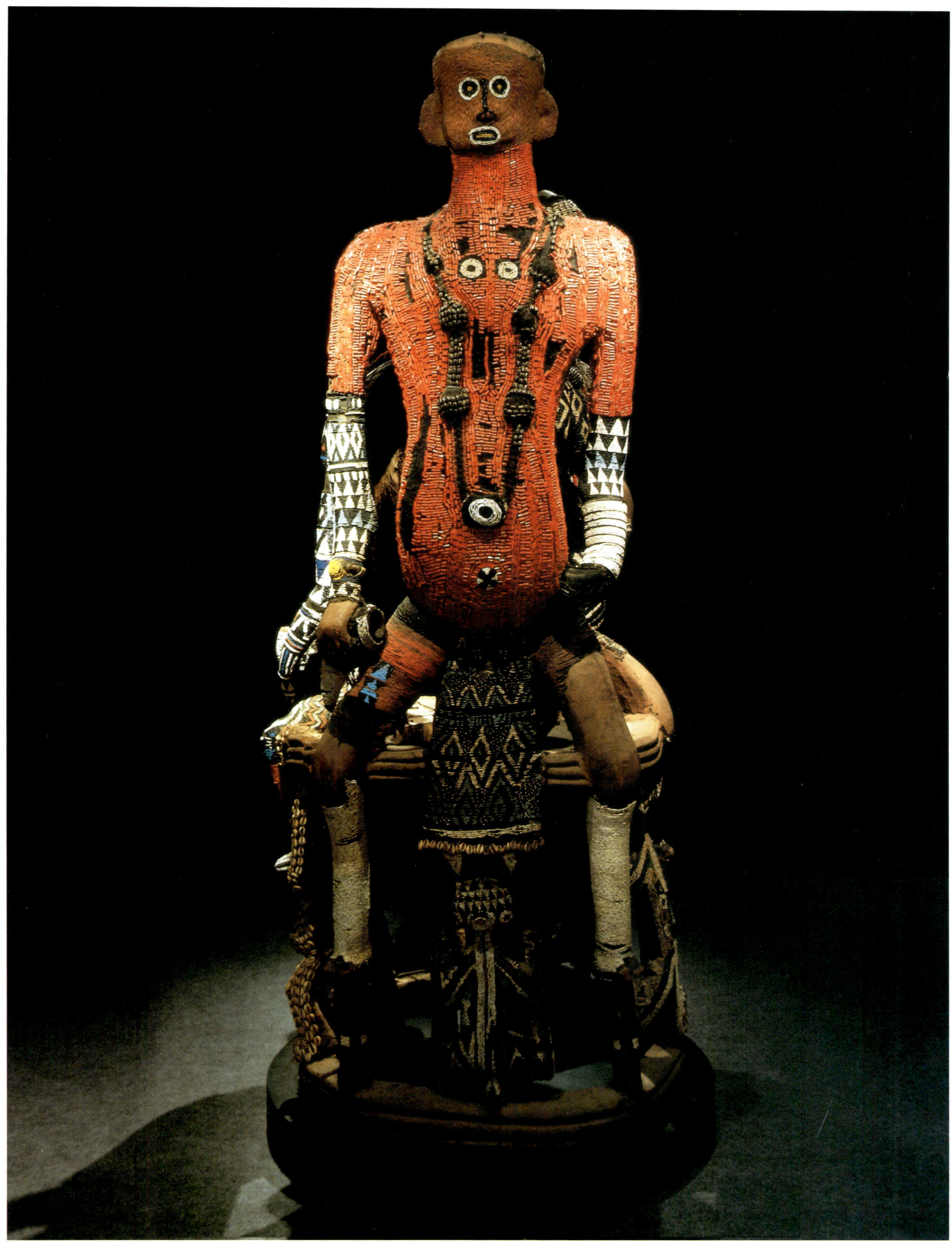

Photograph: Luc Hautecœur, Paris

King's stool (see also plate opposite), with portraits of a king and a queen of the Baham, Cameroon, height 220 cm Cat. 71

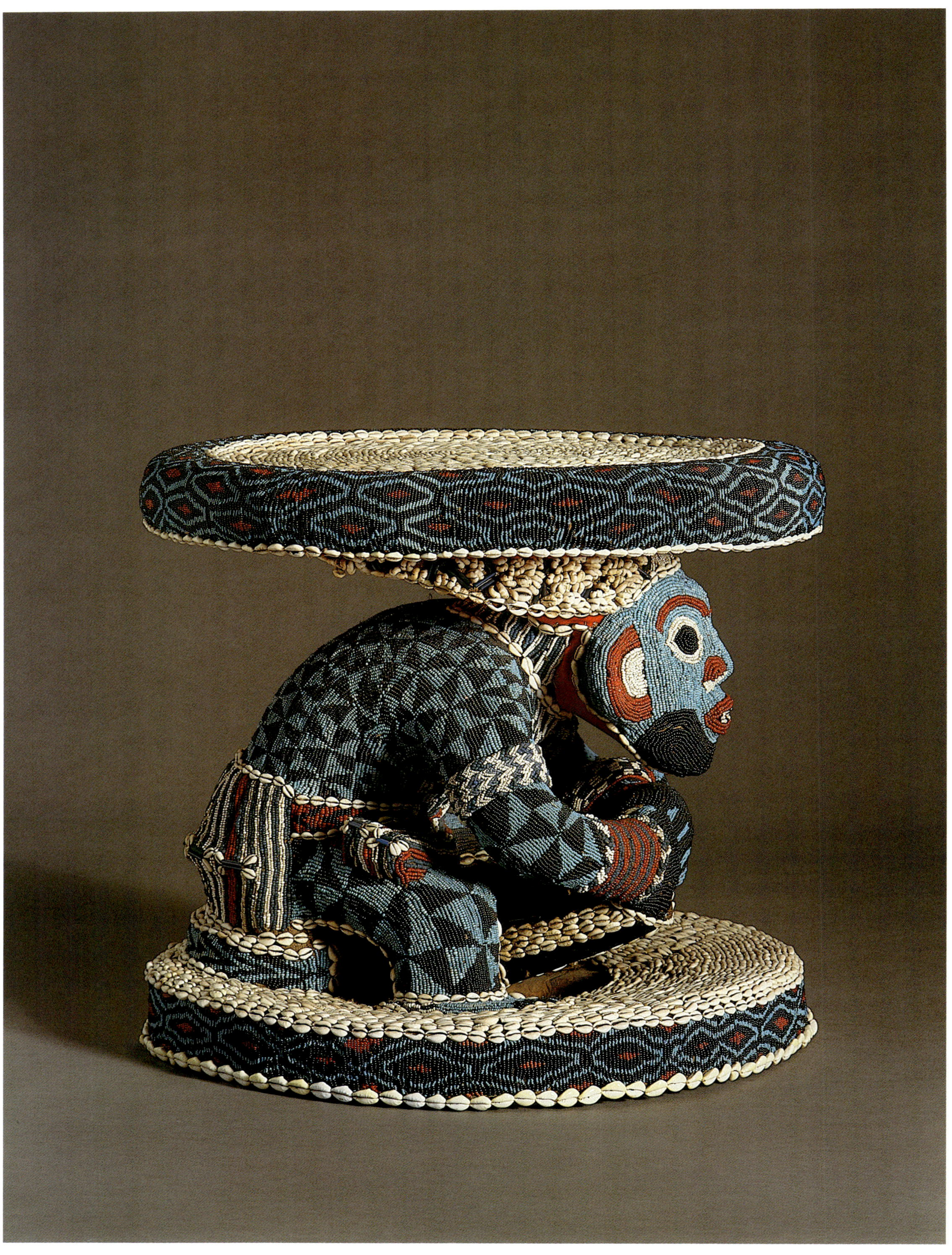

 Stool of King Njoya of the Bamum, Cameroon, height 60 cm Cat. 74

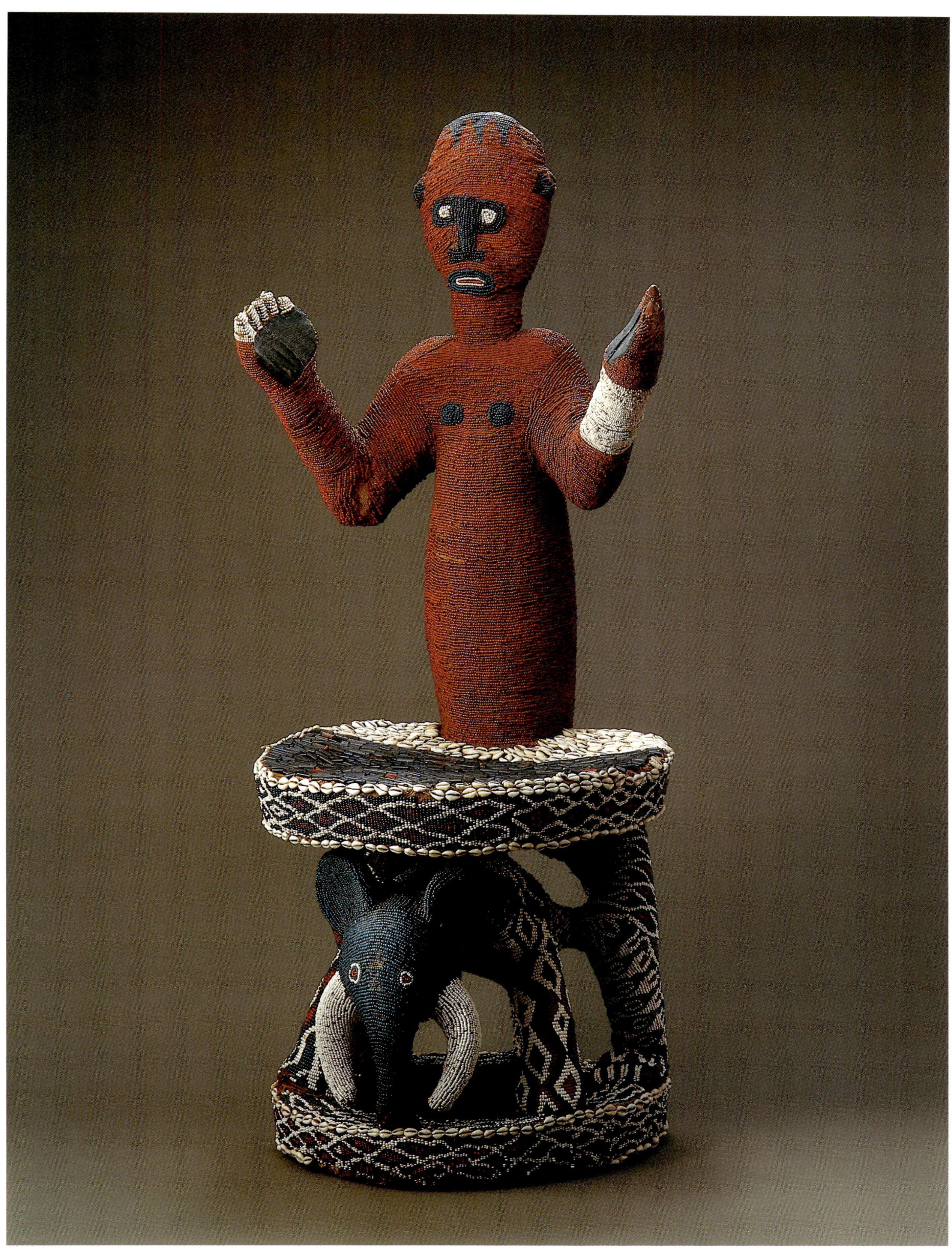

Chair of a notability from the Cameroon grasslands, height 128 cm Cat. 70

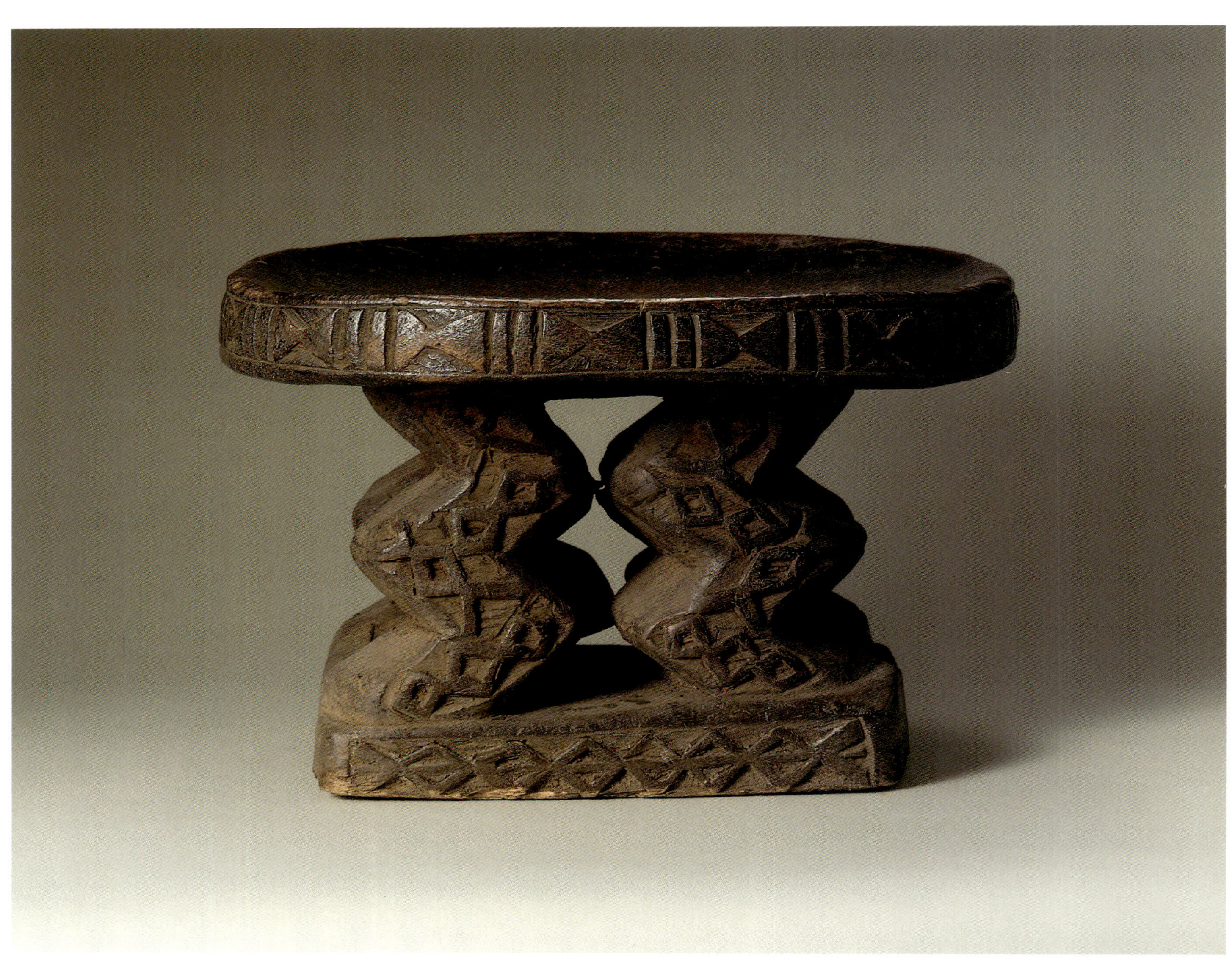

Stool of the Bamileke, Cameroon, height 34.5 cm Cat. 62

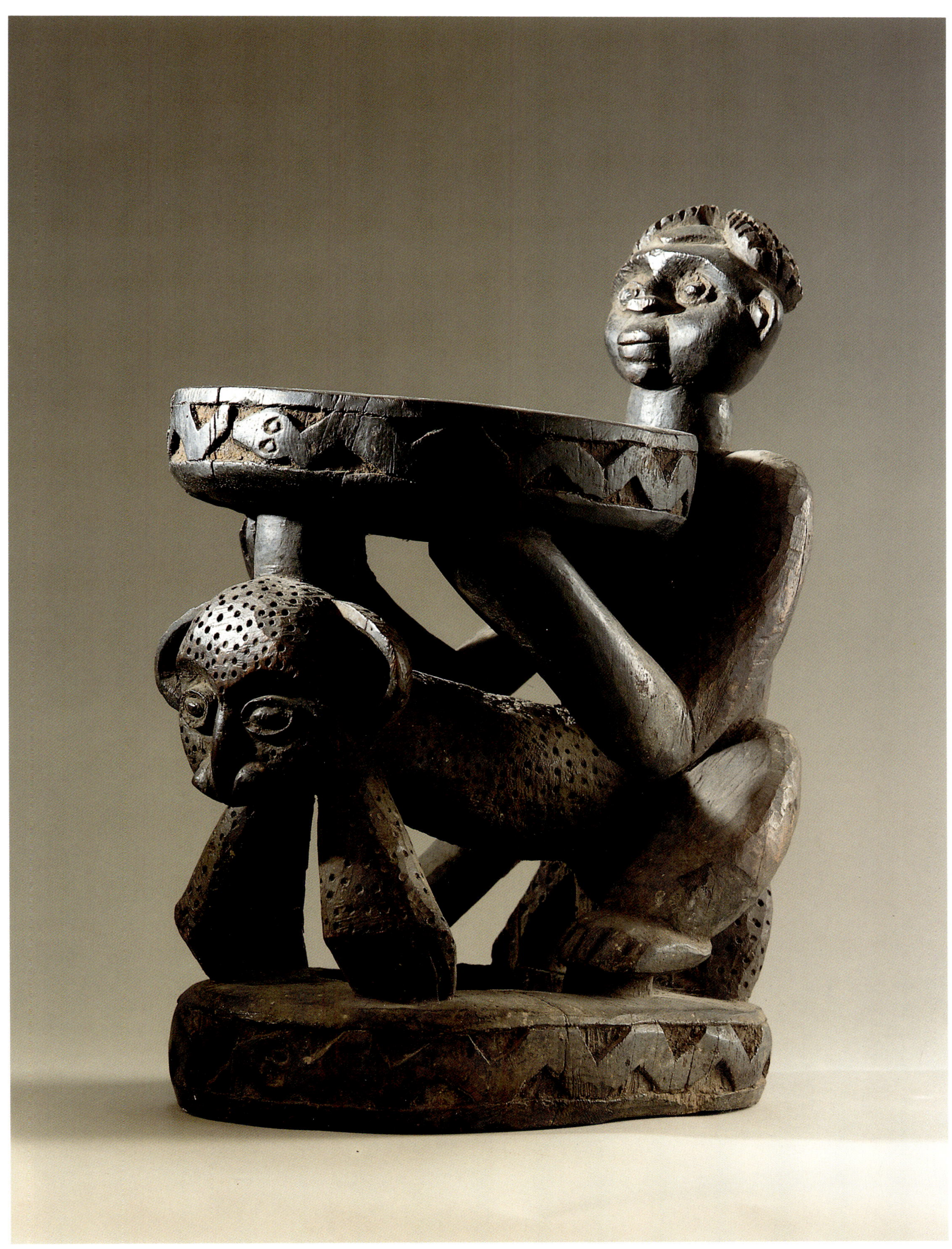

King's chair of the Oku (?), Cameroon, height 54.5 cm Cat. 67

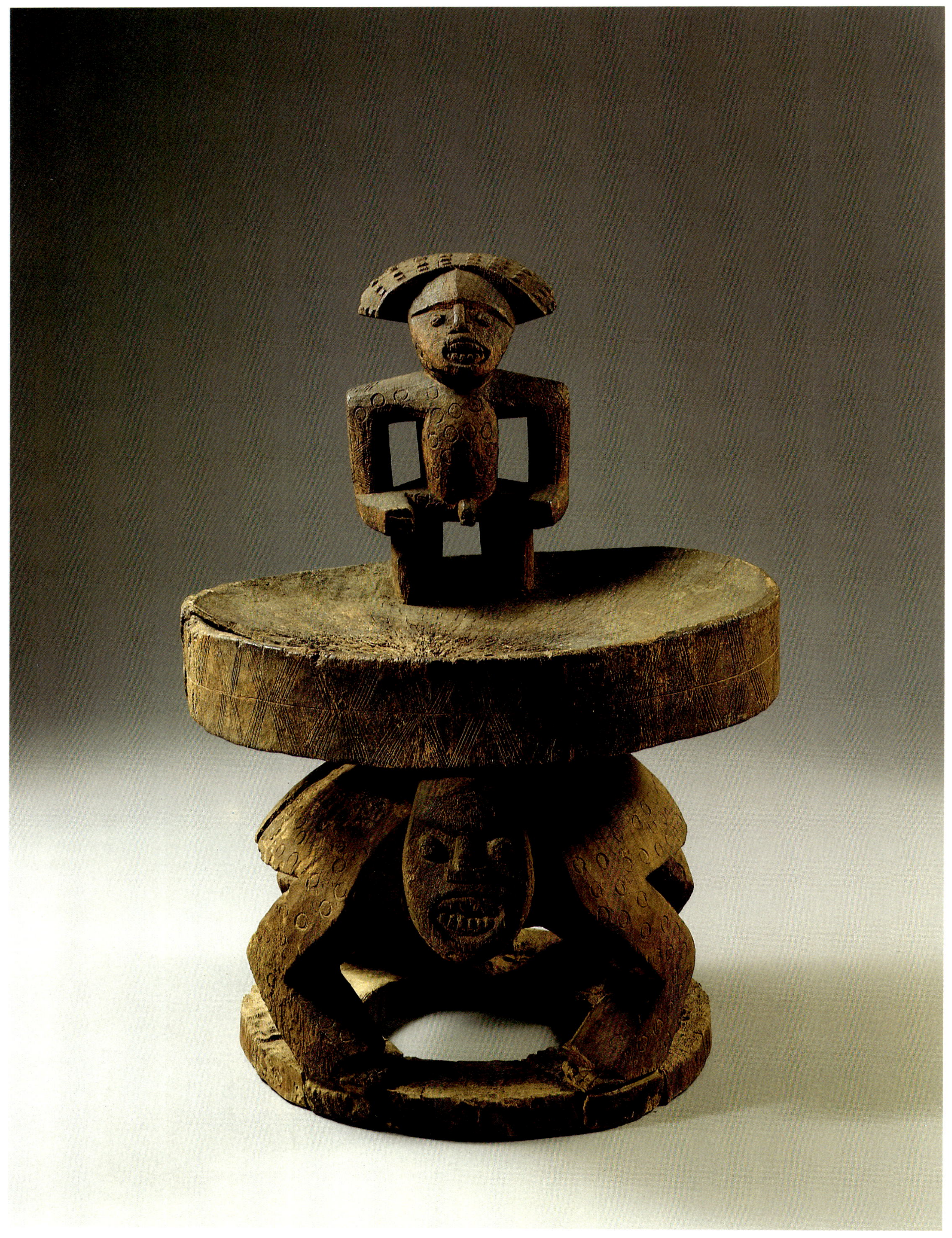

Photograph: Jean Christen, Mannheim

King's chair of the Bamileke (Bana), Cameroon, height 65 cm Cat. 68

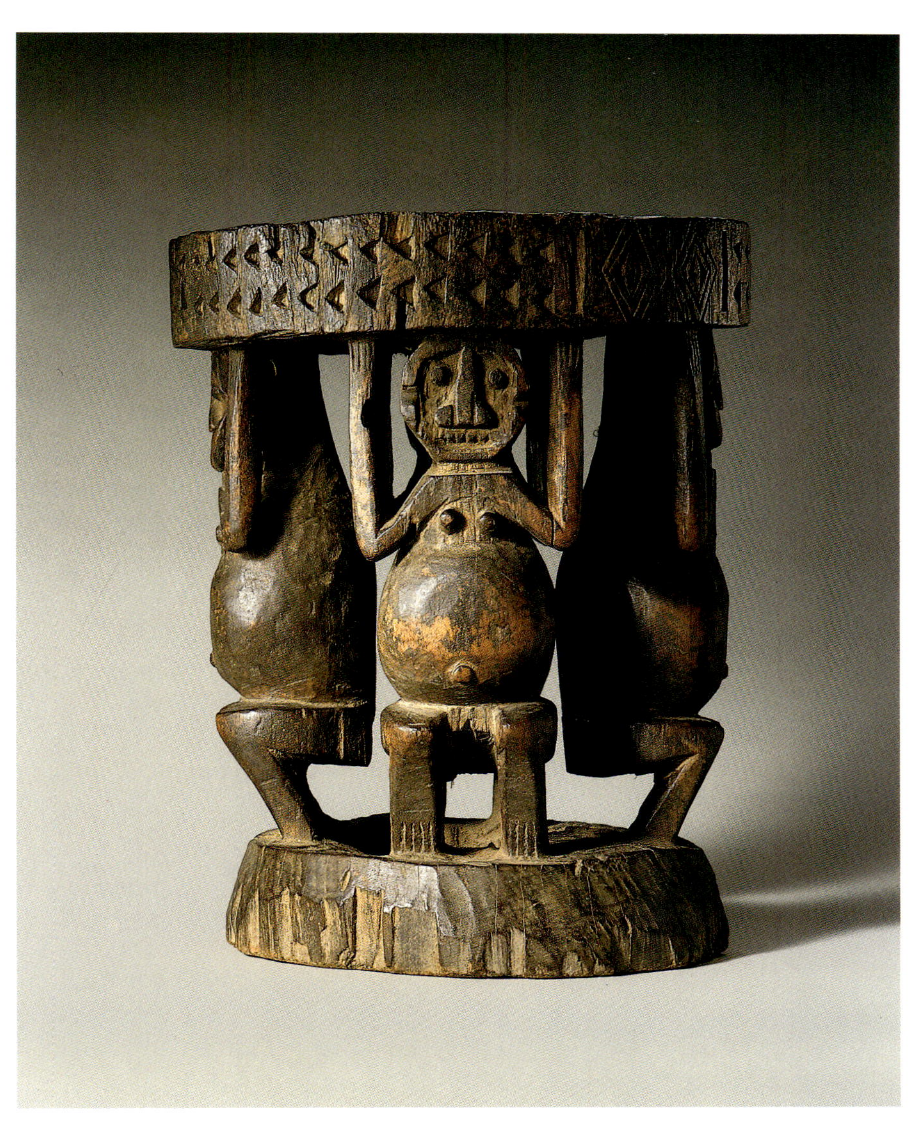

Caryatid stool of the Bamileke, Cameroon, height 43.5 cm Cat. 66

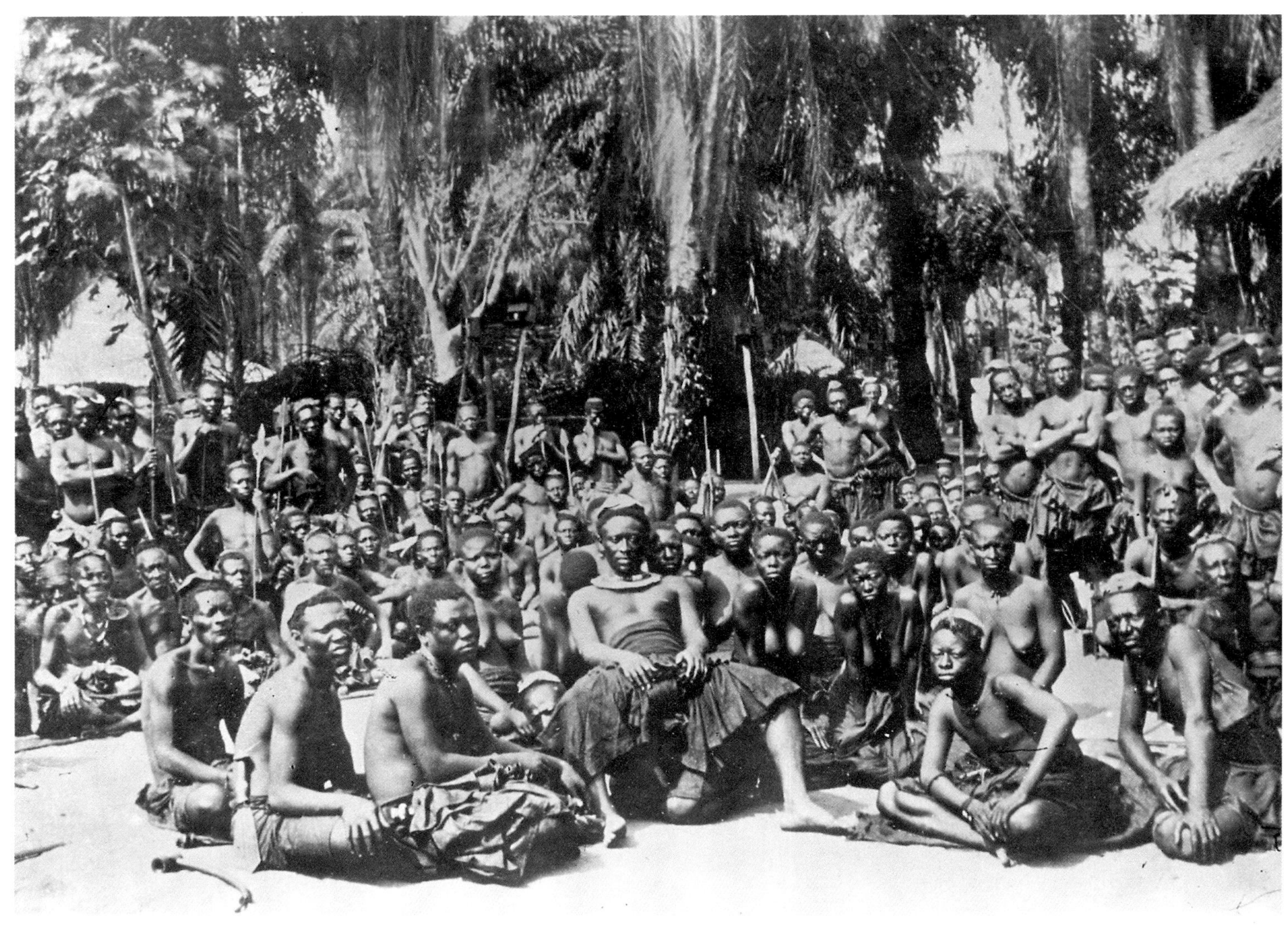

In the past, members of the family of the king of the Kuba were not permitted to sit on the ground. Instead, they sat on an animal skin or a chair or – as in the case of King Kwete Peshanga, shown here, in Nsheng, Zaire – on a slave. The slave can be seen looking out from beyond the king's right knee. (Photograph: W. H. Hilton-Simpson, 1908)

Central Africa

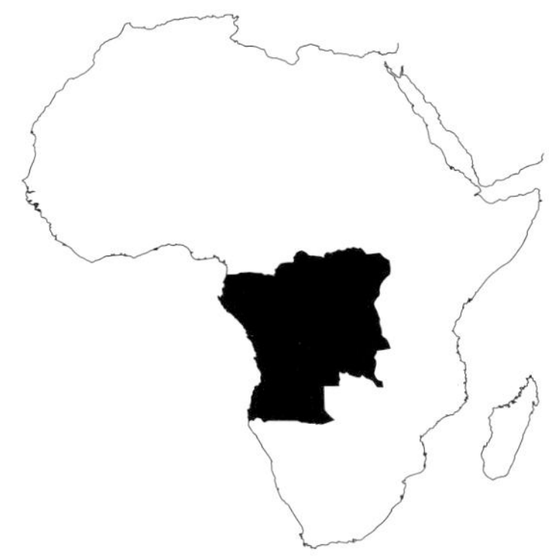

Extending from the Atlantic coast, across the entire catchment basin of the Zaire river, to the lakes in the east, Central Africa embraces a region that is among the most significant in the continent for figural art. A large number of peoples created an astonishing variety of styles and sub-styles here, some of which spread to neighbouring regions, thus hampering the attempt at classification. In Central Africa, as elsewhere, regional styles are therefore of greater significance than those that can be associated with specific peoples. Nor should it be forgotten that, even in a region so rich in art, there remain large areas where little or no figurative art is to be found. None the less, the savannah region, south of the equator, is especially rich in forms of artistic expression. Ritual objects predominate here: masks and figures filled with magic substances used in connection with secret societies and by distinct age groups. This is also an area in which historically significant kingdoms arose. The most important of these – that of the Congo around the mouth of the Zaire river, the Kuba, the Luba and the Lunda in the south and south-east, and the Azande and the Mangbetu in the north-east – are represented here in the form of thrones made for their princes, which function above all as symbols of sovereignty. Like other carefully designed ceremonial implements – sceptres, curved pins, display knives and axes – they signify the status and prestige of members of the royal court.

Among the magnificently carved seats of this region, caryatid stools are especially widespread. The caryatid itself – the form supporting the usually circular seat with its hands or on its head – may take a human or an animal form (plates on pp. 127, 139, 143–8). Caryatid figures are usually female, but this was not intended to impute to women in such societies the rank of merely servile bearers. The scar tattoo patterns on these figures reveal that the depicted women were members of families of the highest rank, so occupying an influential social position. As is often the case among the Bantu peoples, with their matriarchally organized society,

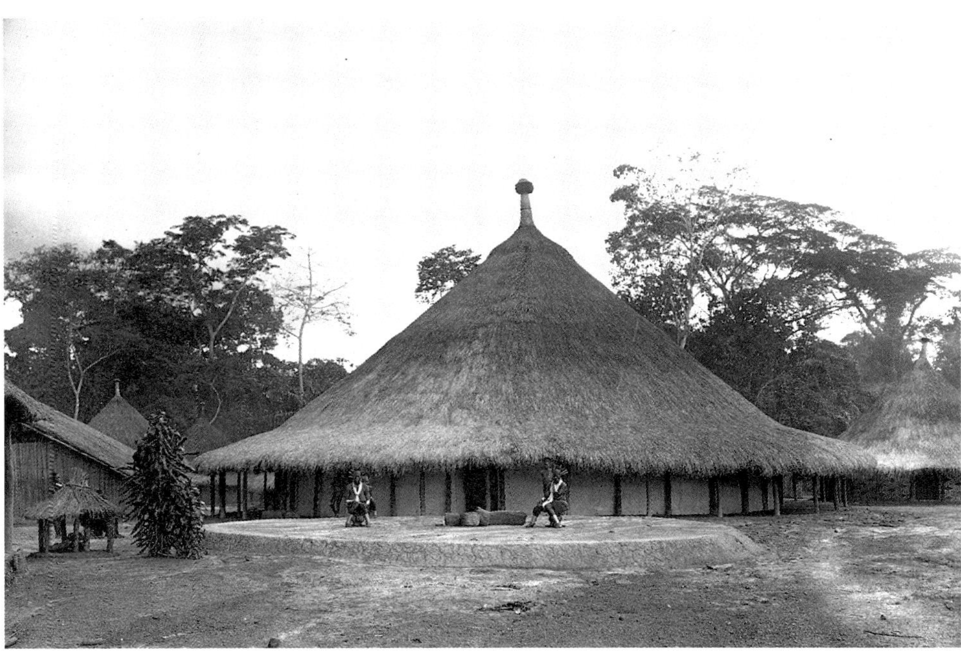

The house of Matubani, one of the wives of the Mangbetu chief Okondo, in Zaire. Men of the Mangbetu who were of noble rank were polygamous. According to reports, Okondo had 180 wives, all of them living in the royal enclosure. The largest house, shown here, belonged to Queen Matubani; and this is where Okondo usually stayed. (Photograph: Herbert Lang, 1910)

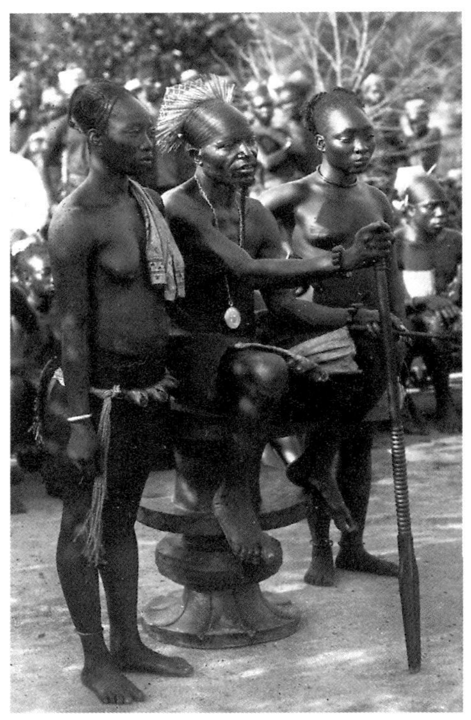

The Mangbetu chief Danga in Rungu on a double-decker stool, which was a symbol of his power. (Photograph: Herbert Lang, 1910)

The Mangbetu chief Okondo waiting to perform his dance. His wives, each seated on a stool, look on; cf. cat. 96 and fig. on p. 30. (Photograph: Herbert Lang, 1913)

women were seen as the pillars of the family and of the clan as a whole. Presented as caryatids, they were thus symbolized as 'Bearers of the Nation'. Possession of such objects was the privilege of high-placed and rich individuals (plates on pp. 112–16, 118–21). These seats usually have neither backs nor arms. The most outstanding examples are perhaps those produced in south-eastern Zaire by the Luba and by their northern and western neighbours, the Hemba, the Chokwe and the Zimba. In the caryatid seats of the Luba and the Songye, the figures are more often presented in a kneeling pose, while those of the Hemba and the Zimba usually stand.

Seats with backs, assembled out of several different pieces of wood, are found above all among the Pende and the Chokwe, who, like both the Luba and the Mangbetu, live in societies with a strictly structured hierarchy among the ruling élite. Such seats have magnificent detailed carving: there may be contemporary genre scenes or perhaps the depiction of mythological figures that may take part in everyday life (as assisting spirits) but are also believed to appear at important events. Such representations were skilfully worked both below the seating surface (on the crossbeams) and also on, and within, the back. The formal design of these chairs is clearly derived from European models (plates on pp. 150–5).

The simple three-legged back-supports carved from a suitably shaped forked branch as semi-reclining chairs for men of the Mangbetu are in some cases mounted, as a mark of prestige, with brass tacks (plate on p. 129). Far more elegant are the two-legged back-supports with a sweeping concave form and also usually a perforated back (plates on pp. 130 and 131). Even more consummate in terms of design are the small circular chairs, with geometrically decorated central supports, used only by women; though exceptionally plain, they are distinguished by their formal tension (plate on p. 127; fig. on p. 30; photograph on p. 126).

Among many other peoples of the Zaire region – for example among the Ngombe and the Chokwe – one finds examples of decoration with brass tacks (plates on pp. 132–4, 139, 145). Although generally intended for everyday use by men, women and children, these seats often took on a specific symbolism, closely linked with the political hierarchy, with social prestige or with religious authority.

Lorenz Homberger

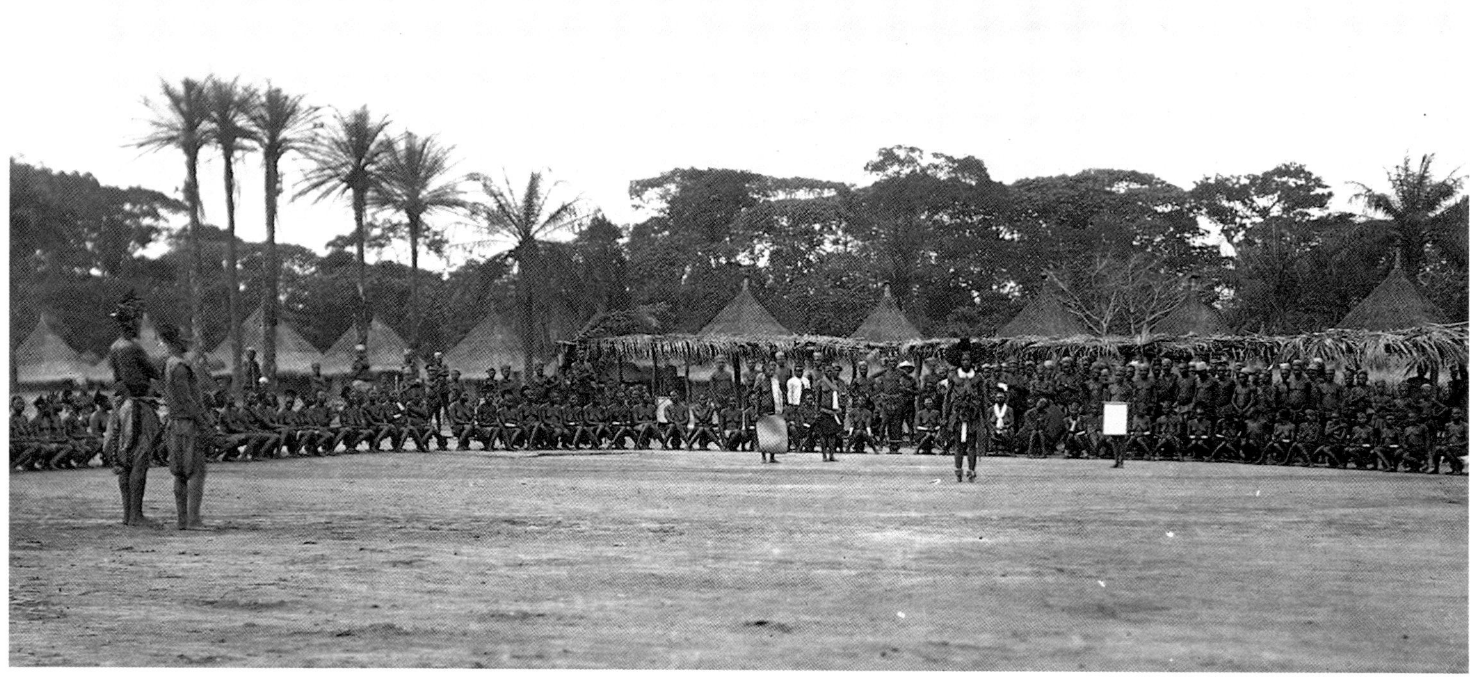

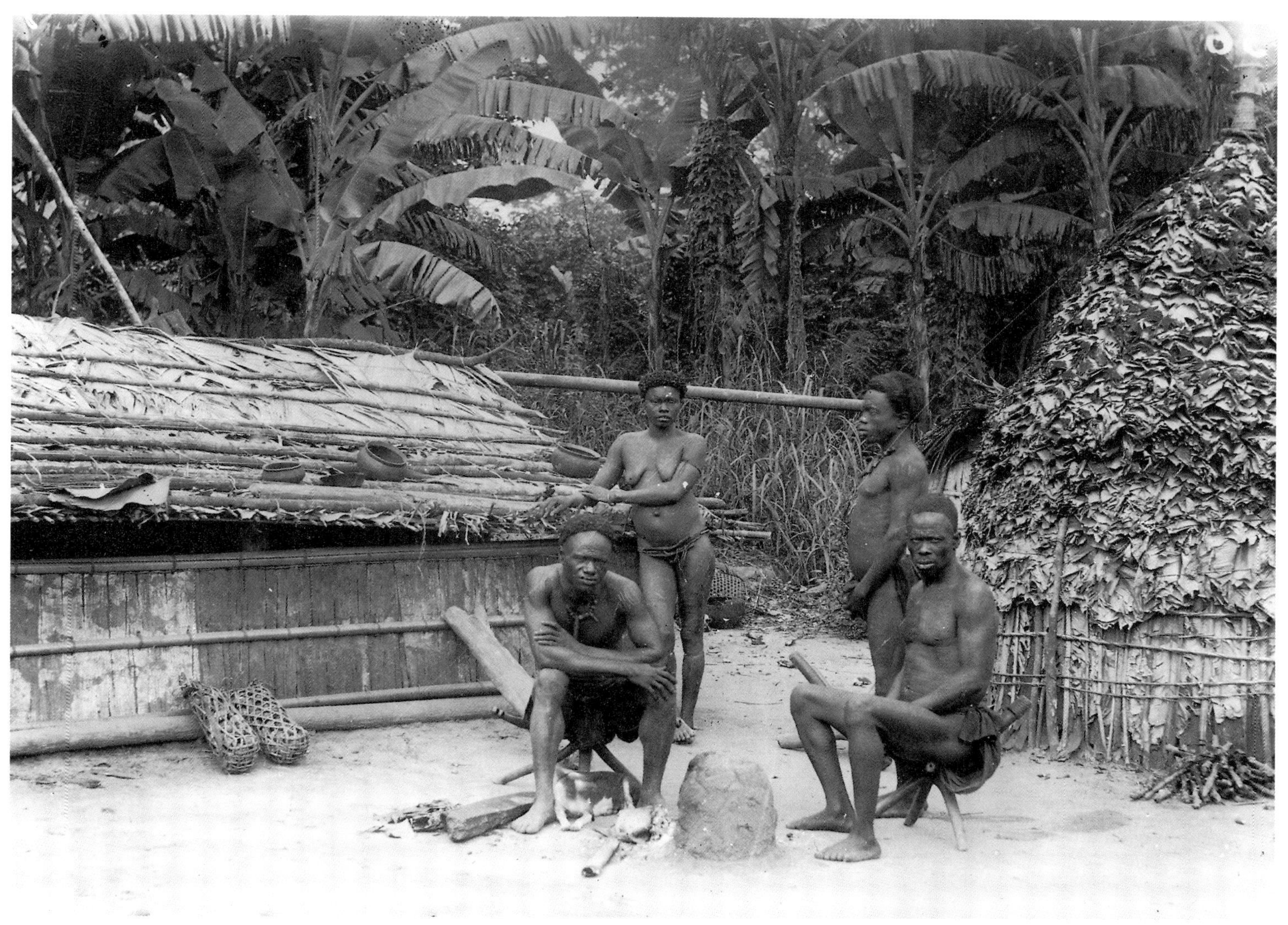

Men seated on three-legged stools in Turumbu (Olombo), Zaire. In Africa, chairs and stools were to some extent regarded as ordinary utensils and, as such, could be used by all members of the society. Often, however, they were symbols of social status or of power and were then reserved for the nobility. (Photograph: Thevoz, 1899)

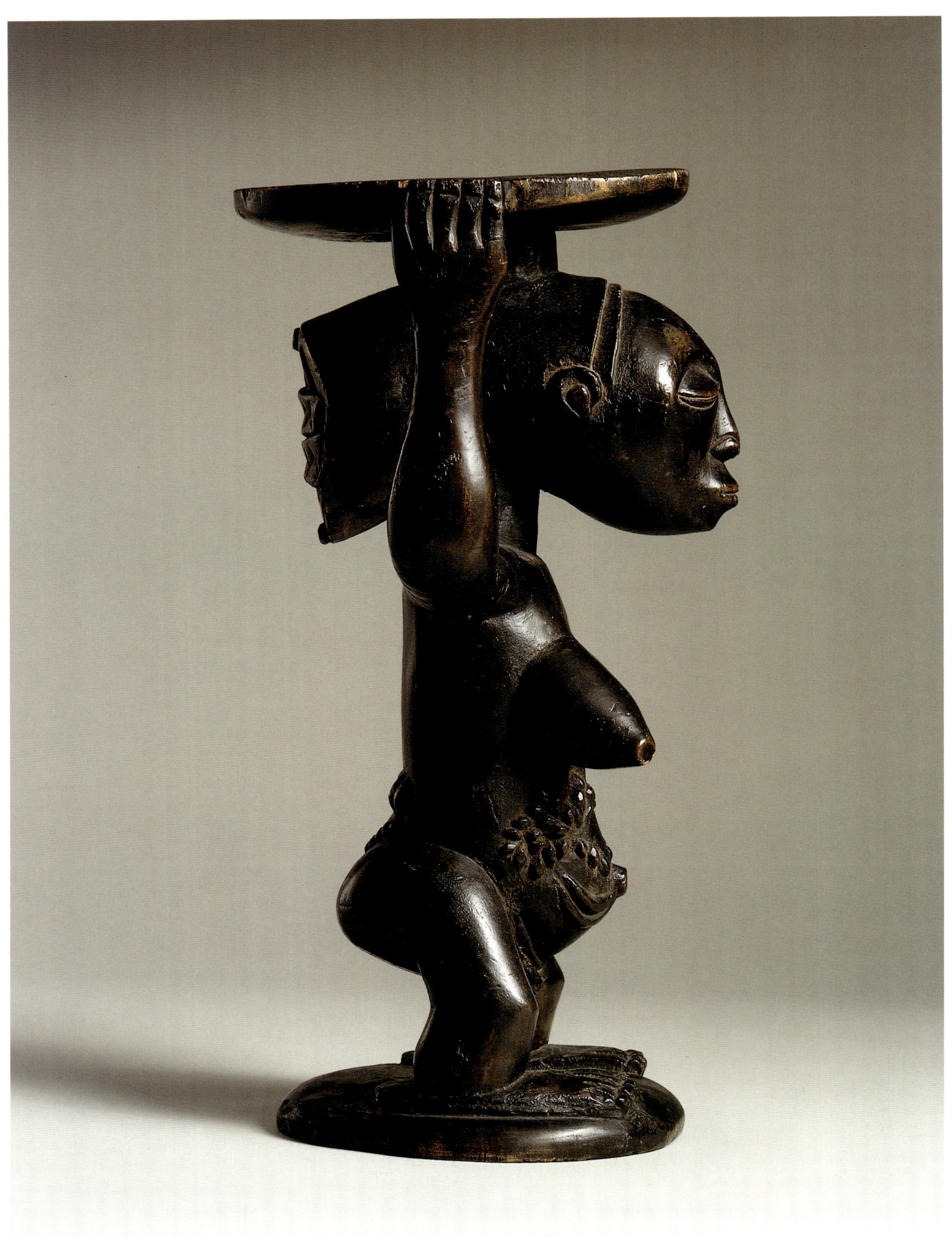

 Caryatid stool of the Luba, Zaire, height 41.5 cm Cat. 128

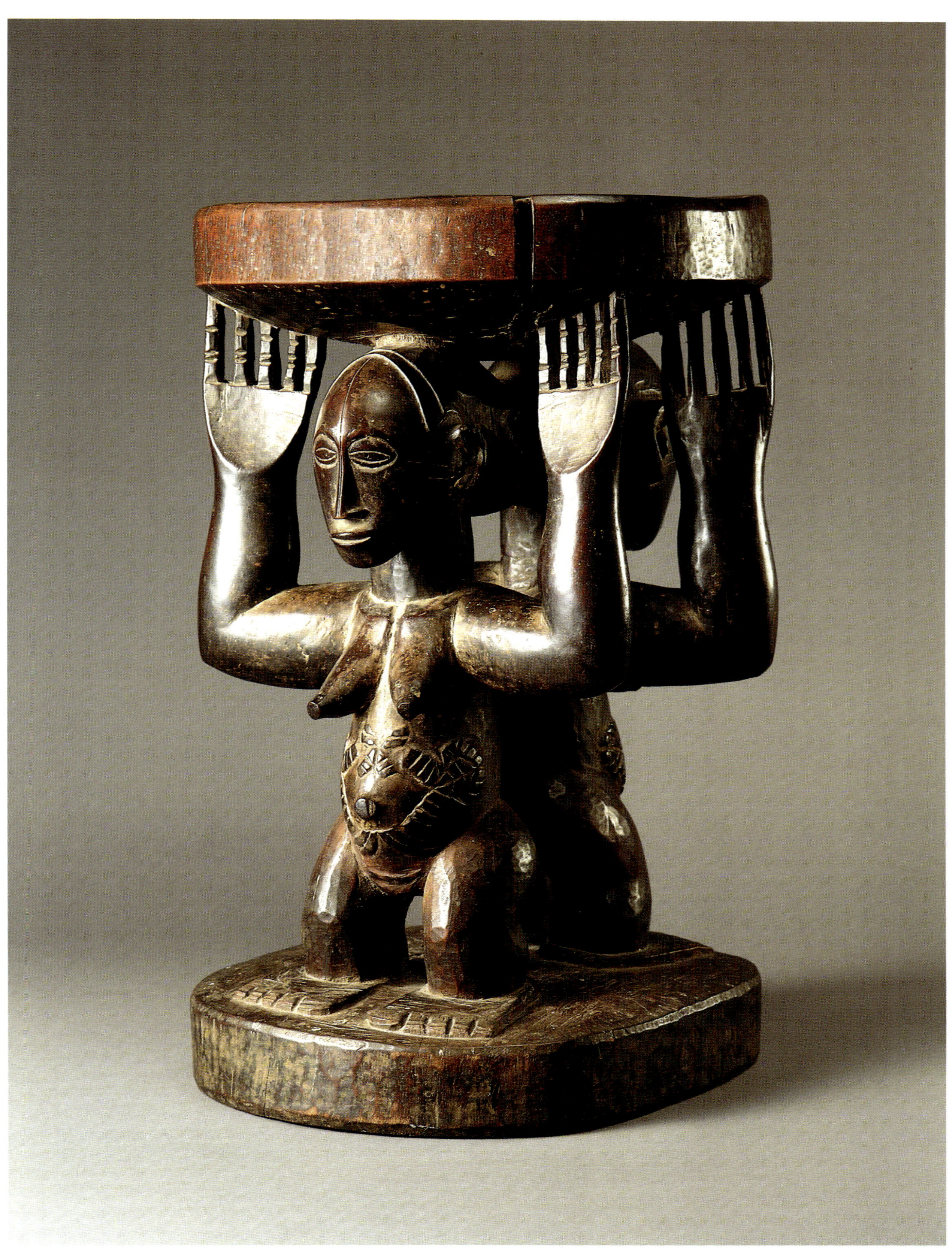

Caryatid stool of the Hemba, Zaire, height 53 cm Cat. 131

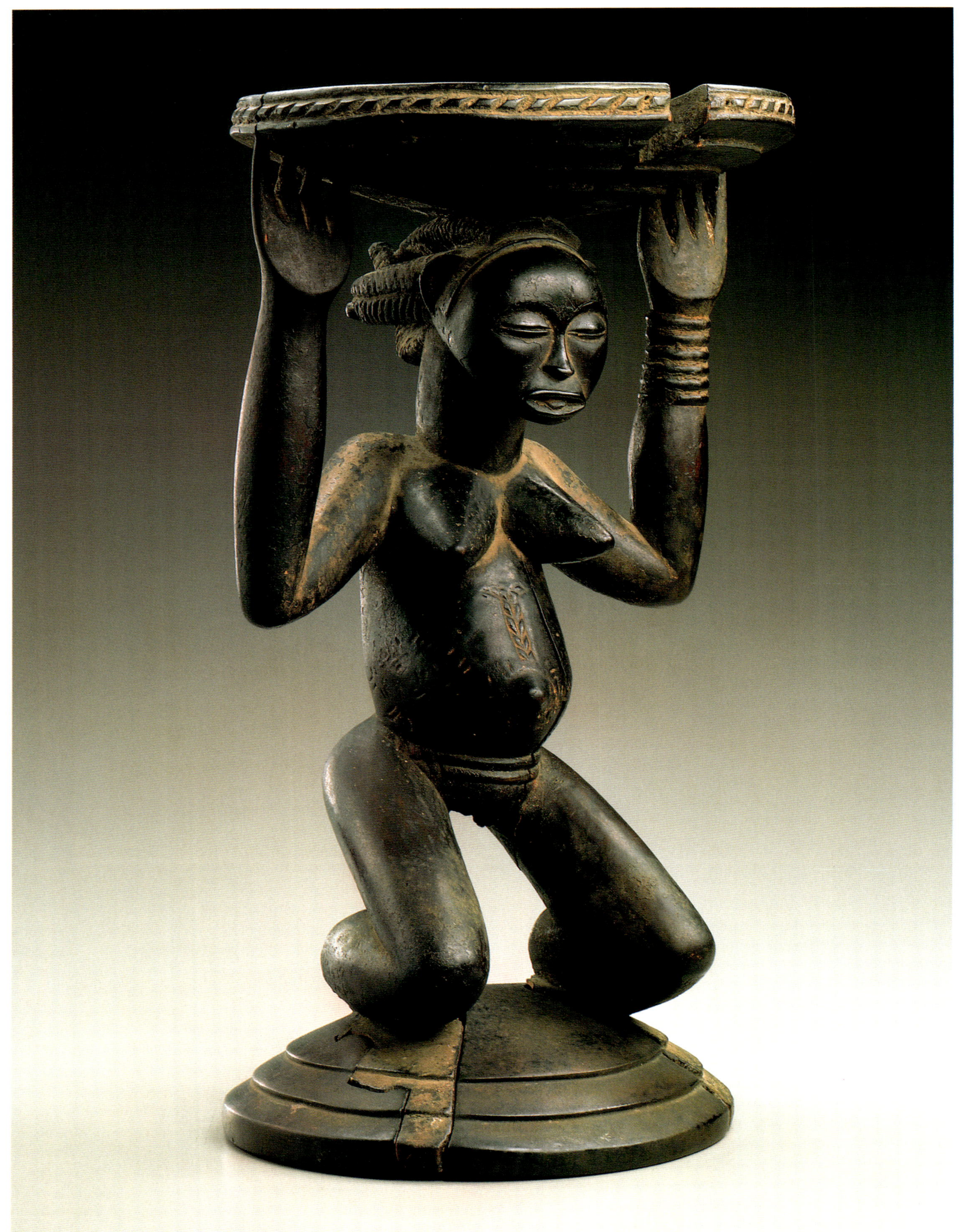

Photograph: Roger Asselberghs, Brussels

Caryatid stool of the Hemba, Zaire, height 46 cm Cat. 129

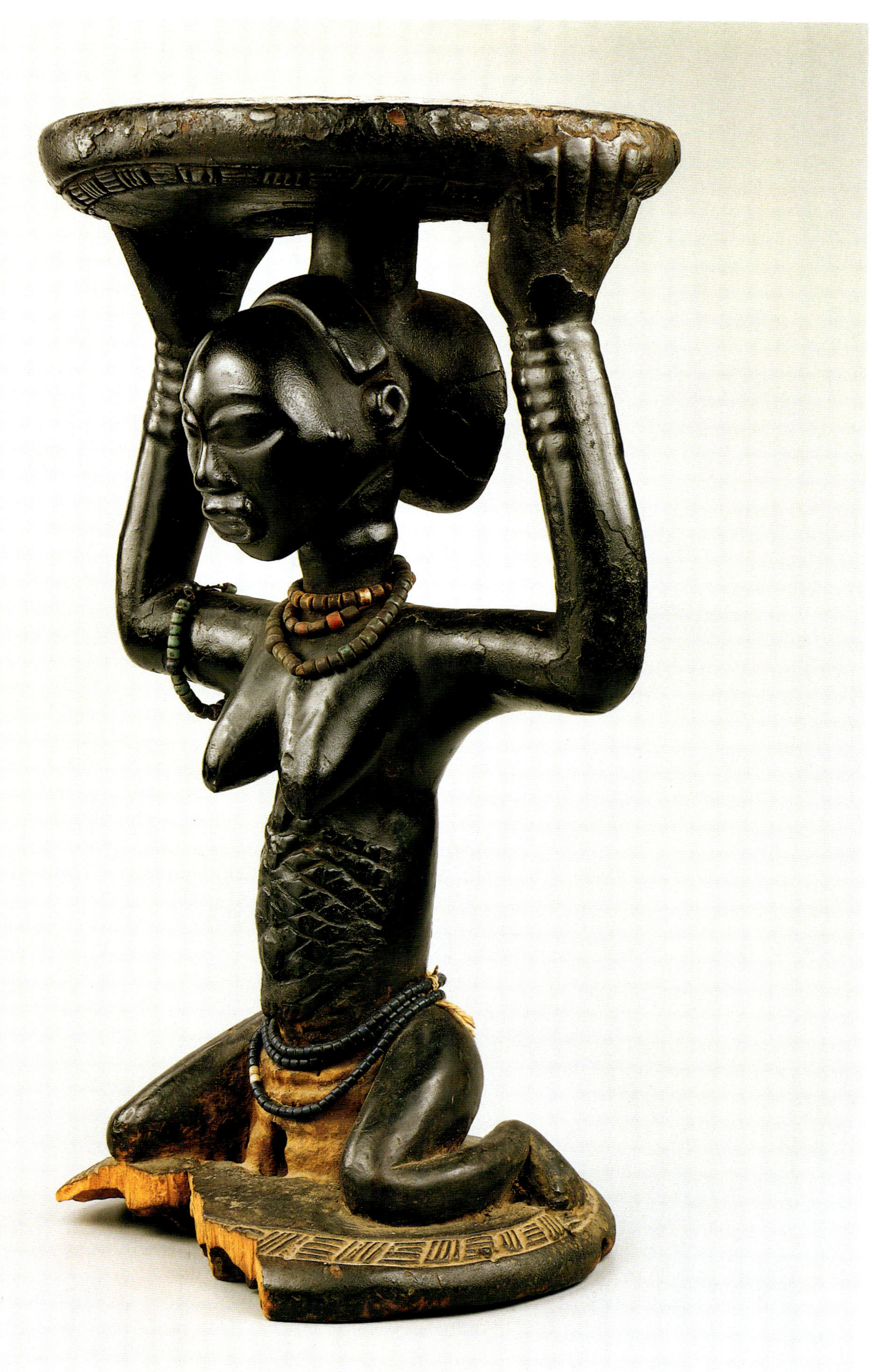

Photograph: Hughes Dubois, Archives Musée Dapper, Paris

Caryatid stool of the Hemba, Zaire, height 53 cm Cat. 130

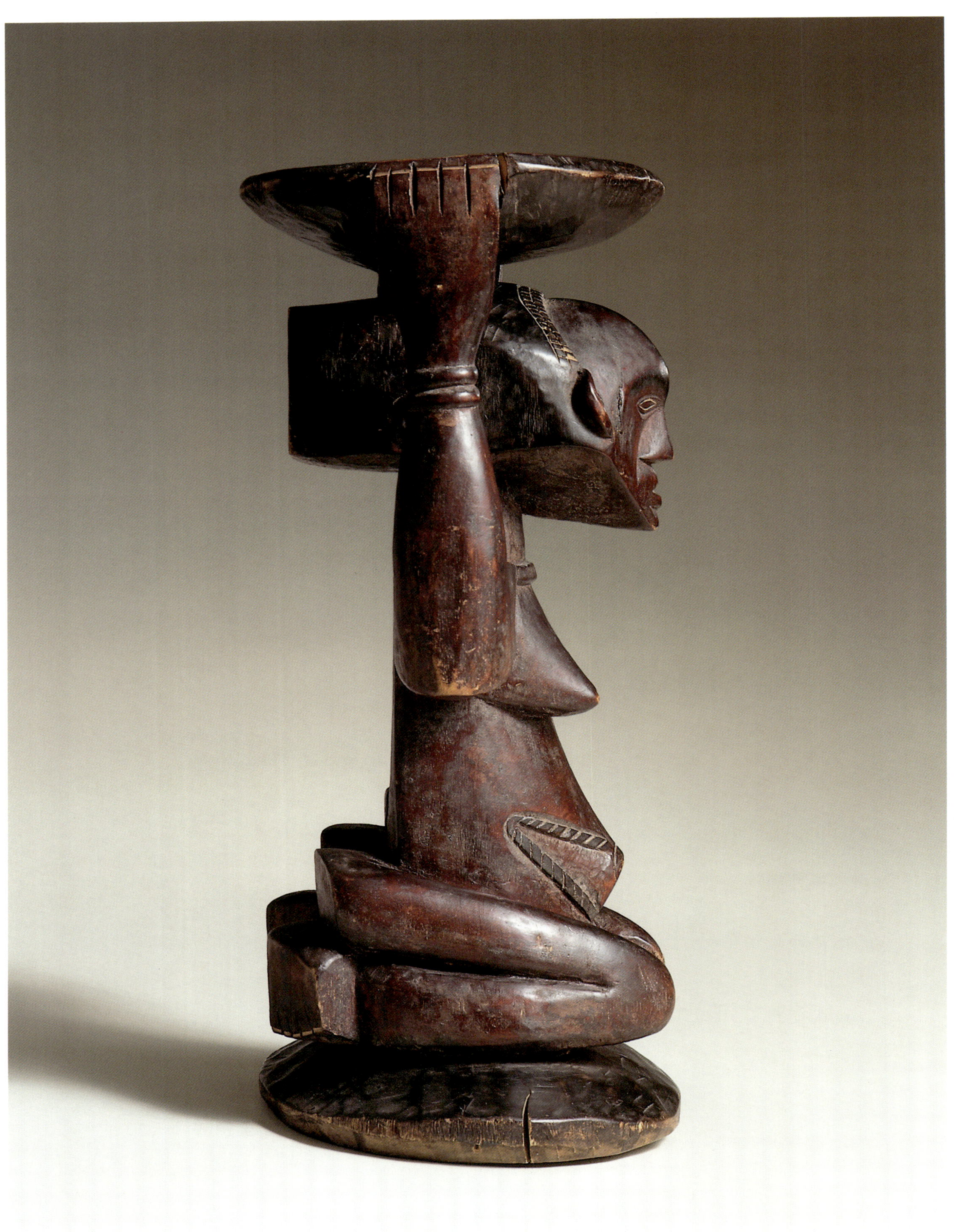

Caryatid stool of the Luba, Zaire, height 48 cm Cat. 136

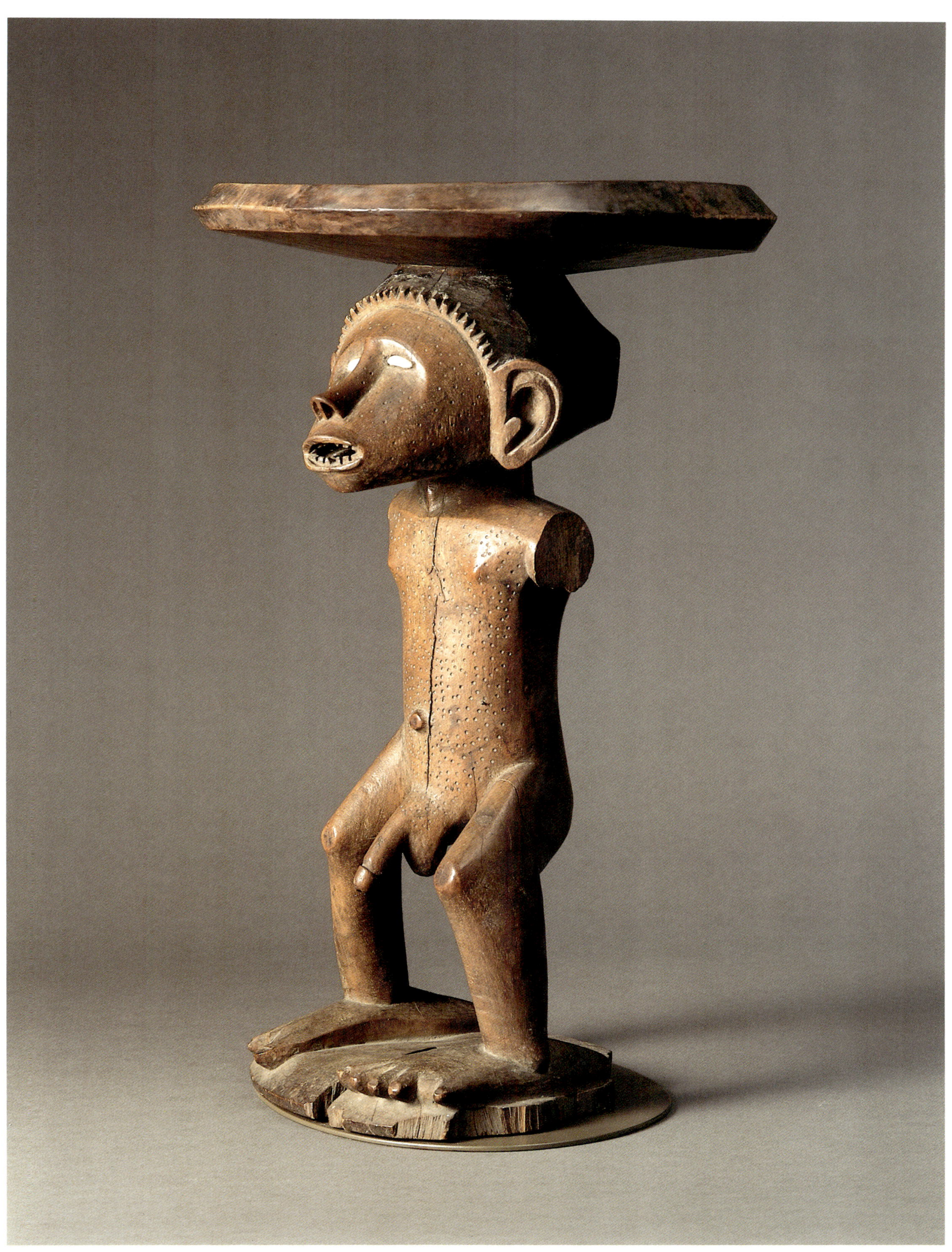

Caryatid stool from Zaire, height 47 cm Cat. 127

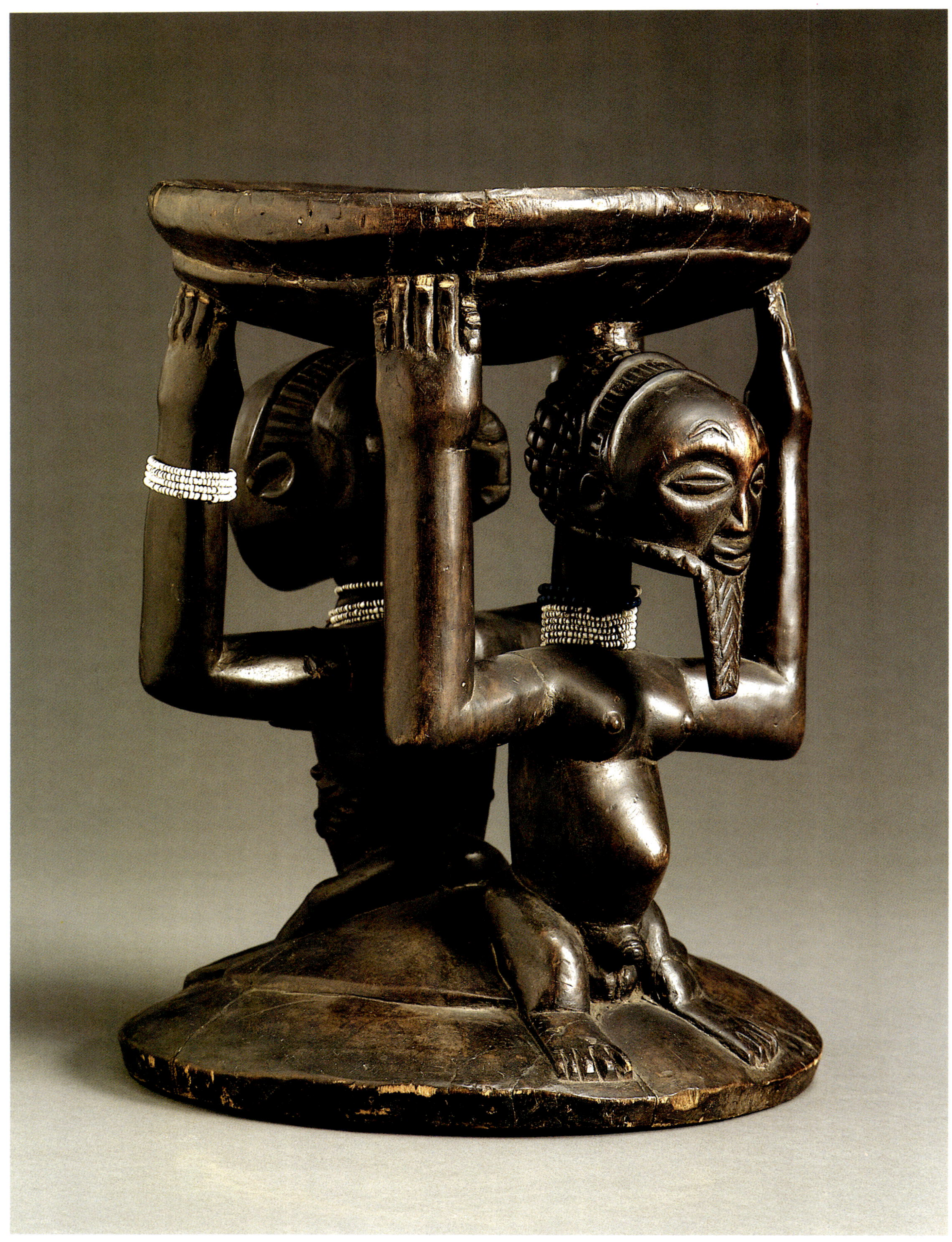

Caryatid stool of the Luba-Katanga, Zaire, height 37 cm Cat. 134

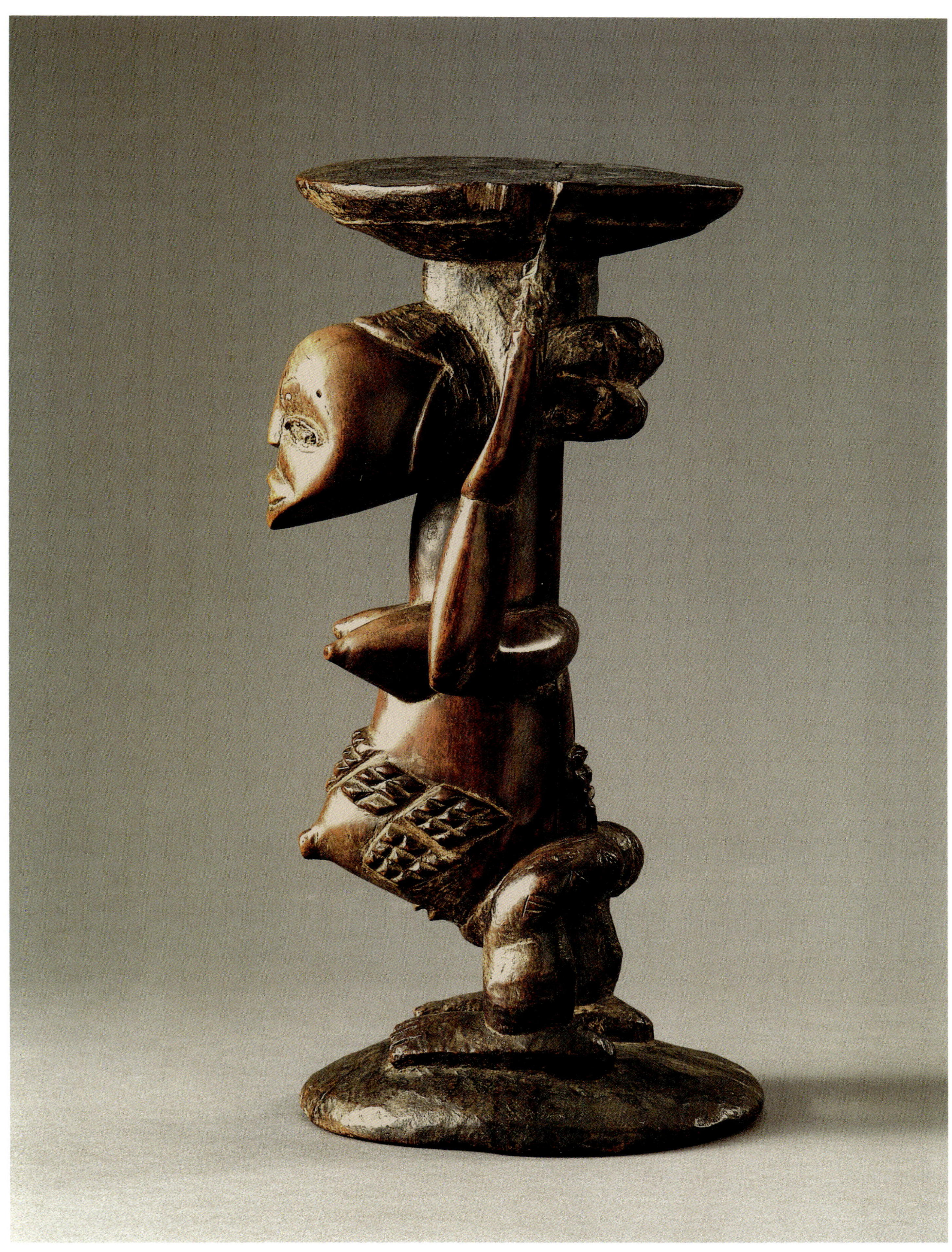

Caryatid stool of the Luba, Zaire, height 43 cm Cat. 133

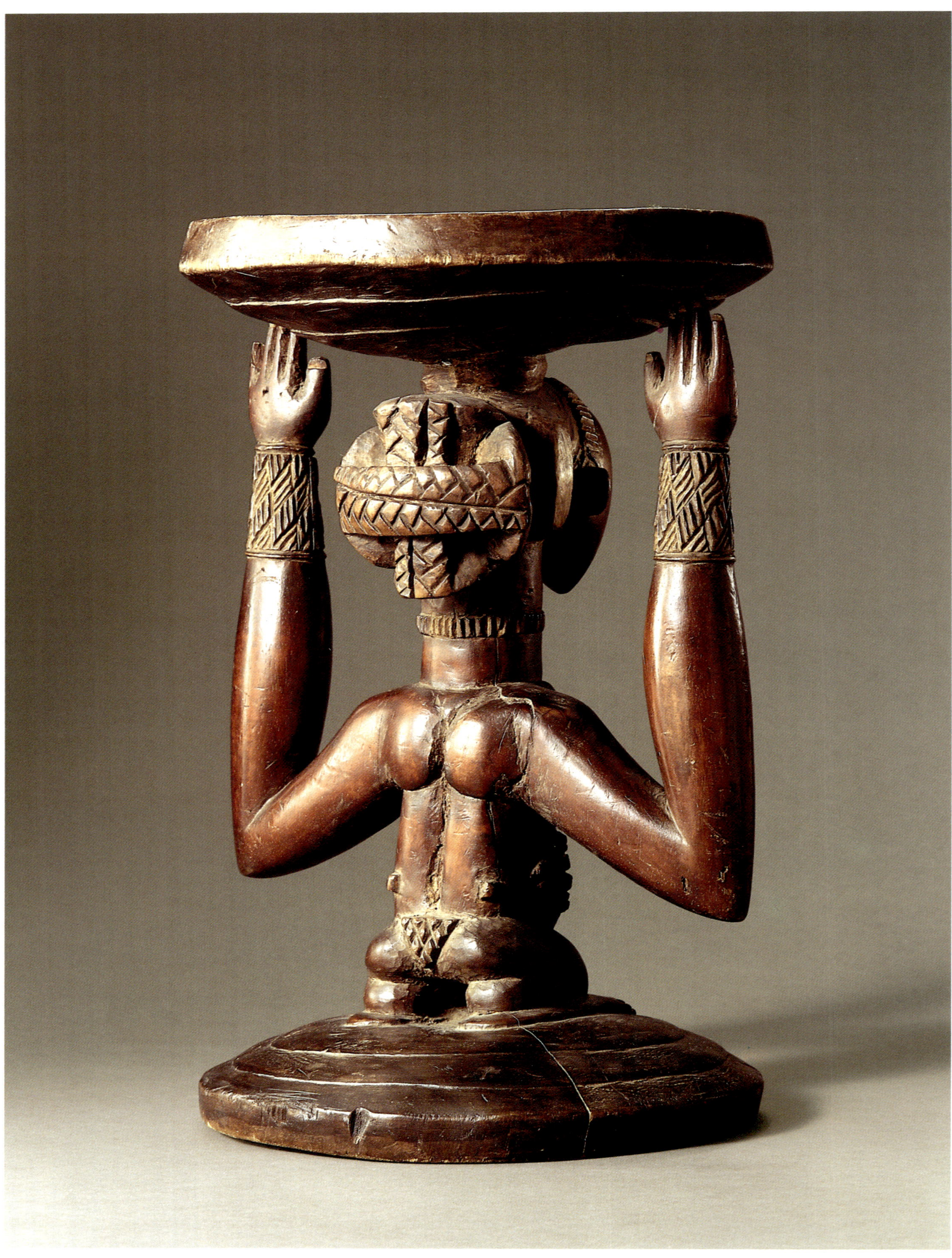

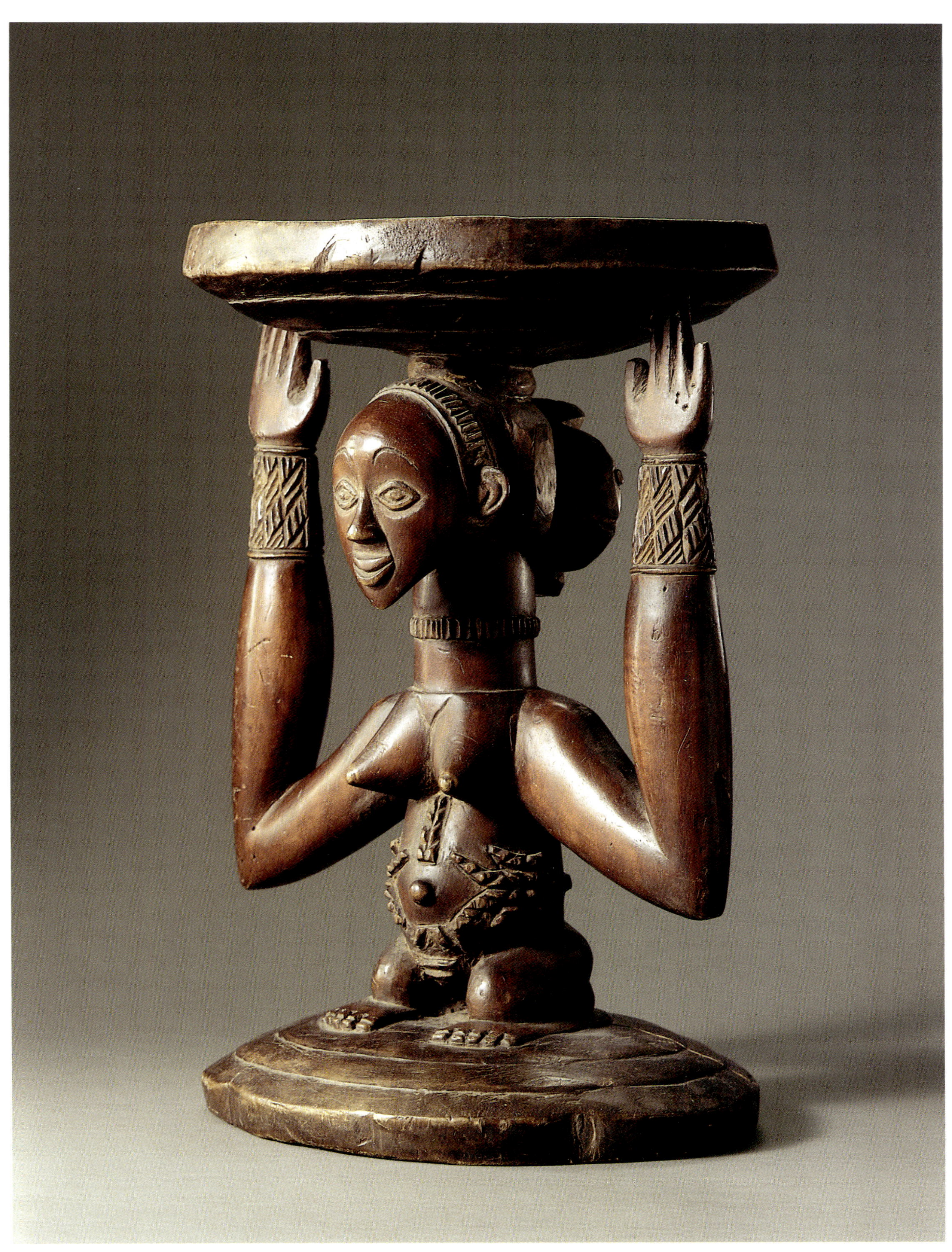

Caryatid stool (see also plate opposite) of the Luba-Hemba,
Zaire, height 48.5 cm Cat. 132

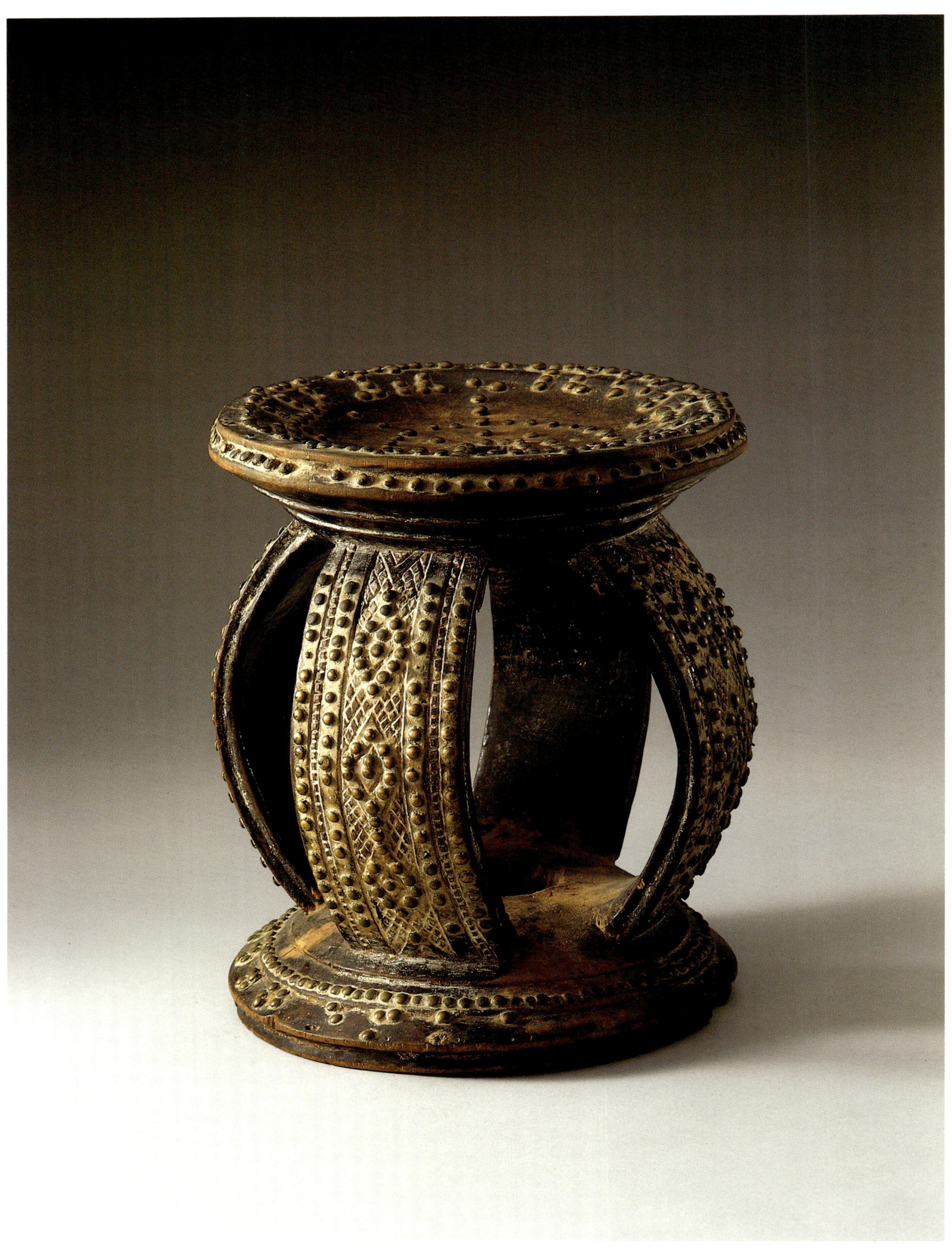

Stool of the Hemba, Zaire, height 34 cm Cat. 125

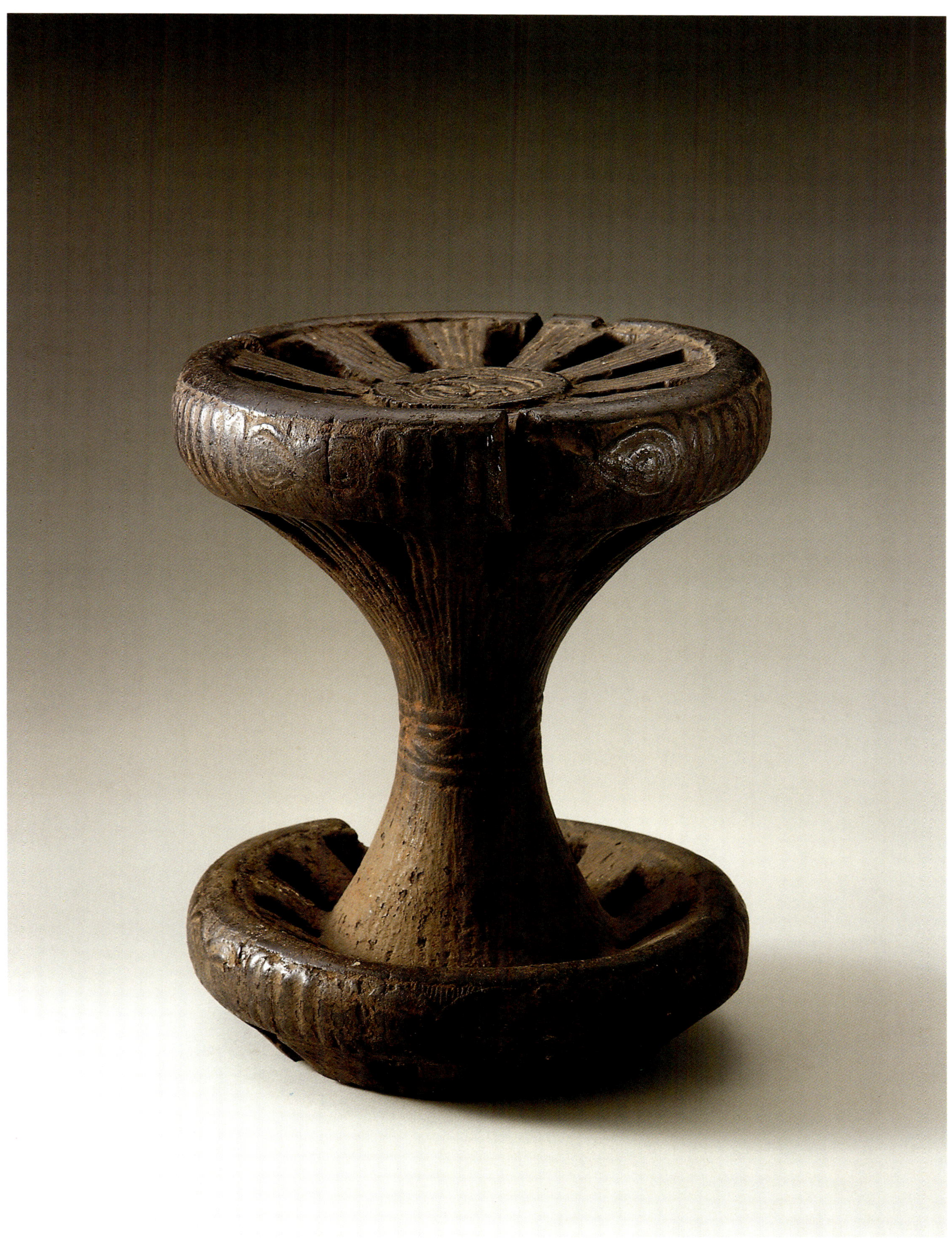

Stool of the Kuba, Zaire, height 45 cm Cat. 83

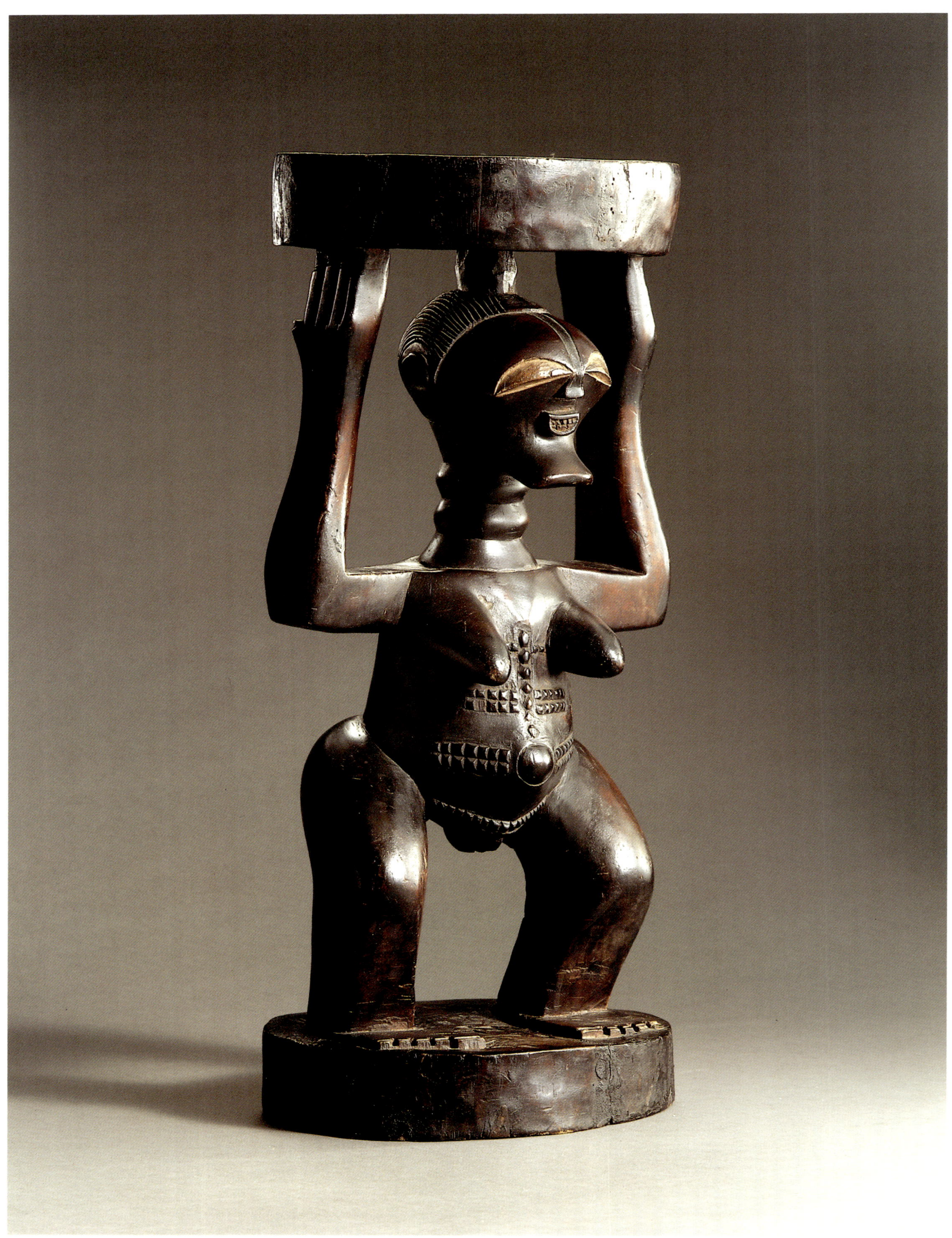

Caryatid stool of the Songye/Luba, Zaire, height 59.8 cm Cat. 137

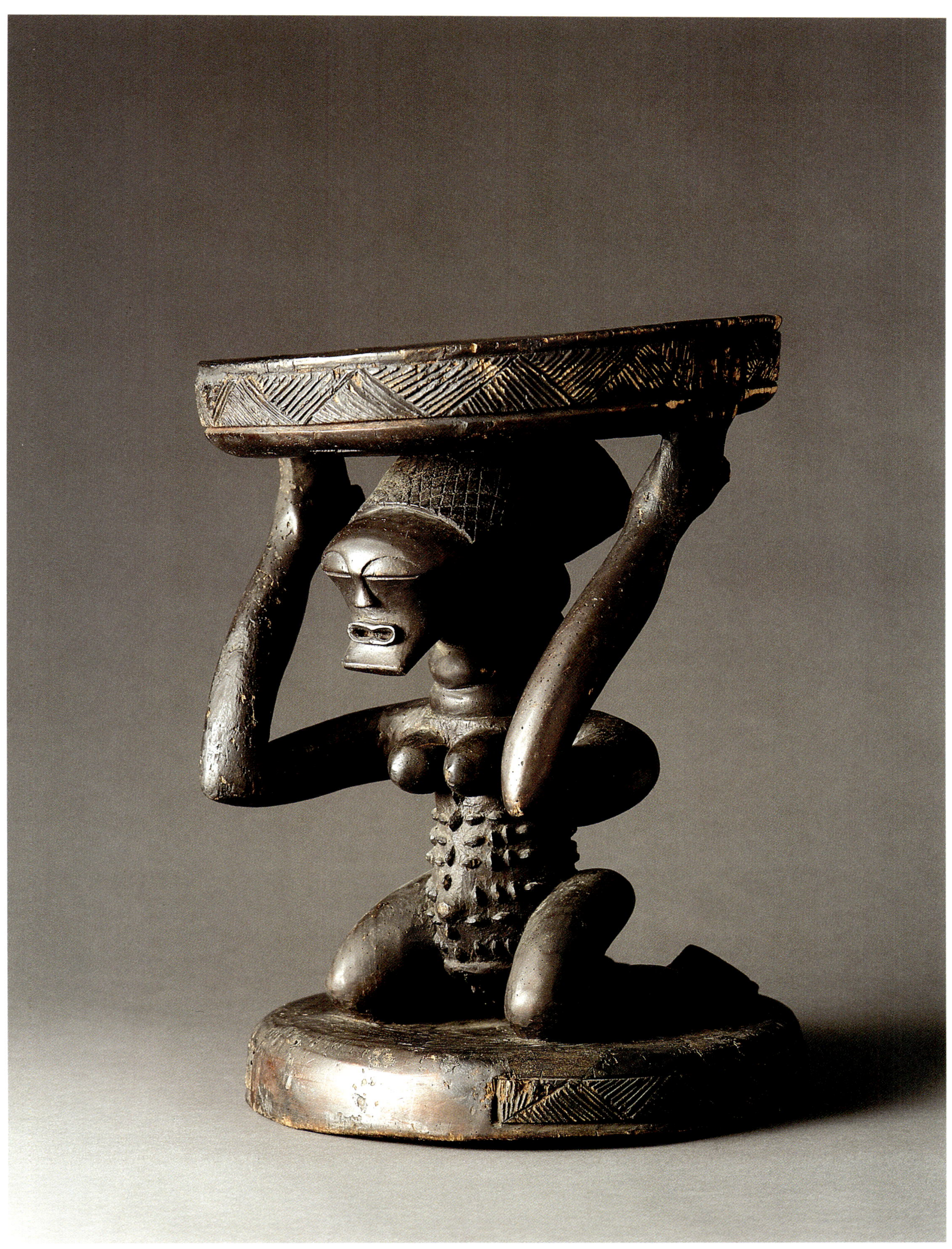

Caryatid stool of the Songye, Zaire, height 51.5 cm Cat. 138

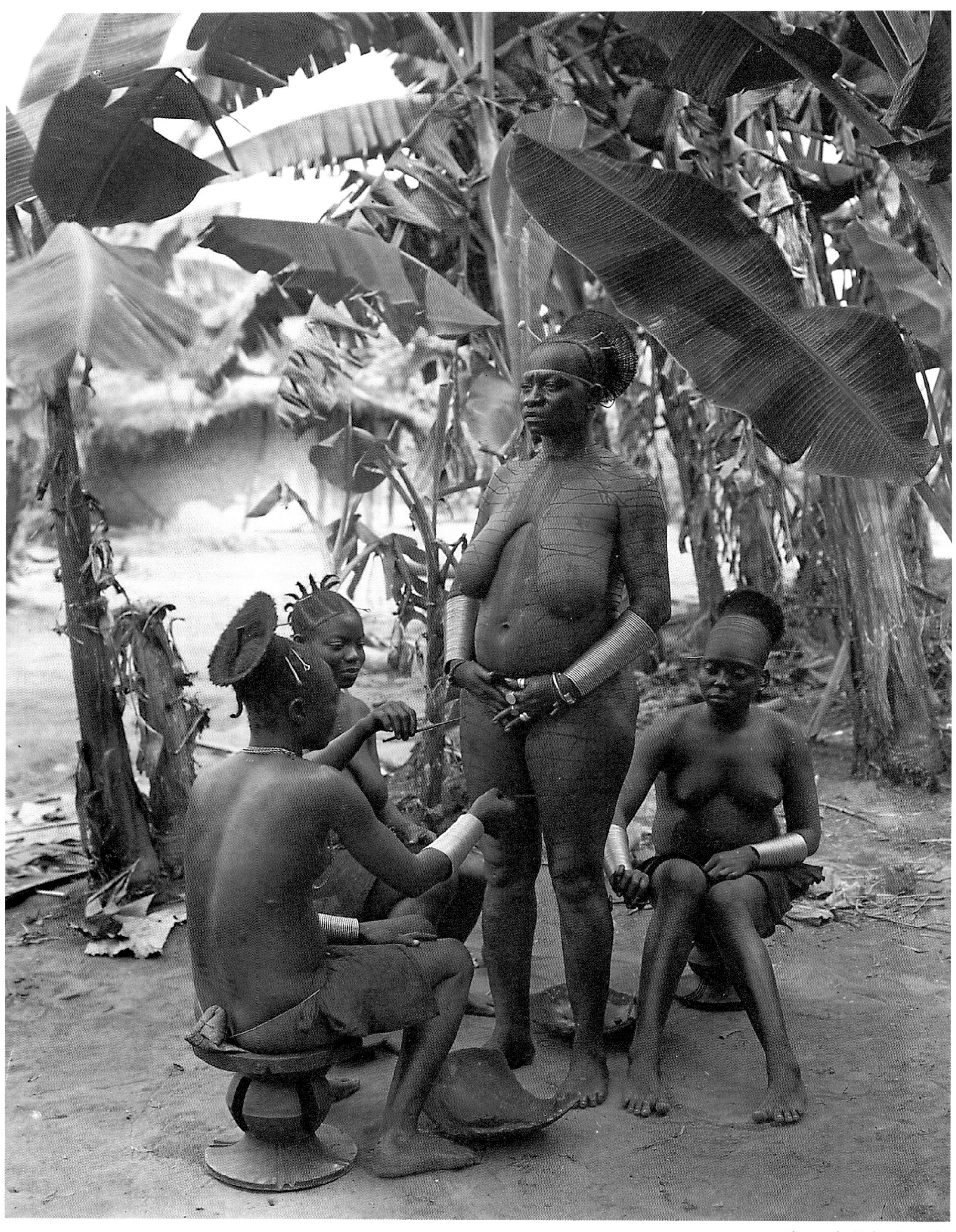

Photograph: Herbert Lang, 1910

126 A group of women applying body paint to Matubani, one of the wives of the Mangbetu chief Okondo, Zaire

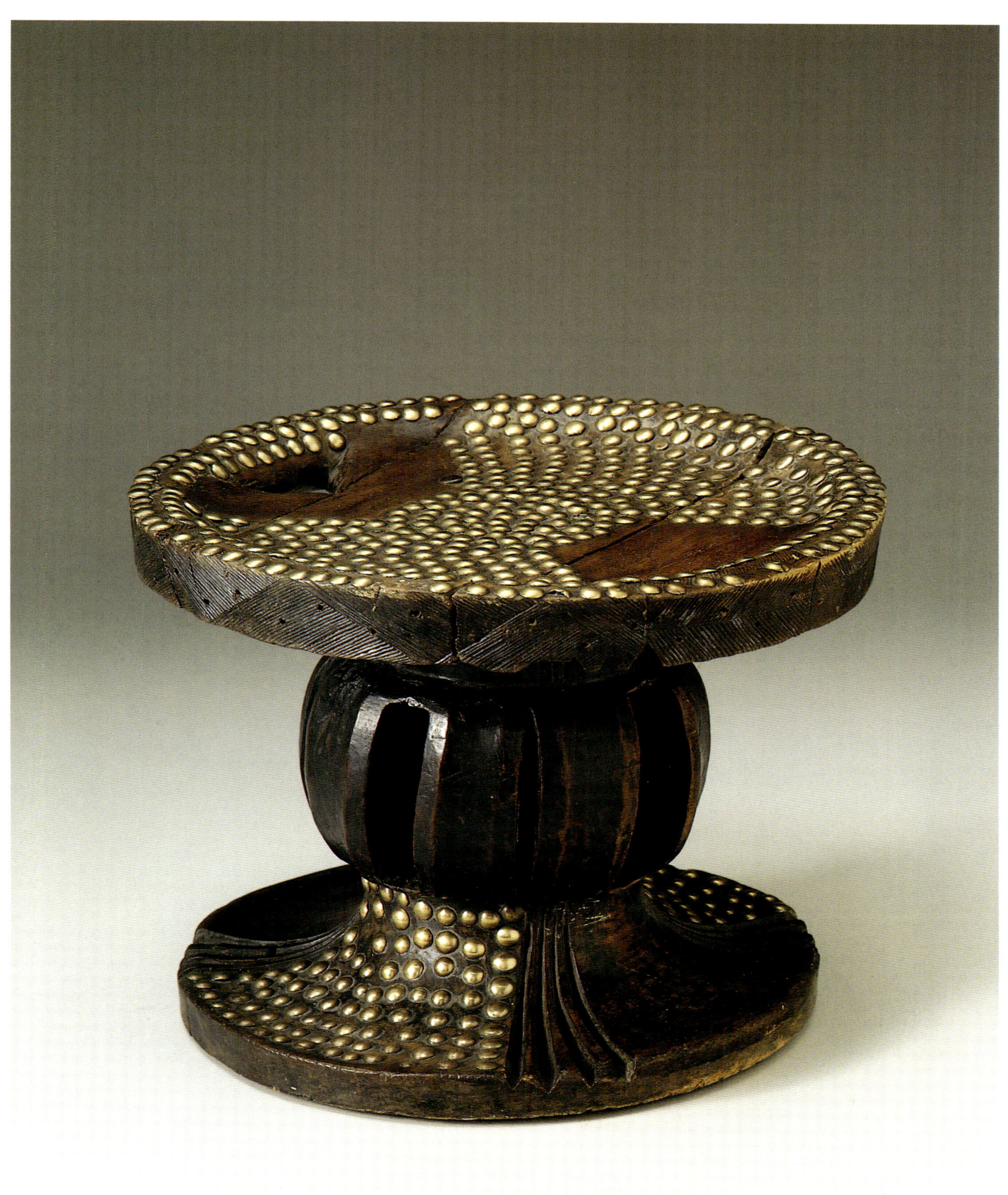

Stool of the Mangbetu, Zaire, height 23.2 cm Cat. 96

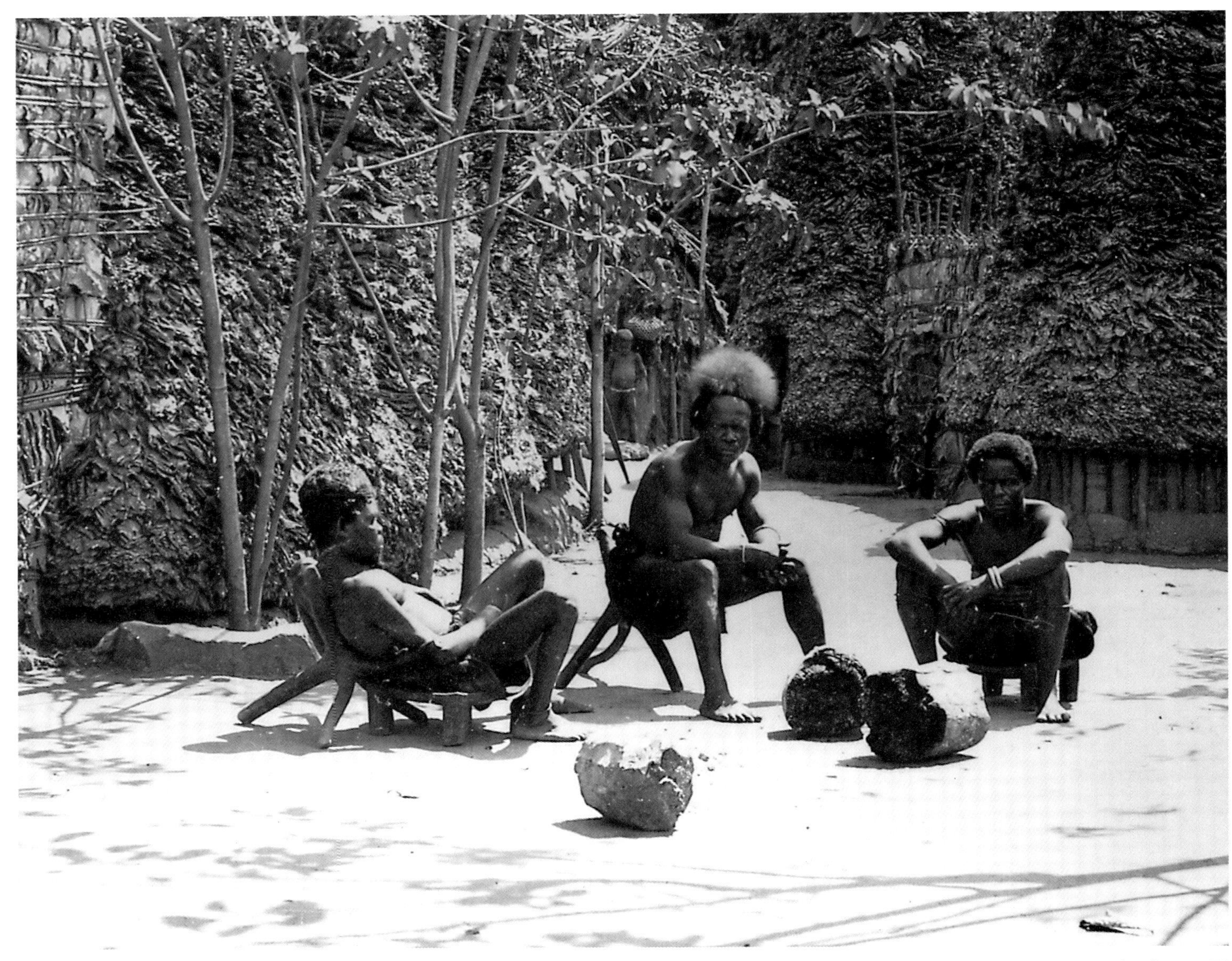

Photograph: Thevoz, 1905

Men of the Ngelima(-Angba) in the village of Bwangwa, near Panga, Zaire, use backrests also as seats

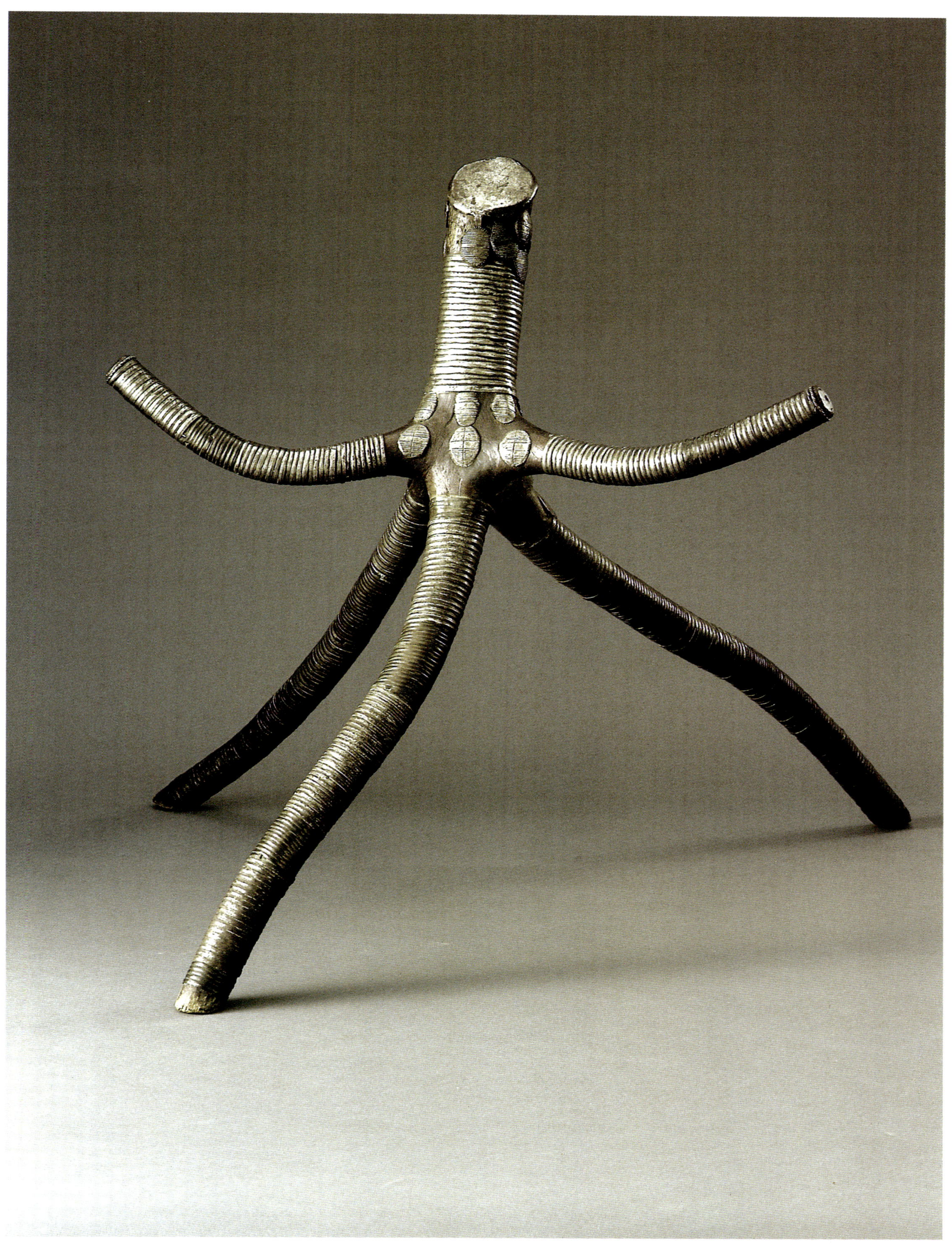

A Mangbetu chief's backrest, Zaire, height 67 cm   Cat. 94

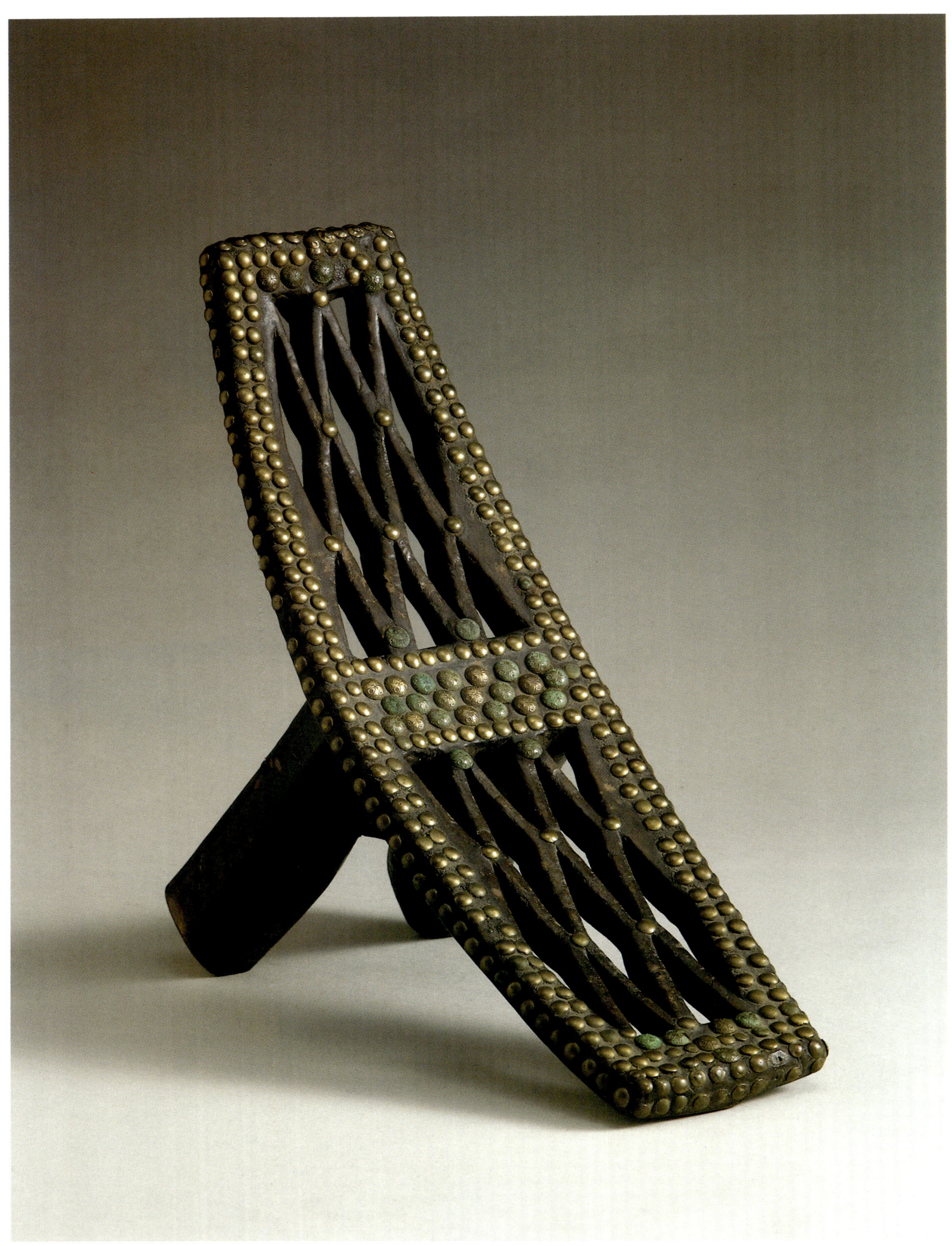

 Backrest/Seat from Zaire, width 49.2 cm Cat. 89

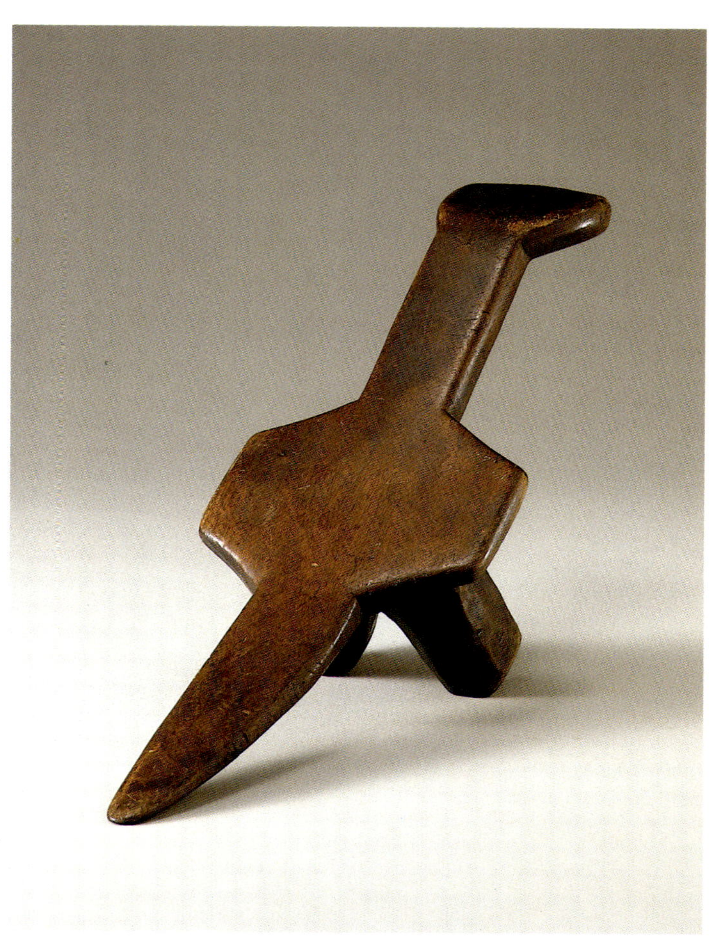
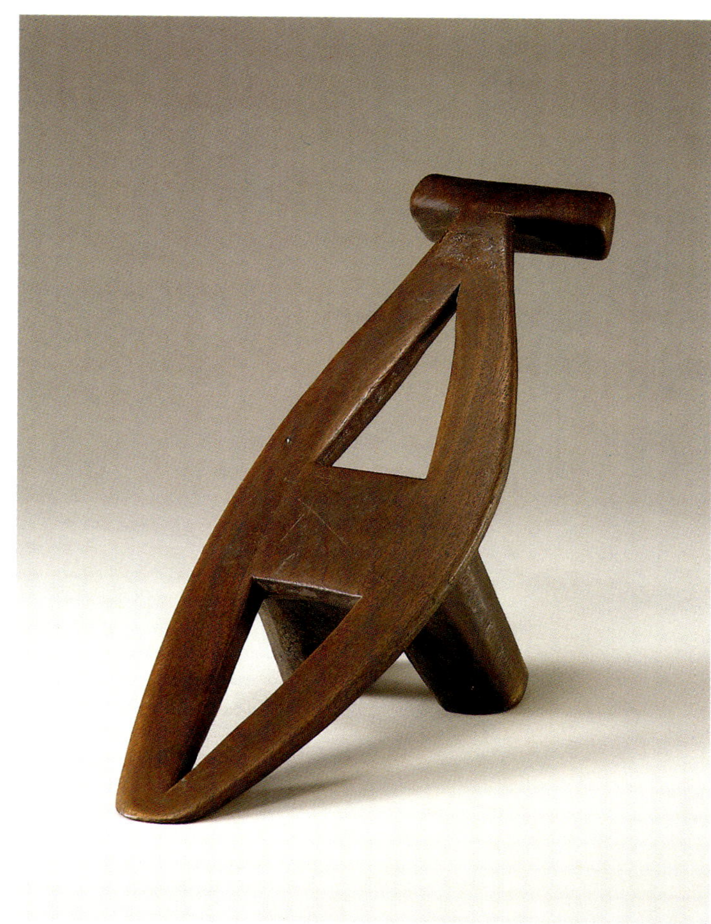
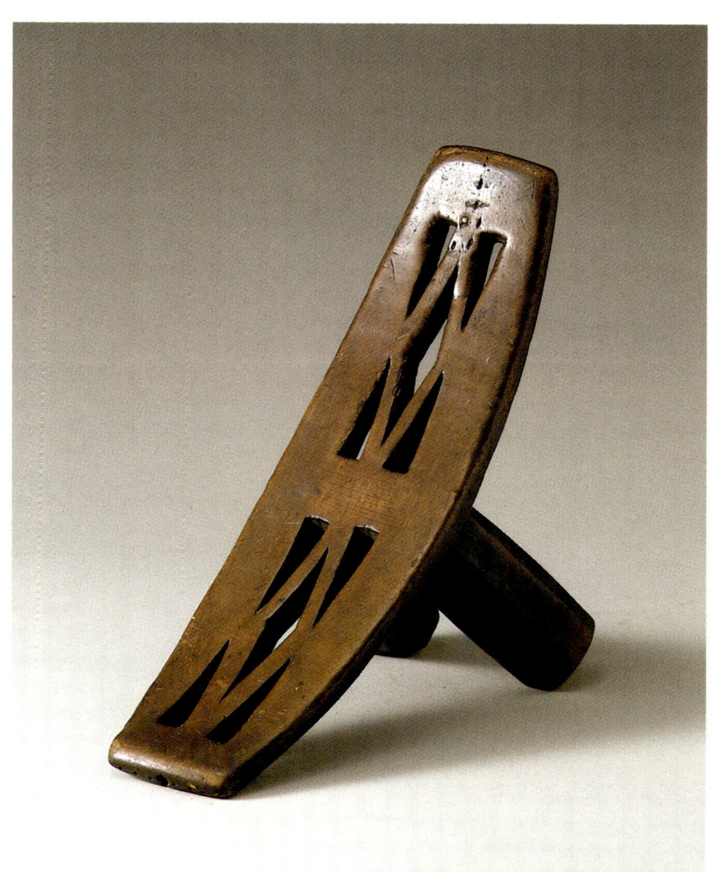
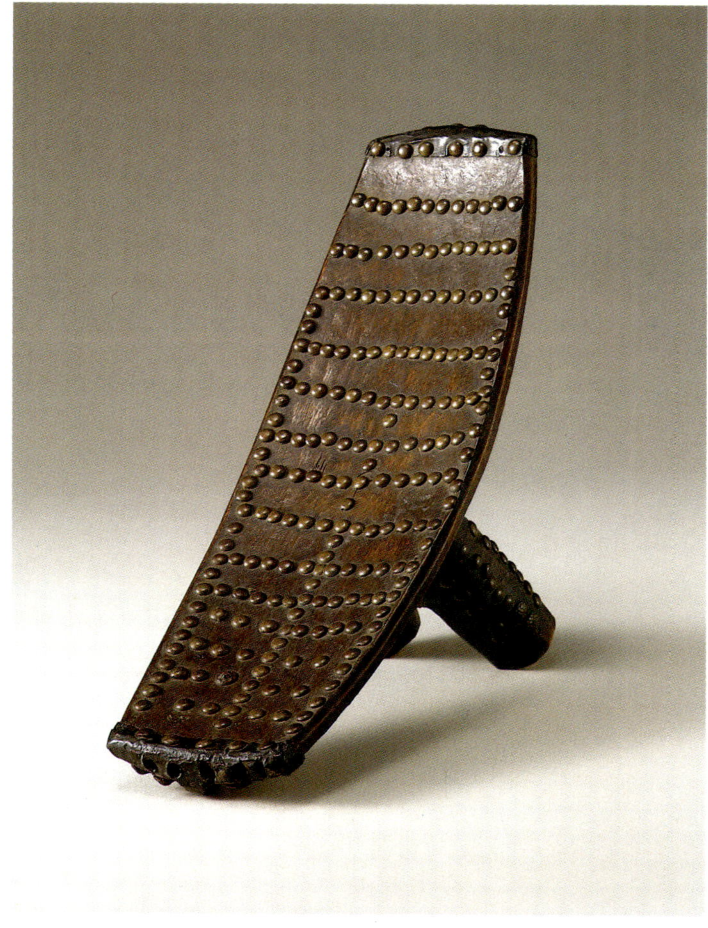

Backrests/Seats from Zaire, width 46 cm, 48.5 cm and 38.5 cm, and 41.5 cm Cats. 93, 92, 91, 90

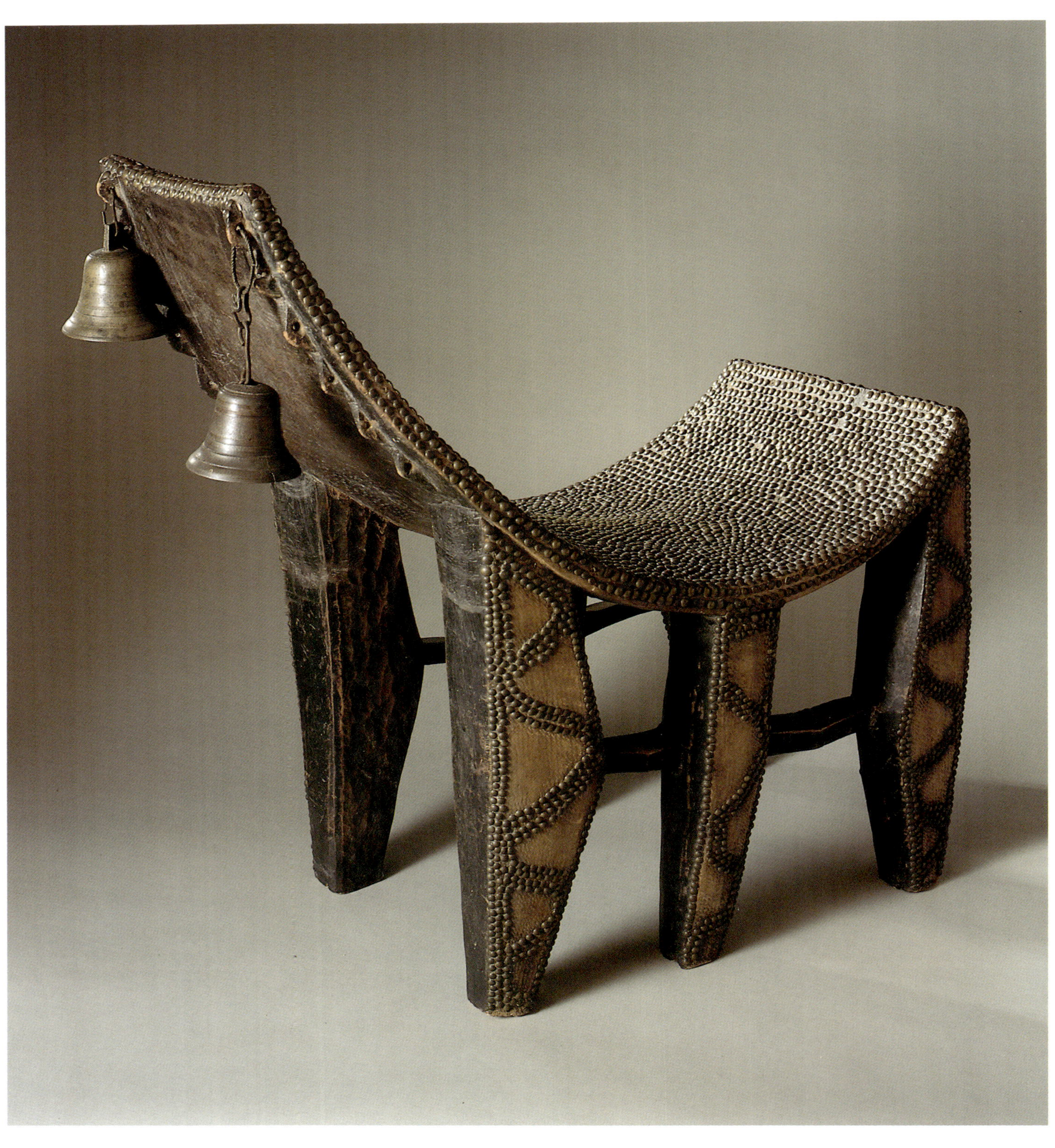

 Semi-reclining chair of the Ngombe, Zaire, height 73 cm Cat. 87

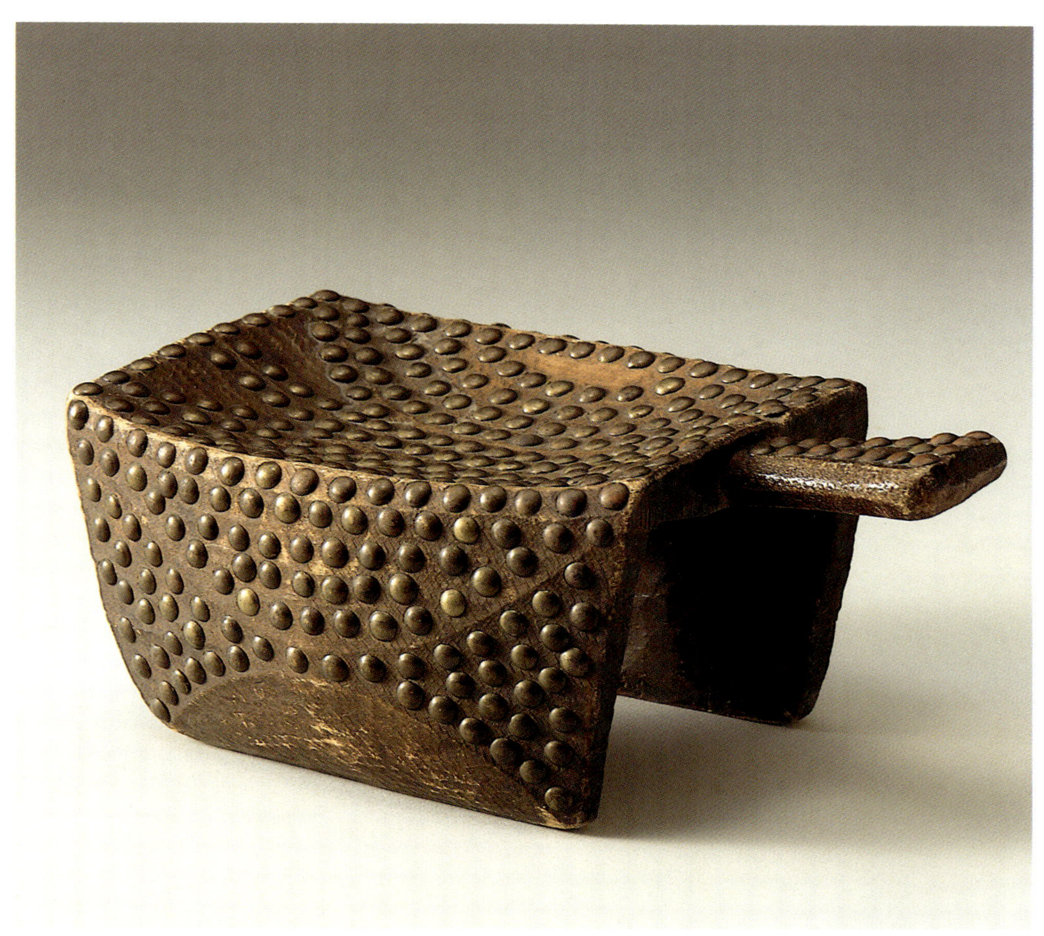

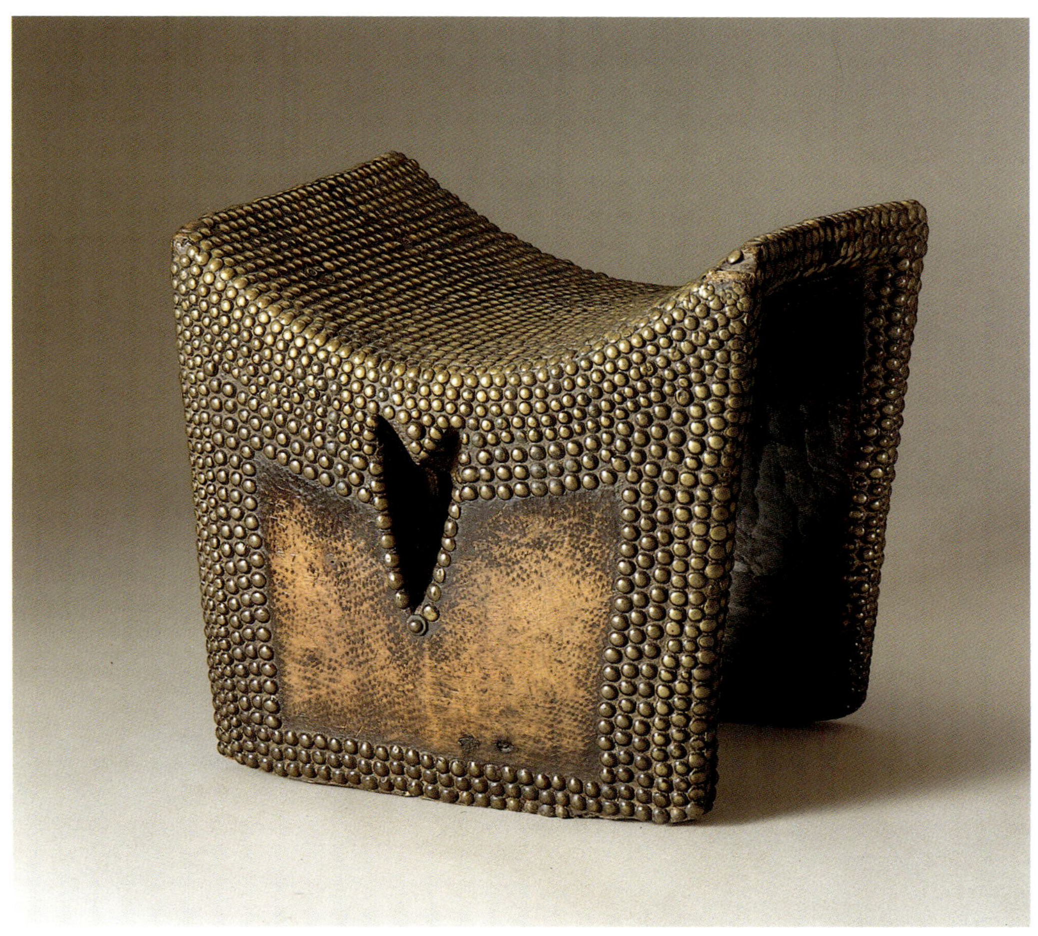

Stools of the Ngombe, Zaire, height 19.2 cm and 31 cm Cat. 85, 84

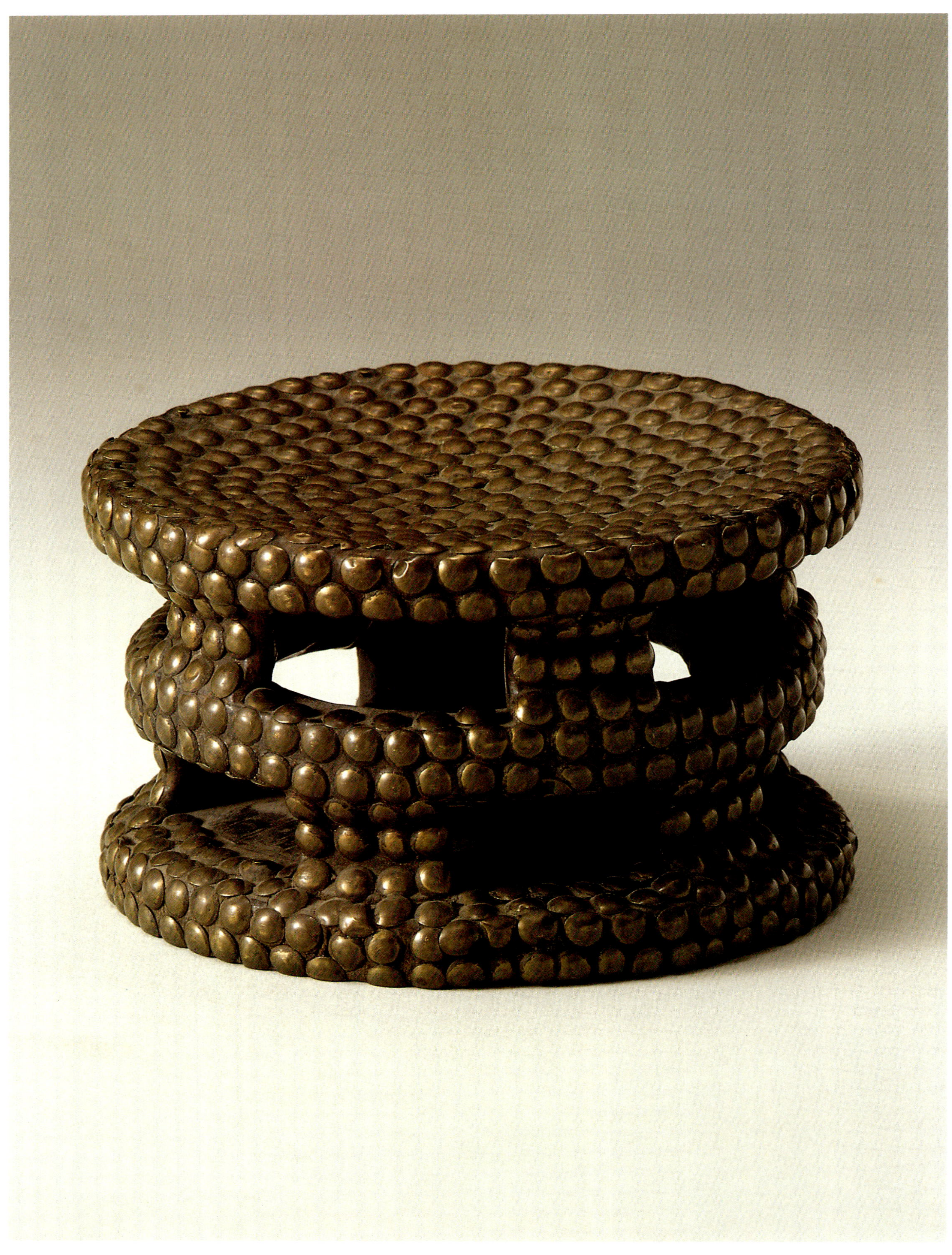

Stool of the Chokwe, Zaire/Angola, height 12.2 cm Cat. 99

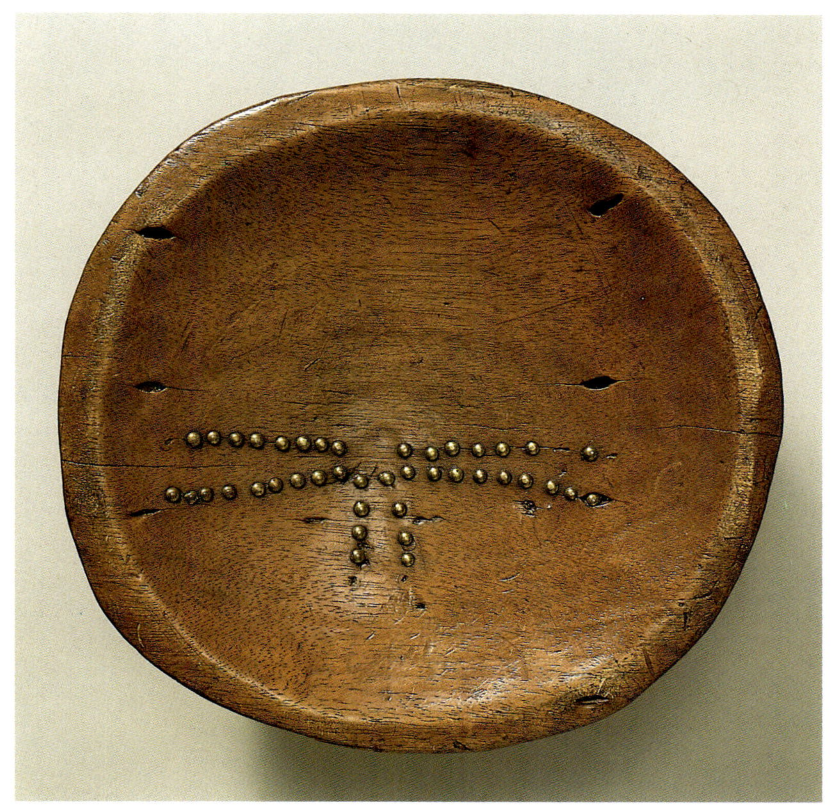

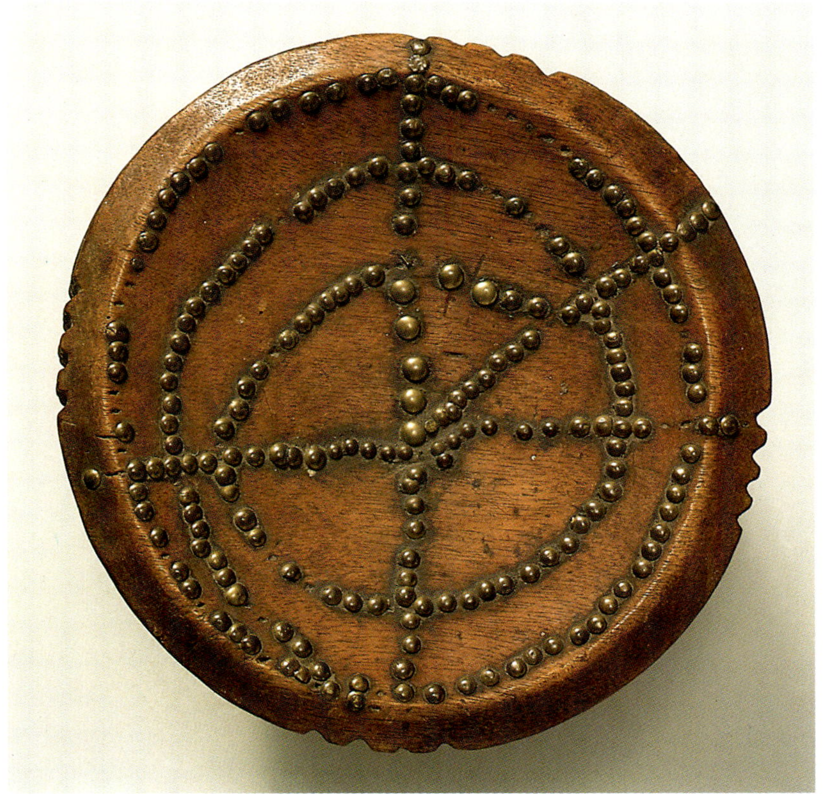

Seating surfaces of a stool from north-eastern Zaire, diameter 29 cm,
and of a stool of the Mabinza, Zaire, diameter 25 cm
(Africa Museum, Tervuren; ex-catalogue)

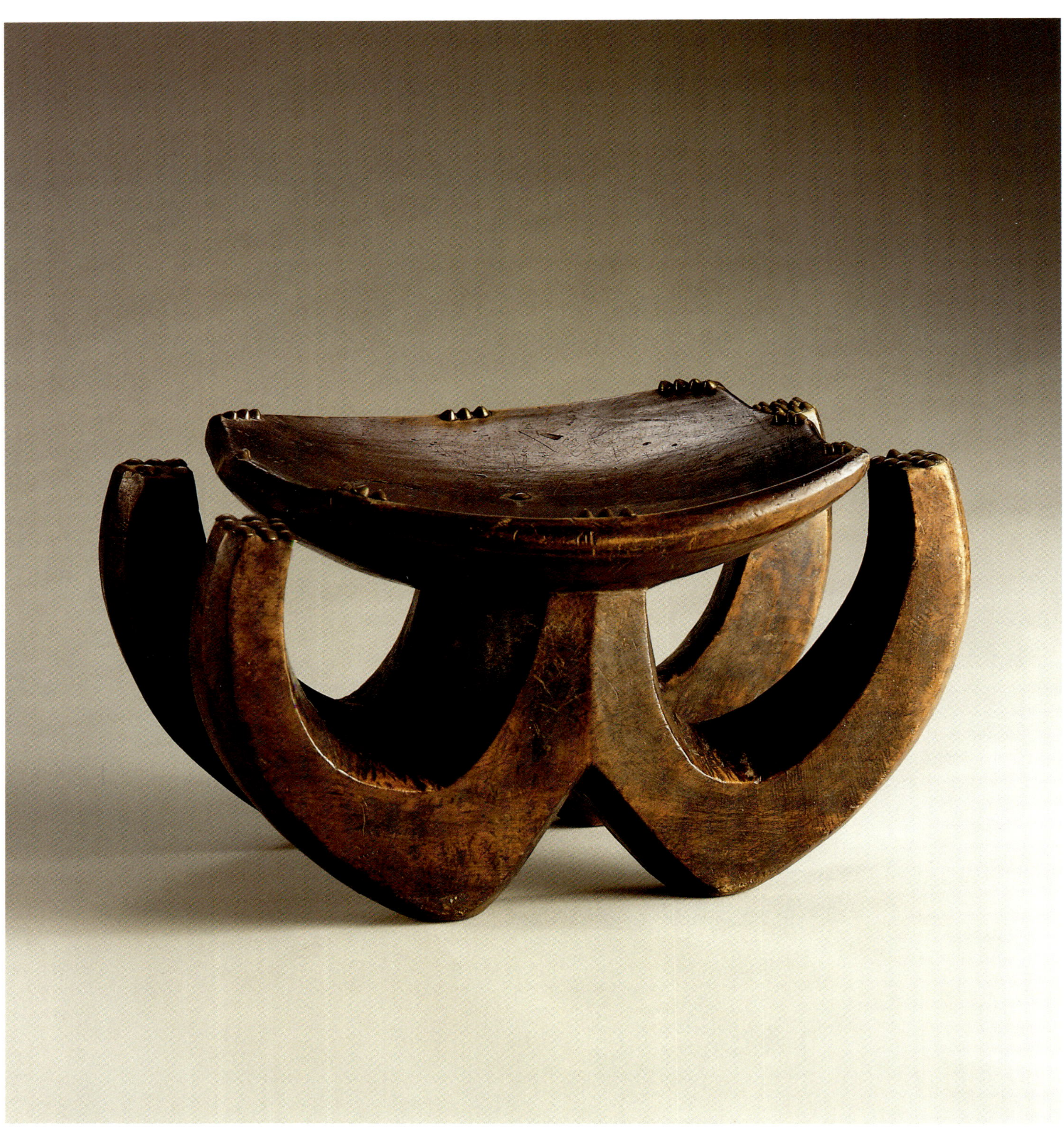

Stool from Zaire, height 23 cm   Cat. 82

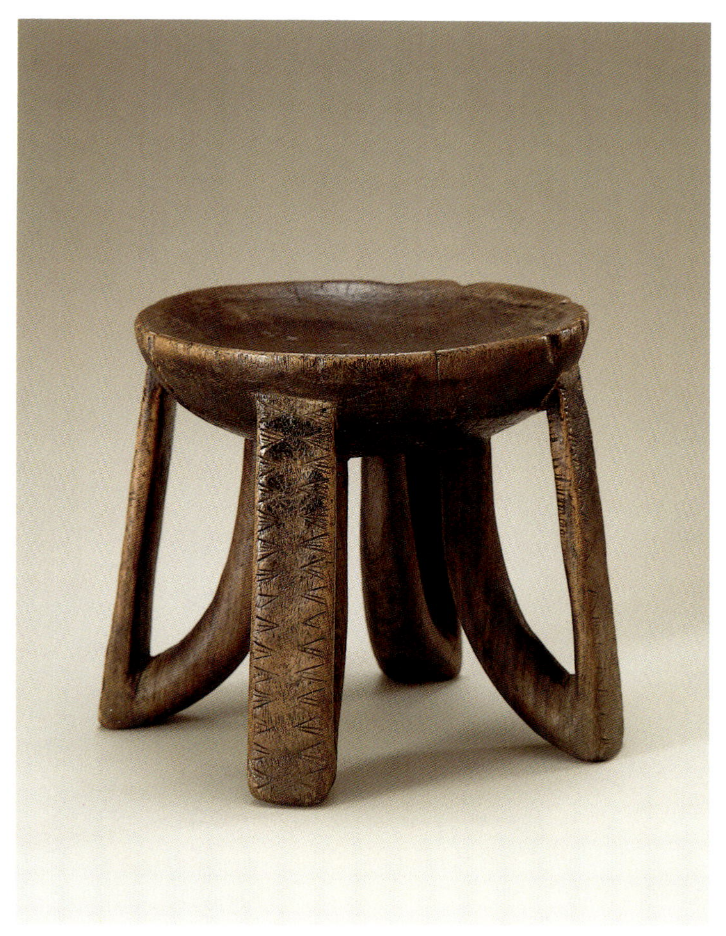

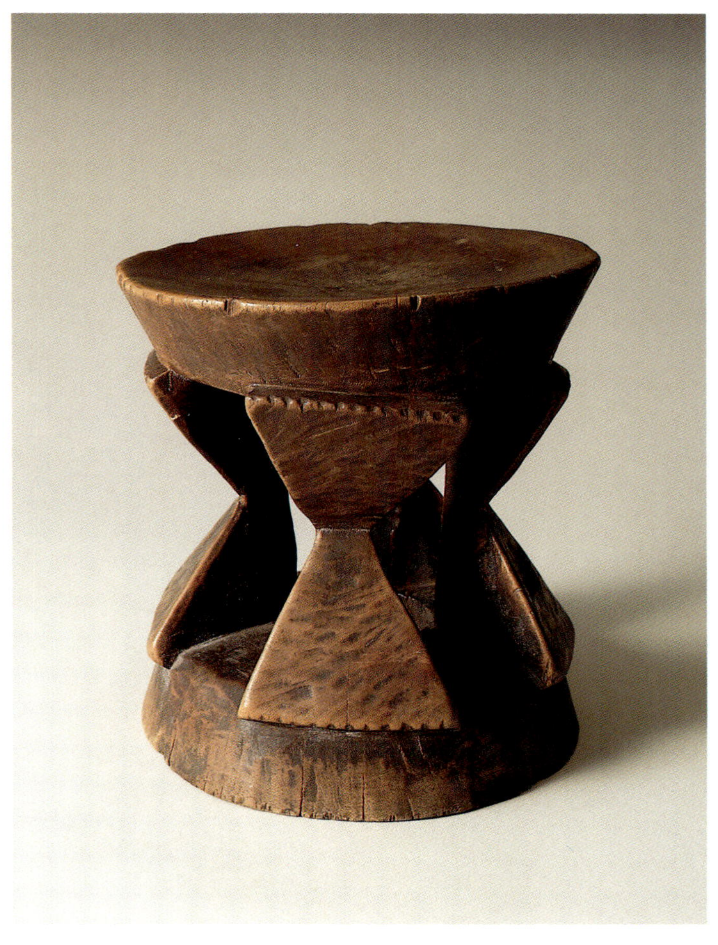

Stool from Zambia, height 24.5 cm Cat. 151
Stool of the Songye, Zaire, height 22.5 cm Cat. 126

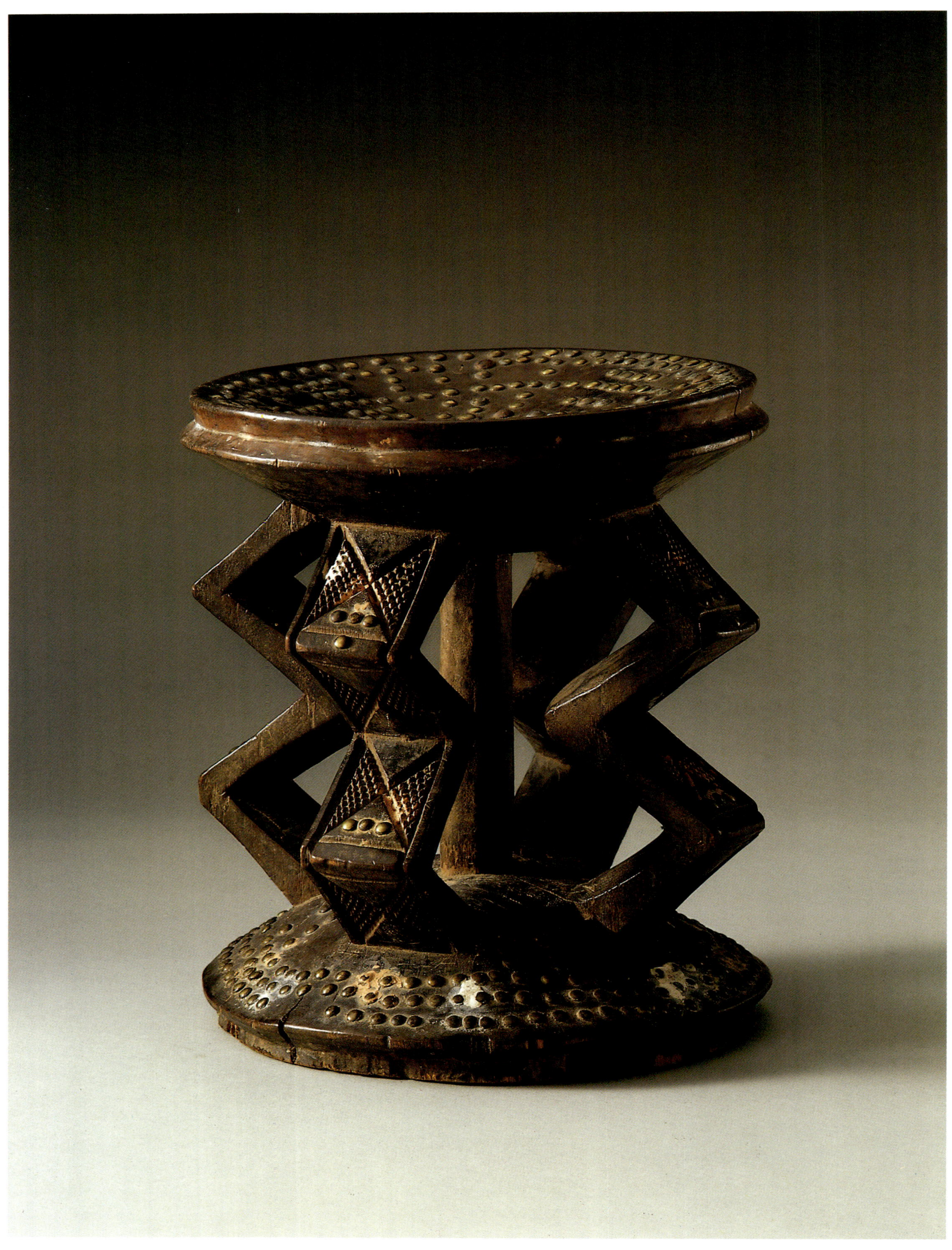

Stool of the Kusu, Zaire, height 31 cm Cat. 124

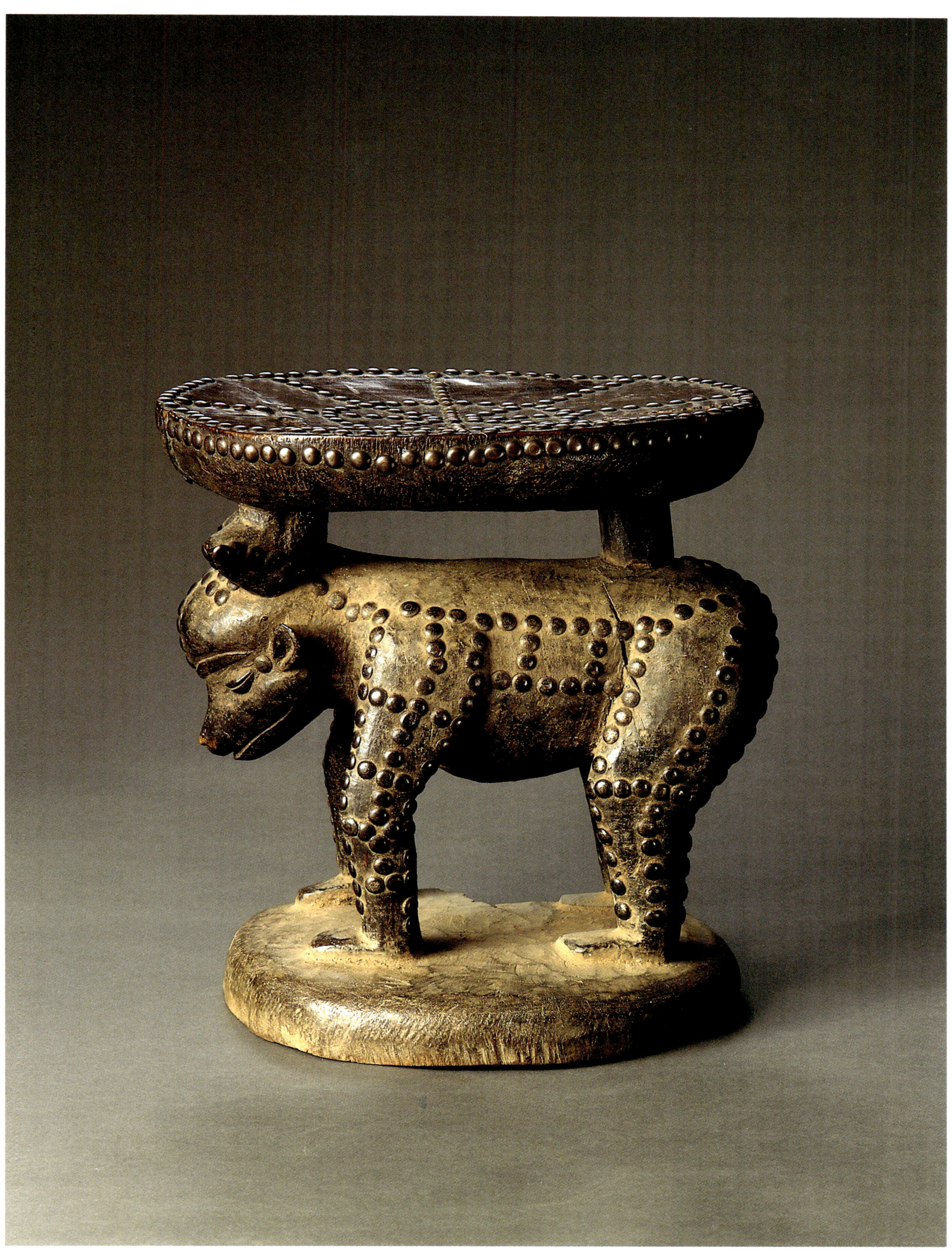

Stool with a buffalo of the Pende, Zaire, height 33 cm Cat. 104

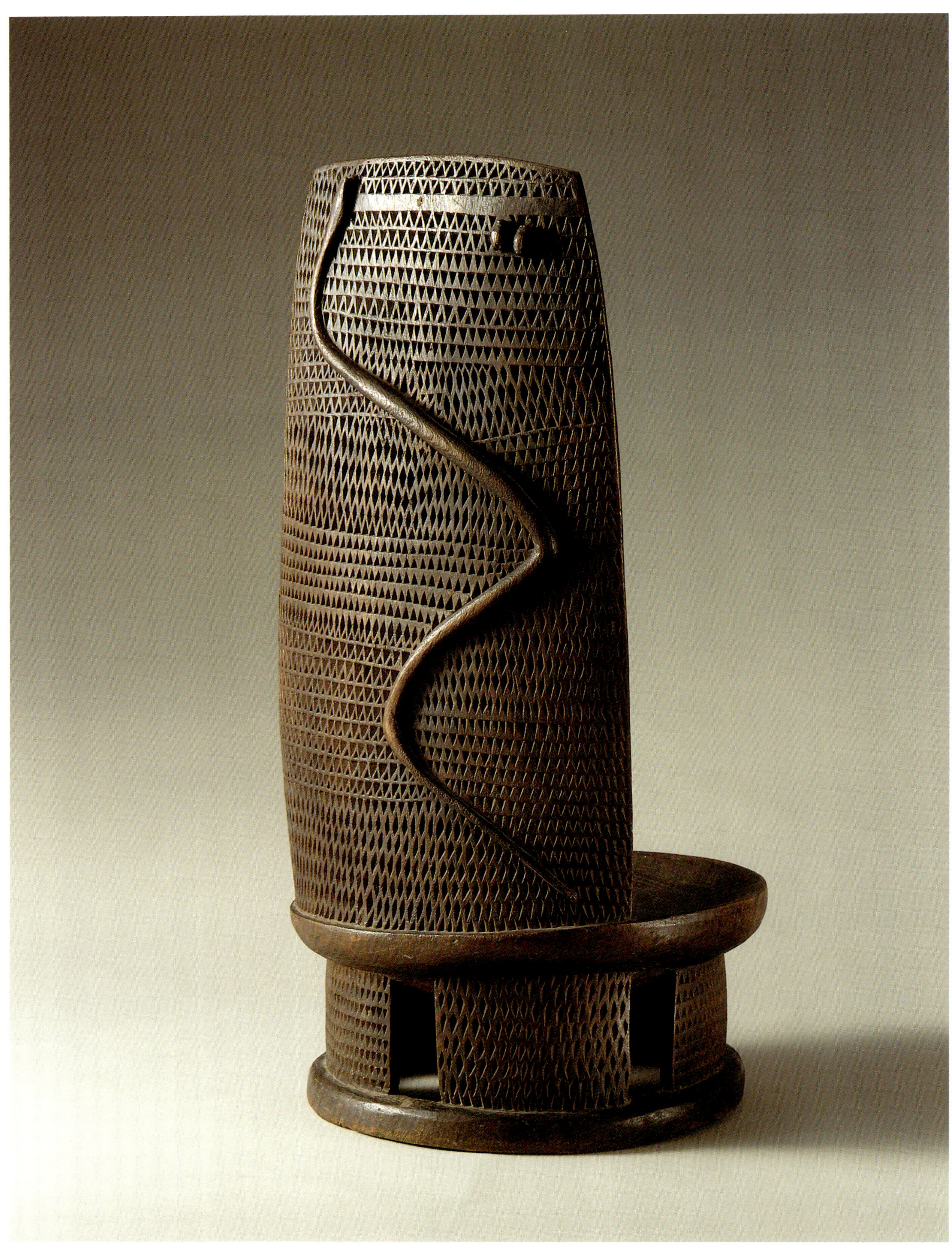

 Chief's chair of the Tabwa, Zaire, height 77 cm Cat. 143

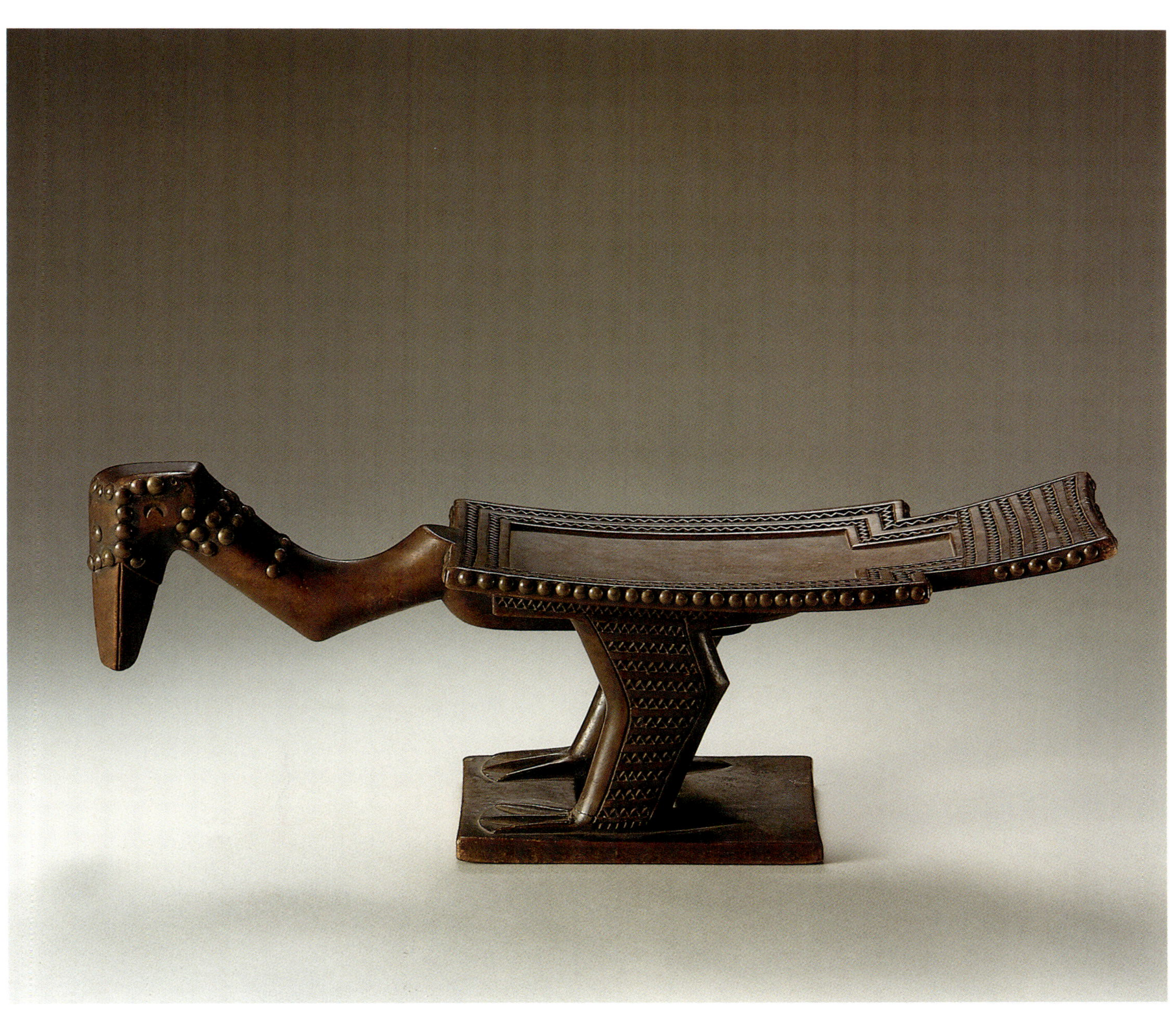

Stool in the form of a bird of the Imbangala, Angola, width 54 cm Cat. 113

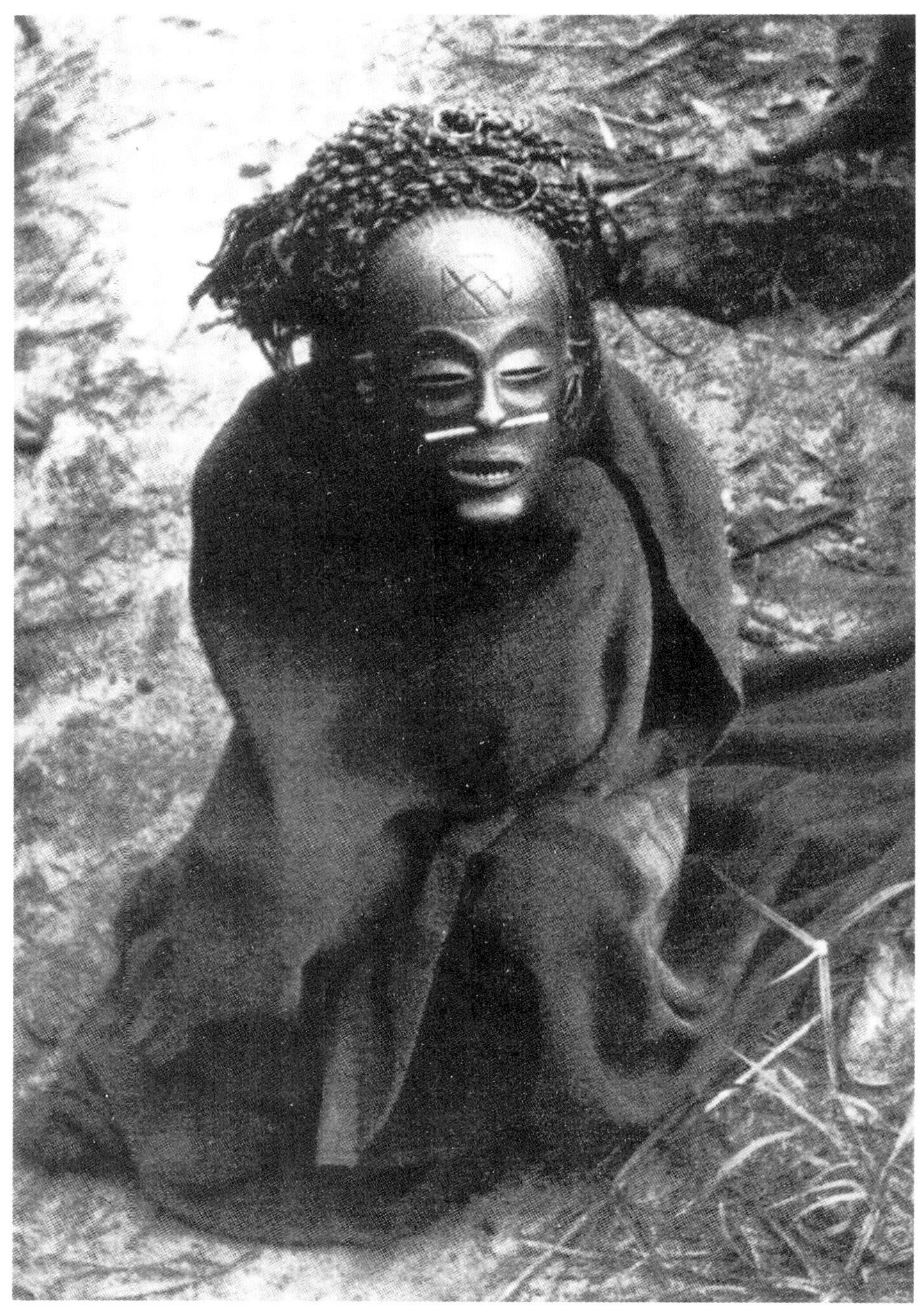

Photograph: Hans Himmelheber, 1938/39

A Mwana-po masked figure of the Chokwe with a 'beautiful' female face, Zaire; cf. the caryatid stool in the plate opposite

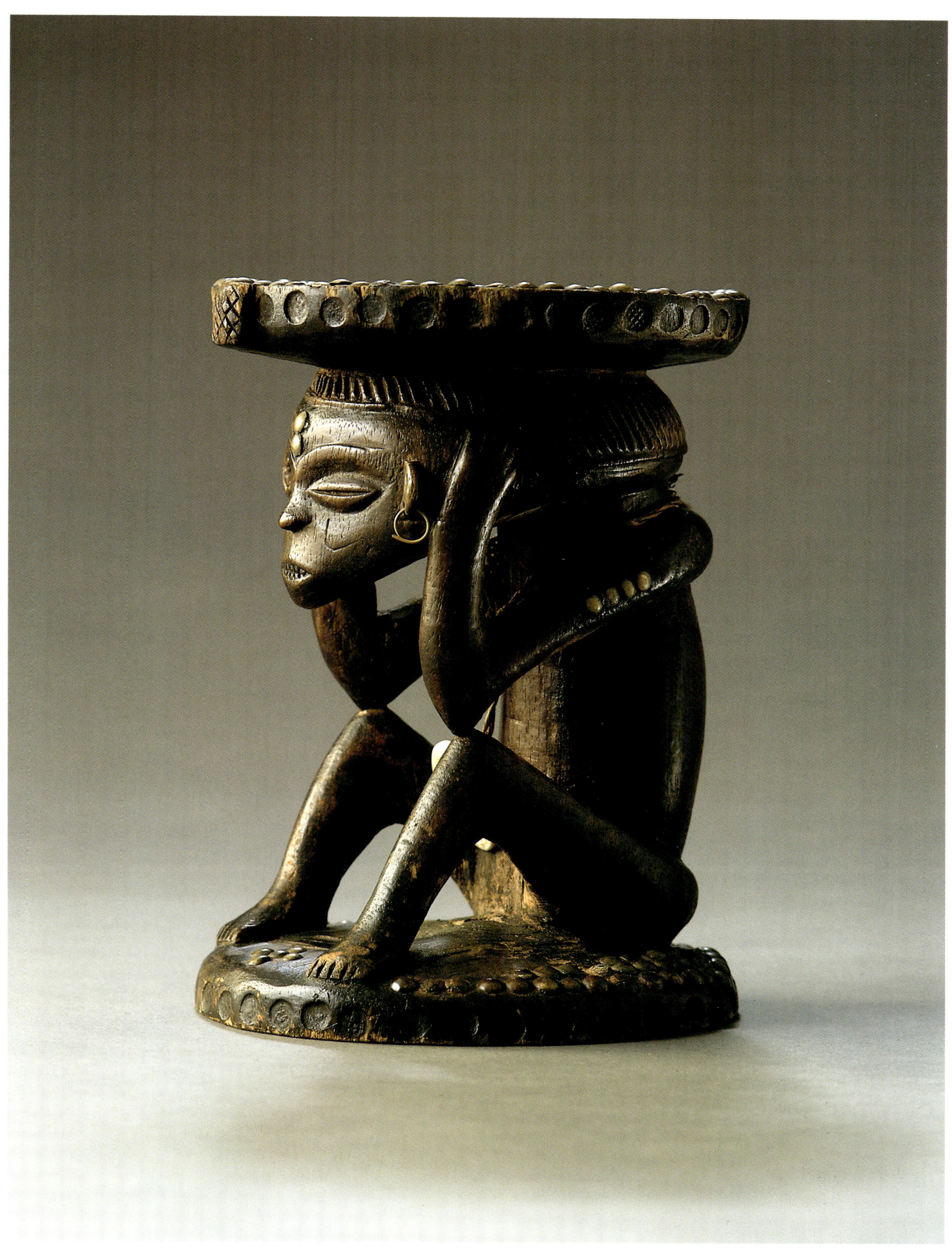

Caryatid stool of the Chokwe, Angola, height 22.5 cm Cat. 108

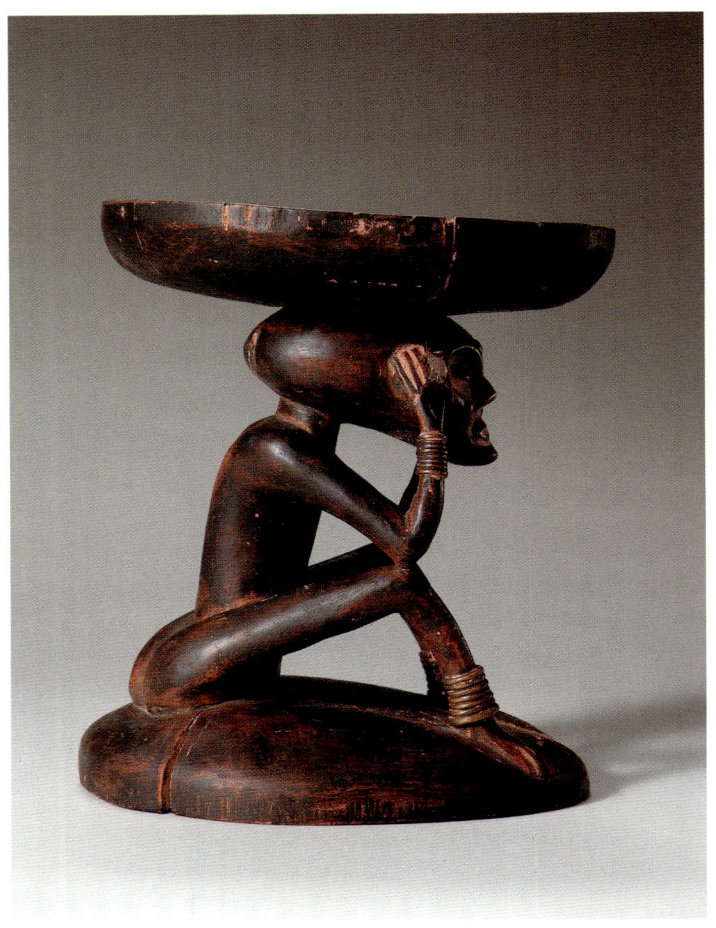

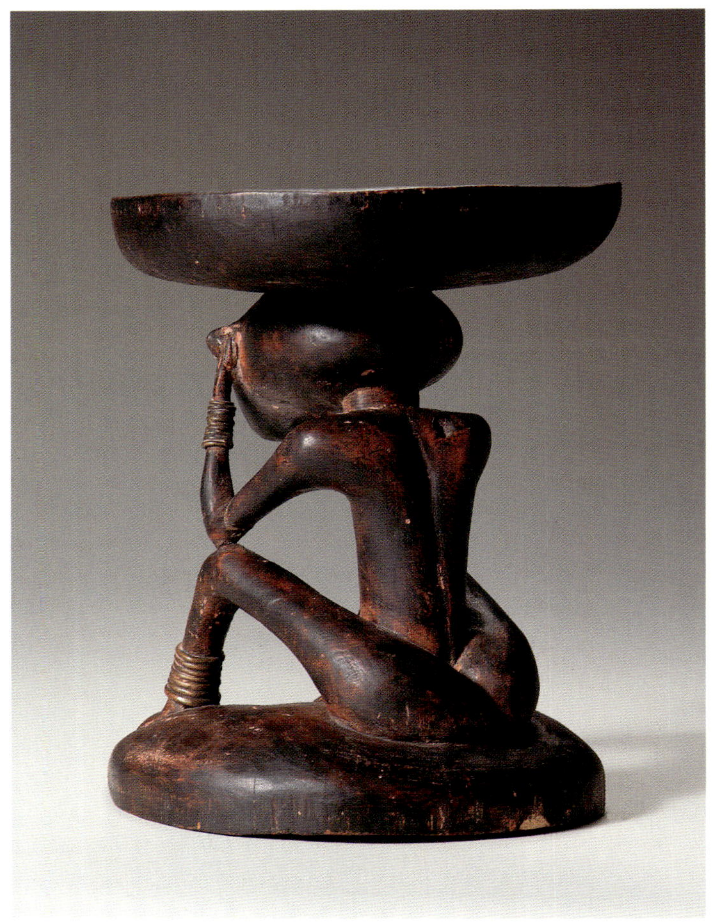

Caryatid stool of the Chokwe/Pende, Zaire, height 25 cm Cat. 107

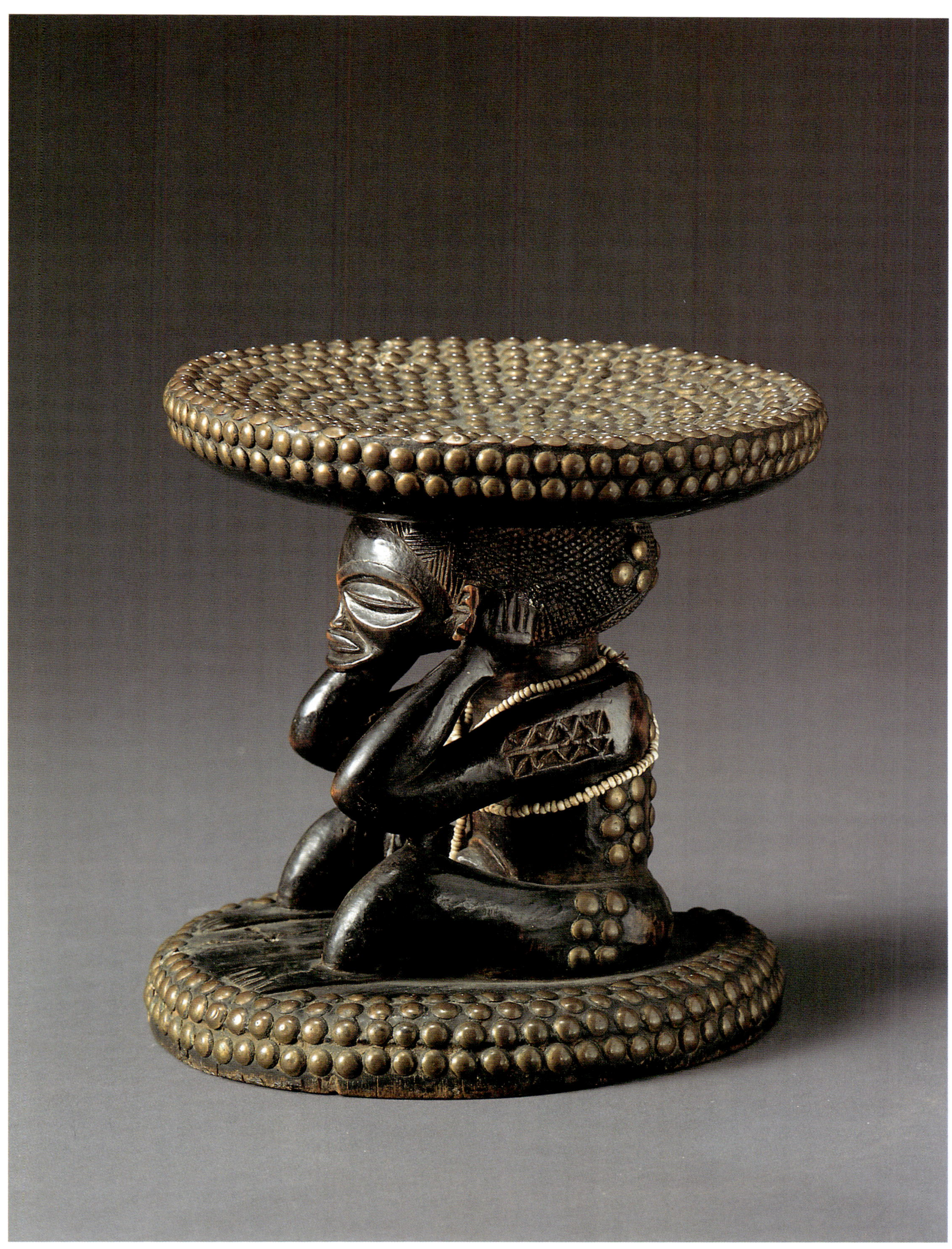

Caryatid stool of the Chokwe, Zaire, height 21.3 cm Cat. 105

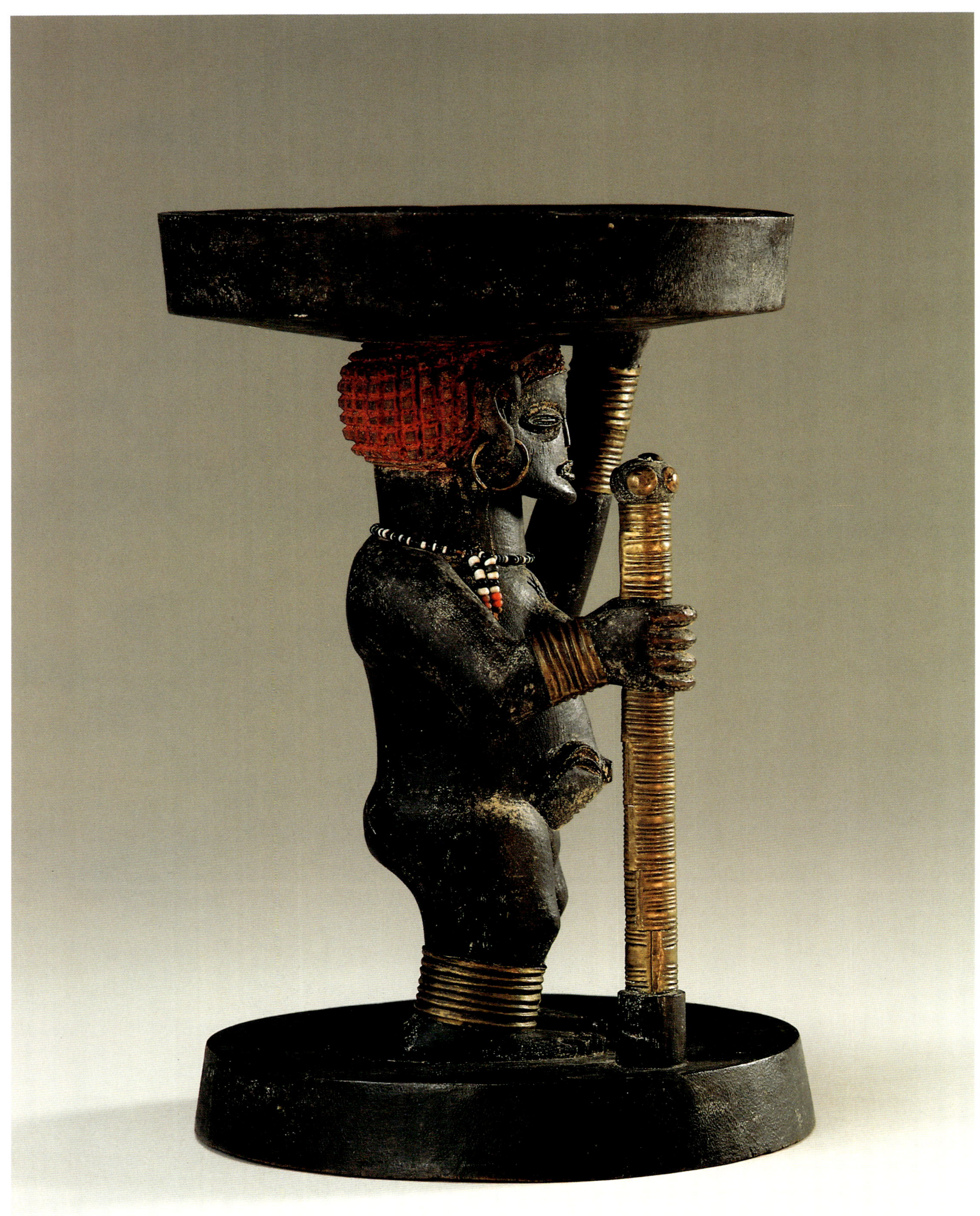

Caryatid stool of the Chokwe, Zaire/Angola, height 31.5 cm Cat. 109

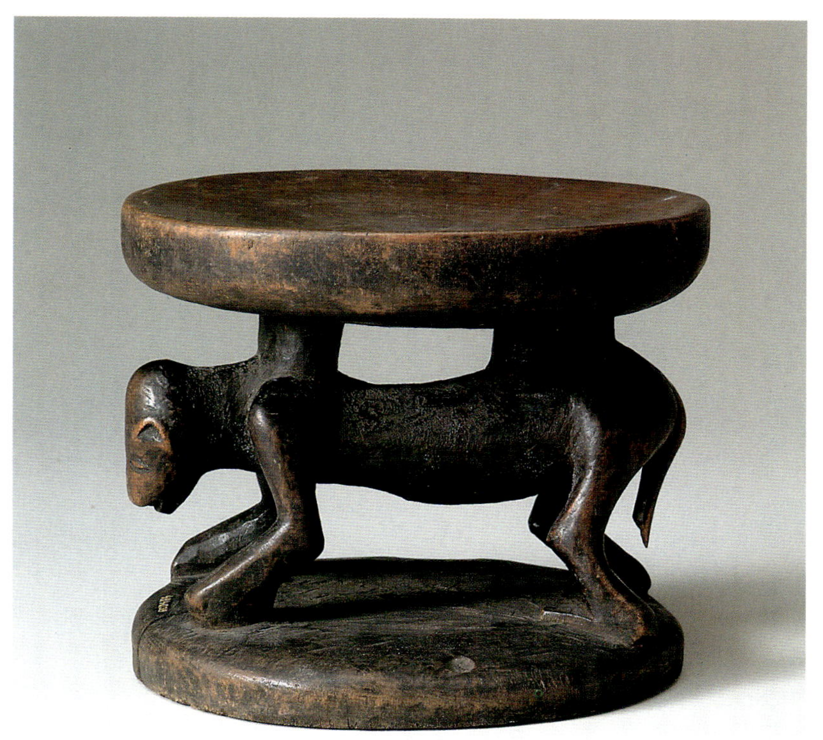

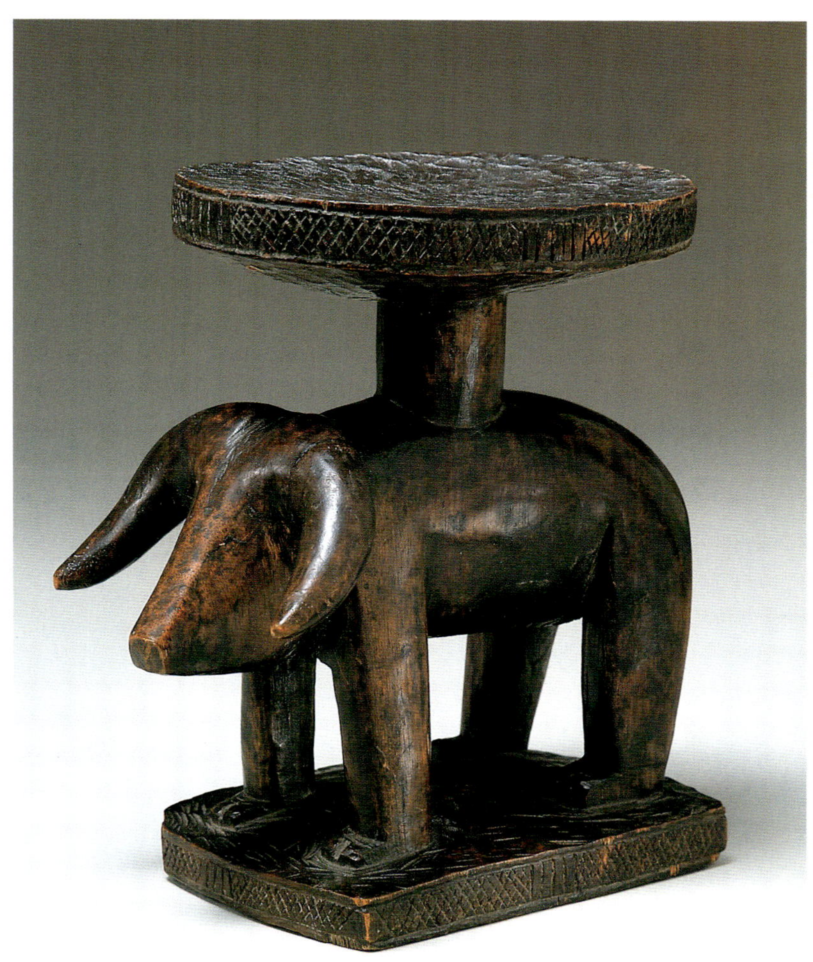

Stools of the Chokwe, Zaire/Angola, height 20.5 cm and 25 cm Cats. 101, 102

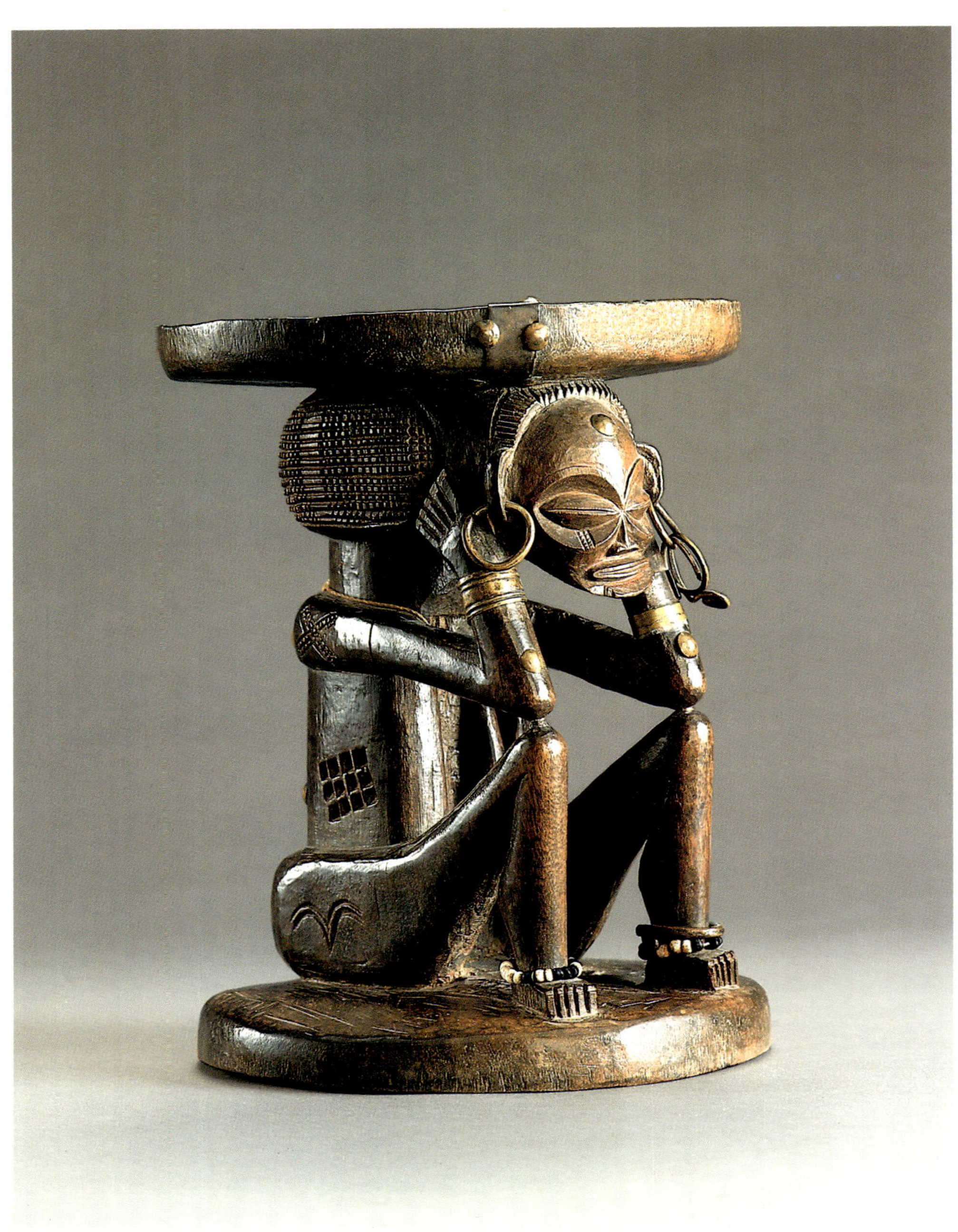

Caryatid stool of the Chokwe, Angola, height 24 cm Cat. 106

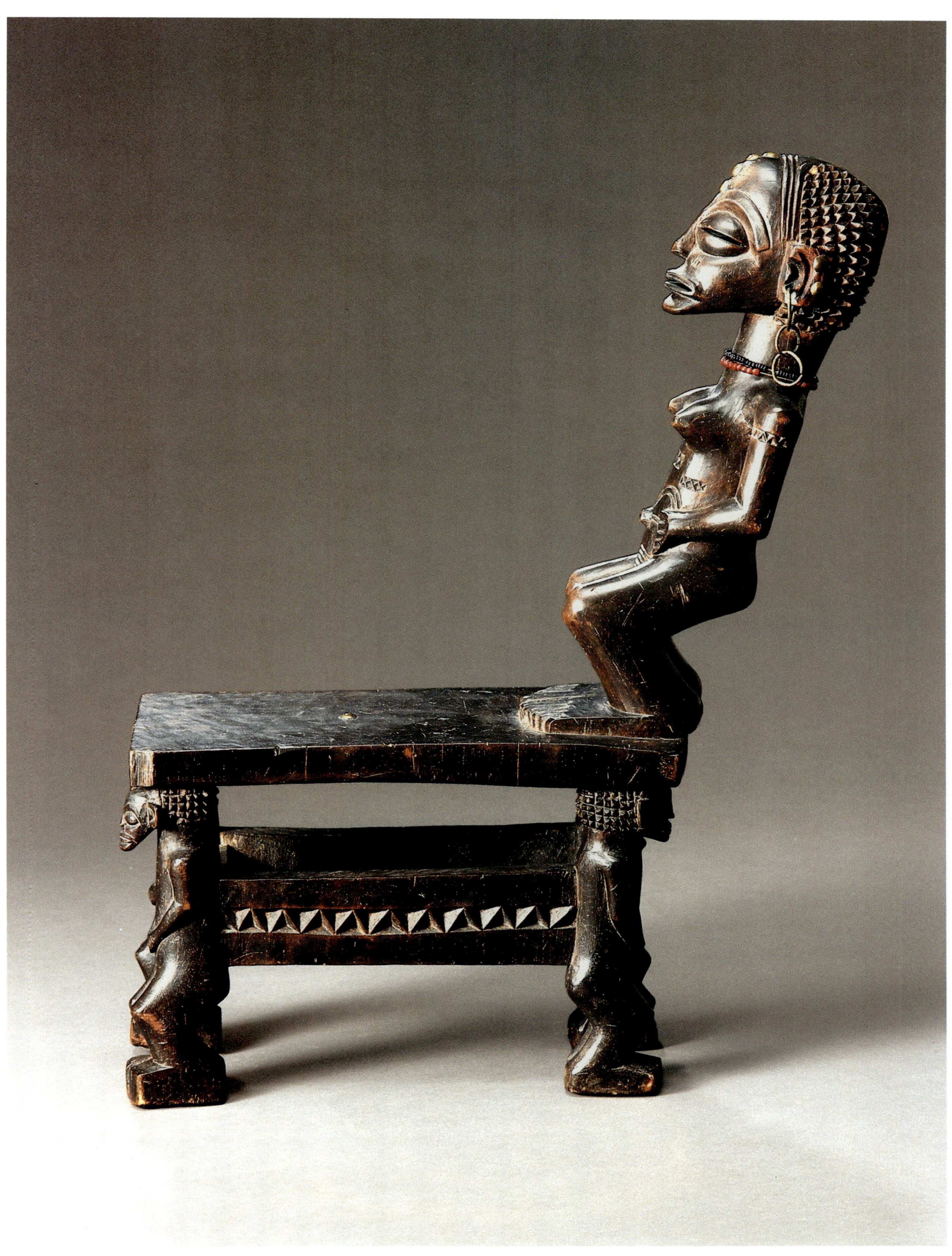

Chair of the Chokwe, Zaire, height 55 cm Cat. 110

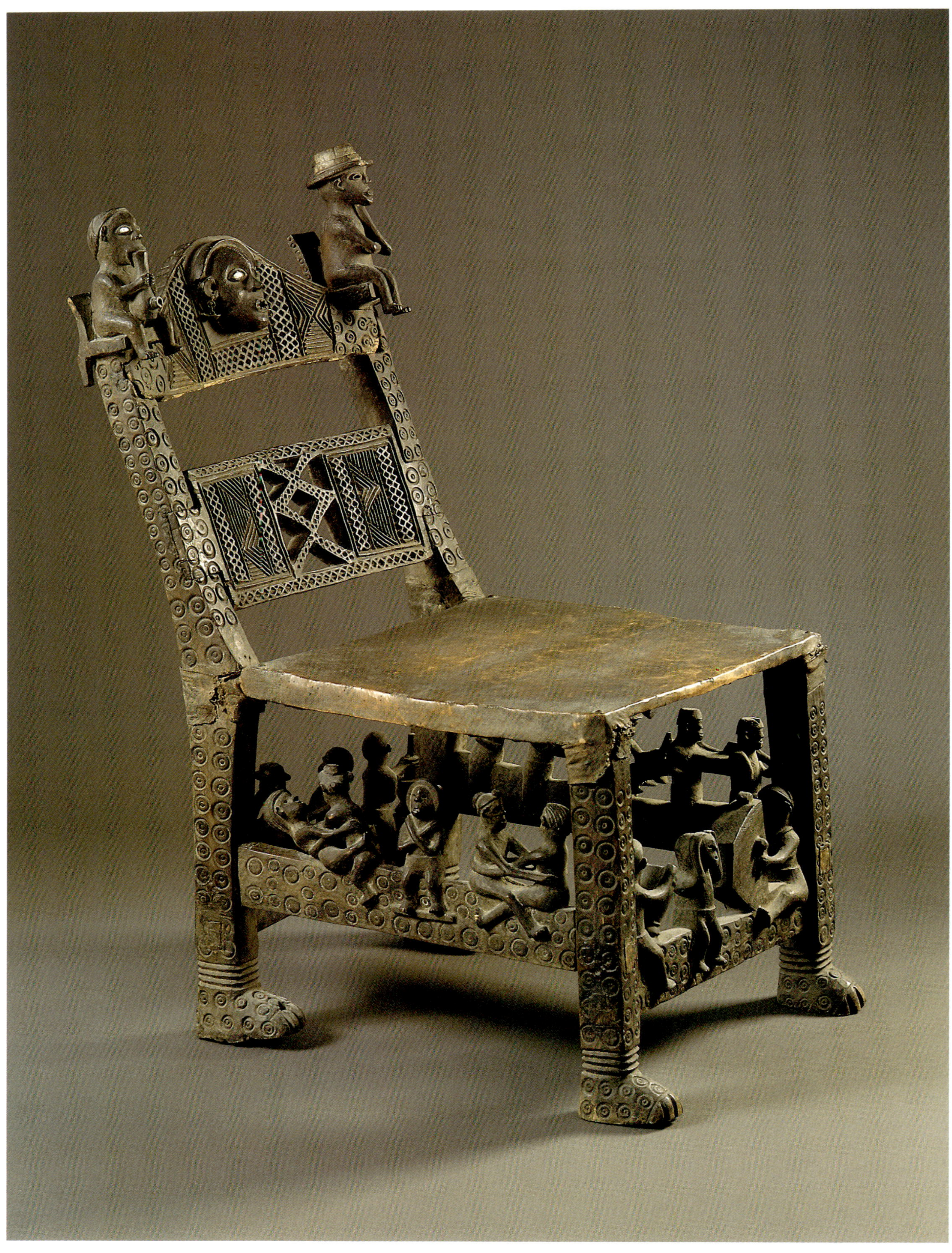

Chair of the Pende, Zaire, height 27 cm Cat. 114

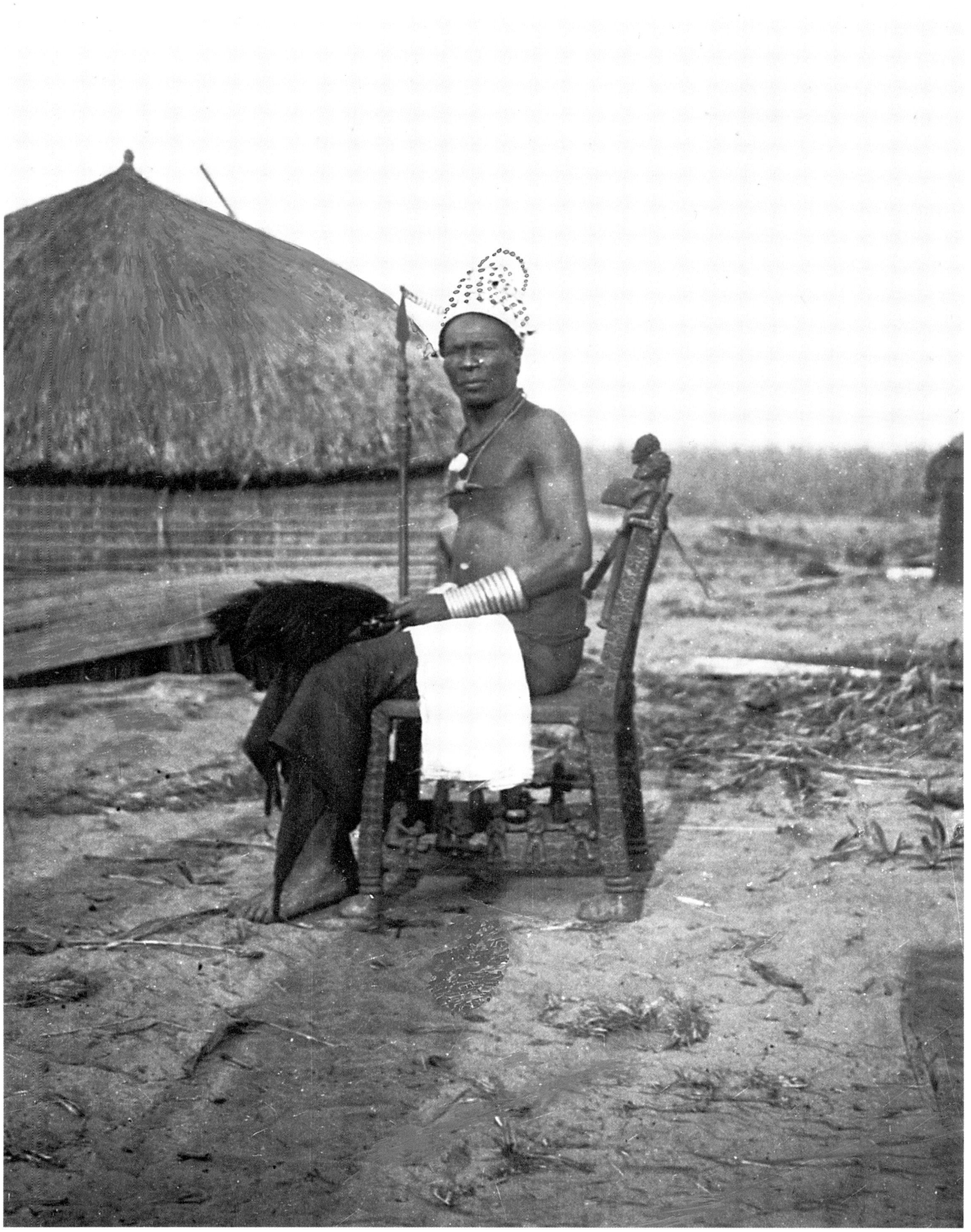

Photograph: Mukulu-Nzambi, Gungu, Zaire, 1925

The Pende chief Sintshinga seated on a chair with leopard paws, Mukulu-Nzambi, Gungu, Zaire

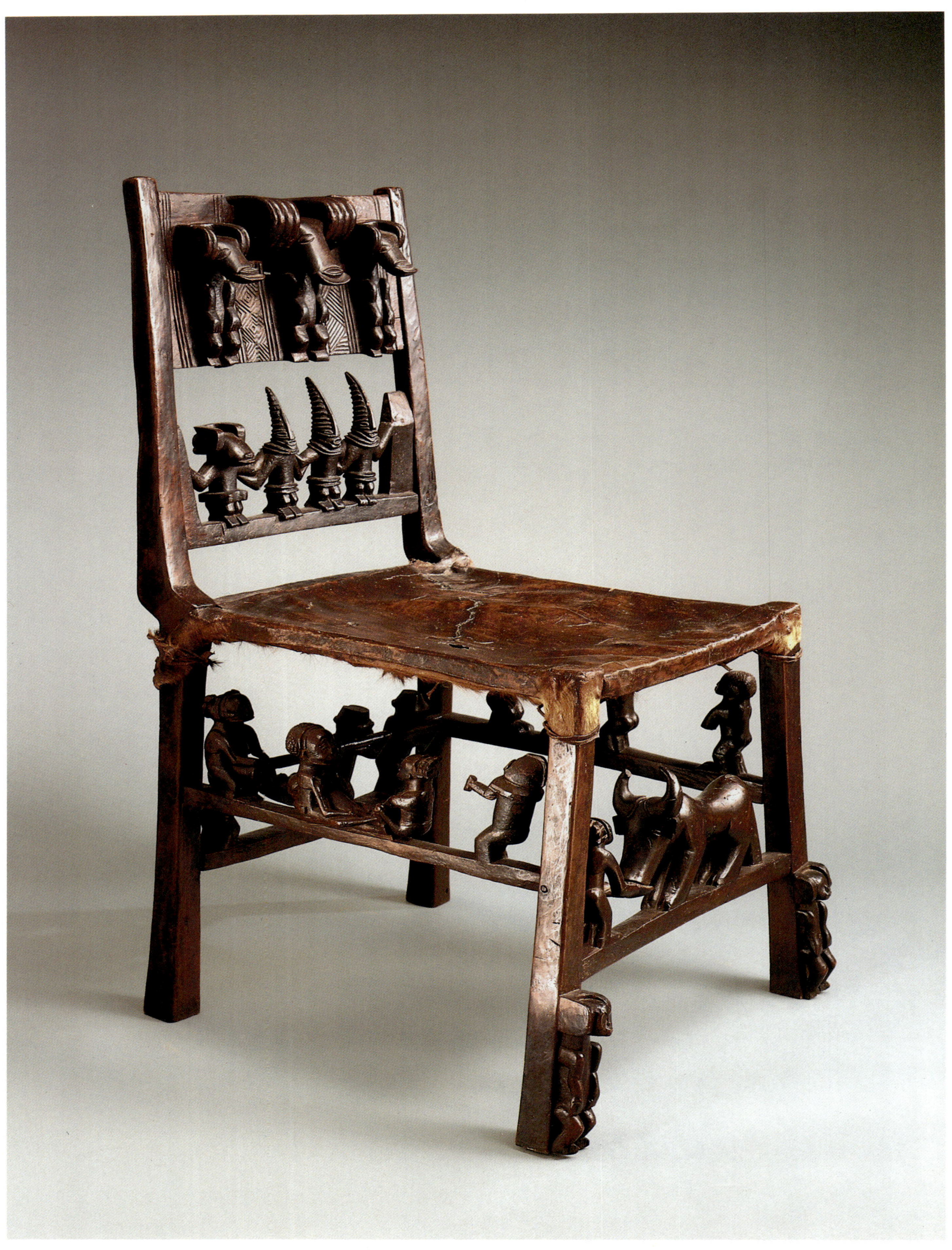

Chair of the Chokwe, Zaire, height 93.5 cm Cat. 115

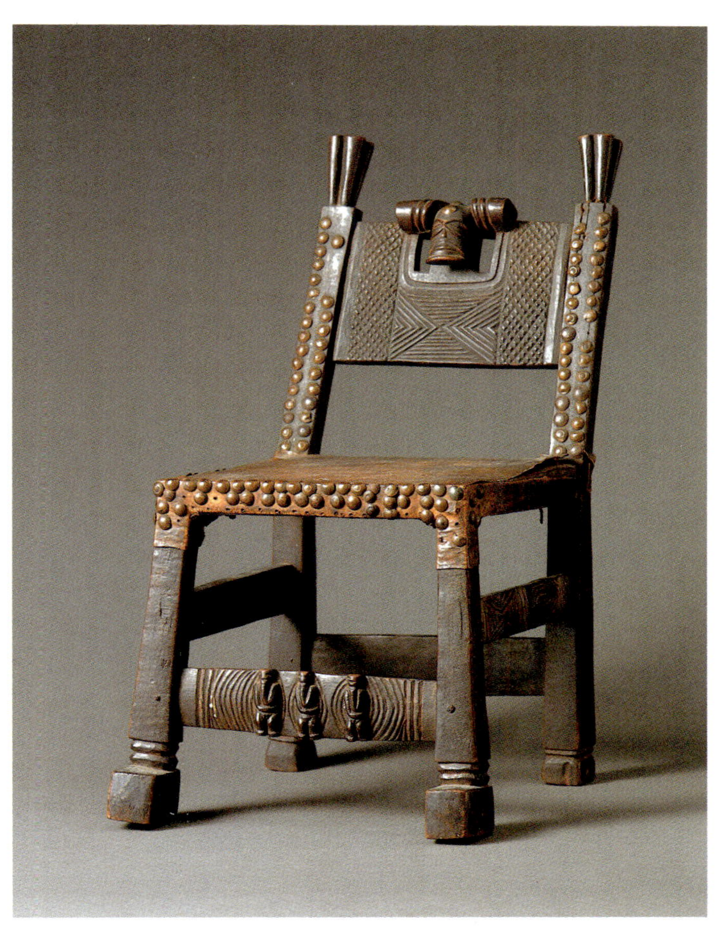

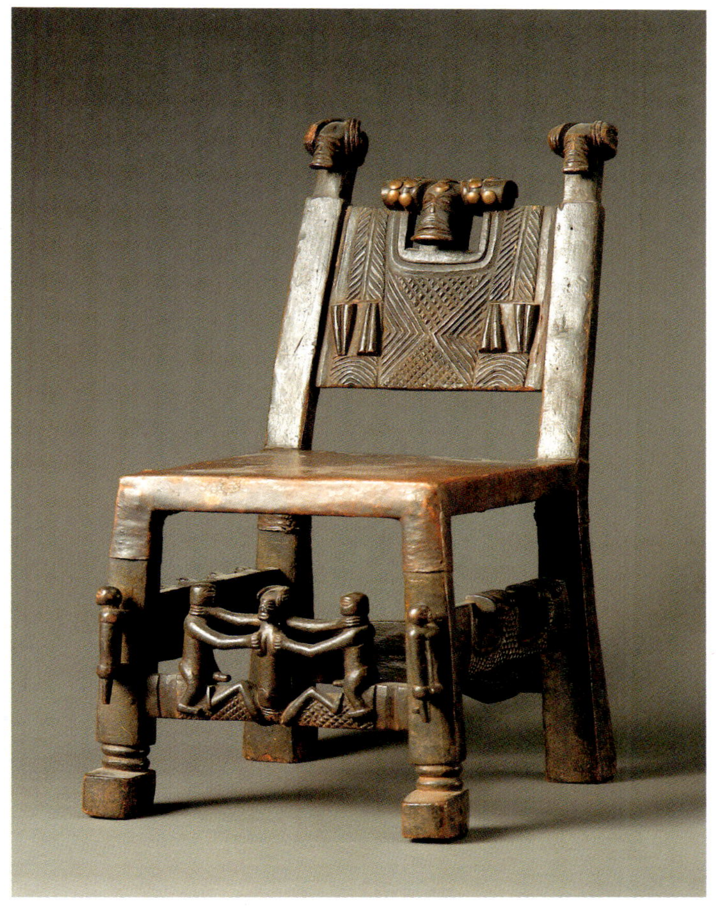

Chairs of the Chokwe, Zaire/Angola, height 41 cm and 41.5 cm Cats. 117, 116

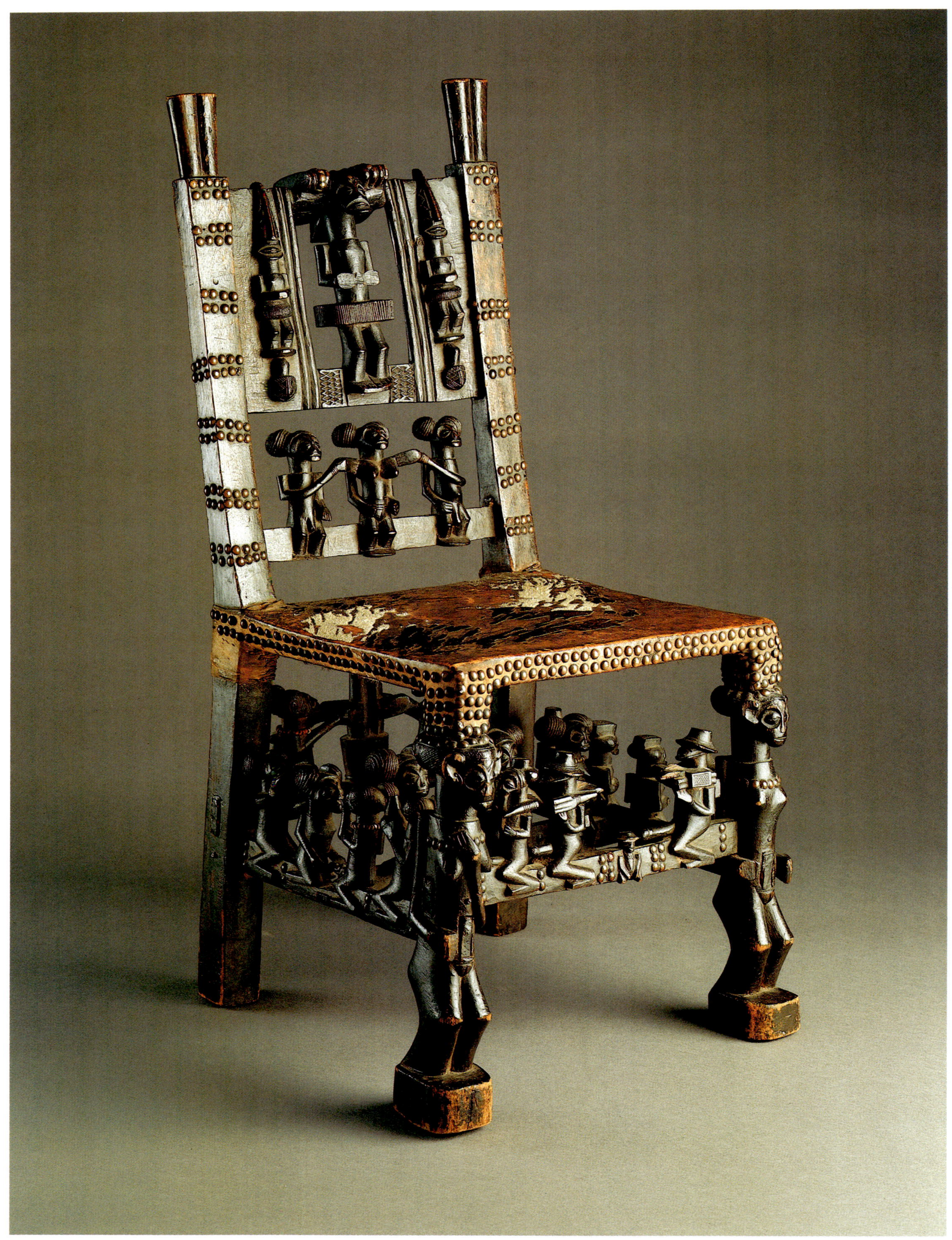

Photograph: Grund & Flum, Basle

Chair of the Chokwe, Zaire/Angola, height 79 cm Cat. 121

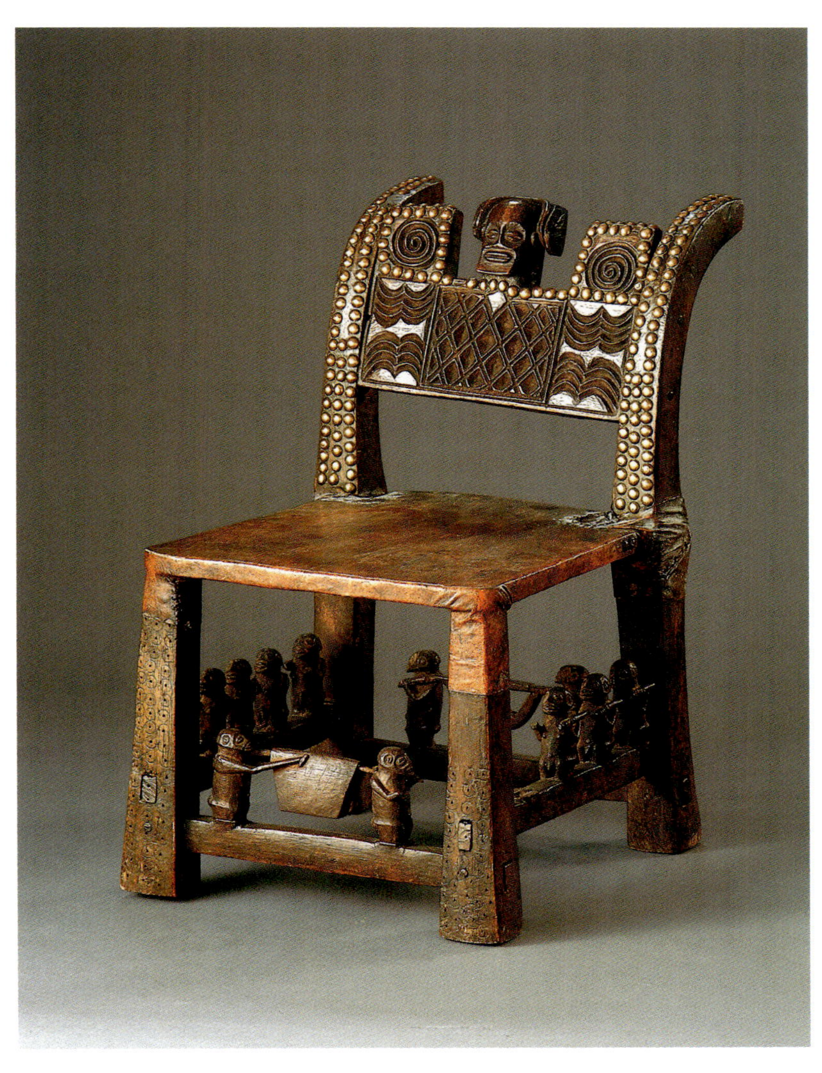

Chair of the Chokwe, Zaire, height 51.5 cm Cat. 118

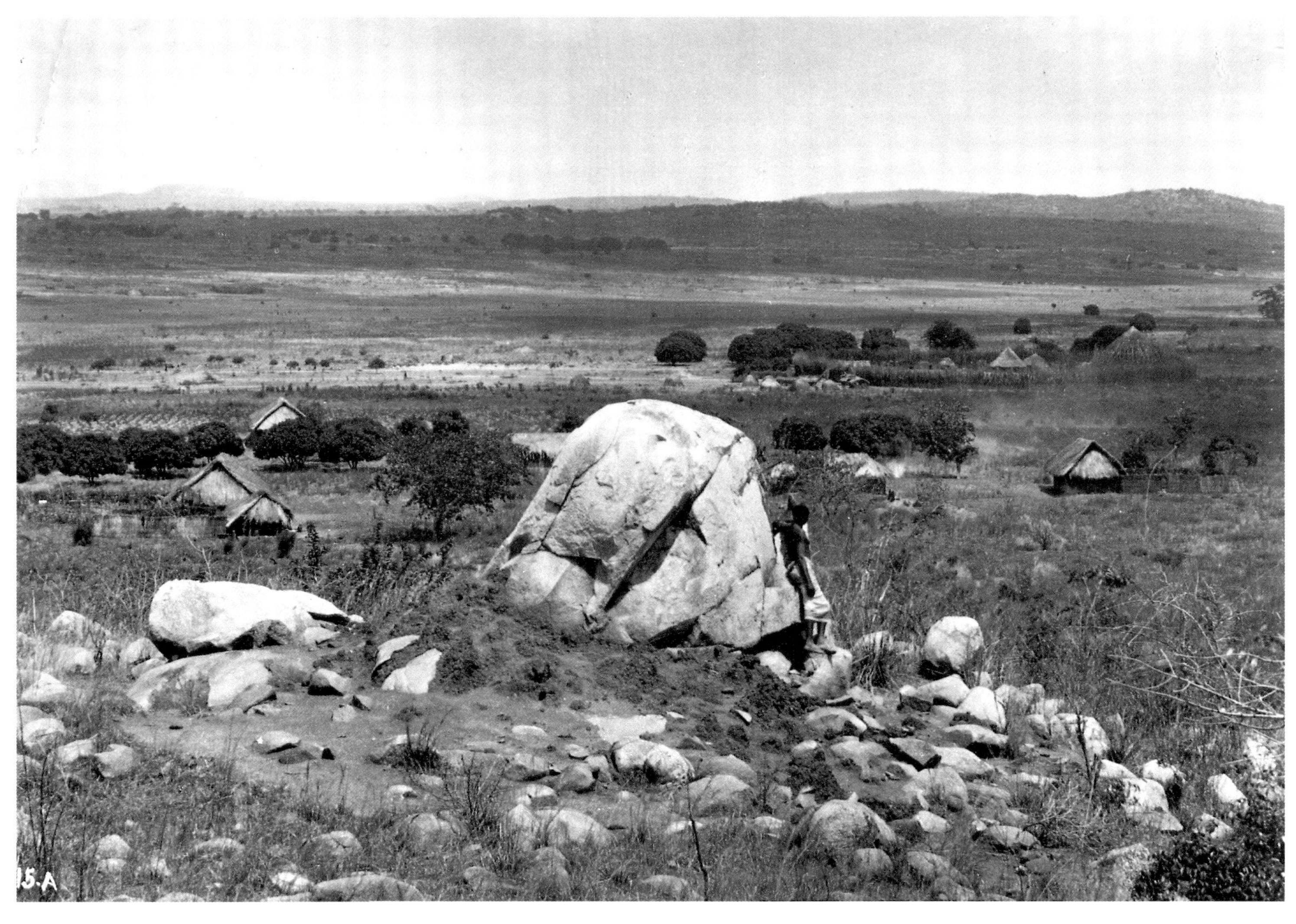

Landscape of Unyamnyembe, near Tabora: Nyamwezi village with mango trees, Tanzania. (Photograph: Mösenbacher, *c.* 1910)

East and Southern Africa

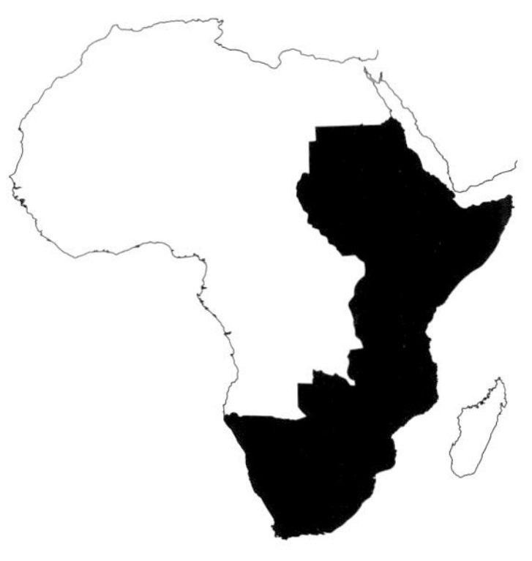

It is now regarded as certain that it was from East Africa that the first human beings set out to settle the earth; their traces have been found in the Kenyan highlands. Just as fascinating as this anthropological discovery are the splendid rock paintings from the neolithic period found in southern Africa, and also the enigmatic ruined cities in what is now Zimbabwe, which still resist attempts to establish their age and identify their builders. They are testimony to empires that once flourished in the southern part of this continent and, along with many further archaeological finds, to the lively cultural past of this region.

In spite of these early traces, East Africa and southern Africa have for long been regarded as relatively unfruitful regions in artistic terms. The great nomadic peoples of East Africa created no figurative art at all. Moslem immigrants, whose iconophobe convictions led them to tolerate no representation of man and beast, spread relentlessly along the eastern coast during the first millennium AD, ridding large regions of their cultural artefacts. Indeed, if one compares the cultures in the east and south of the continent with those of Central and West Africa, it is apparent that the peoples of the latter were far more devoted to rituals with masks and to the veneration of ancestors and of the soil, and were thus much more productive from the point of view of art connected with ritual. Only a few peoples in the south-east of Africa – for example the Makonde in Tanzania (plate on p. 165) – employed traditional types of masks.

None the less, it is precisely among such peoples, with their very few sacred objects, that we encounter an astonishing wealth of outstandingly designed everyday utensils: spoons, figurally and ornamentally carved calabashes and ostrich eggs, tobacco pipes, jewellery and, not least, neck-rests, stools and chairs.

Both expressive, archaic masks and figures of extremely simplified form, were produced in the region of the Upper Nile. Alongside such ritual implements, the Shilluk, and to their south the Bari, the Bongo and the Nuba, have also made objects for everyday use – out of wood, clay and calabash gourds. A number of examples shown here (e. g. cat. 139) testify to the high artistic quality of such items.

Figurative forms are also to be found among seating furniture. One of the greatest examples, perhaps, is the chief's throne from a workshop of the Nyamwezi, discovered in 1898 in the palace of the Sultana of Buruku, and now in Berlin (plate on p. 158). Placed asymmetrically on its high back, with head and arms stretching beyond the edges, is a human figure carved in high relief, which guards the sitter from behind. The formal design of this truly regal throne appears to be related to that of a seat from the Tabwa region (plate on p. 140). As in the case of the Nyamwezi throne, the back again rises as a solid wedge out of the seating surface. In place of a human figure, however, a snake zigzags across the back.

More unusual forms of seats and stools are those with removable backs, found in Ethiopia (e. g. plate on p. 167). The plainer stools from this region have plate-like seating surfaces. Comparable seats are also produced in Sudan and in Kenya among the Kamba and the Maasai, while similar forms are found in Malawi, in Zambia and in Tanzania (plates on pp. 159, 163–4). In these, the very varied design of both the seating surfaces and their supports offer constant delight. Whether resting on three, four or eight legs, these seats – hardly ever taller than 20 centimetres – are among the most aesthetically appealing to be found in southern Africa.

Lorenz Homberger

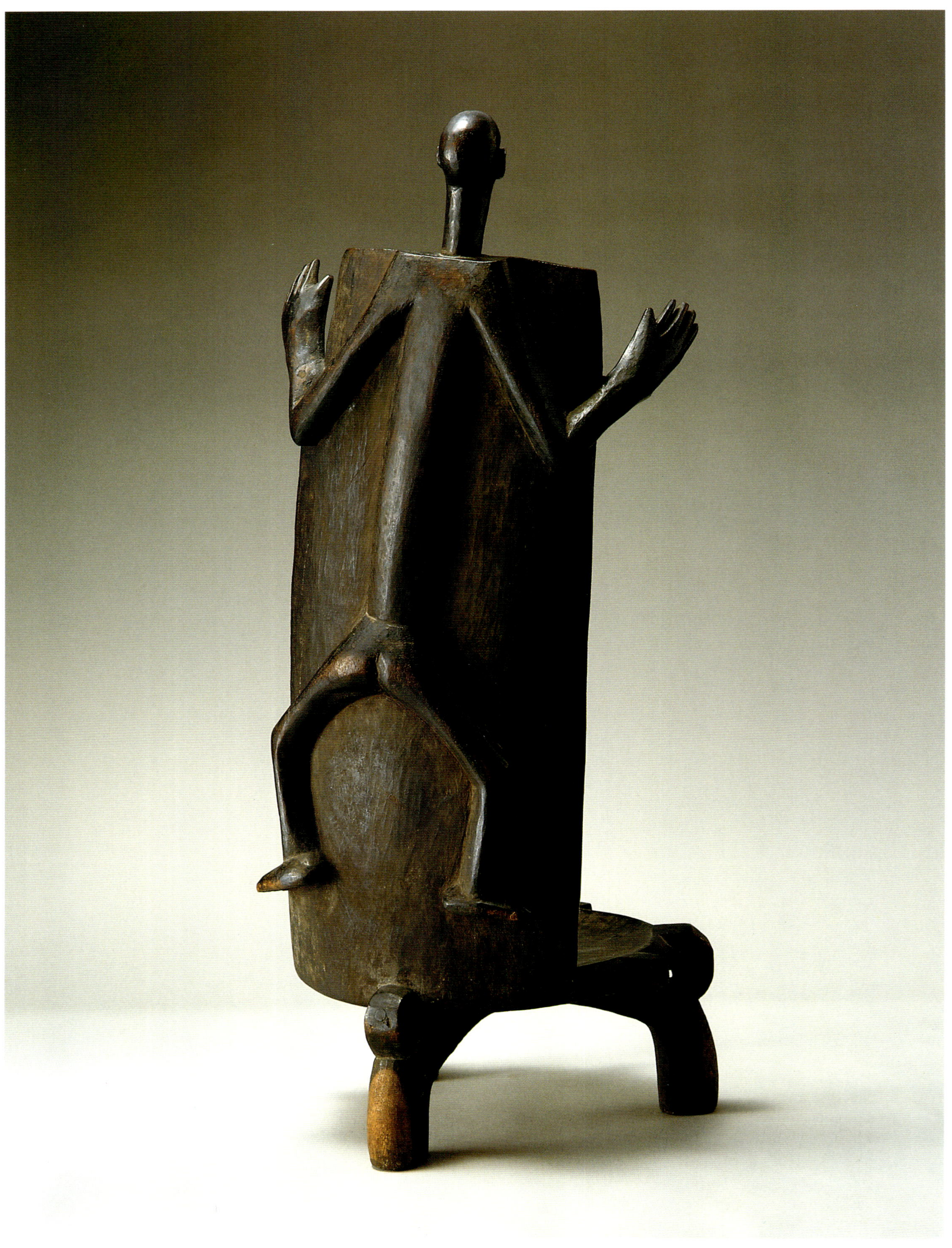

Chair of the Nyamwezi, Tanzania, height 107 cm Cat. 145

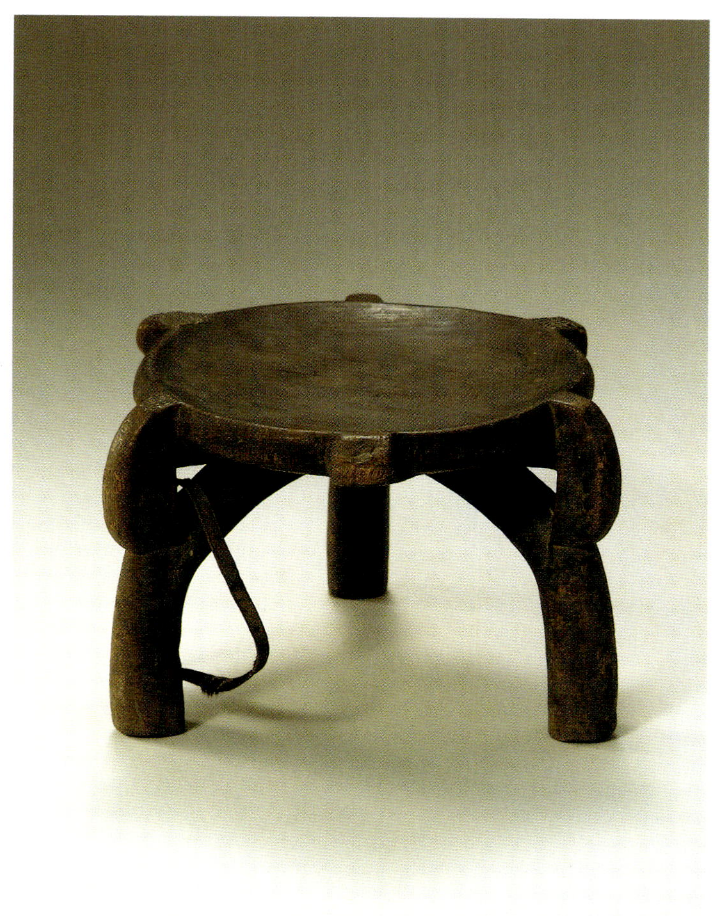

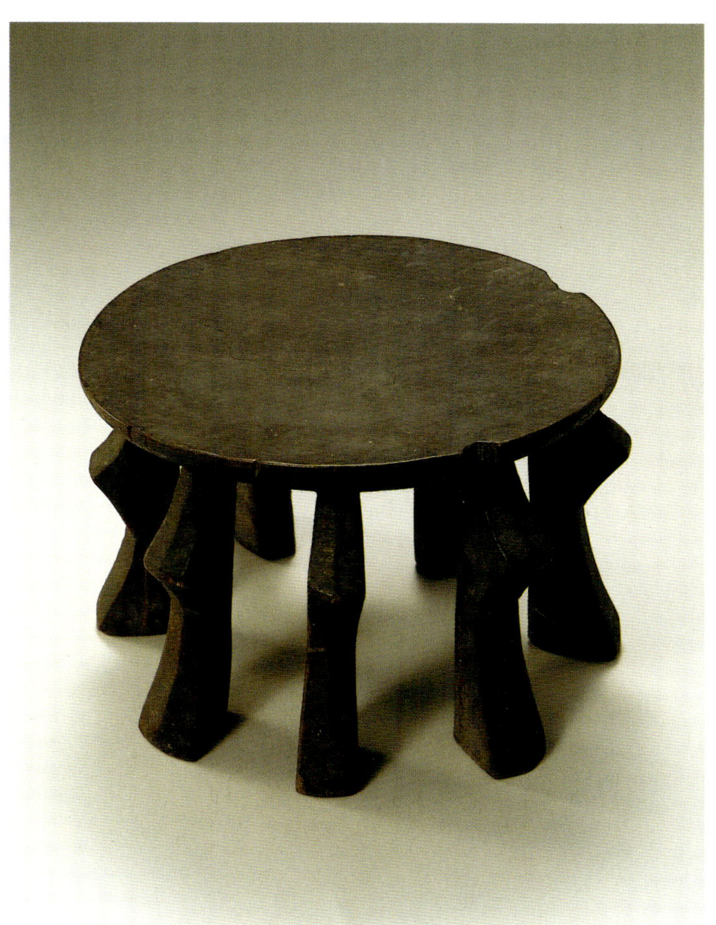

Stools of the Hehe, Tanzania, height 22 cm and 25 cm Cats. 146, 148

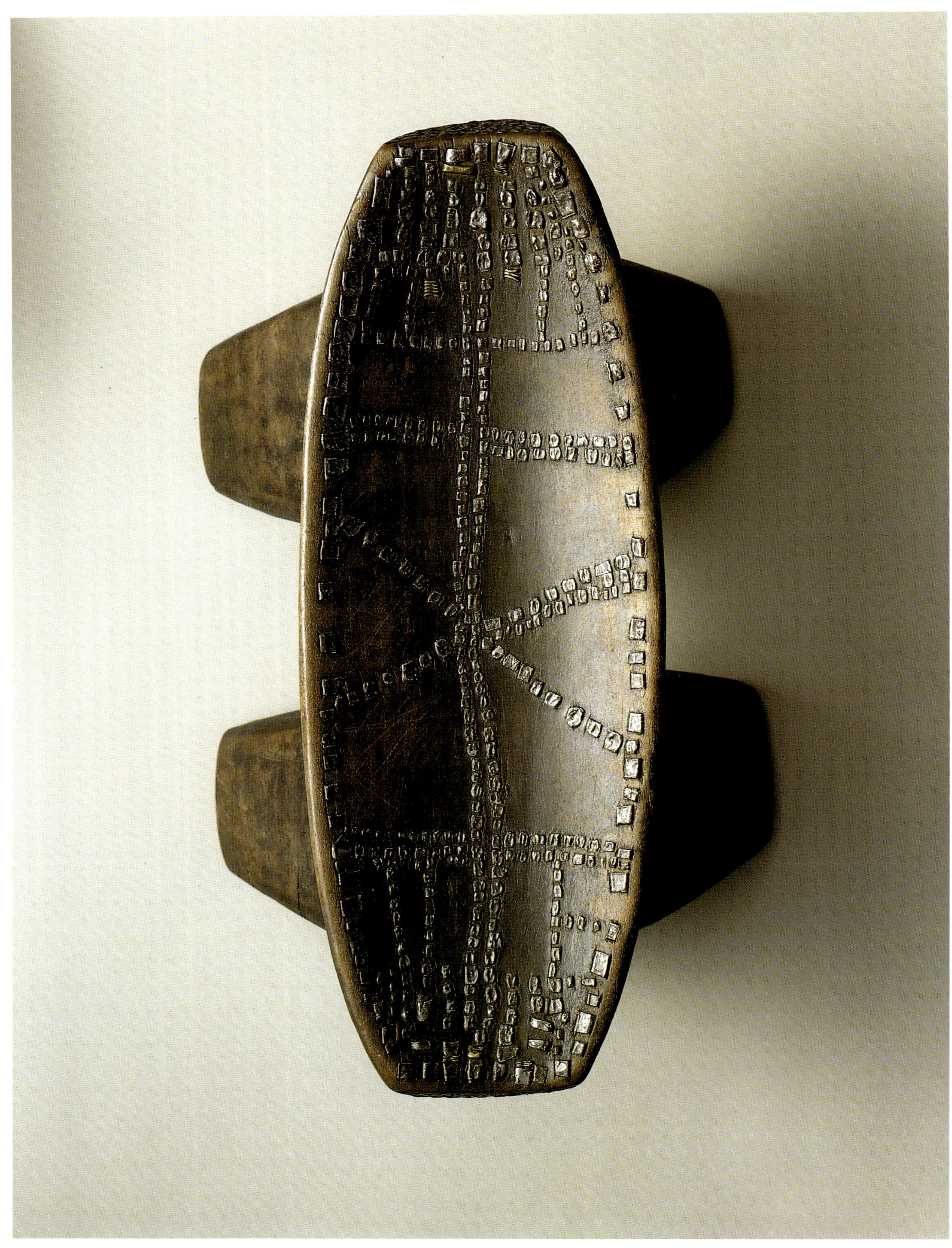

 Stool of the Safwa/Poroto, Tanzania, width 36 cm Cat. 150

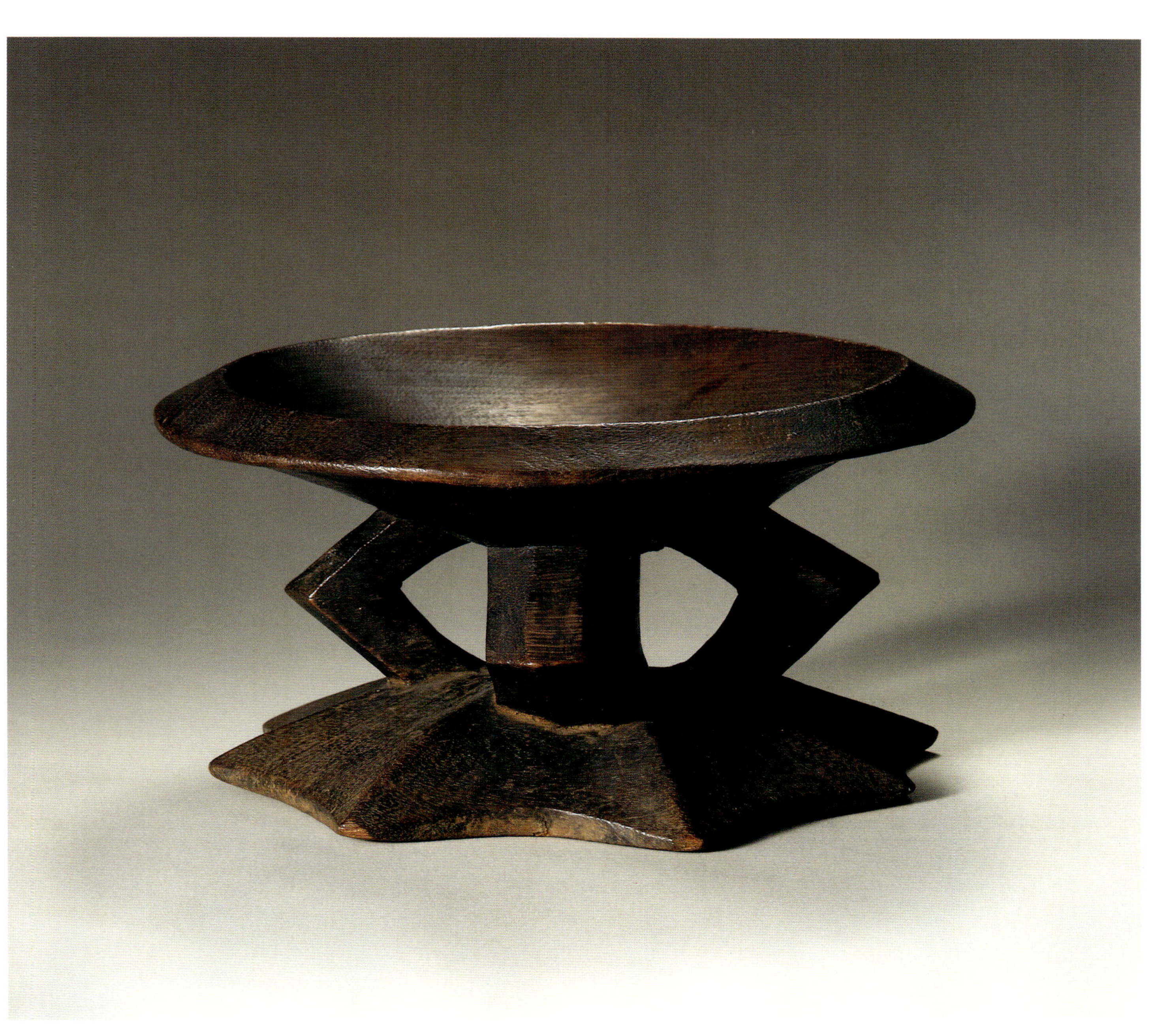

Stool of the Zande, Zaire, height 19 cm Cat. 98

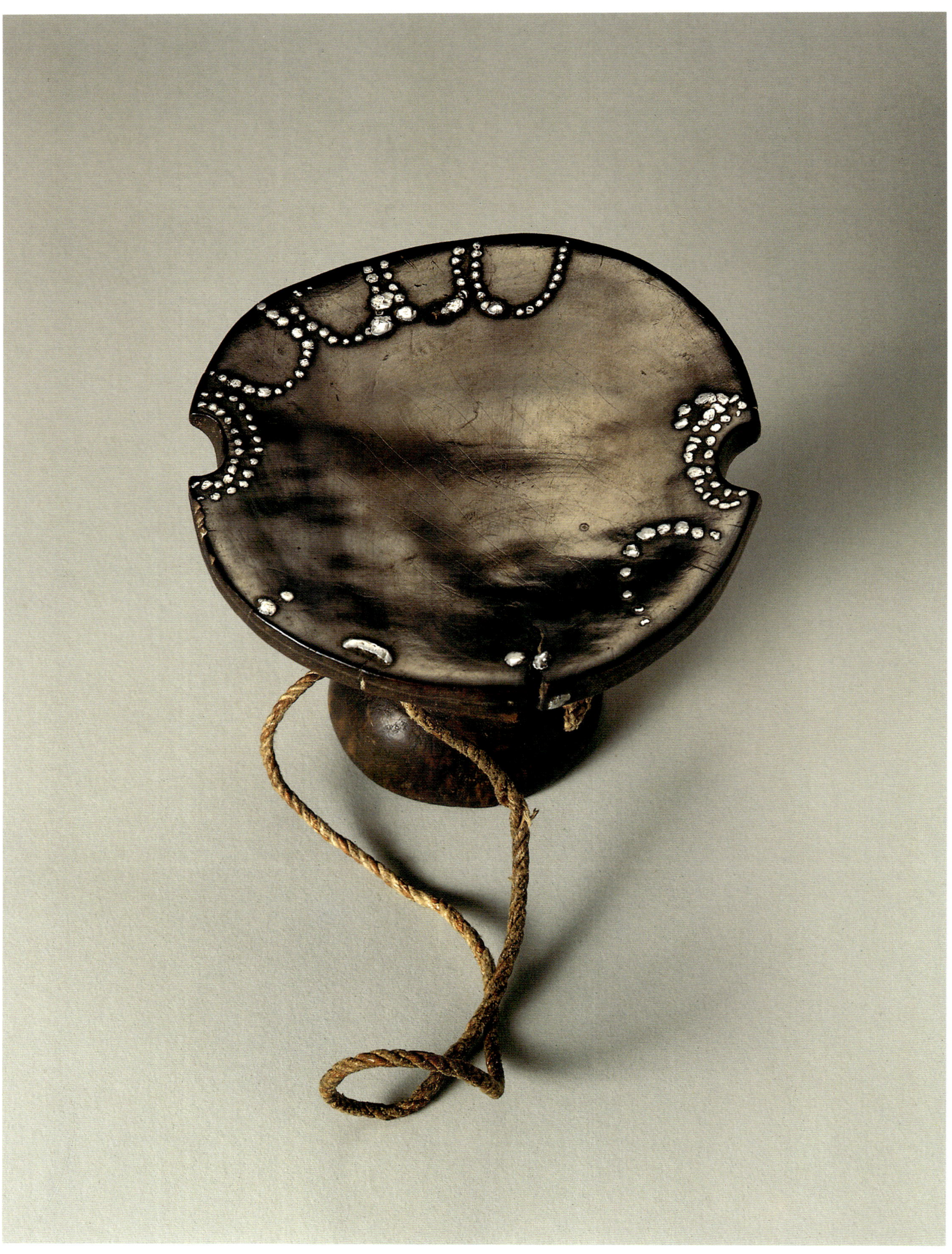

 Stool of the Gurage, Ethiopia, height 12 cm Cat. 140

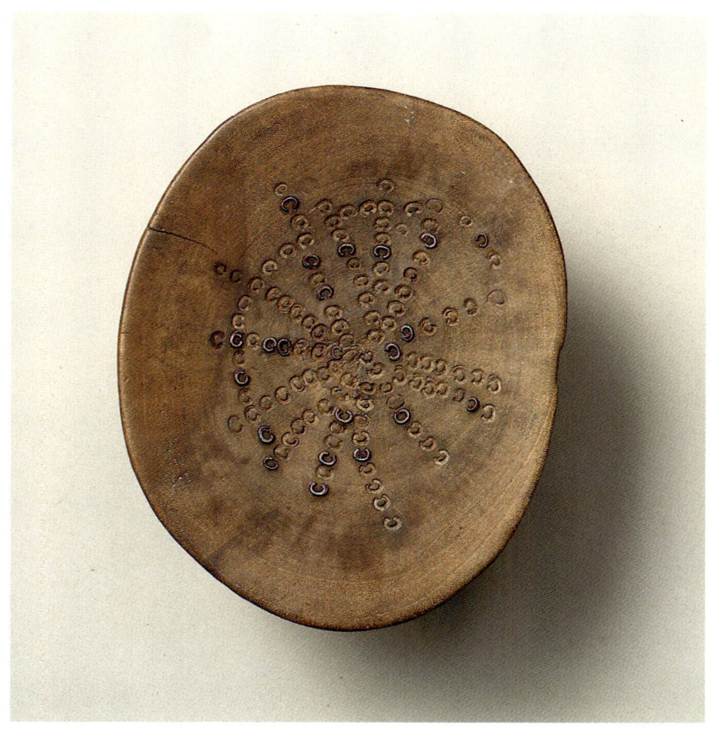

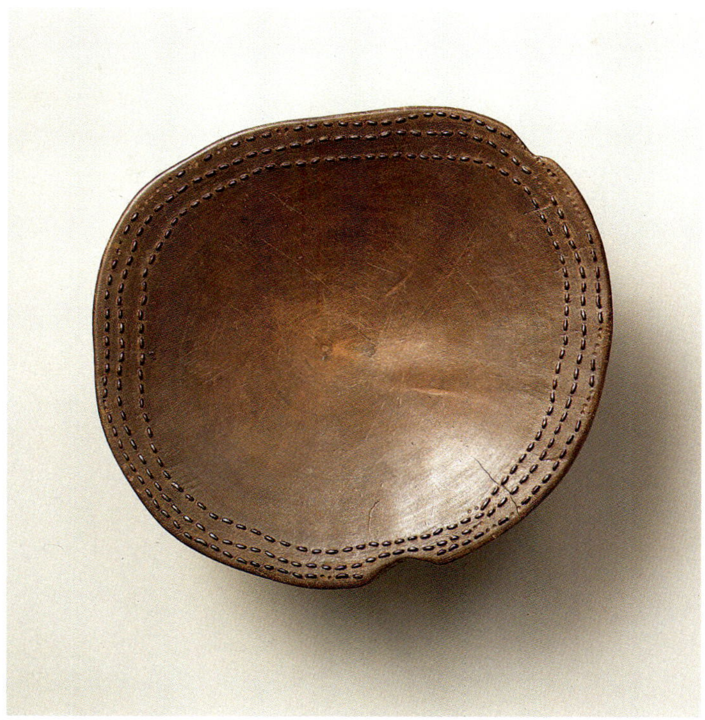

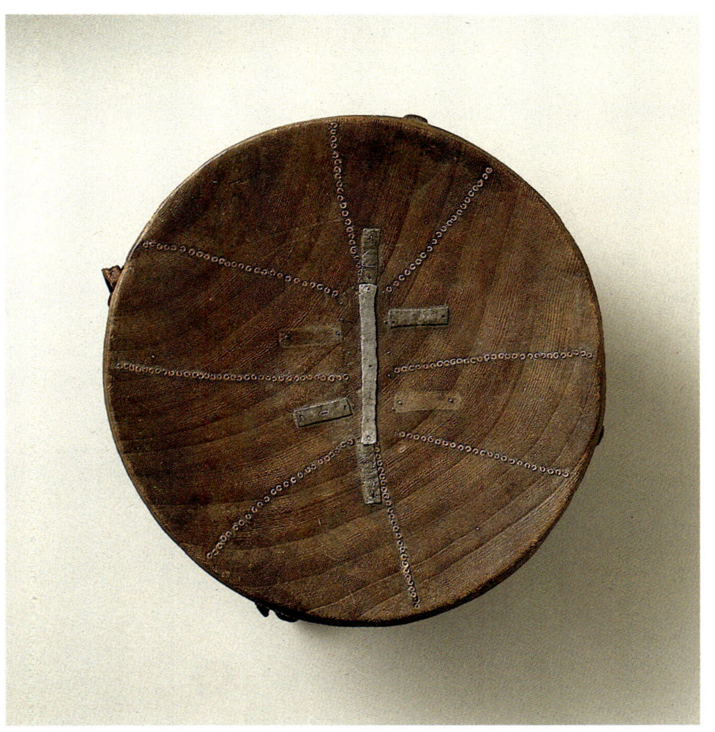

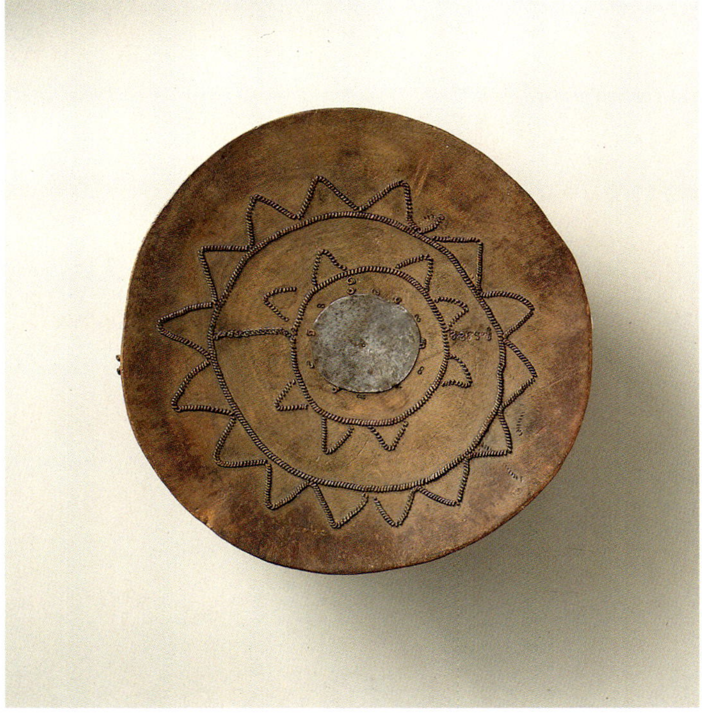

Seating surfaces of stools of the Kamba, Kenya, diameter 18–22 cm Cats. 154, 157, 156, 155

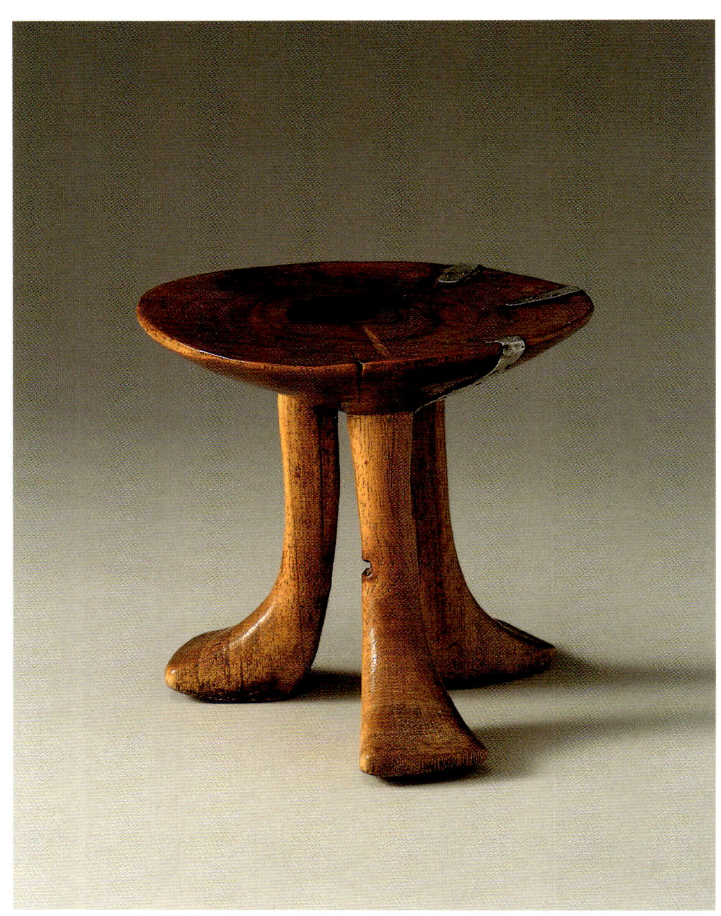

 Stool of the Maasai, Kenya, height 18 cm Cat. 158

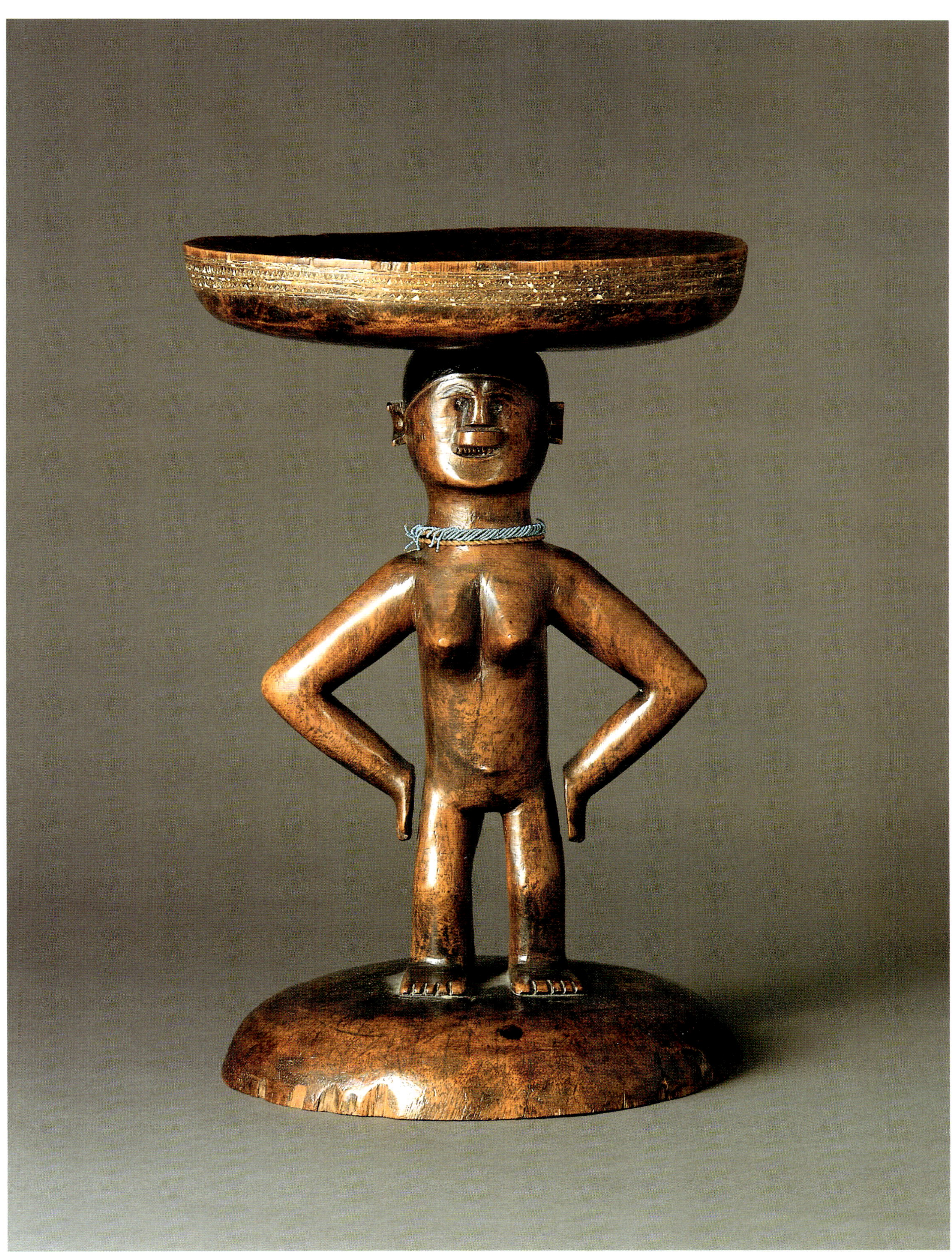

Caryatid stool of the Makonde, Tanzania, height 48 cm Cat. 160

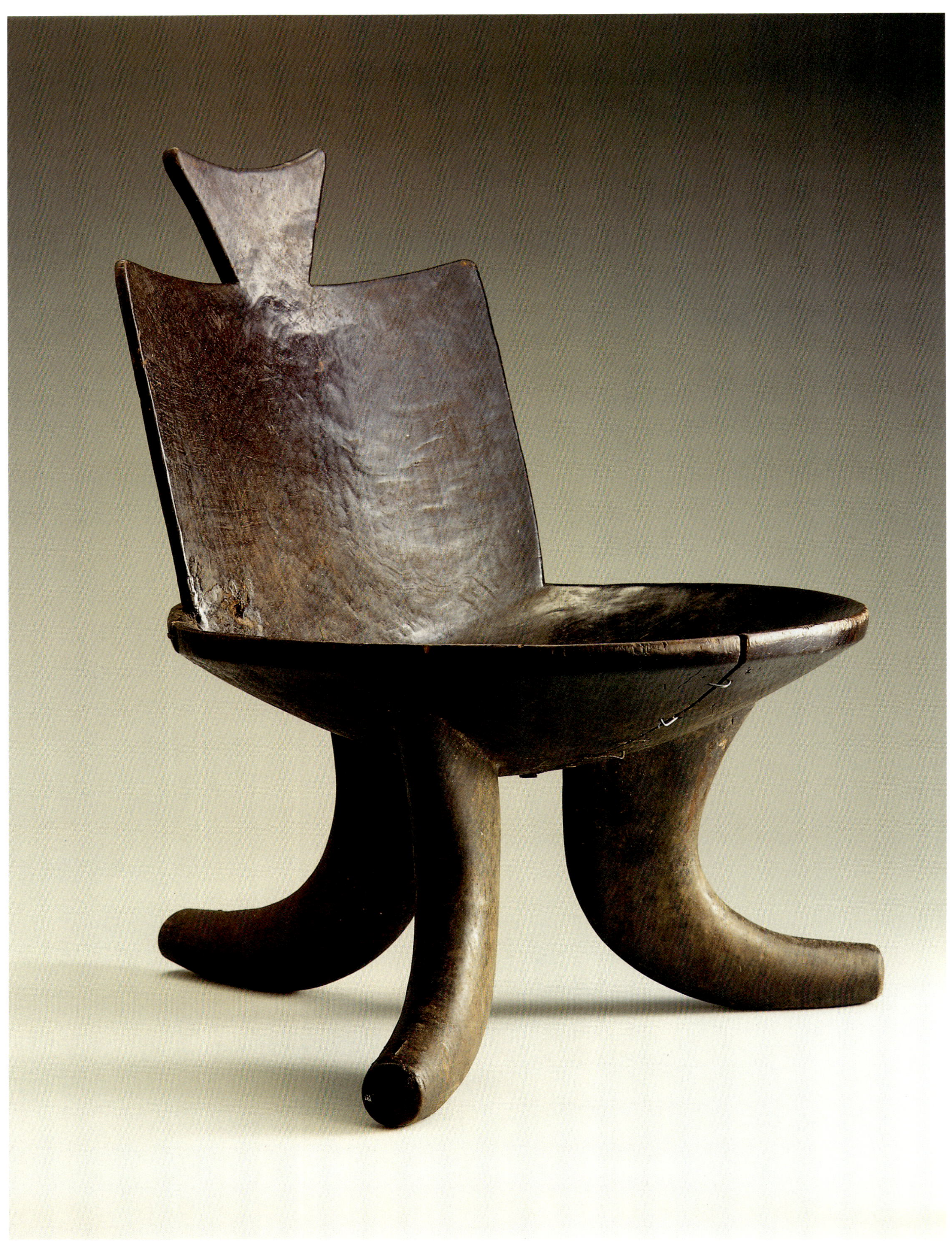

Chair of the Galla (?), Ethiopia, height 88 cm Cat. 142

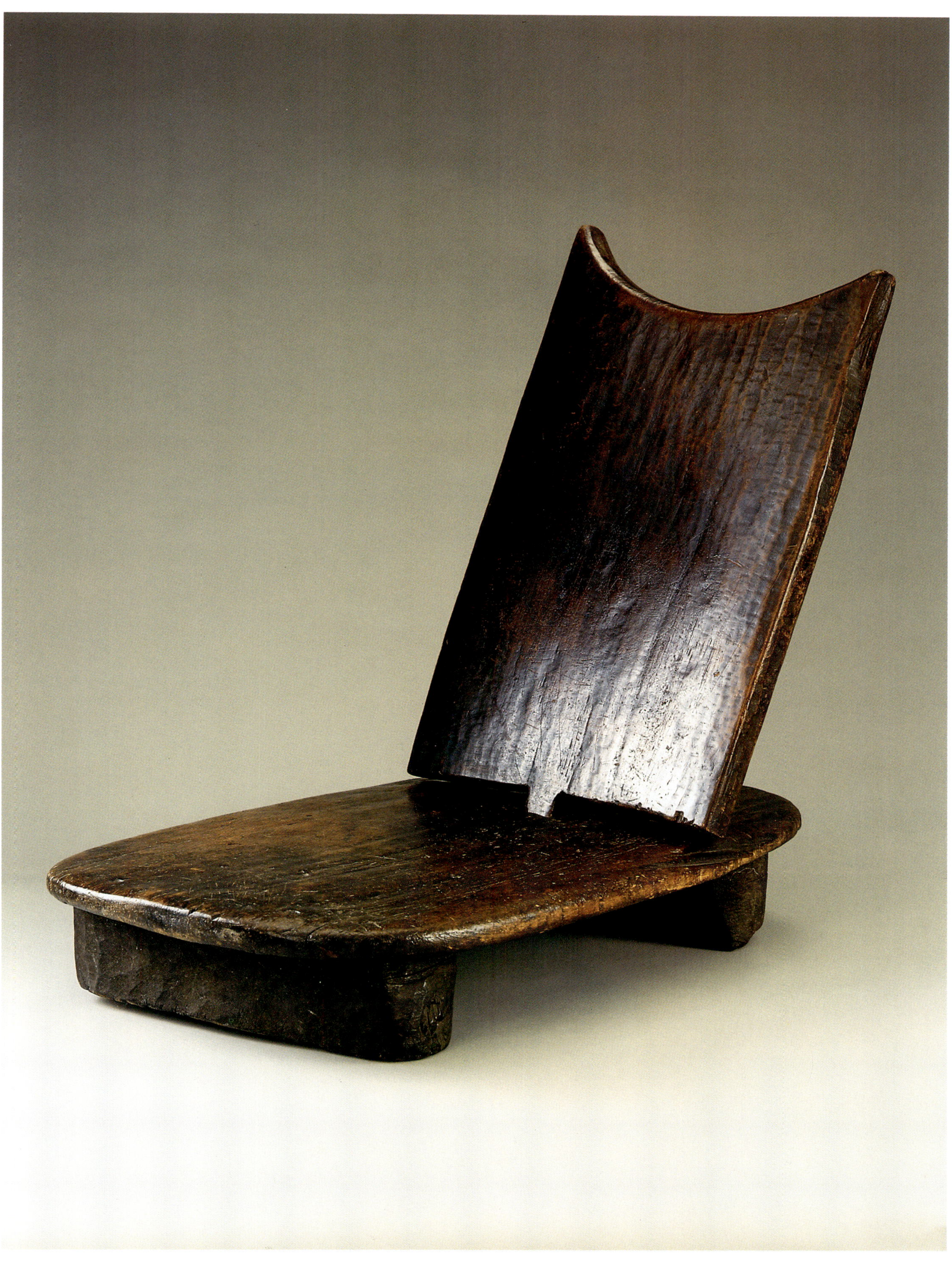

Semi-reclining chair from Ethiopia, height 76 cm Cat. 141

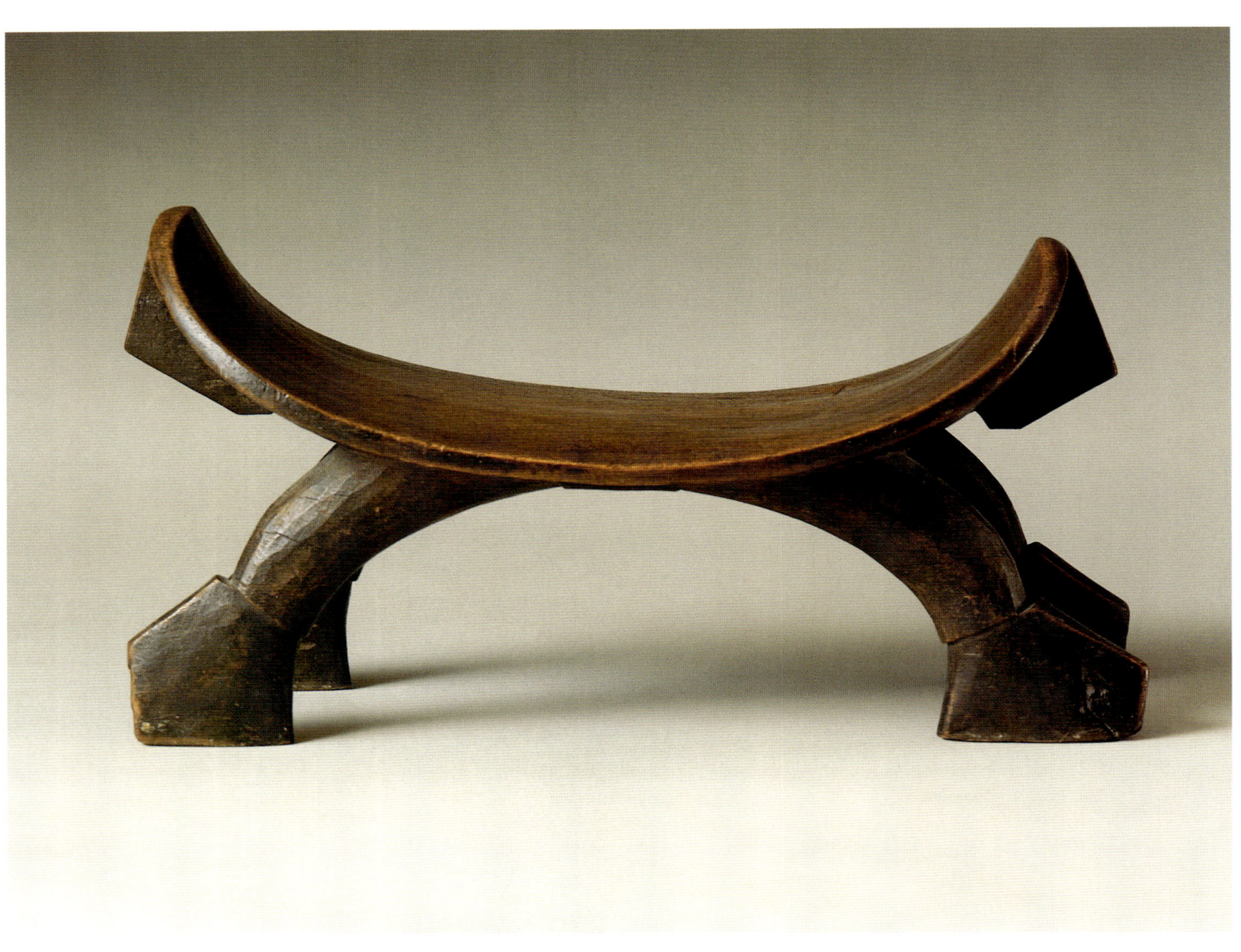

Stool of the Bongo, Sudan, width 47 cm Cat. 139

Catalogue

Unless otherwise indicated, di-mensions are given in the ord[er] height, width, depth. Where [only] two dimensions are given, the[y] are in the order: height, widt[h]

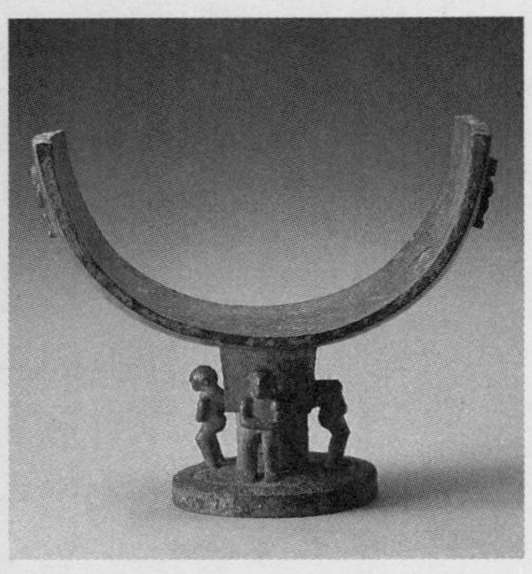

1 King's stool
Bidjogo, Guinea-Bissau
Wood, 39.5 x 46.5 x 21.4 cm
Museum für Völkerkunde, Berlin
Inv. III C 45047
Plate on p. 68

The king, the priestess of the worldly chief, the chief drummer, and all other important elderly persons each possessed a carved stool as a token of their rank, on which they would sit at assemblies. (cf. Duquette 1983, p. 67.)

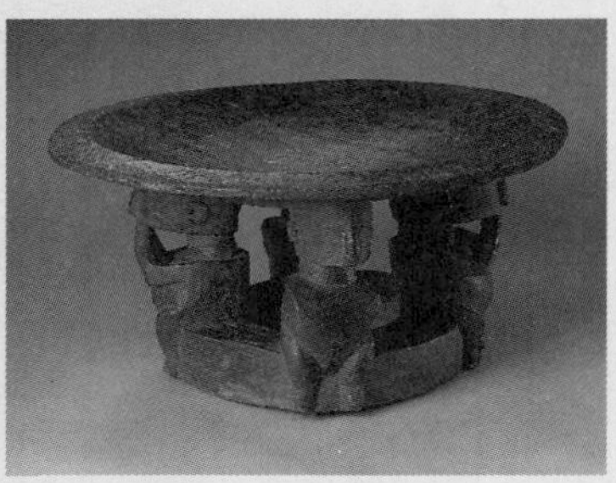

2 Stool
Baga, Guinea
Wood, height 32, diam. 63.5 cm
Musée Barbier-Mueller, Geneva
Inv. 1001-26

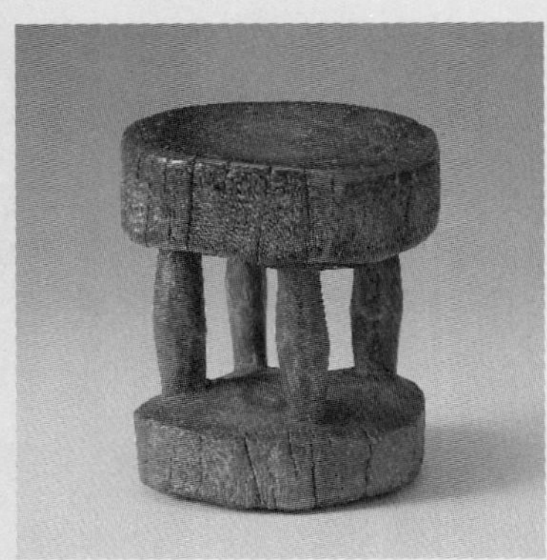

3 Stool
Guinea (Youkounkoun)
Wood, height 27.2, diam. 20 cm
Africa Museum, Tervuren
Inv. 69.59.145
Plate on p. 56

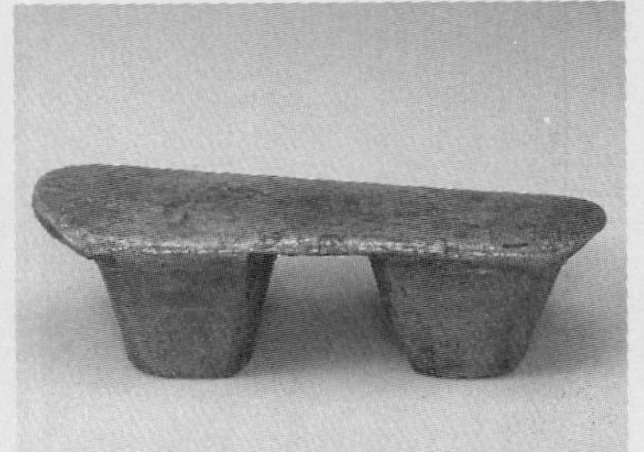

4 Stool
Guerze, Guinea (Macenta)
Wood, 6.8 x 26.6 x 10.7 cm
Africa Museum, Tervuren
Inv. 69.59.130
Plate on p. 57

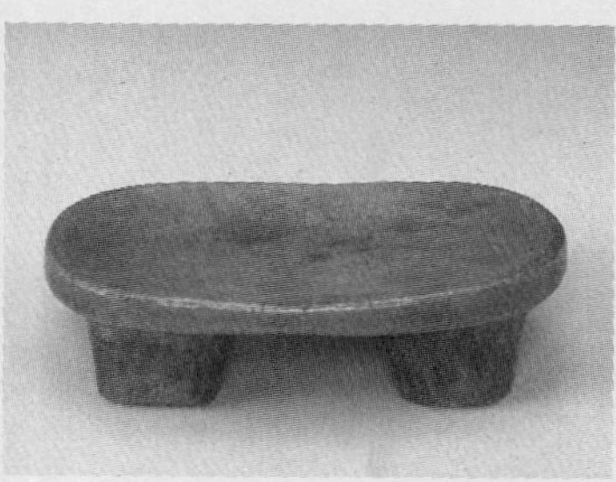

5 Stool
Guerze, Guinea (Looma)
Wood, 7 x 28 x 18 cm
Africa Museum, Tervuren
Inv. 69.59.122, acquired in 1934
Plate on p. 57

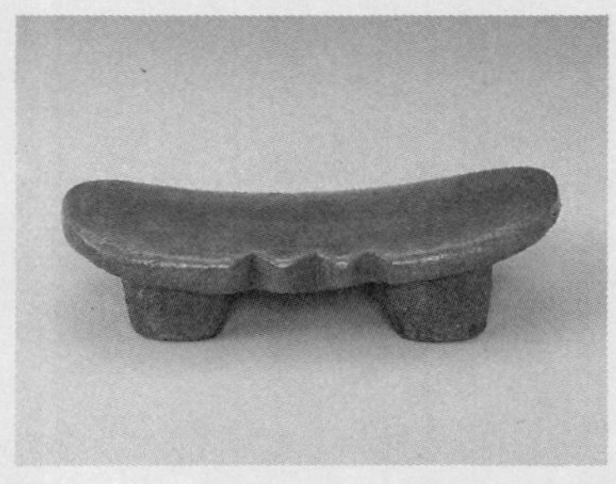

6 Stool
Guerze, Guinea (Looma)
Wood, 8 x 31.1 x 13.5 cm
Africa Museum, Tervuren
Inv. 69.59.128
Plate on p. 57

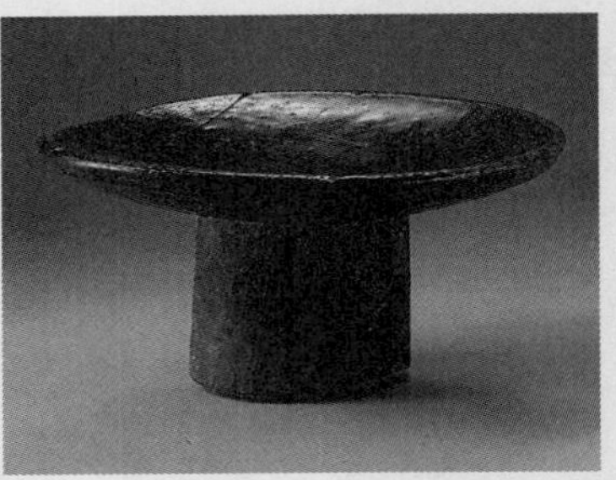

7 Wedding stool
Malinke, Guinea (Kouroussa)
Wood, 20 x 39 x 36 cm
Private collection, Zurich

Malinke women possessed many stools that their menfolk were also allowed to use. None the less, each woman, on her marriage, received a special stool from her husband: she alone used it during the wedding ceremonies. It then became her personal possession and no one else was allowed to sit on it. (Information kindly supplied by Mme Maine-Durieu, Paris.)

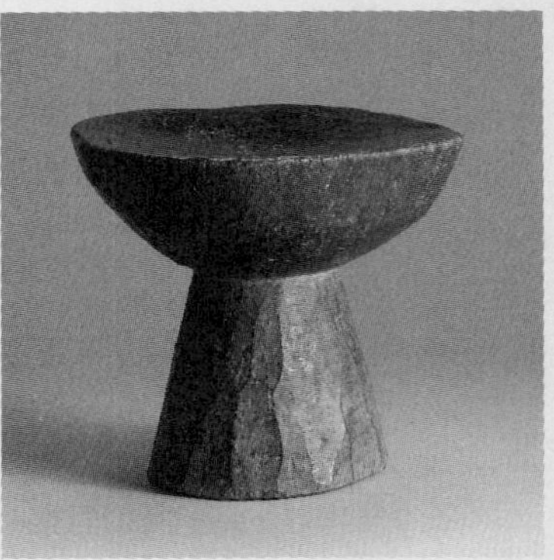

8 Wedding stool
Malinke, Guinea (Kouroussa)
Wood, height 30, diam. 33 cm
Private collection, Zurich
Plate on p. 55

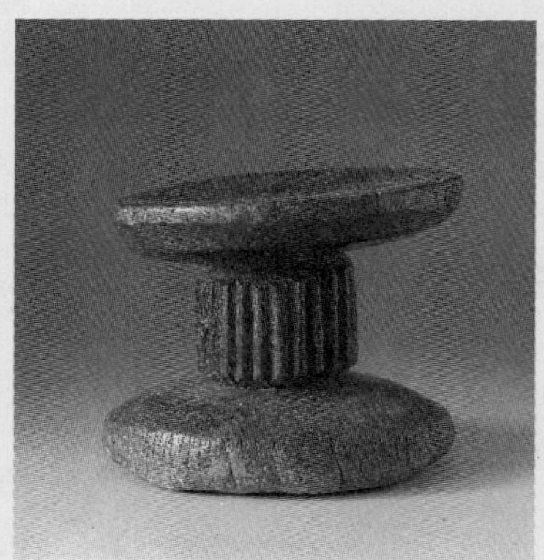

9 Stool
Malinke, Guinea (Kouroussa)
Wood, 21 x 24 x 24 cm
Private collection, Zurich
Plate on p. 55

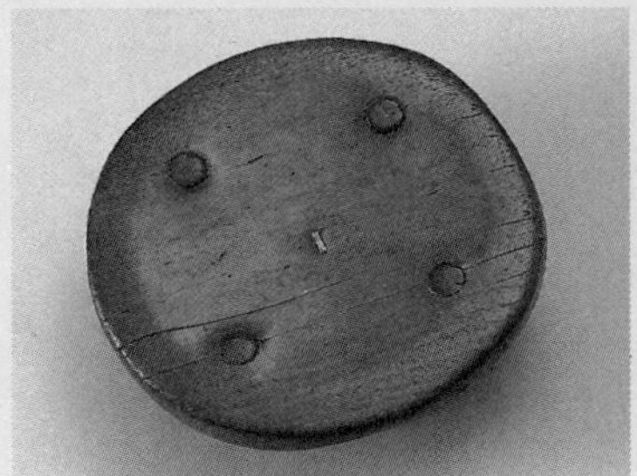

10 Stool
Malinke, Guinea (Koukou)
Wood, height 9, diam. 22 cm
Private collection, Zurich

This stool consists of a seating surface into which are inserted the upper ends of four legs. It is therefore one of the very rare examples of a stool for everyday use that was not monoxylous – that is to say, carved from a single block of wood.

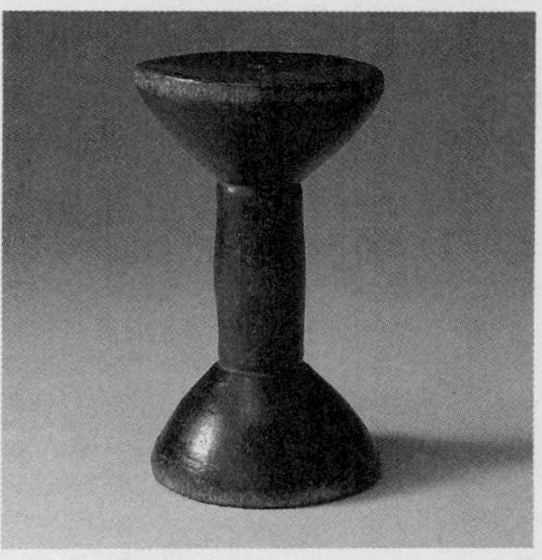

11 Stool
Dan (Yacuba), Ivory Coast (Man-Danane)
Wood, height 27.5, diam. 15.5 cm
Africa Museum, Tervuren
Inv. 69.59.165, acquired in 1934
Plate on p. 58

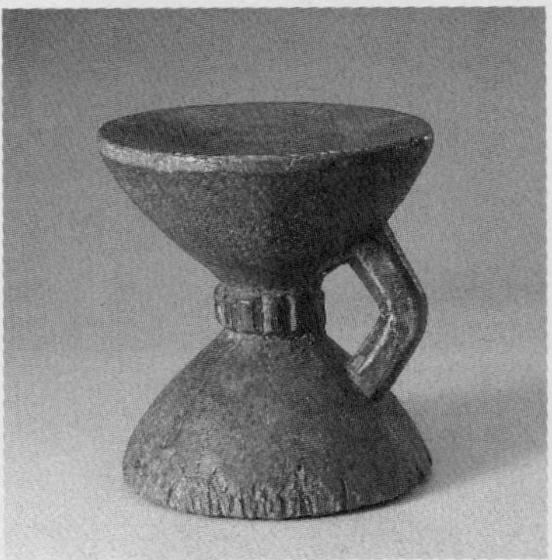

12 Stool
Dogon, Mali
Wood, height 26.5, diam. 25 cm
Collection of Sandro Bocola, Zurich
Plate on p. 55

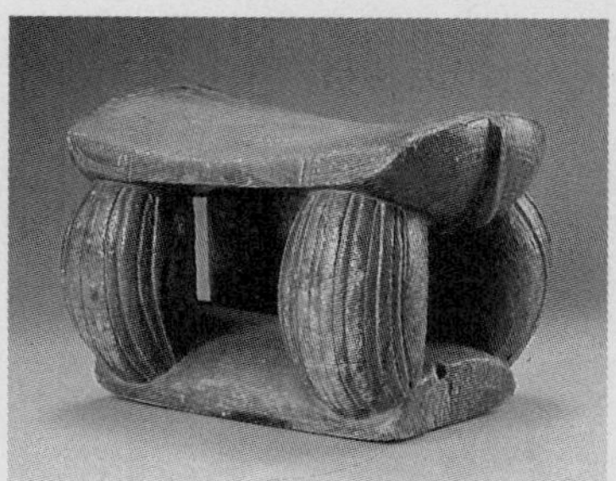

13 Stool
Gere/We, Liberia
Wood, width 45 cm
Musée Barbier-Mueller, Geneva
Inv. 1003-25
Plate on p. 69

This sort of stool was used during female circumcision by the person carrying out the operation.
(cf. P. Harter, in: Barbier 1992, p. 84.)

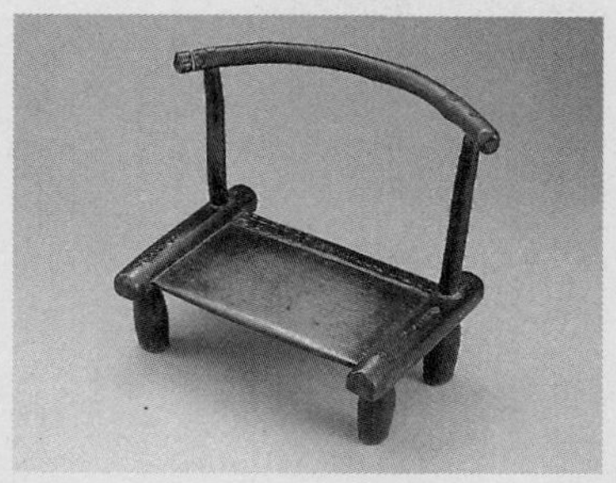

14 Chair
Dan, Ivory Coast (Man)
Wood, brass tacks, 35 x 40 x 23 cm
Private collection, Zurich

Small, multi-part chairs are found among the Guro, the Gere, the Baule and the Dan. In the case of the Gere, we know that these small chairs played an important part in the rituals accompanying female circumcision. The girls would borrow them from their grandfathers and perform a dance with them.
(cf. Himmelheber 1965, p. 539; also the present volume, pp. 42–3)

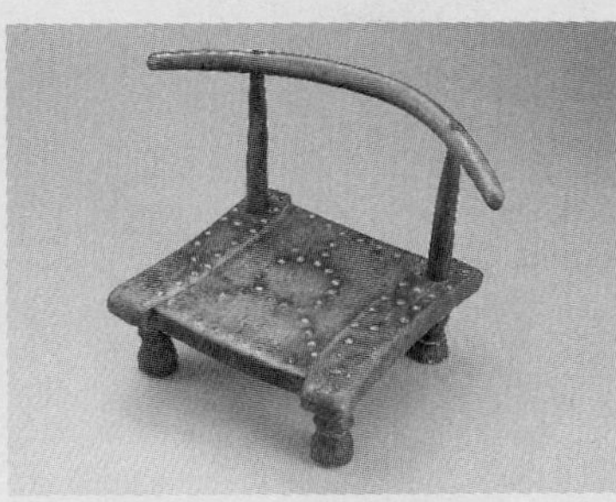

15 Chair
Dan, Ivory Coast (Man)
Wood, brass tacks, 30 x 41 x 28.5 cm
Private collection, Zurich
Plate on p. 73

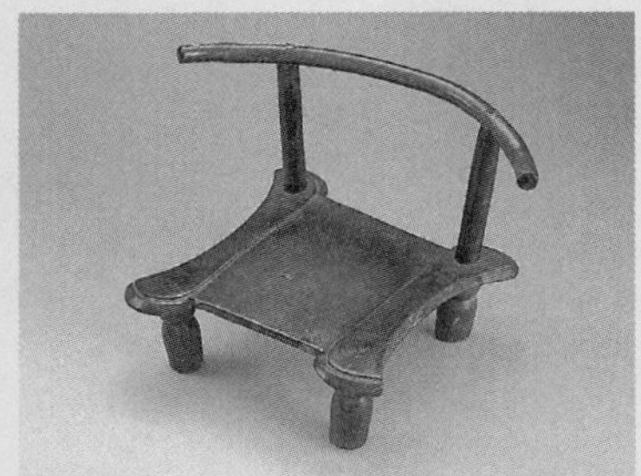

16 Chair
Dan, Ivory Coast (Man)
Wood, 31 x 42 x 32 cm
Private collection, Zurich
Plate on p. 73

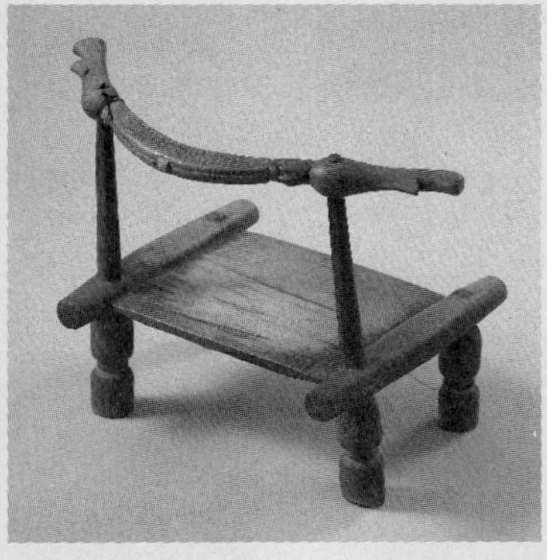

17 Chair
Guro, Ivory Coast (Duizra)
Wood, 53 x 68 x 44 cm
Private collection, Zurich
Plate on p. 71

'The small chairs of the Guro, which are up to sixty centimetres in height, consist almost always of eight individual parts. . . The wooden horizontal bar forming the back, bent into a smooth curve when newly cut, and then dried under pressure, is the most attractive part of the chair. . . . These small chairs are usually part of the household effects of a distinguished family. They are regarded as private property and may belong to older people, men and women. One has to ask the owner's permission if one wishes to sit on such a chair. Some individuals, however, have "sacred chairs", which only their owners may use.' (Fischer and Homberger 1985, p. 293.)

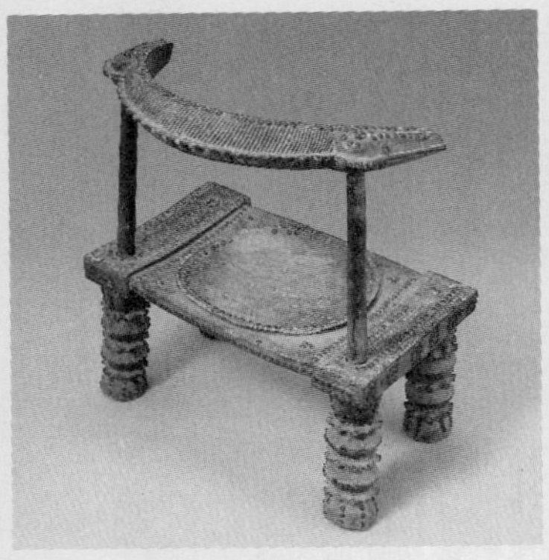

18 Chair
Baule, Ivory Coast
Wood, brass tacks,
61.5 x 52 x 31.5 cm
Private collection, Munich
Plate on p. 72

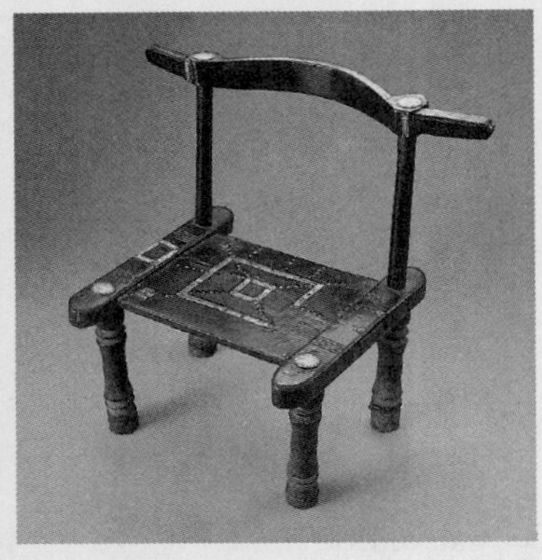

19 Chair
Toma, Guinea
Wood, aluminium, 53 x 55 x 35 cm
Private collection, Zurich

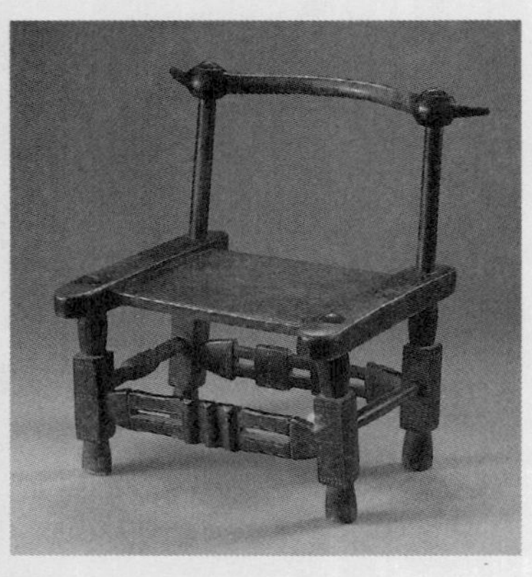

20 Chair of a notability
Malinke, Guinea
Wood, 57.5 x 45 x 43 cm
R. & D. David, Kilchberg

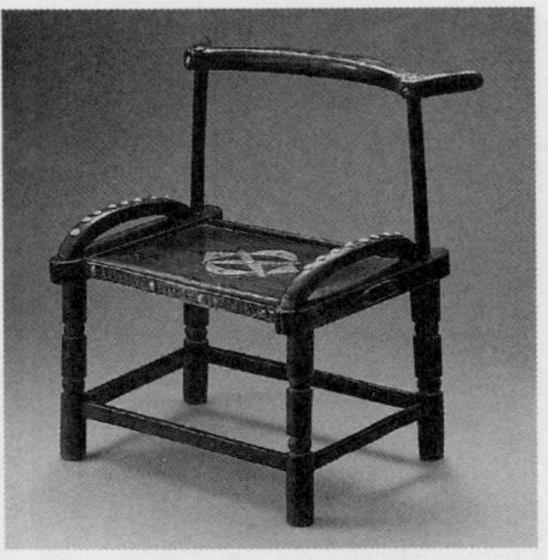

21 Chair
Malinke, Guinea
Wood, aluminium, 60 x 54 x 43 cm
Ghysels Collection, Brussels

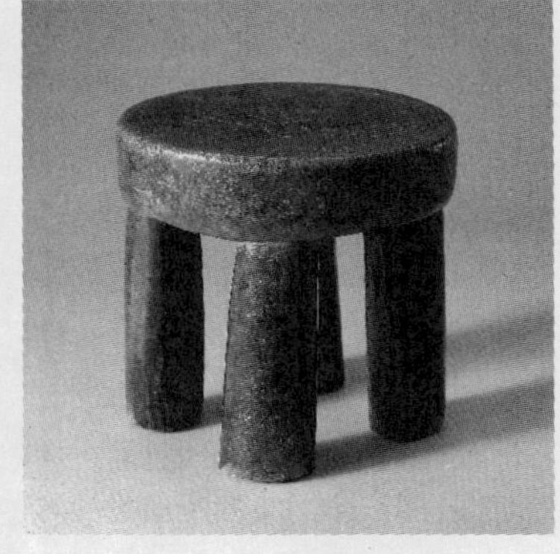

22 Stool
Senufo, Ivory Coast
Wood, height 22, diam. 22 cm
Collection of Sandro Bocola, Zurich
Plate on p. 55

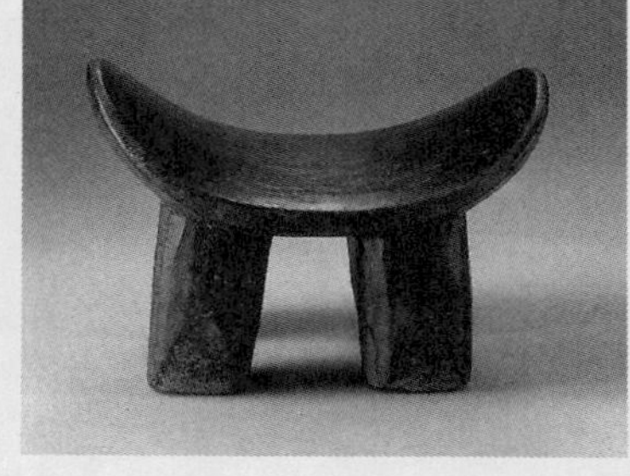

23 Stool
Senufo, Ivory Coast (Korhogo)
Wood, 22 x 32 x 22.5 cm
Collection of Sandro Bocola, Zurich
Plate on p. 61

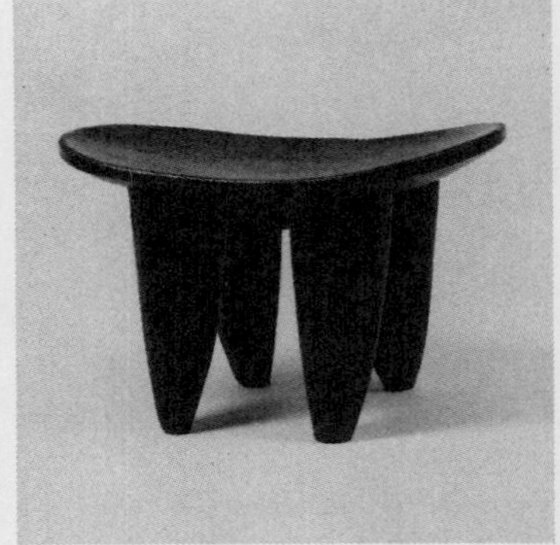

24 Stool
Senufo, Ivory Coast
Wood, 45 x 68 x 45 cm
Vitra Design Museum, Weil am Rhein

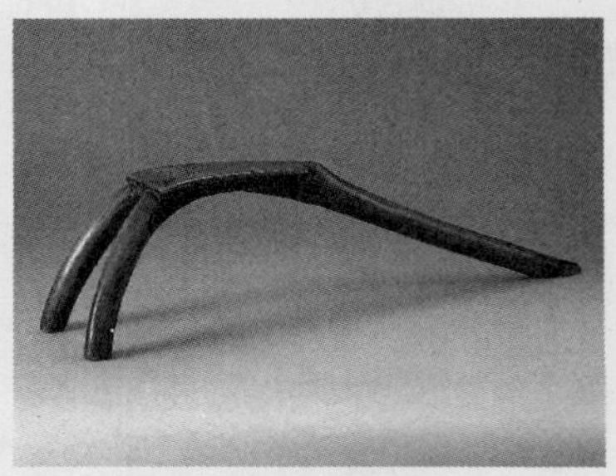

25 Stool
Lobi, Ivory Coast
Wood, height 19 cm
Private collection, Basle
Plate on p. 59

Every man of the Lobi who had undergone initiation is said to have possessed one of these stools. When approached by older people, he would beat on the ground with the stool as a sign of respect. A Lobi would carry his three-legged stool on his left shoulder when travelling. In an emergency such a relatively unstable form of seating could be used as a weapon. (cf. Meyer 1981, p. 121; Sieber 1980, p. 87.)

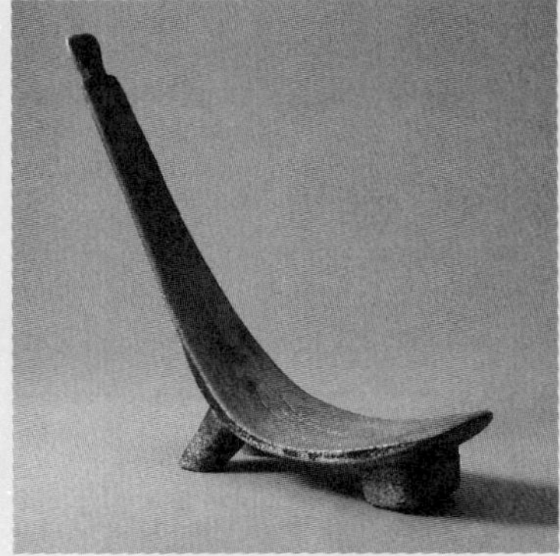

26 Semi-reclining chair
Lobi, Ivory Coast
Wood, 59 x 17 x 80 cm
Private collection, Zurich
Plate on p. 54

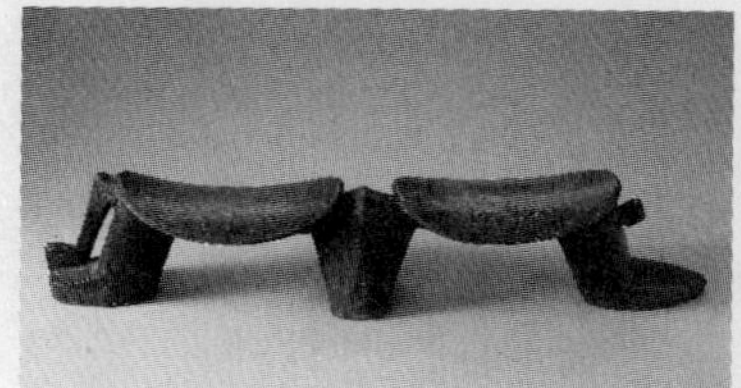

27 Double stool
Gurunsi, Burkina Faso
Wood, 20.3 x 101.8 x 21.4 cm
Africa Museum, Tervuren
Inv. 77.52.1, acquired in 1934
Plate on p. 59

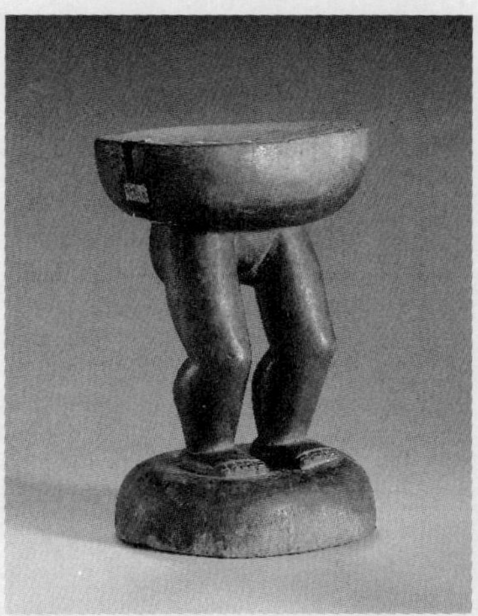

28 Stool
Dan, Ivory Coast
Wood, height 30, diam. 20 cm
Africa Museum, Tervuren
Inv. 67.63.1746
Plate on p. 60

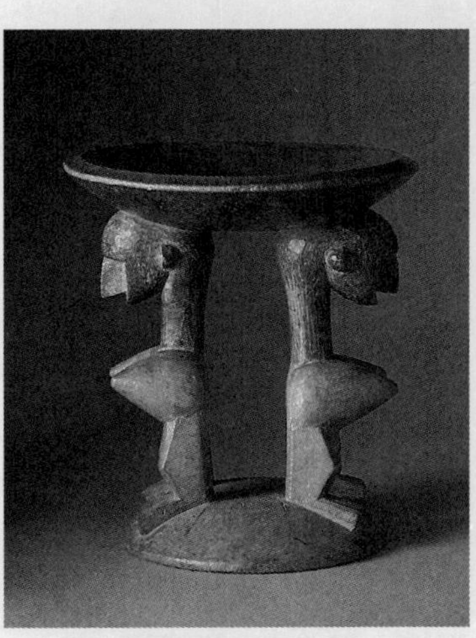

29 Caryatid stool
Bambara, Mali
Wood, height 41 cm
Musée Barbier-Mueller, Geneva
Inv. 1004-40

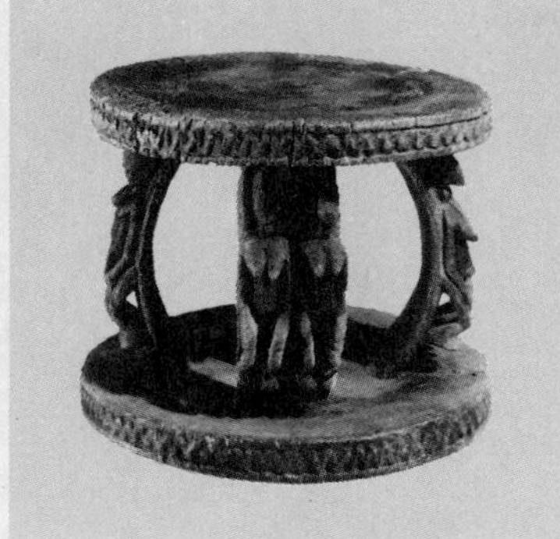

30 Ritual seat with four pairs of figures
Dogon, Mali
Wood, height 28 cm
Kofler-Erni Collection, Riehen, acquired 1946 in Paris

Small wooden stools serve the Dogon for everyday use. In some cases, the seating surface is supported by four figures, or pairs of figures representing ancestors (*nommo*). Such stools used to be symbols of the authority of the priests (*hogons*) – who had great political influence within the society – and were apparently never used as seats. The seating surface and the base were understood to represent, respectively, heaven and earth, and to be linked by a tree, the *axis mundi*, represented by the column at the centre. Each motif in the design of such stools is suggestive of the rich mythology of the Dogon. (cf. Ezra 1988, p. 98; Imperato 1978, p. 28; Laude 1973, fig. 35.)

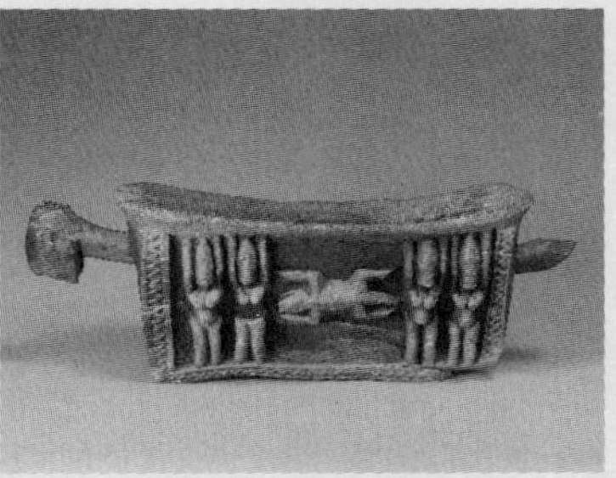

31 Ritual seat
Dogon, Mali (Douentza-Hombori)
Wood, 24.5 x 67 cm
Museum Rietberg, Zurich
Inv. RAF 256
Plate on p. 67

'The figures in relief below the seating surface, representing worshipping female figures, retain a tense relation to the horizontally positioned lizard, an animal viewed as the protector of the village. This seat, elevated to the rank of an instrument of ritual, is used during initiation ceremonies.' (Leuzinger 1978, p. 44.)

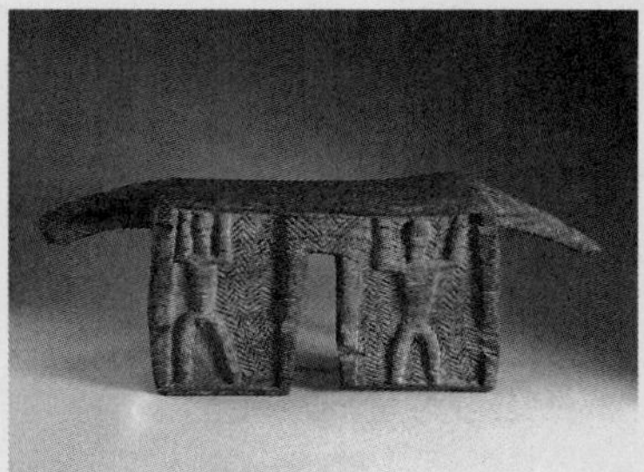

32 Ritual seat
Dogon, Mali
Wood, 43 x 115 x 24 cm
Musée Barbier-Mueller, Geneva
Inv. 1004-96, acquired before 1942

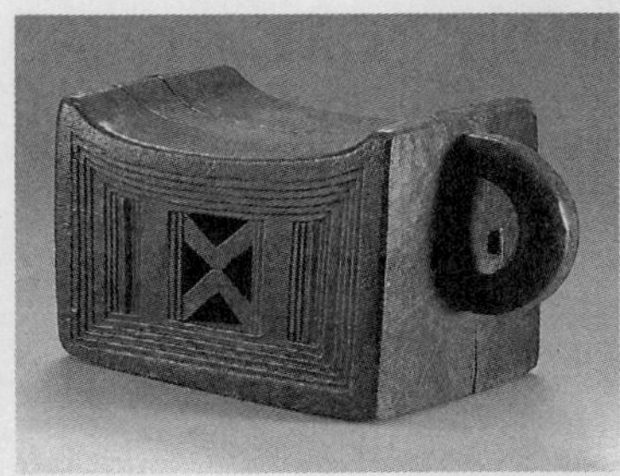

33 Stool
Baule, Ivory Coast (Bouaké)
Wood, 24 x 42 x 22.5 cm
Private collection, Zurich

The Baule use various sorts of seats. One of these is a solid bench without legs, carved out of a single rectangular block of wood. On one side a handle is carved into the body of the stool so that it can be picked up and carried. This sort of seat was not intended for general everyday use, but was reserved for the use of the oldest in the community, for the heads of families and for important chiefs. A chief's *umele* might be blackened after his death as was usual in the case of the seats of the Asante in Ghana. (cf. Timothy F. Garrard, in: Barbier 1992, p. 140)

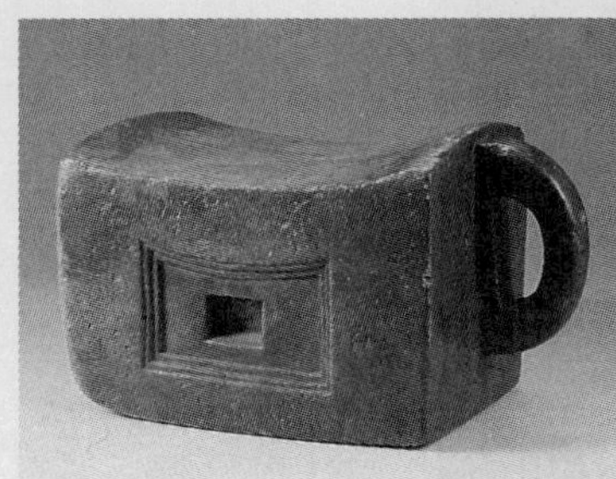

34 Stool
Baule, Ivory Coast (Central-East Region)
Wood, 25 x 42 x 23.5 cm
Collection of Sandro Bocola, Zurich
Plate on p. 69

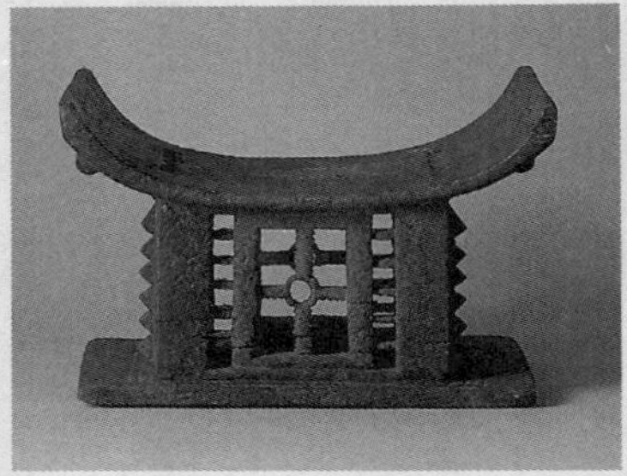

35 Stool
Asante, Ghana (Kumasi)
Wood, 27.5 x 41 x 29.5 cm
British Museum, London
Inv. AF 1896, 0511.6, acquired in 1896
Plate on p. 79

Now, as in the past, stools have a spiritual significance as well as a purely practical use. The stool was understood to be the seat of its owner's soul. When not in use it was therefore placed at a slant against a wall so that none of the souls passing by could settle on it. The Asante say that there are no secrets between a man and his stool. Each member of Asante society possessed a stool. Such stools were each carved out of a single piece of light wood. If a king died a natural death during his own reign, one of his stools was blackened and would, in future, be regarded as an ancestral seat. Sacrifices would then be made to it.

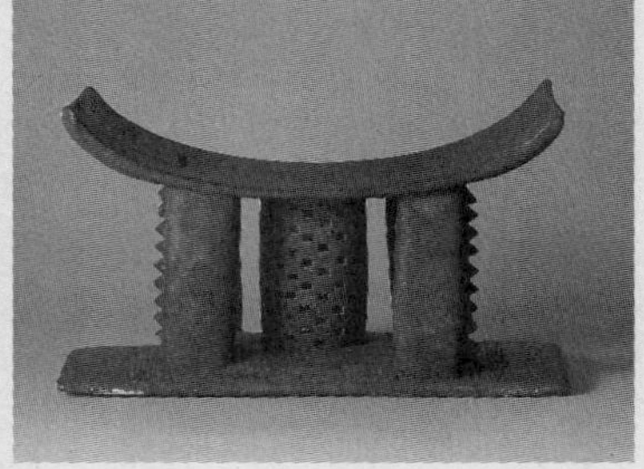

36 Stool
Asante, Ghana (Kumasi)
Wood, 27.5 x 46 x 24 cm
British Museum, London
Inv. AF 1896, 0511.7, acquired in 1896
Plate on p. 79

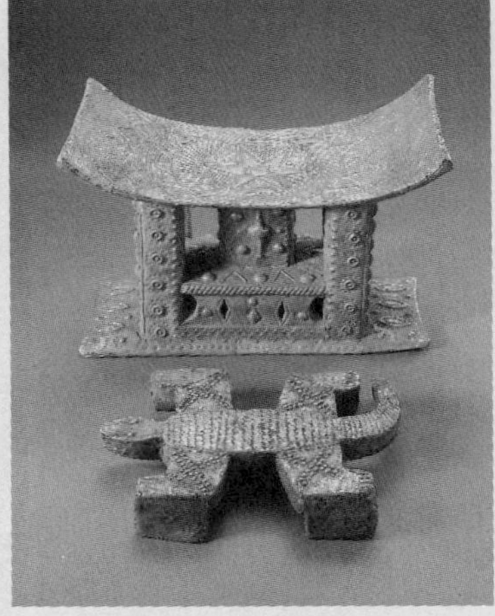

37 Stool and footrest
Asante, Ghana
Wood, brass; stool: 46 x 65.5 x 37 cm; footrest: height 9, width 59 cm
R. & D. David, Kilchberg
Plate on p. 75

As soon as a king had been appointed (in the local language, 'placed on his chair'), he was no longer allowed to touch the ground. This meant that he could no longer sit on the ground and that he had to wear sandals. Direct contact with the ground signified a form of pollution and would have invoked unfortunate consequences for the society as a whole, in the form of illness and famine. If a king was dethroned, this change of status was signified by removing his sandals and placing him on the ground.

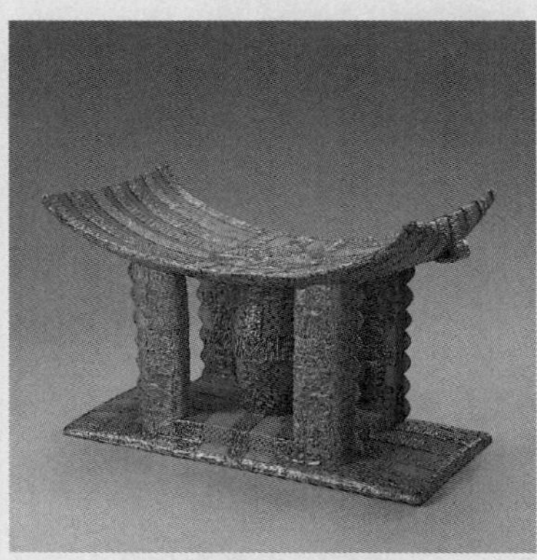

38 Stool
Asante, Ghana
Wood, silver, 48.3 x 68.5 x 42 cm
R. & D. Kilchberg

Objects decorated with chiselled silver plates were reserved for the most exalted queen mother (of the Asantehene's family) and only a few honoured dignitaries.

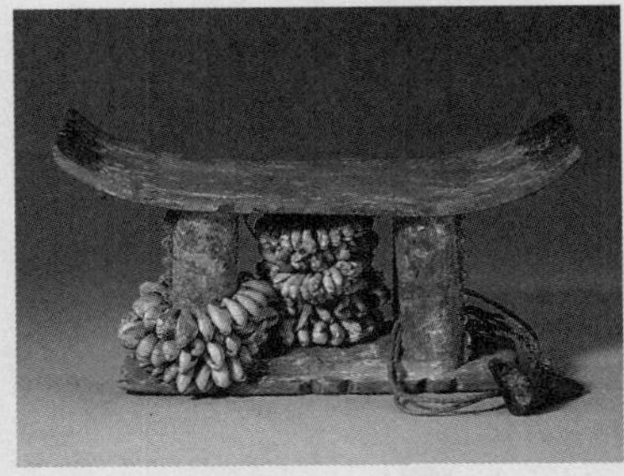

39 Stool with patina left by sacrifices
Kuwe, Togo
Wood, cowrie shells, leather cord, horn, plant fibres, 16.5 x 32.5 x 13 cm
Staatliches Museum für Völkerkunde, Munich
Inv. 15-8-30, acquired in 1915

'A stool with the patina left by sacrifices, intended for use in ritual. The cowrie shells strung on leather laces and the piece of horn may themselves be regarded as offerings.' (Information kindly supplied by Maria Kecskési, Munich.)

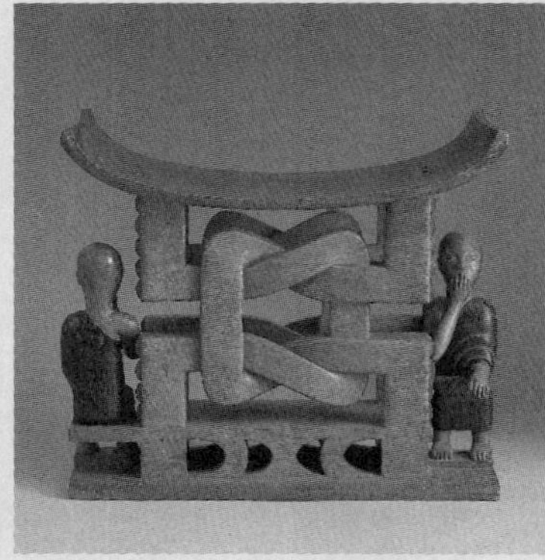

40 Stool
Asante, Ghana
Wood, 53.5 x 59.5 cm
R. & D. David, Kilchberg
Plate on p. 82

On the central section of this stool there are to be found incised symbols; these may be verbalized in the form of traditional sayings. In daily, as in political, life, such sayings were keenly employed. This is a wisdom knot stool (*nyansapow dwa*) and signifies: only the wise man can untie the wisdom knot. The king concerned wanted, by this means, to show his subjects that he sought to rule through wisdom and not through force. (cf. Kyerematen 1964, p. 24; 1969, p. 9.)

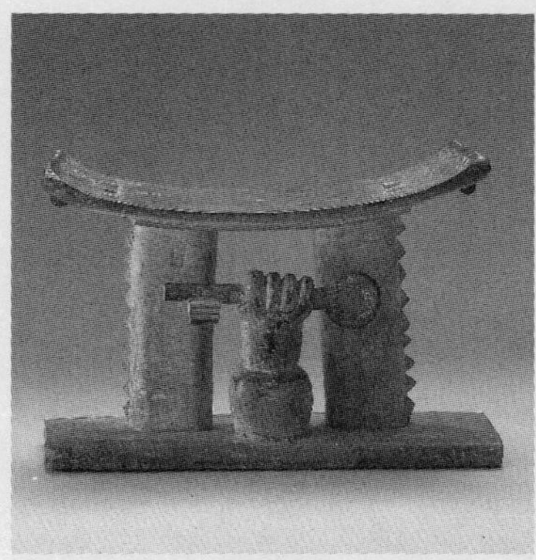

41 Stool
Asante, Ghana
Wood, 32 x 46.5 cm
Galerie Walu, Zurich
Plate on p. 82

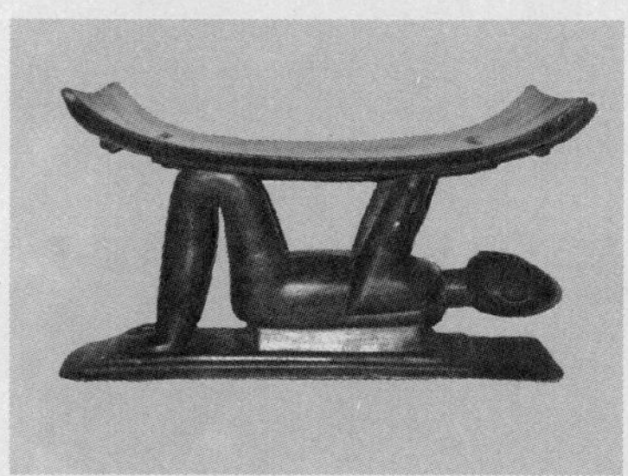

42 Stool
Asante, Ghana
Wood, 34 x 56 x 25.5 cm
R. & D. David, Kilchberg

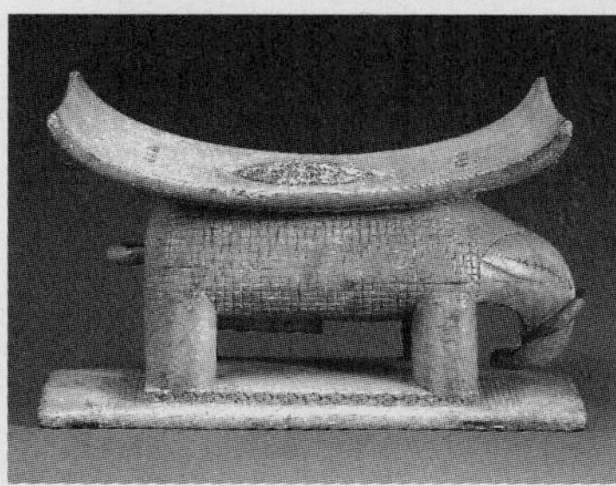

43 Stool with an elephant
Asante, Ghana
Wood, brass (silver alloy), 32.9 x 54.7 x 27.5 cm
Africa Museum, Tervuren
Inv. 76.38.112
Plate on p. 78

The elephant indicates the king's power and authority. In the past only the Asantehene was permitted to use a stool with its seating surface supported by the figure of an elephant. Only certain kings (*omanhene*) and the queen mother on the Asantehene's side were allowed to use silver in any form.

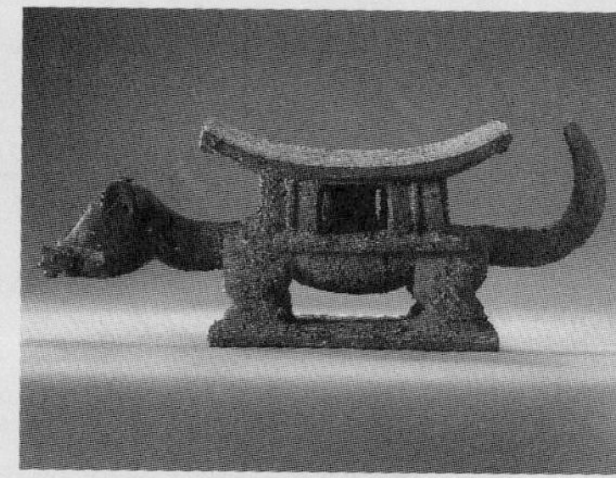

44 Stool with figure of an animal
Baule, Ivory Coast
Wood, 26 x 63 x 23.5 cm
Museum für Völkerkunde, Berlin
Inv. III C 44916
Plate on p. 81

In the last hundred years Asante stools have been imitated beyond the borders of Asante territory, and variations on them have appeared among neighbouring peoples. The stool illustrated here has a form typical of an Asante seat: that is to say, with the seating surface placed on the back of an animal. Should we see this as the utmost symbol of power?

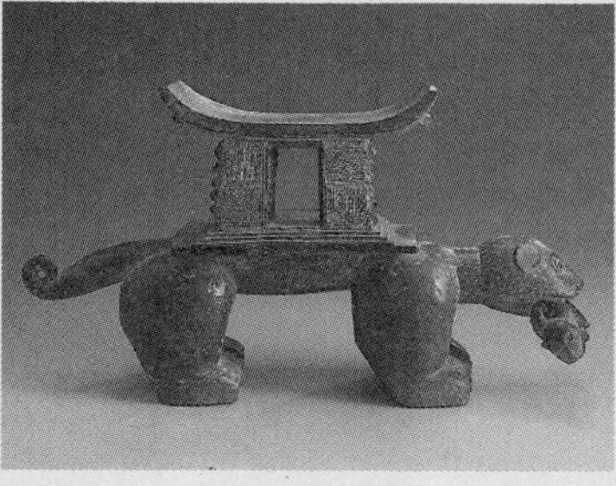

45 *Ulimbi bia* stool
Baule, Ivory Coast
Wood, width 73.5 cm
Musée Barbier-Mueller, Geneva
Inv. 1007-187
Plate on p. 80

This royal seat symbolizes the highest power: a panther with a small ram between its teeth.

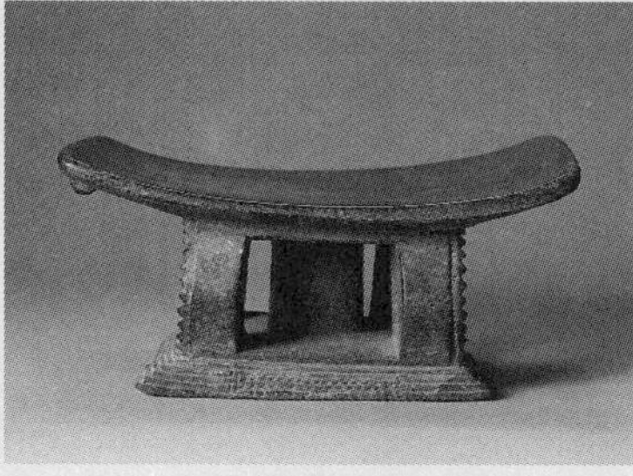

46 Stool
Yohure, Ivory Coast
Wood, 16.5 x 25 x 36 cm
Private collection, Zurich

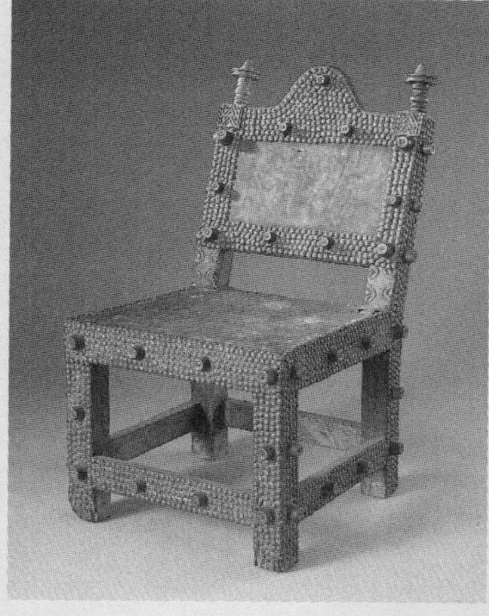

47 *Asipim* chair
Asante, Ghana
Wood, leather, brass tacks, height 68 cm
Musée Barbier-Mueller, Geneva
Inv. 1009-9
Plate on p. 76

The *asipim* is a chair with no arms and a slightly inclined back. The wood has not been stained, nor has the leather seat-covering. The word *asipim* signifies: I stand firm. This is the most widespread sort of chair. Each local king possesses one or more of this type. It is reserved for the use of the ruling élite at the most important assemblies and debates. Its form is based on European styles of the seventeenth and eighteenth centuries.

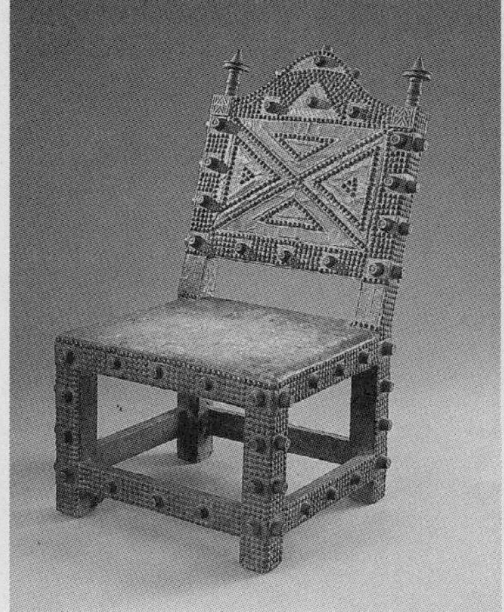

48 *Asipim* chair
Asante, Ghana
Wood, brass, leather, height 76.8 cm
Musée Barbier-Mueller, Geneva
Inv. 1009-30

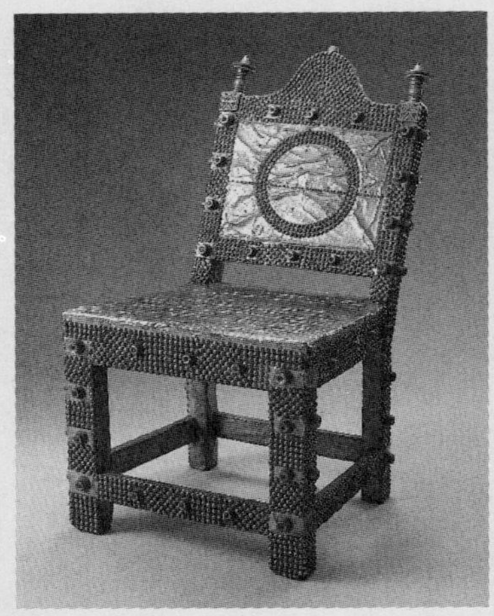

49 *Asipim* chair
Asante, Ghana
Wood, brass, 88 x 46.5 x 43 cm
Galerie Walu, Zurich
Plate on p. 76

With this *asipim*, both the seating surface and the back are completely covered in brass and not, as is usually the case, in leather.

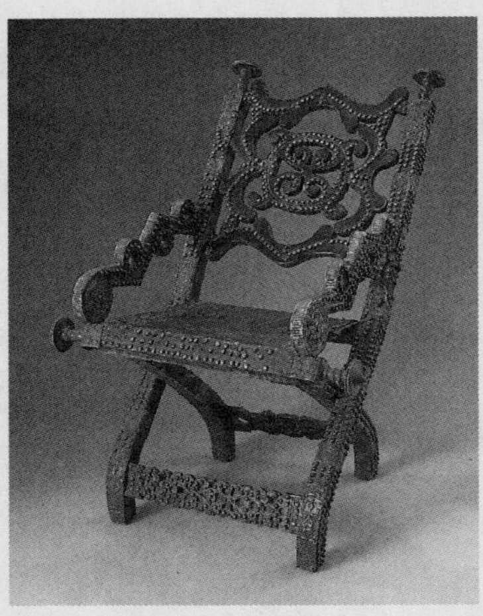

50 *Akonkromfi* chair
Asante, Ghana
Wood, leather, brass tacks, height 91.8 cm
Musée Barbier-Mueller, Geneva
Inv. 1009-134

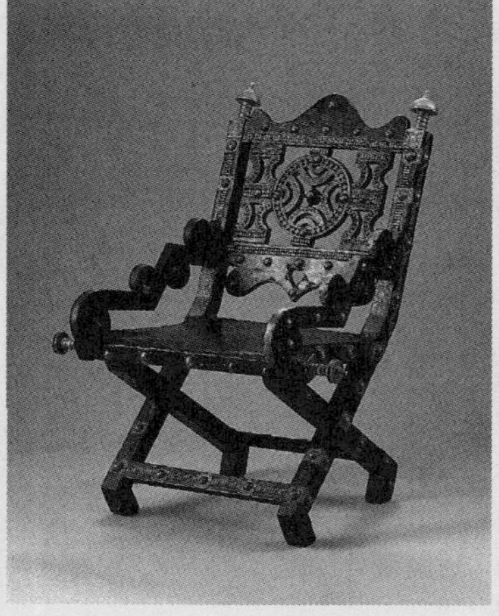

51 *Akonkromfi* chair
Asante, Ghana
Wood, brass, leather, height 87, depth 81 cm
Galerie Walu, Zurich
Plate on p. 77

The *akonkromfi* has the form of a folding chair; seen from the side, its legs form a cross. Such seats are assembled using various techniques of joining. They are generally decorated with brass tacks and metal parts. The back is carved in a perforated pattern and often recalls the form of European coats of arms. Folding chairs with coats of arms were very popular in Europe in the seventeenth century and are seen as models for the *akonkromfi*. This word means 'praying mantis', perhaps referring to the articulated nature of this insect. The *akonkromfi* was used predominantly for festive occasions and ceremonials at the royal court. (cf. Cole and Ross 1977, p. 142.)

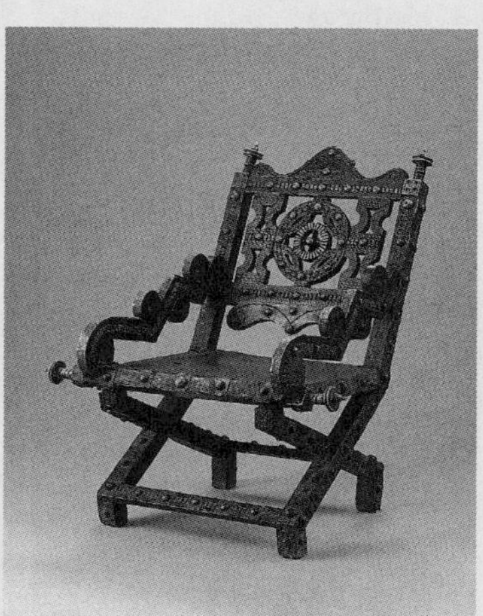

52 *Akonkromfi* chair
Asante, Ghana
Wood, brass, leather, height 97, depth 76.5 cm
Galerie Walu, Zurich

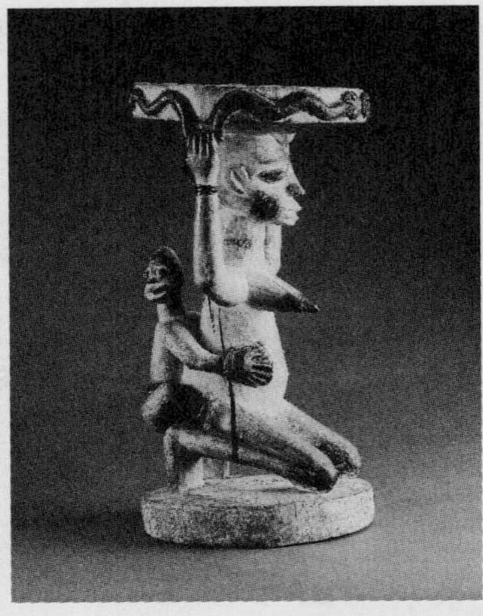

53 Caryatid stool
Yoruba (?), Benin
Wood, height 52, diam. 26 cm
Musée National des Arts Africains et Océaniens, Paris
Inv. 66-22-1, acquired in 1913–17
Plate on p. 64

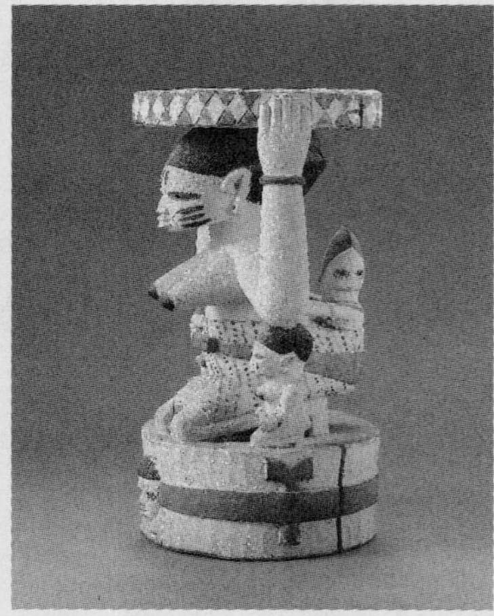

54 Caryatid stool
Nago, Benin
Wood, height 60, diam. 32 cm
Collection of Dr Michael Storrer, Zurich
Plate on p. 63

The form of this Nago stool corresponds to the typical Yoruba style: protruding eyes, the infant carried on the woman's back looking sideways, and painted wood. The Nago live very near to the Yoruba and have been influenced artistically by them.

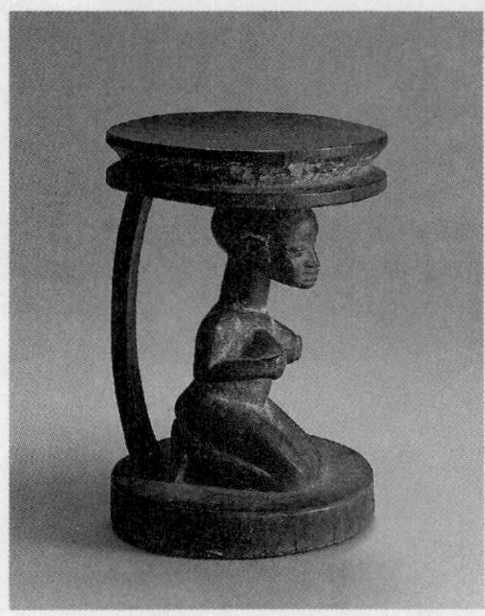

55 Caryatid stool
Yoruba, Nigeria
Wood, height 32, diam. 21 cm
Linden-Museum, Stuttgart
Inv. L 2738; F 51.622
Plate on p. 62

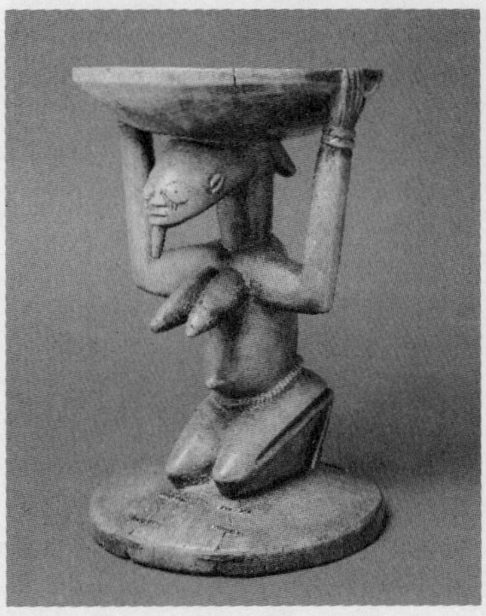

56 Caryatid stool
Yoruba, Nigeria (Owu)
Wood, height 46.7 cm
Collection of Gaston T. de Havenon, New York
Plate on p. 65

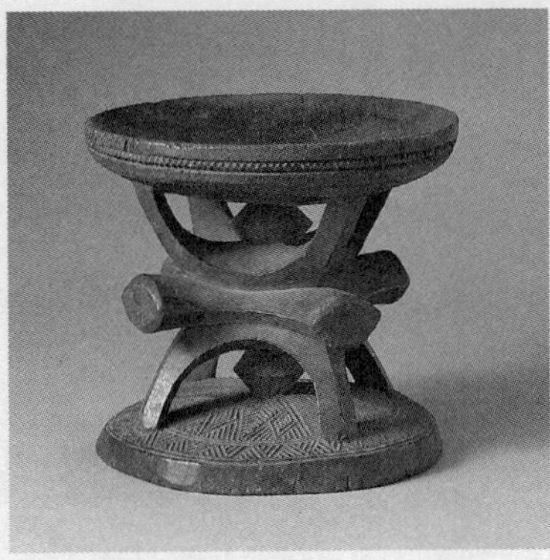

57 Stool
Nupe, Nigeria
Wood, height 28.8 cm
Musée Barbier-Mueller, Geneva
Inv. 1014-86

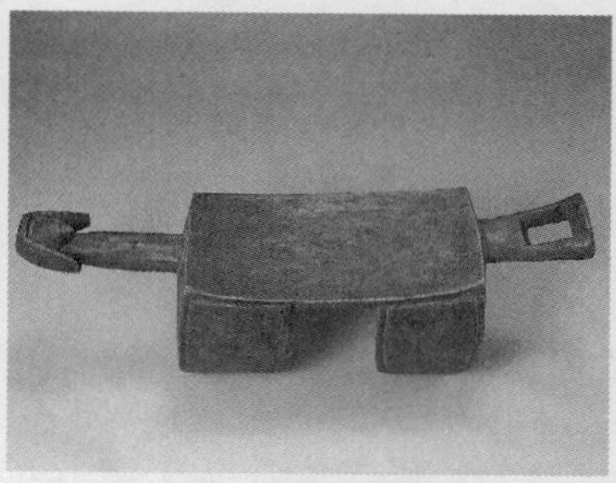

58 Stool
Mumuye, Nigeria
Wood, 22 x 86 cm
Musée Barbier-Mueller, Geneva
Inv. 1015-67

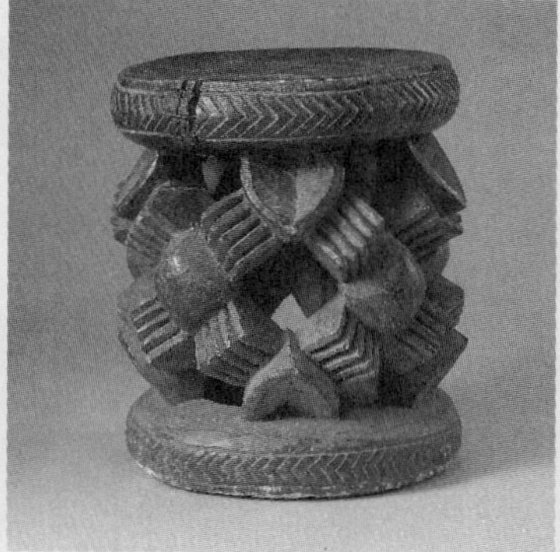

59 Stool
Bamileke, Cameroon
Wood, height 37 cm
Musée Barbier-Mueller, Geneva
Inv. 1018-67
Plate on p. 93

In the Cameroon grasslands the spider is a symbol of wisdom, and it plays an important part in soothsaying. As an abstracted form, the motif of the spider is found on a number of objects, e. g. masks and stools. The spider, which lives in a hole in the ground, was seen to have an especially close relationship to the ancestors, who were also understood to live in a world below the earth. (cf. Geary 1981, p. 94.)

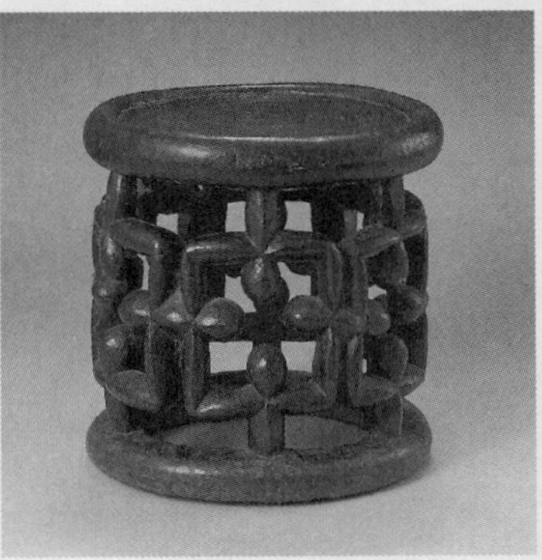

60 Stool
Cameroon
Wood, height 37 cm
Musée Barbier-Mueller, Geneva
Inv. 1018-51

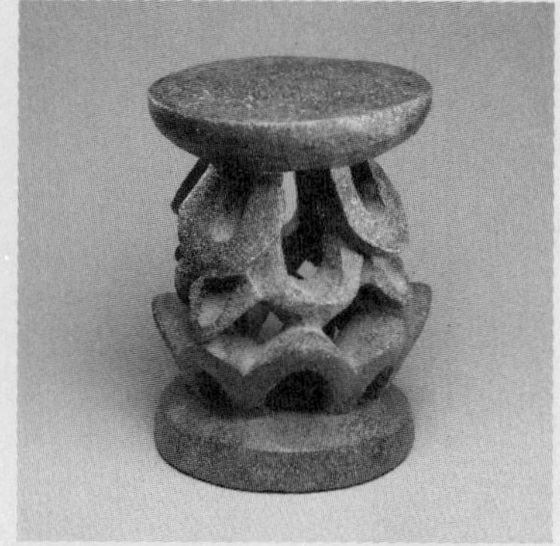

61 Stool
Cameroon
Wood, height 30, diam. 25 cm
Musée Barbier-Mueller, Geneva
Inv. 1018-50
Plate on p. 93

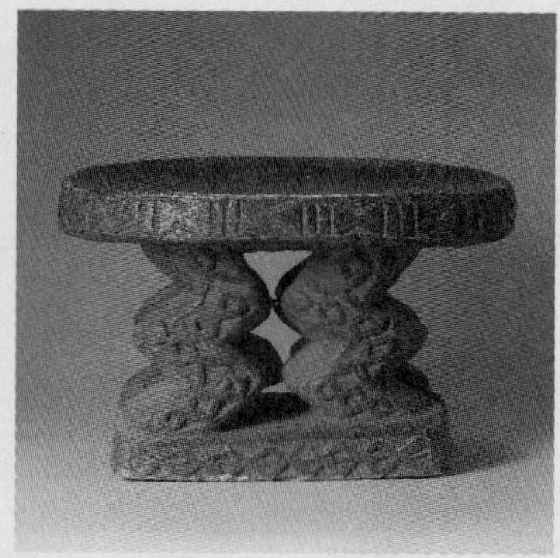

62 Stool
Bamileke, Cameroon
Wood, 34.5 x 49 x 41 cm
Private collection, Zurich
Plate on p. 104

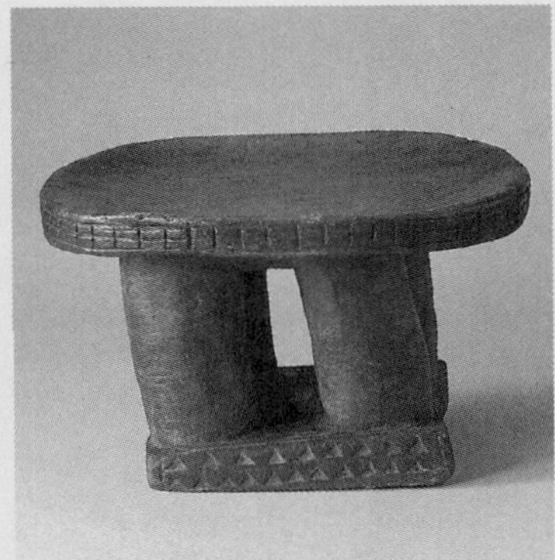

63 Stool
Bamileke, Cameroon
Wood, 31 x 52 x 44 cm
Collection of Sandro Bocola, Zurich

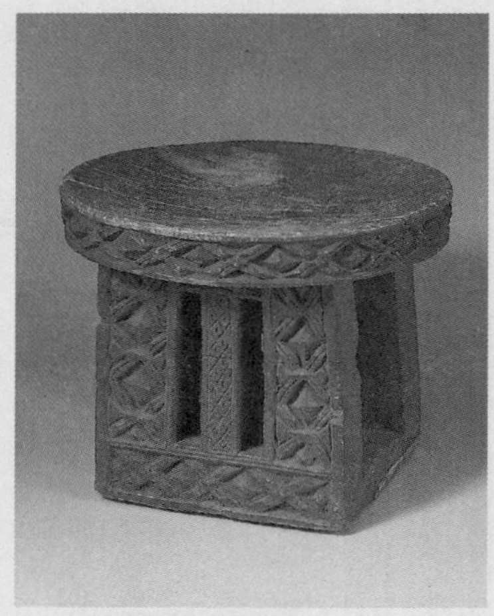

64 Stool
Tikar (Bamenda ?), Cameroon
Wood, height 44, diam. 52 cm
Staatliches Museum für Völkerkunde, Munich
Inv. 05.245, acquired in 1905

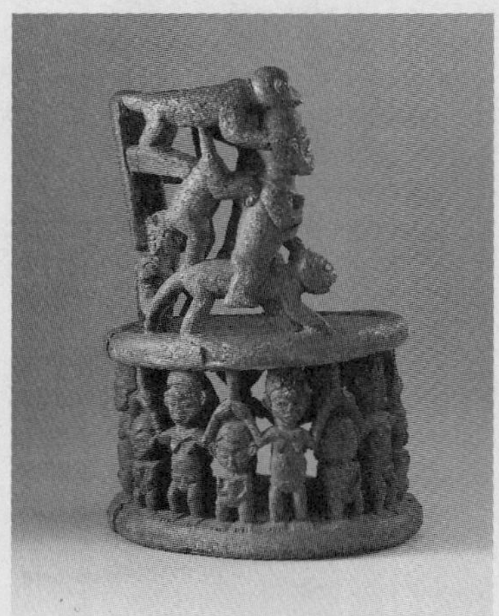

65 Chair
Babanki, Cameroon
Wood, 89 x 66 x 57 cm
British Museum, London
Inv. AF 1969, 13.1
Plate on p. 92

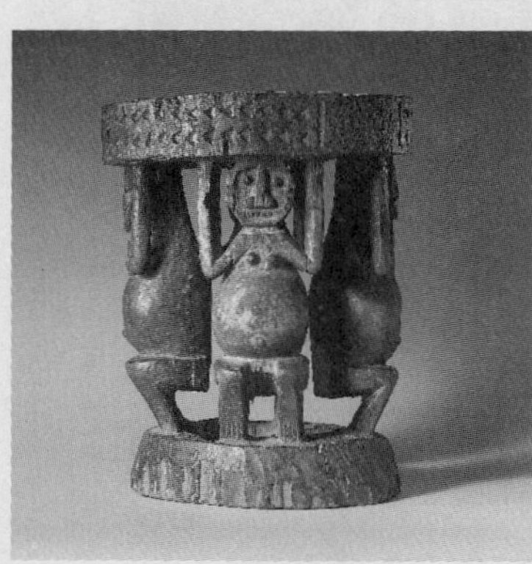

66 Caryatid chair
Bamileke, Cameroon
Wood, height 43.5, diam. 34 cm
Africa Museum, Tervuren
Inv. 76.38.161
Plate on p. 107

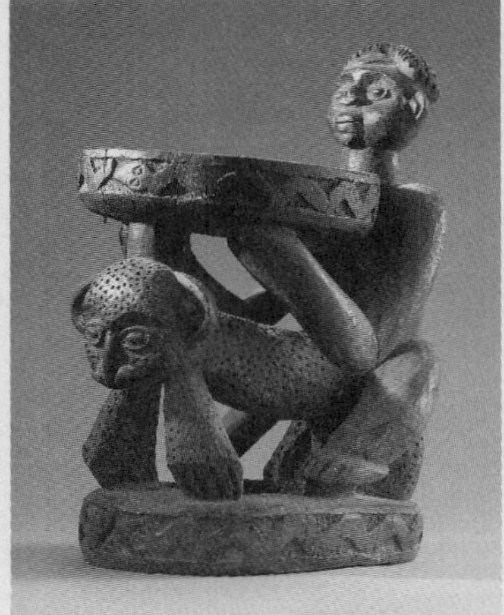

67 King's chair
Oku (?), Cameroon
Wood, with gleaming incrusted patina, height 54.5, diam. 49 cm
Musée Barbier-Mueller, Geneva
Inv. 1018-59
Plate on p. 105

'The figure of the king is wearing the sort of cap associated with royal ancestor figures. He is shown mounted on a leopard, an animal that signifies the ability to survive, expressed in a guarded aggressiveness, speed, cunning and mobility – qualities that are thus transferred to the king himself. The leopard therefore became one of the most important royal symbols, and could, indeed, even be regarded as the king's *alter ego*. Another important royal symbol, the snake, recurs in myths concerning the foundation of several kingdoms in the Cameroon grasslands, among them Oku.' (Tamara Northern, in: Schmalenbach 1988, p. 191.)

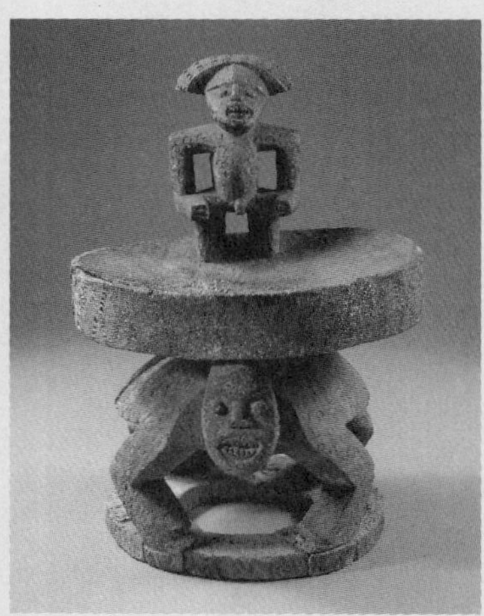

68 King's chair
Bamileke (Bana), Cameroon
Wood, height 65 cm
Städtisches Reiß-Museum, Mannheim
Inv. IV Af 7441, acquired in 1913
Plate on p. 106

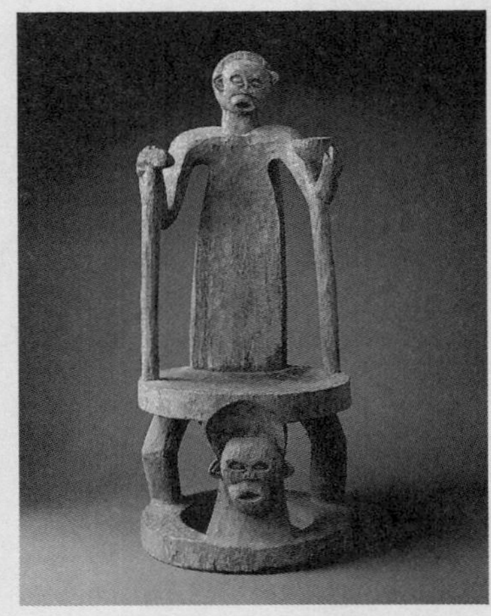

69 Chair
Cameroon grasslands, Cameroon
Wood, height 120 cm
Musée Barbier-Mueller, Geneva
Inv. 1018-47
Plate on p. 95

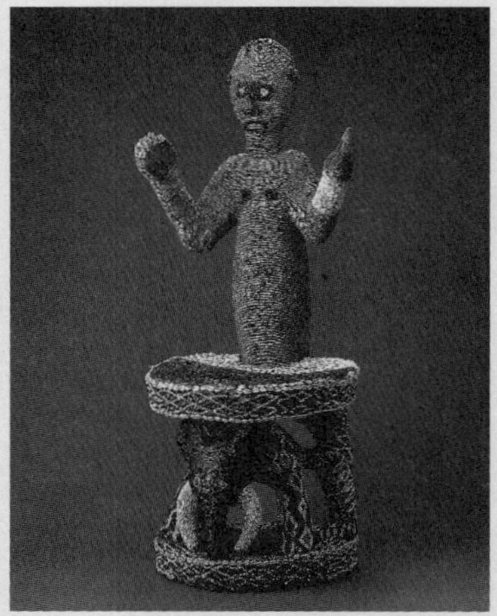

70 Chair of a notability
Cameroon grasslands, Cameroon (Bafusam)
Wood, beads, cowrie shells, textile, height 128, diam. 50 cm
Linden-Museum, Stuttgart
Inv. 43018, acquired in 1905
Plate on p. 103

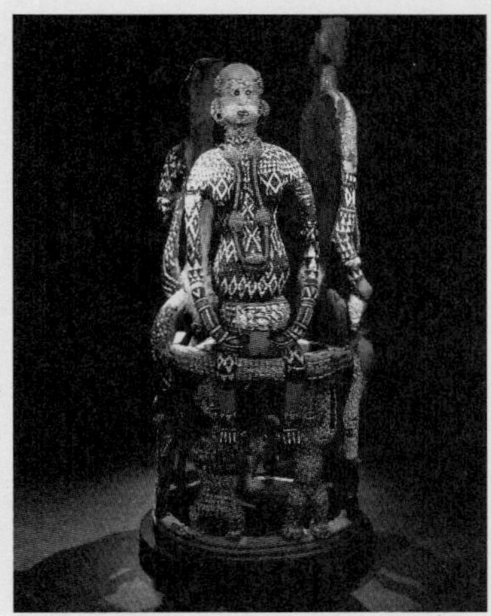

71, 72 King's stool with the representation of the *fon* Kamwa Mars and two queens
Baham, Cameroon
Wood, glass beads, cowrie shells, textile, 220 x 100 x 100 cm
Collection of Philippe Guimiot, Brussels
Plates on pp. 100, 101

A king and two queens are shown sitting on the throne, their legs hanging down, thus indicating that the king and the throne are inseparable. A throne would often be used to demonstrate a close connection with the king's ancestors and, in this respect, can substitute for an ancestor statue and so become a ritual object (information kindly supplied by Philippe Guimiot). This object was produced by the king's own appointed carver, Kwanu, and is seen as his masterpiece. In 1934 it was covered in glass beads and cowrie shells by a master of such beadwork, Kandep. Pierre Harter photographed the stool in situ in 1957.
(cf. Harter 1986, p. 287.)

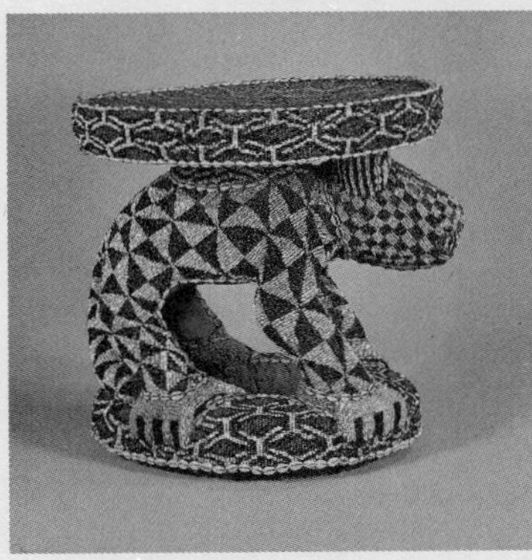

73 Leopard stool
Bamum, Cameroon
Wood, glass beads, jute, cowrie shells, height 54, diam. 55 cm
Städtisches Reiß-Museum, Mannheim
Inv. Af 8554, acquired in 1910

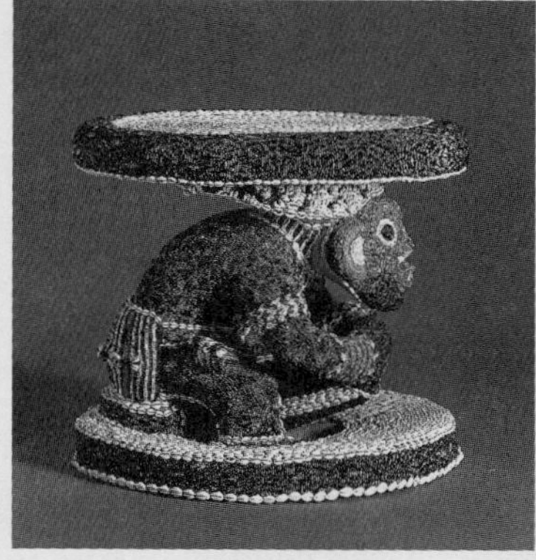

74 Stool of King Njoya
Bamum, Cameroon
Wood, glass beads, cowrie shells, height 60, diam. 64 cm
Museum für Völkerkunde, Berlin
Inv. III C 19141, acquired in 1905
Plate on p. 102

Presented by King Njoya to Kaiser Wilhelm II.

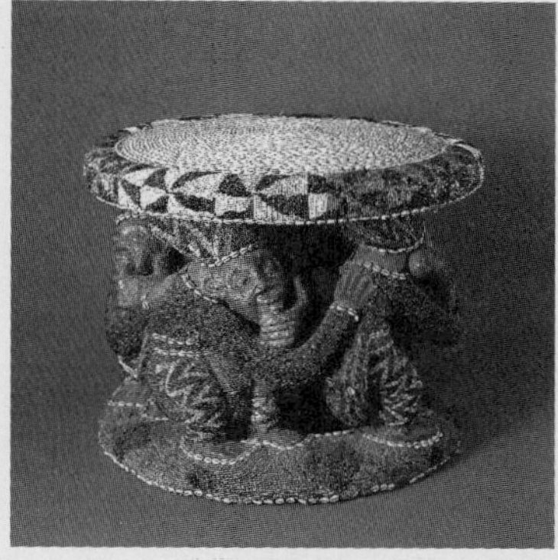

75 King's stool
Bamum, Cameroon
Wood, beads, cowrie shells, embossed copper, height 57, diam. 70 cm
Musée Barbier-Mueller, Geneva
Inv. 1018-73
Plate on p. 90

This royal 'travelling chair' was given by King Njoya to his friend Captain Glauning. The caryatid figures represent servants adopting a respectful pose, each with his right hand placed on the shoulder of the figure in front. The faces covered with copper plate and the beaded hoods recall the anthropomorphic masks that, in the past, would appear on particular occasions. The seating surface of this king's stool is covered with cowrie shells.
(cf. Pierre Harter, in: Schmalenbach 1988, p. 193.)

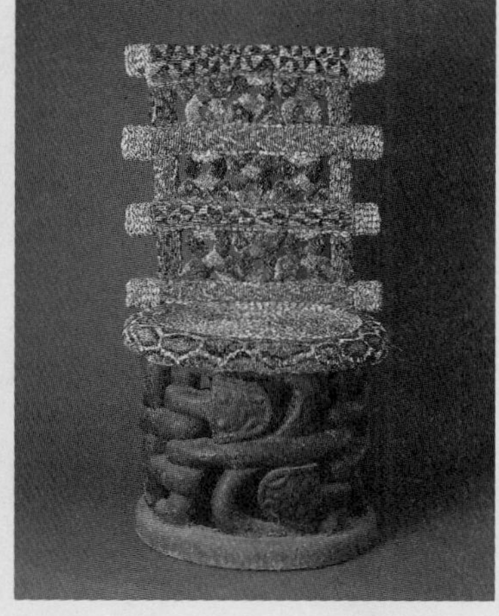

76 Chair
Bamum, Cameroon
Wood, beads, cowrie shells, embossed copper, height 119, diam. 62 cm
Musée Barbier-Mueller, Geneva
Inv. 1018-21
Plate on p. 91

This seat, carved out of a single block of wood, is covered with beads, cowrie shells and copper foil. The shape of the back recalls the traditional chair made of bamboo and raffia. The motif of the snake with two heads is a royal emblem. This sort of chair appears not to have been intended for the king, but rather to have been assigned to the second most important person in the Bamum kingdom – the queen mother. Chairs of this sort were produced during the reign of King Njoya.
(cf. Pierre Harter, in: Schmalenbach 1988, p. 192.)

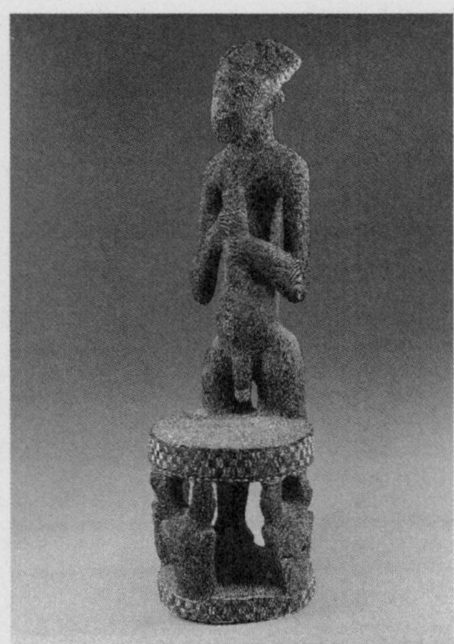

77 King's chair
Bamum, Cameroon
Wood, glass beads, cowrie shells, height 175, diam. 50 cm
Museum für Völkerkunde, Vienna
Plate on p. 97

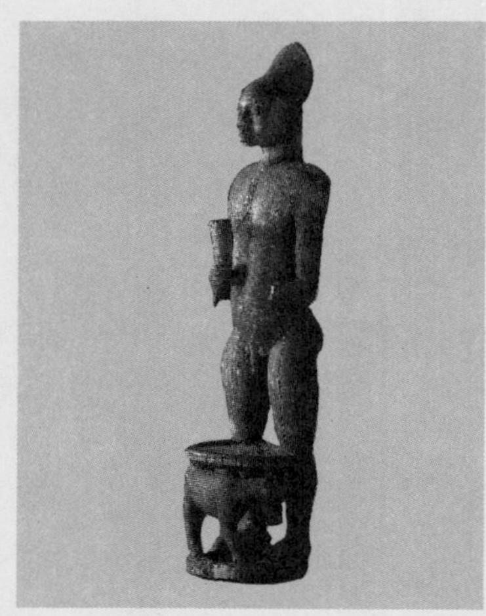

78 Chair with standing male figure
Kom, Cameroon
Wood, copper plate, 190 x 40 cm
Museum für Völkerkunde, Berlin
Inv. III C 20681, acquired in 1905
Plate on p. 99

The figure seen here is a king. The whole figure was once covered in beads in the manner of the stool in cat. 73. These seats were not used for sitting on, but only publicly displayed on special occasions. Figurative representations of this sort were not individual portraits; they presented, rather, idealized figures – of the king, his mother and his first wife, or the most important of his wives. This chair, along with other objects, was carried off to Europe by the German colonial forces after the sacking of the palace of Laikom in January 1905 (see photograph on p. 98). (cf. Hans-Joachim Koloß, in: Beumers and Koloß 1992, p. 301; Armand Duchâteau, in: Baum 1990, p. 172; Geary 1991, p. 38)

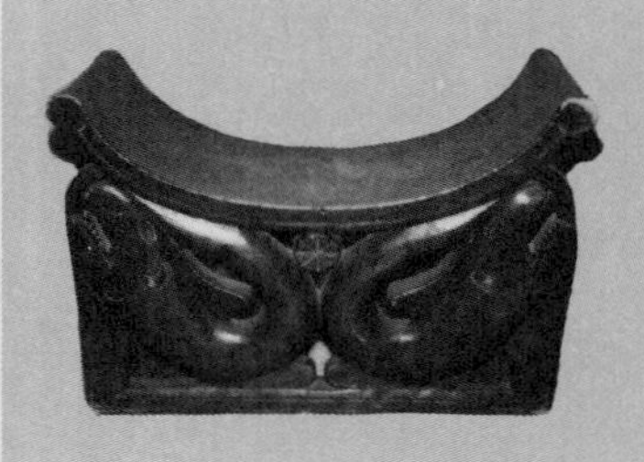

79 Stool
Duala, Cameroon
Wood, height 44 cm
Musée Barbier-Mueller, Geneva
Inv. 1018-70

Large stools of this kind are found in three regions of Western Africa: on the Arquipélago dos Bijagós; among the Akan on the Ivory Coast and in Ghana, and in what was formerly the kingdom of Dahomey; and among the Duala in Cameroon. Historical connections between the types of stools found in each of these locations have not been established. The prestige seats found among the Duala are unique in this part of Africa because the peoples of the south-western part of Cameroon had a segmentary system rather than a hierarchical one and did not recognize leaders with political or priestly power. The emergence of obvious leaders only became necessary after the first contacts with Europeans. By this means, the leading figure among the oldest men evolved into a sort of ruling chief. (cf. Sieber 1980, p. 128; Northern 1984, p. 178; Jack 1991, p. 16)

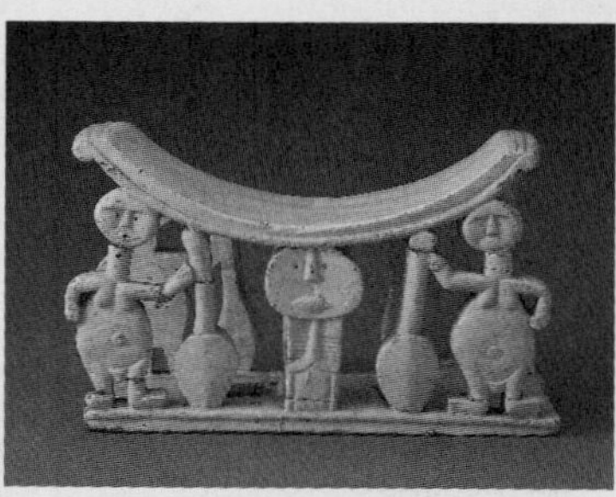

80 Stool
Duala, Cameroon
Wood, oil paint, 30 x 45 x 22.5 cm
Staatliches Museum für Völkerkunde, Munich
Inv. 73-1-115; plate on p. 83

'The use of stools of this sort was a privilege of the oldest in the community. The lacquer is atypical and, like the strengthening of the seat with a metal plate, appears to have been introduced after the stool had been in use for some time.' (Information kindly supplied by Maria Kecskési, Munich; cf. Ardener, 1956.)

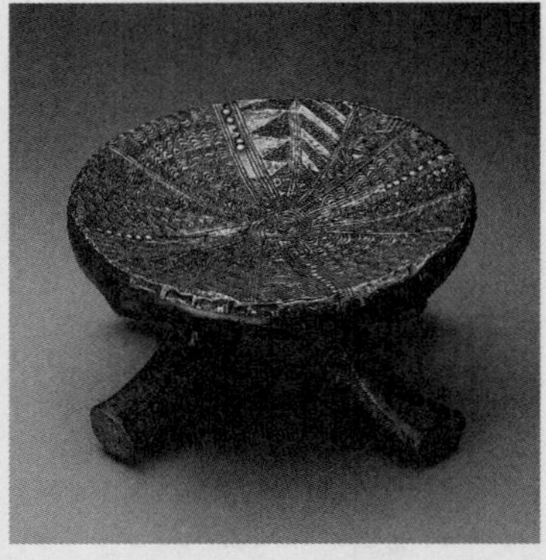

81 *Kwanga* stool
Kota, Gabon
Wood, embossed copper, nails, diam. 36 cm
Musée Barbier-Mueller, Geneva
Inv. 1019-54, acquired in 1941 in Paris

There are various forms of Kota stools. They are always carved out of a single block of wood. The most commonly used are stools of the form shown here: a circular, slightly depressed seating surface supported by four outward curving legs. This sort of stool was generally used by women. This particular example is an exception on account of its unusual, finely embossed copper decoration; it would certainly have been reserved for high dignitaries. The motifs used in the decoration clearly recall the form of those used in connection with ancestor figures. (cf. Perrois 1985, p. 188.)

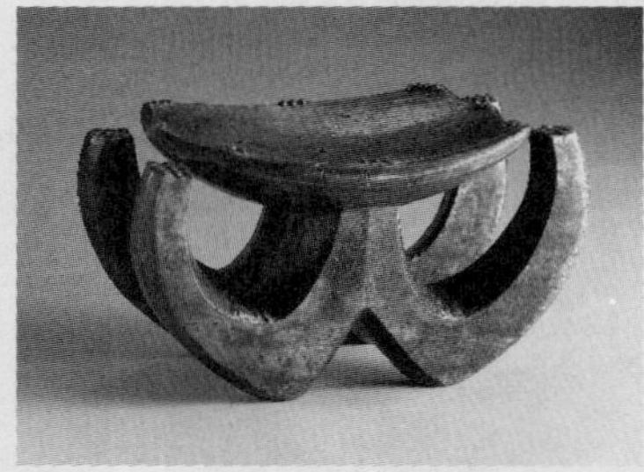

82 Stool
Zaire (Central Oubangui, Northern Zaire)
Wood, brass tacks, 23 x 39 x 27.5 cm
Musée National des Arts Africains et Océaniens, Paris
Inv. AF 8 849, acquired in 1905
Plate on p. 136

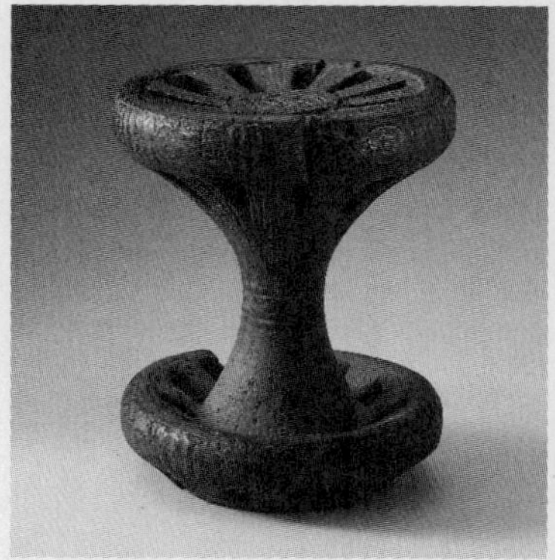

83 Stool
Kuba, Zaire
Wood, height 45, diam. 39 cm
Private collection, Brussels
Plate on p. 123

The king of the Kuba and the chiefs of the Bushong use a throne – the *ipon*, its shape recalling that of a large bobbin. Such a stool usually has a large vertical handle. The throne always rests on a raised platform and is covered with an animal skin because the Bushong nobility – under whose hegemony the kingdom of Kuba arose – always sit on animal skins. (cf. Cornet 1982, p. 301)

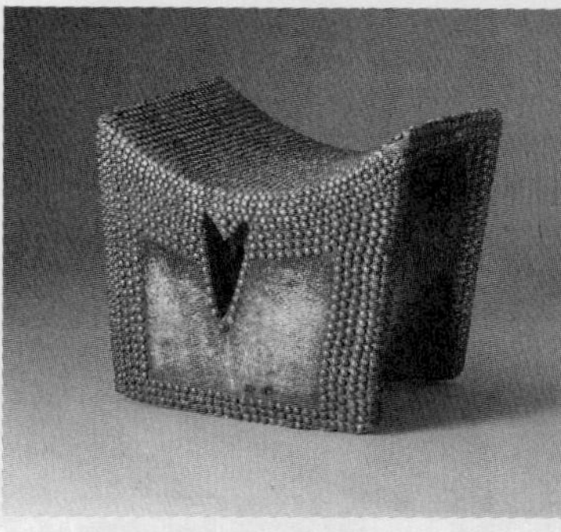

84 Stool
Ngombe, Zaire
Wood, brass tacks, 31 x 31.4 cm
Musée Barbier-Mueller, Geneva
Inv. 1026-240
Plate on p. 133

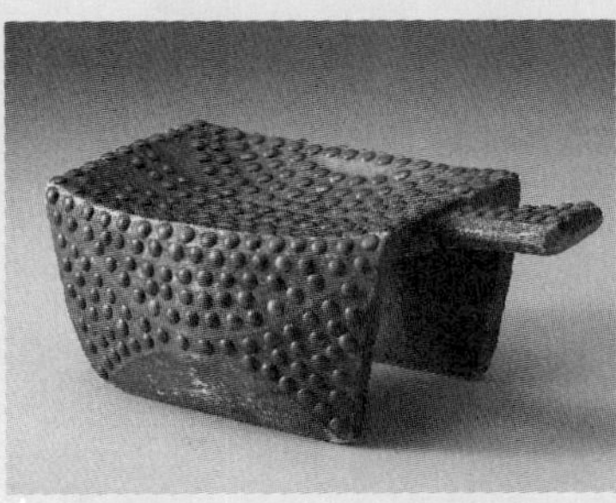

85 Stool
Ngombe, Zaire
Wood, brass tacks, 19.2 x 32.6 cm
Africa Museum, Tervuren
Inv. 53.4.15
Plate on p. 133

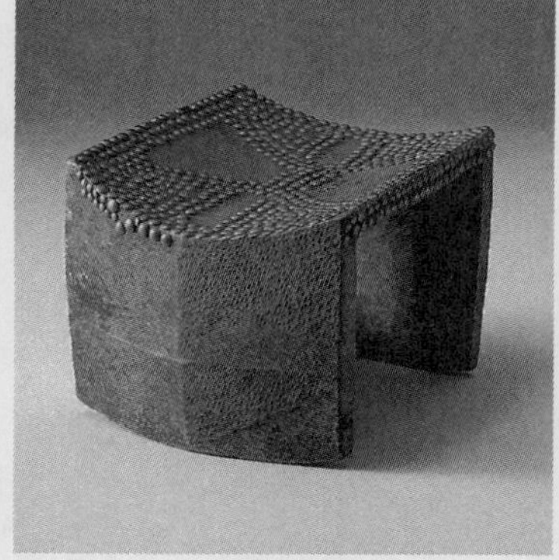

86 *Ebonga* stool for women
Ngombe, Zaire (Lusengo, Makanza)
Wood, brass tacks, 26.3 x 22.5 x 20.5 cm
Africa Museum, Tervuren
Inv. 296, acquired in 1901–3

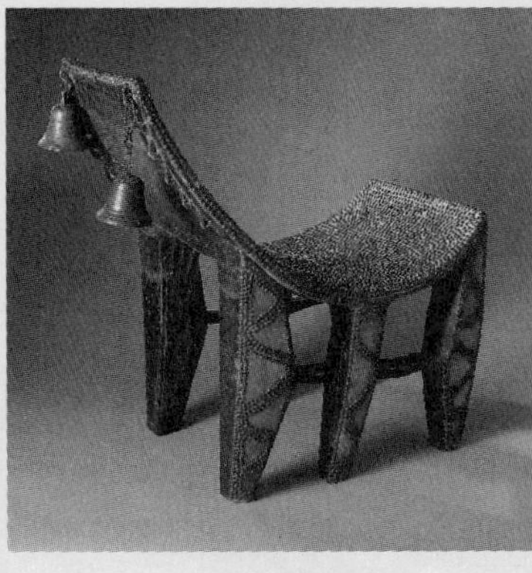

87 Semi-reclining chair
Ngombe, Zaire
Wood, brass tacks, brass bells, 73 x 70 x 39 cm
Musée Barbier-Mueller, Geneva
Inv. 1026-125
Plate on p. 132

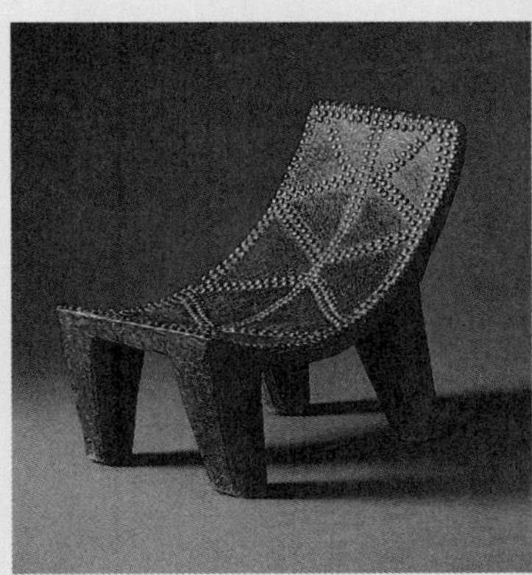

88 Semi-reclining chair
Ngombe (?)/Biondjos, Zaire (Lower Oubangui)
Wood, brass tacks, 39 x 26 x 46 cm
Musée National des Arts Africains et Océaniens, Paris
Inv. AF 8850, collected in 1905 and acquired by Museum in 1935

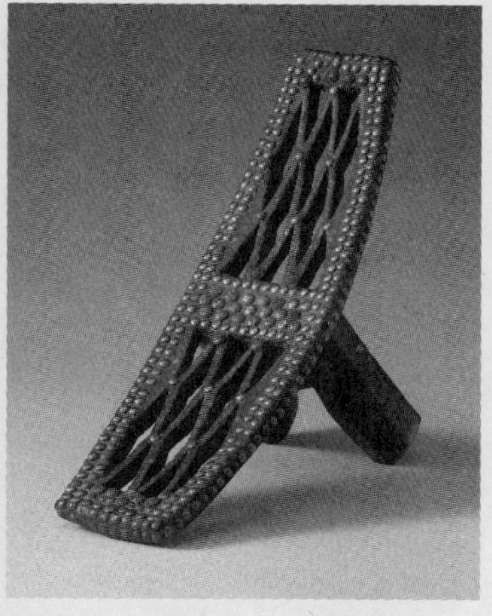

89 Backrest/Seat
Zaire (Sankuru, Lomela)
Wood, brass tacks, width 49.2, depth 15 cm
Africa Museum, Tervuren
Inv. 34075, acquired in 1932
Plate on p. 130

Objects of this sort could be placed in an upright position for use as stools or inclined to one side for use as backrests. The decoration of this example with brass tacks suggests that the stool belonged to a distinguished individual or to a chief. (cf. Sieber 1980, p. 136)

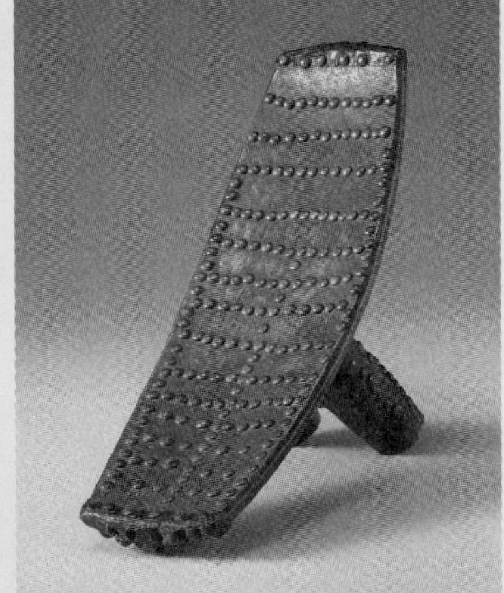

90 Backrest/Seat
Zaire
Wood, brass tacks, width 41.5, depth 13.8 cm
Africa Museum, Tervuren
Inv. 40695, acquired in 1945
Plate on p. 131

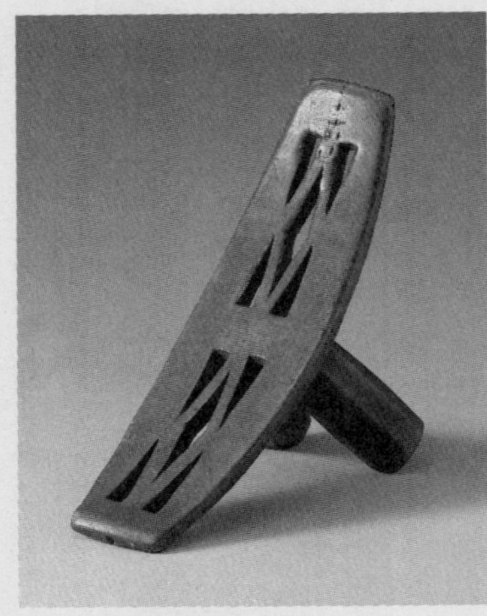

91 Backrest/Seat
Jonga, Zaire (Équateur, Moma)
Wood, width 38.5, depth 11 cm
African Museum, Tervuren
Inv. 29711
Plate on p. 131

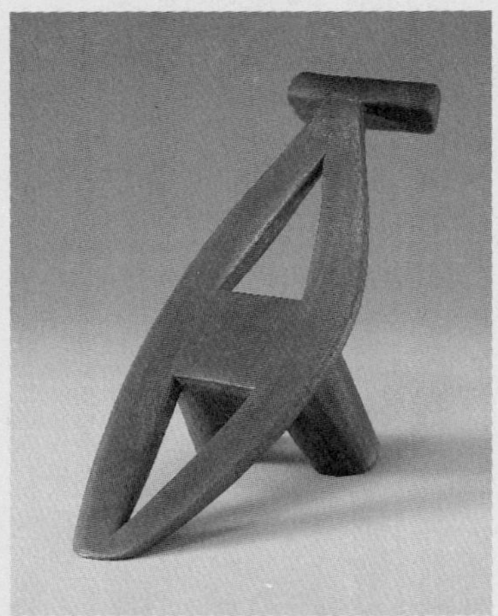

92 Backrest/Seat
Songye, Zaire (Kasai)
Wood, width 48.5, depth 14.5 cm
Africa Museum, Tervuren
Inv. 19263
Plate on p. 131

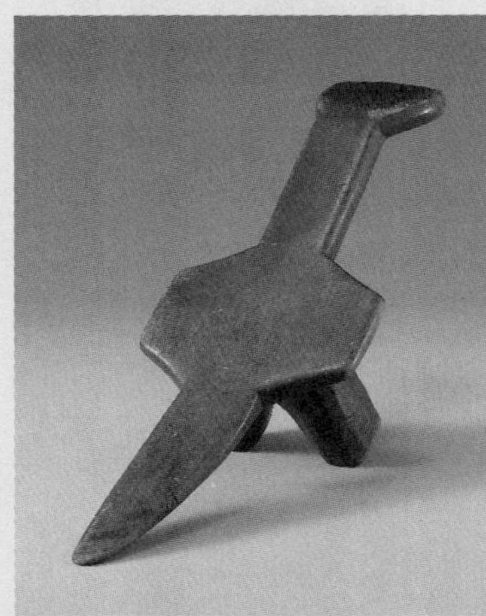

93 Backrest/Seat
Songye, Zaire (Lukenge)
Wood, width 46, depth 14.8 cm
Africa Museum, Tervuren
Inv. 17170, acquired in 1914
Plate on p. 131

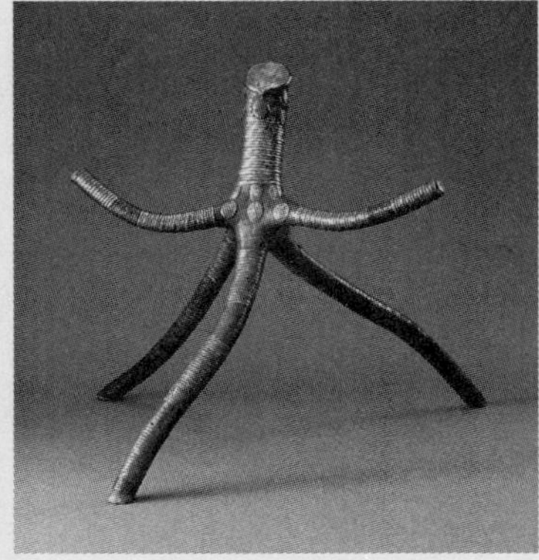

94 Chief's backrest
Mangbetu, Zaire (Uele)
Wood, iron and copper wire, iron, 67 x 70 x 70 cm
British Museum, London
Inv. AF 1898/294, acquired in 1898
Plate on p. 129

Men placed three-legged backrests behind their stools. Those backrests belonging to chiefs were generously wound with wire and/or mounted with nails. (cf. Schildkrout, Keim et al. 1990, pp. 41, 160.)

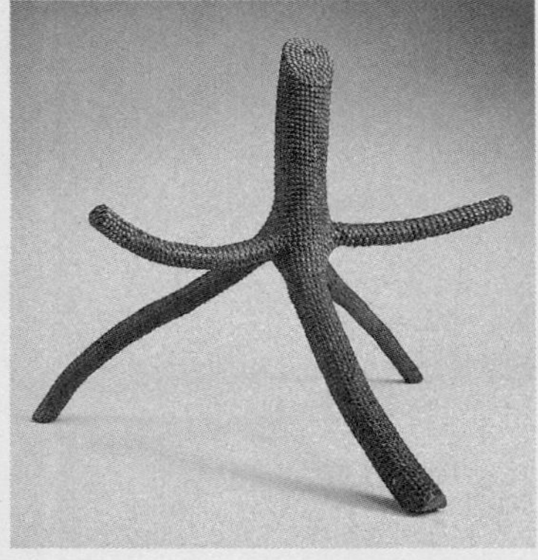

95 Backrest
Meje, Zaire (Uele)
Wood, brass tacks, 90 x 78 cm
Africa Museum, Tervuren
Inv. 10912, acquired in 1913

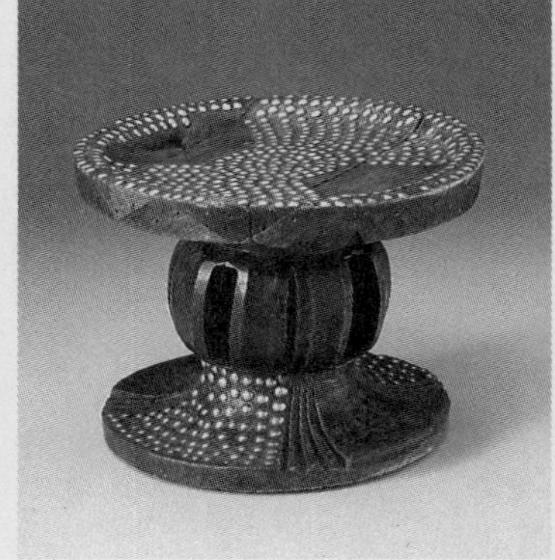

96 Stool
Mangbetu, Zaire (Uele)
Wood, brass tacks, height 23.2, diam. 28.9 cm
Africa Museum, Tervuren
Inv. 85.19.1
Plate on p. 127

Wherever they went, women of the Mangbetu carried wooden stools, each carved out of a single block. Only the stools owned by the most important women, however, were decorated with metal nails. The female members of a chief's court had stools that were especially finely worked. Men of the Mangbetu did not sit on stools. Only chiefs owned large, double-decker versions of these stools, so that they could always sit a little higher than the women who surrounded them (see photograph on p. 110). (cf. Schildkrout, Keim et al. 1990, pp. 119–21.)

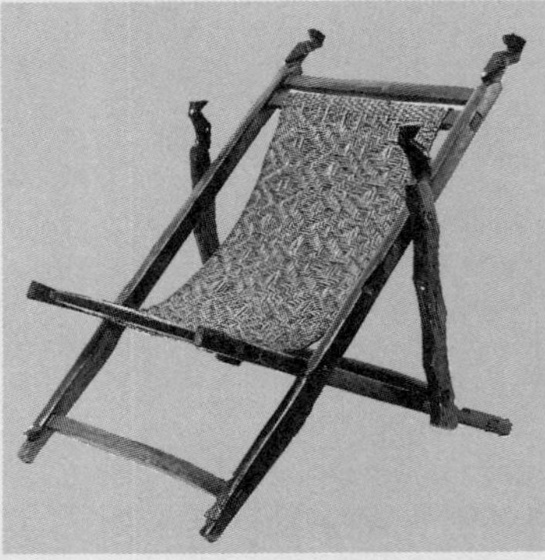

97 Semi-reclining chair
Mangbetu, Zaire
Wood, rattan, 87 x 77 x 87 cm
Galerie Daffos-Estournel, Paris

Semi-reclining chairs of this sort, produced following the European model, were in use at the beginning of this century. The upper ends of the wooden slats in the example illustrated are finished with heads worked in a style typical for the Mangbetu (see photograph on p. 35). (cf. Schildkrout, Keim et al. 1990, p. 42.)

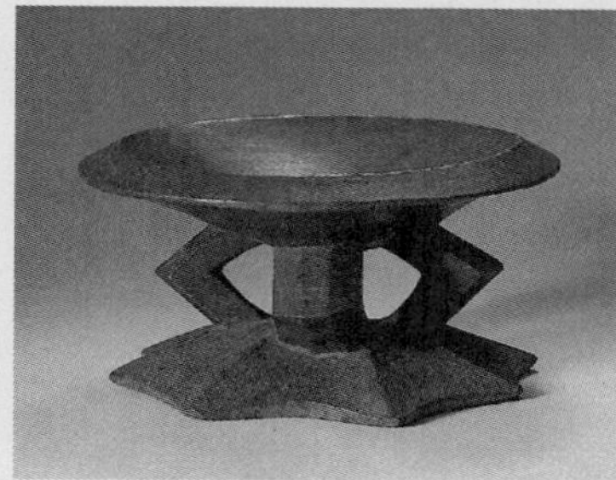

98 Stool
Zande, Zaire (Uele, Sagi)
Wood, height 19, diam. 35 cm
Africa Museum, Tervuren
Inv. 6417
Plate on p. 161

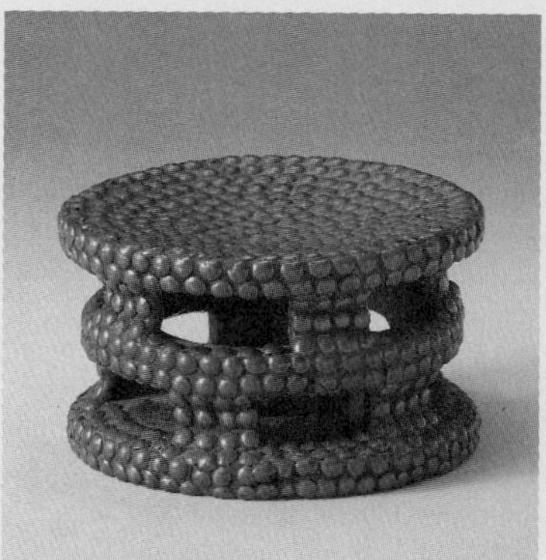

99 Stool
Chokwe, Zaire/Angola
Wood, brass tacks, height 12.2, diam. 19.2 cm
Africa Museum, Tervuren
Inv. 48.40.28
Plate on p. 134

Among the art works of the Chokwe, the chief's stool is regarded as a symbol of power. Earlier Chokwe stools were small, carved out of a single block of wood and often decorated with brass tacks. The tacks had to be imported and were a valuable commodity: in a sense, they were gold for the Chokwe. (cf. Bastin 1984, p. 320.)

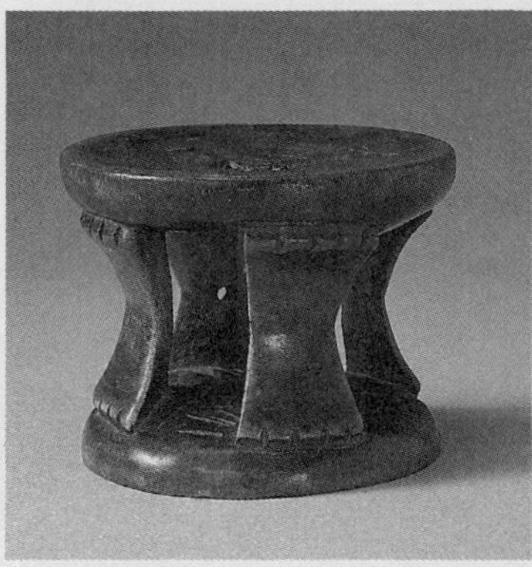

100 Stool
Chokwe, Zaire/Angola
Wood, height 13, diam. 16.2 cm
Africa Museum, Tervuren
Inv. 48.40.45, acquired in 1948

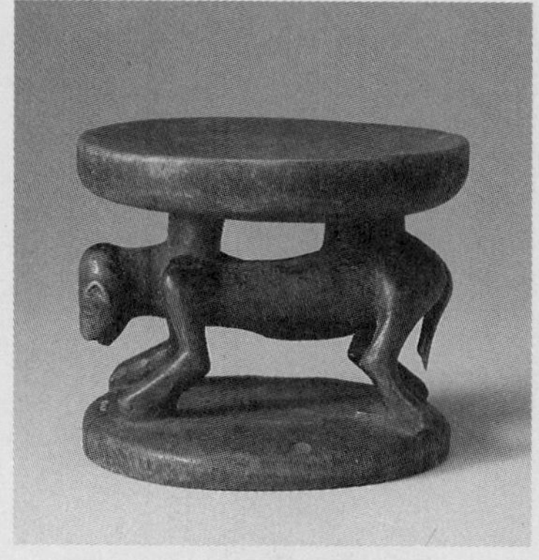

101 Stool
Chokwe, Zaire/Angola
Wood, 20.5 x 24 cm
Africa Museum, Tervuren
Inv. 48.40.39
Plate on p. 147

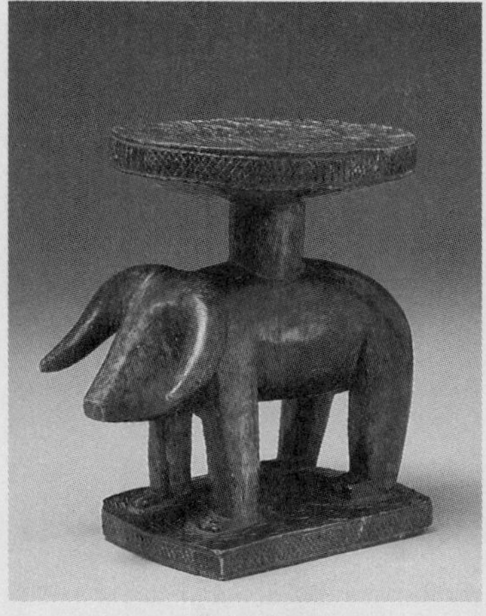

102 Stool with a buffalo
Chokwe, Zaire/Angola
Wood, height 25, diam. 14.3 cm
Africa Museum, Tervuren
Inv. 70.11.3
Plate on p. 147

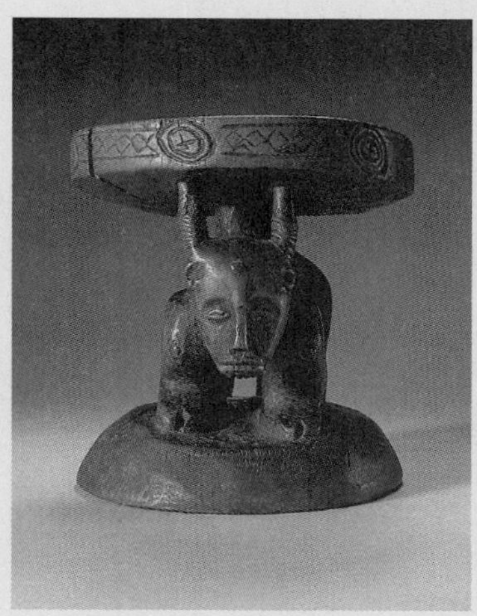

103 Stool
Chokwe, Zaire/Angola
Wood, height 20.9, diam. 21.3 cm
Africa Museum, Tervuren
Inv. 48.40.38

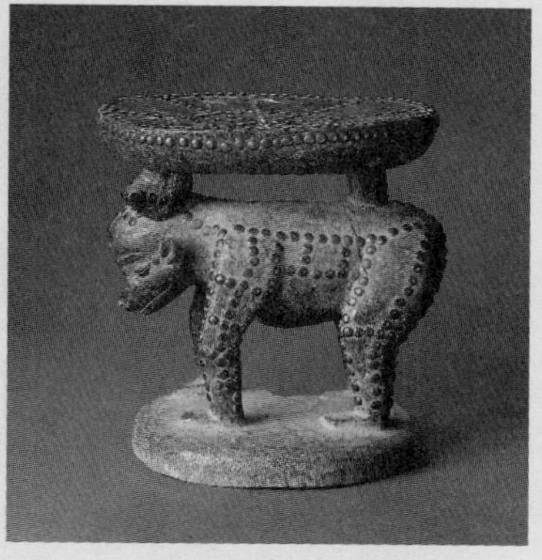

104 Stool with a buffalo
Pende, Zaire
Wood, iron nails, brass tacks, height 33, diam. 30 cm
Musée National des Arts Africains et Océaniens, Paris
Inv. MNAN 77.4.1
Plate on p. 139

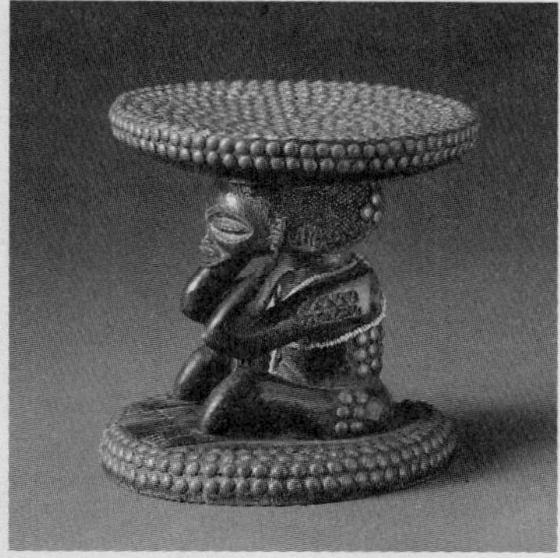

105 Caryatid stool
Chokwe, Zaire (Kasai)
Wood, brass tacks, bead necklace, height 21.3, diam. 20.3 cm
Africa Museum, Tervuren
Inv. 43161
Plate on p. 145

'The caryatid has long occurred in the art of the Chokwe. None the less, we know of no object from the nineteenth century in which a caryatid bears the seat on the crown of its head as is frequently to be found in the art of the Luba and sometimes of the Pende. . . . We can, therefore, assume that it was only during the course of their spread to the north, and through contact with their new neighbours there, that the Chokwe started producing caryatid stools with the seating surface borne on the caryatid's head. . . . The seated female figure . . . represents the female ancestor of a family who expected veneration from her descendants. If they failed to worship her, there was a danger of bad luck or illness. This example reveals traces of consecrated white clay – a token of veneration – that was spat at the caryatid's face.' (Marie-Louise Bastin, in: Schmalenbach 1988, p. 253.)

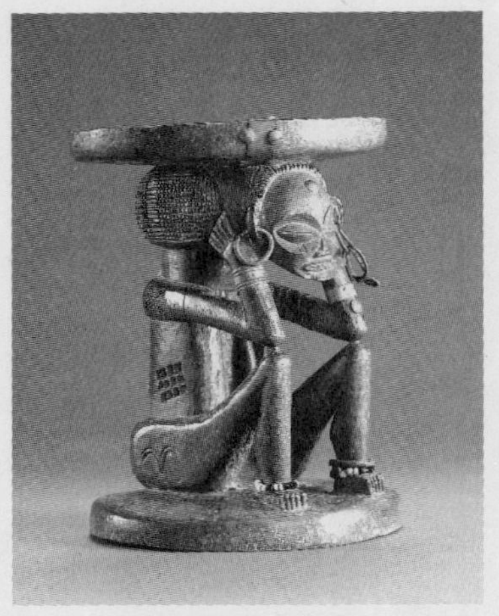

106 Caryatid stool
Chokwe, Angola
Wood, brass, height 24, diam. 18 cm
Bernisches Historisches Museum, Berne
Inv. Co 659, acquired in 1927
Plate on p. 148

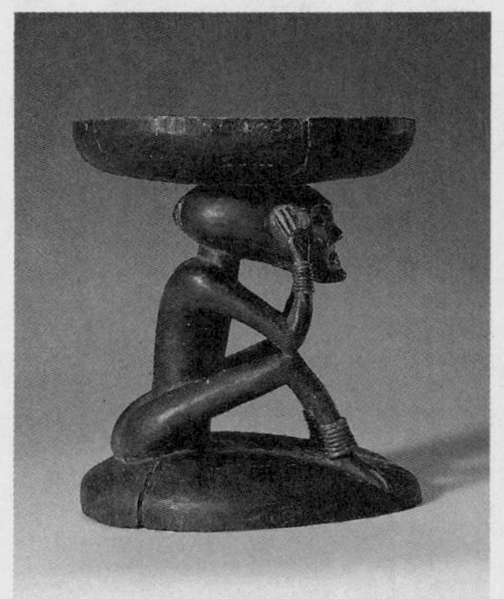

107 Caryatid stool
Chokwe/Pende, Zaire
Wood, height 25, diam. 21 cm
Africa Museum, Tervuren
Inv. 49.68.3
Plates on p. 144

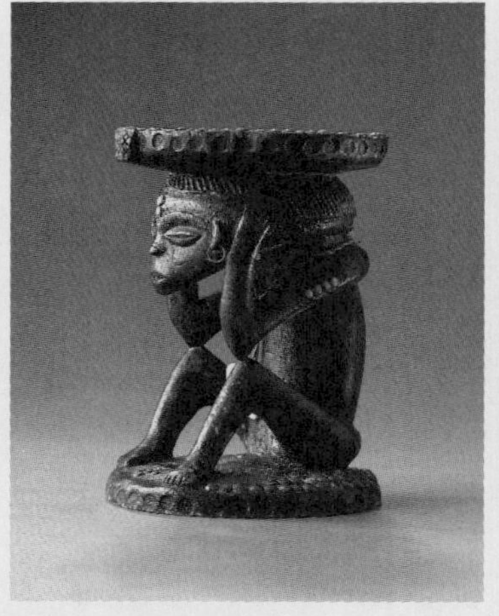

108 Caryatid stool
Chokwe, Angola
Wood, brass, height 22.5 cm
Leloup Collection, Paris
Plate on p. 143

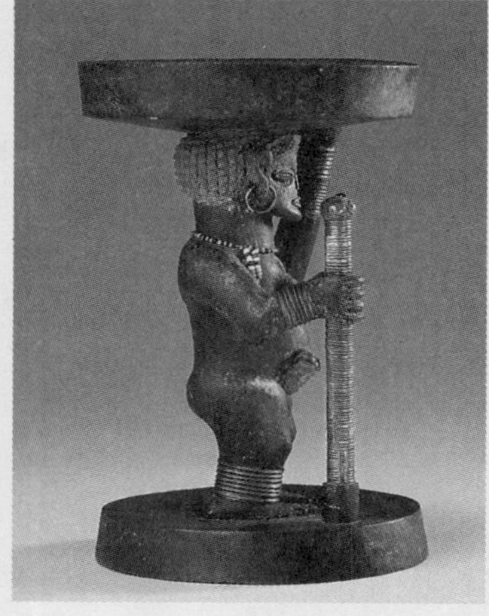

109 Caryatid stool
Chokwe, Zaire/Angola (Kasai)
Wood, brass tacks, copper wire, height 31.5, diam. 20.7 cm
Africa Museum, Tervuren
Inv. 43157, acquired in 1946
Plate on p. 146

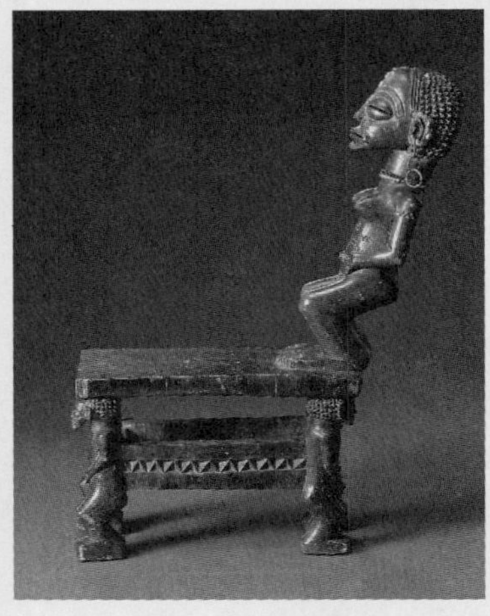

110 Chair
Chokwe, Zaire (Kasai)
Wood, brass, bead necklace, 55 x 30.3 x 13.5 cm
Africa Museum, Tervuren
Inv. 15743, acquired in 1913
Plate on p. 149

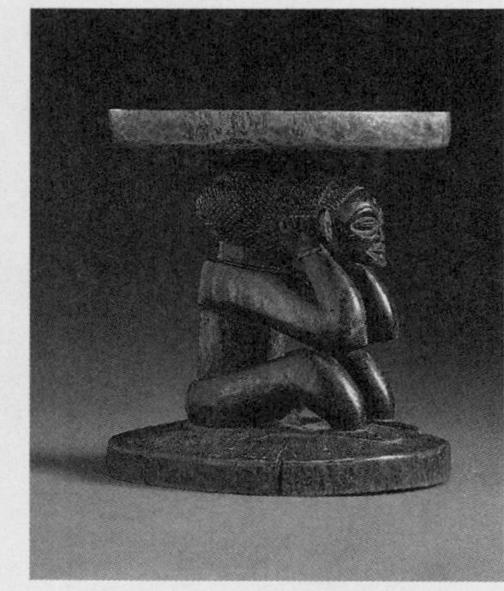

111 Caryatid stool
Chokwe, Zaire/Angola
Wood, height 28.2, diam. 25.5 cm
Africa Museum, Tervuren
Inv. 48.40.26, acquired in 1948

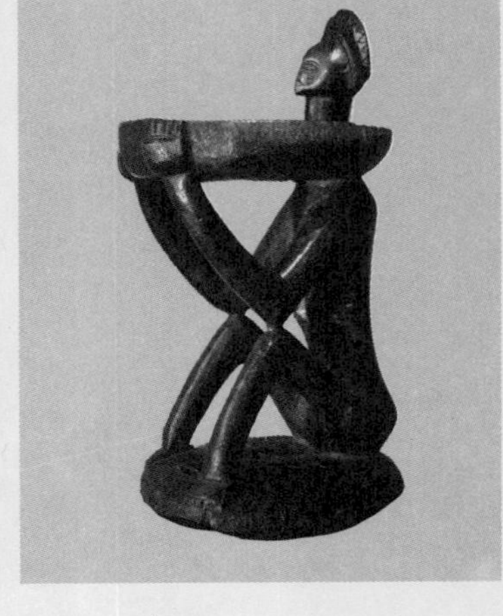

112 Stool
Lwena, Zaire
Wood, 50 x 26 x 28 cm
Leloup Collection, Inc., New York

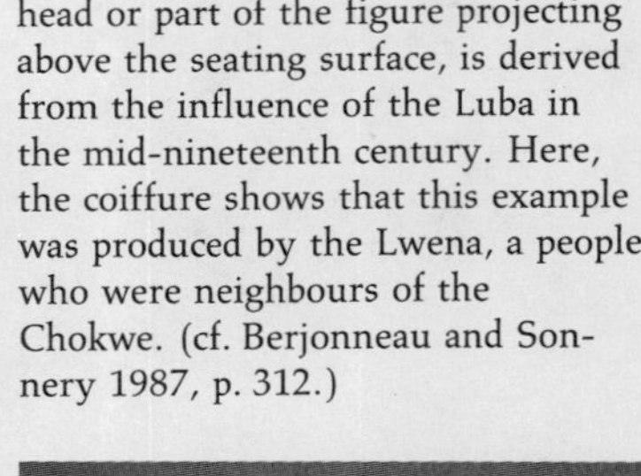

This sort of Chokwe seat, with the head or part of the figure projecting above the seating surface, is derived from the influence of the Luba in the mid-nineteenth century. Here, the coiffure shows that this example was produced by the Lwena, a people who were neighbours of the Chokwe. (cf. Berjonneau and Sonnery 1987, p. 312.)

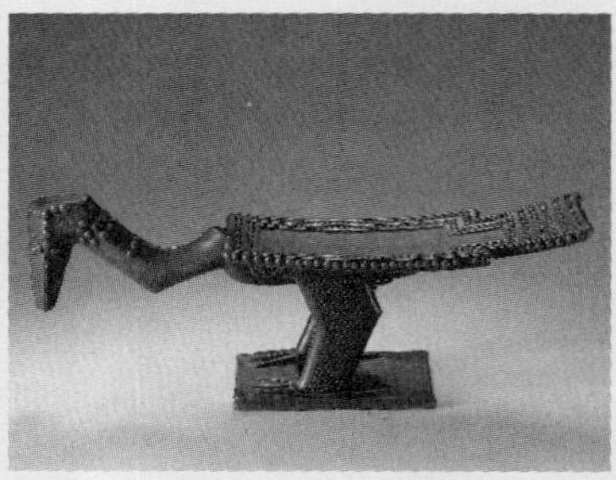

113 Stool in the form of a bird Imbangala, Angola
Wood, brass tacks, 21 x 54 x 20.7 cm
Museum für Völkerkunde, Berlin
Inv. III C 34406, acquired in 1932
Plate on p. 141

This stool, attributed to the Imbangala, has much in common with the bird-shaped stools and neck-rests of the neighbouring Chokwe. This is the case with regard both to the decoration with the brass tacks obtained through trade with the Portuguese and to the rows of incised zigzags. (cf. Koloß 1990, p. 56.)

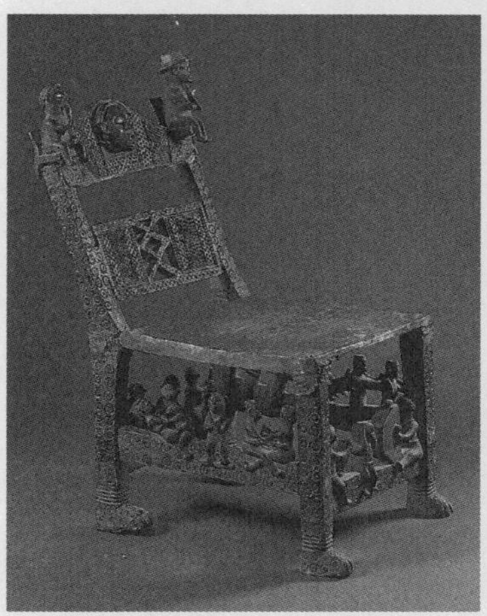

114 Chair
Pende, Zaire
Wood, leather, 27 x 49.5 x 70 cm
Museum Rietberg, Zurich
Inv. RAC 804
Plate on p. 150

'In the sixteenth and seventeenth centuries, European chairs of Renaissance style and shape had already been brought deep into the African bush, and they were there elevated to the rank of chiefs' thrones through the addition of figural and decorative details. The back of the imposing example shown here is dominated by a chief's mask; to the right and left of this there sit the figures, respectively, of a European in a pith helmet and an African with a water pipe. Below the seat we find scenes from the everyday life of the Africans . . . and the legs end in animal paws.' (Leuzinger 1978, p. 206.) See also the photograph of such a chair in use on p. 151.

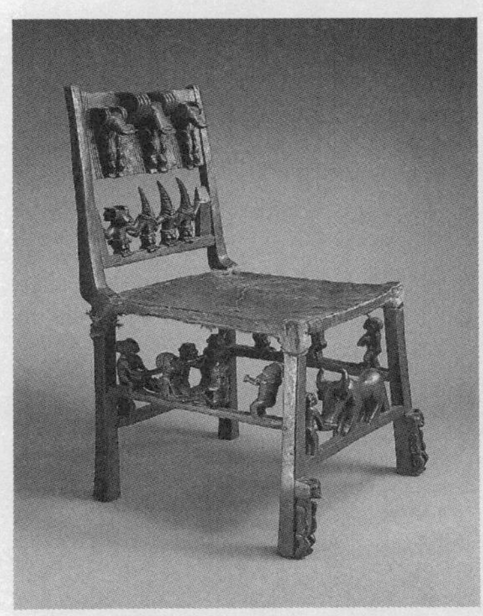

115 Chair
Chokwe, Zaire
Wood, metal nails, cord, animal skin/leather, 93.5 x 49 cm
Africa Museum, Tervuren
Inv. 15995
Plate on p. 152

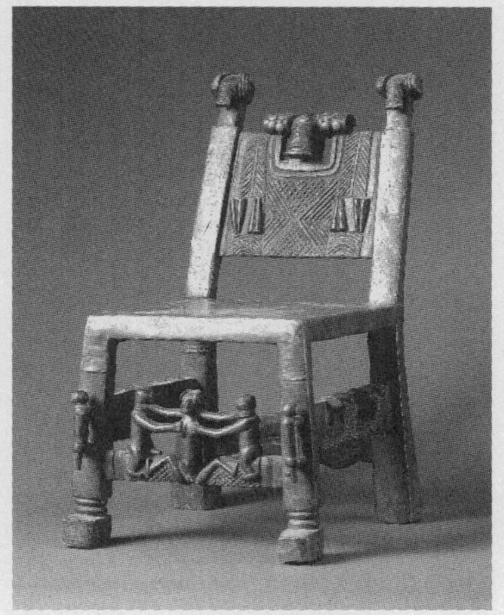

116 Chair
Chokwe, Angola
Wood, leather, 41.5 x 21 cm
Museum Rietberg, Zurich
Plate on p. 153

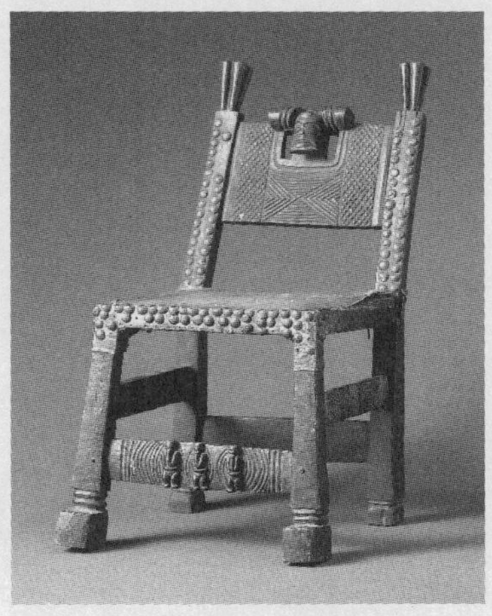

117 Chair
Chokwe, Zaire/Angola
Wood, leather, nails, 41 x 21 cm
Museum Rietberg, Zurich
Plate on p. 153

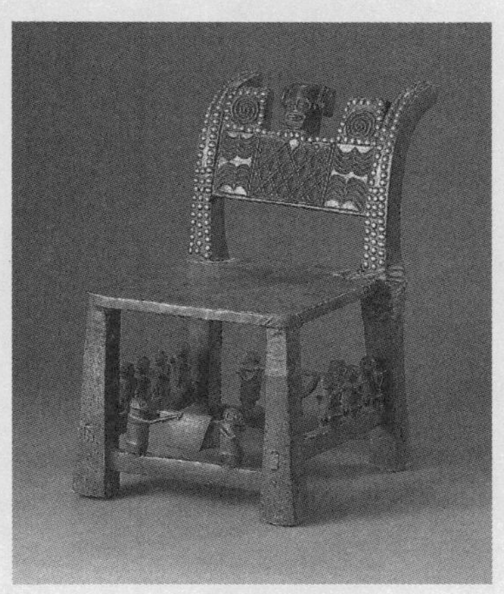

118 Chair
Chokwe, Zaire
Wood, leather, brass tacks, 51.5 x 31 x 42.5 cm
British Museum, London
Inv. AF 1910, 0420.597, acquired in 1910; plate on p. 155

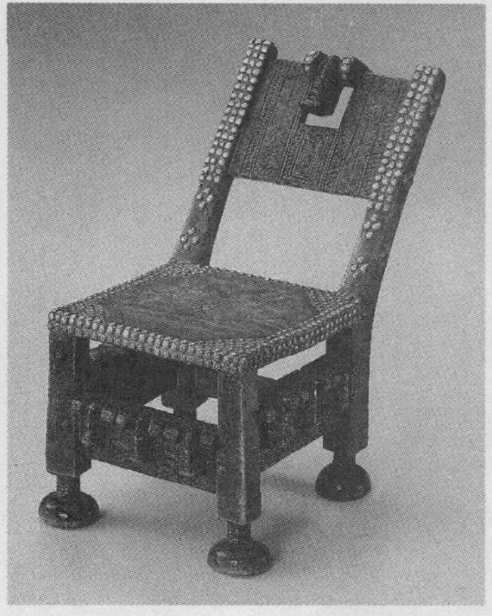

119 Chair
Chokwe, Zaire
Wood, leather, brass tacks, 39 x 21 x 36 cm
Linden-Museum, Stuttgart
Inv. F 51/839 L

Small Chokwe chairs of this sort were taken along when the chief made his rounds of the village or went to the market. Such chairs were richly carved with motifs from everyday life, or from the history, religion and mythology of the Chokwe. They were a status symbol for village chiefs and an expression of their power and authority as well as a token of the highest spiritual power. The leather used in their manufacture was fastened with imported brass tacks. (cf. Crowley 1972, p. 32; Kauenhoven-Janzen 1981.)

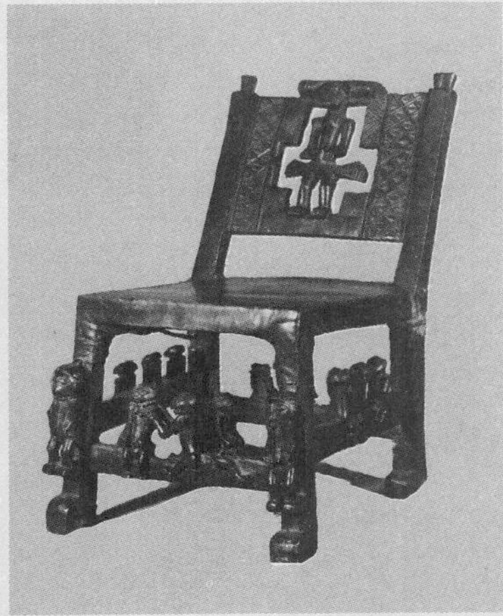

120 Chair
Chokwe, Zaire/Angola (Kasai)
Wood, leather, brass tacks, 43 x 26.5 cm
Africa Museum, Tervuren
Inv. 43165

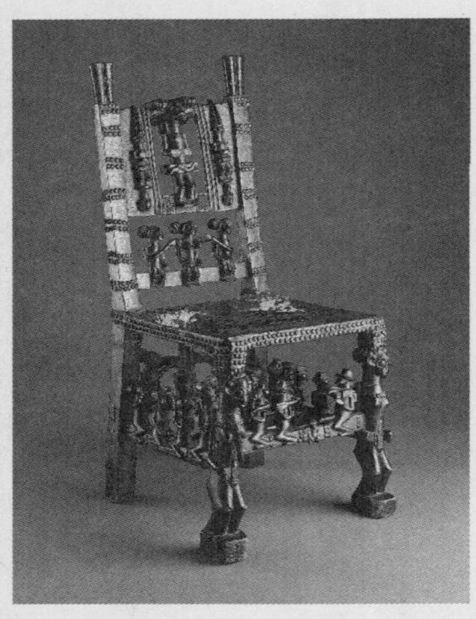

121 Chair
Chokwe, Zaire/Angola
Wood, metal nails, cord, animal skin/leather, 79 x 39 x 37 cm
Private collection, Basle
Plate on p. 154

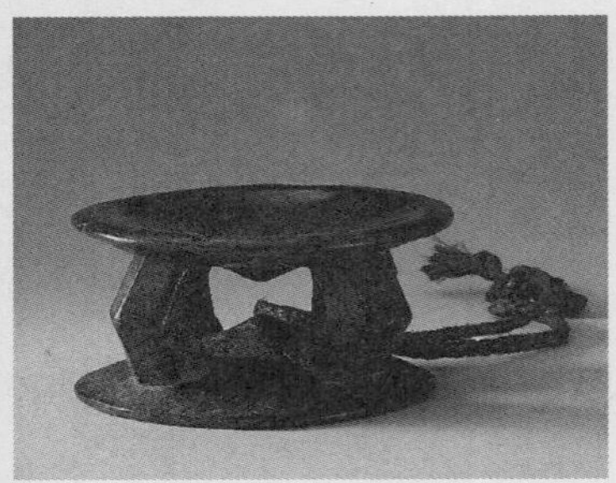

122 Stool
Lega, Zaire
Wood, string, height 10, diam. 20.5 cm
Private collection, Brussels

Among the Lega, the disposal of works of art and their use is exclusively in the hands of the members of the two uppermost degrees of the *bwami* associations – the court of last appeal in political and legal decision-making in public life. Unlike other Lega seats, the small, well-polished *kisumbi* stools were associated with an altogether specialized symbolic significance: they were used for various rituals within the association. *Kisumbi* stools were owned by individuals from the two highest degrees in the *bwami* association, and they remained a life-long possession – in contrast to other objects, which were exchanged as their owner rose to a higher rank. The *kisumbi* stool was a token of status, wealth and intelligence – qualities that, in addition to a certain age, were fundamental preconditions for advancement within the *bwami* association. (cf. Biebuyck 1973, pp. 186 ff.; 1977.)

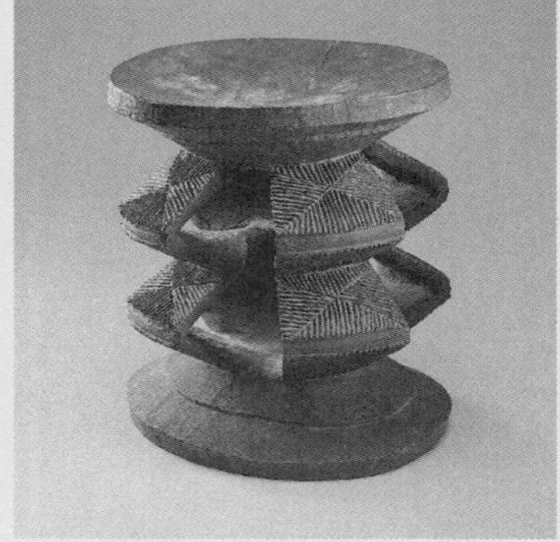

123 Stool
Kusu, Zaire
Wood, height 42 cm
Musée Barbier-Mueller, Geneva
Inv. 1026-186

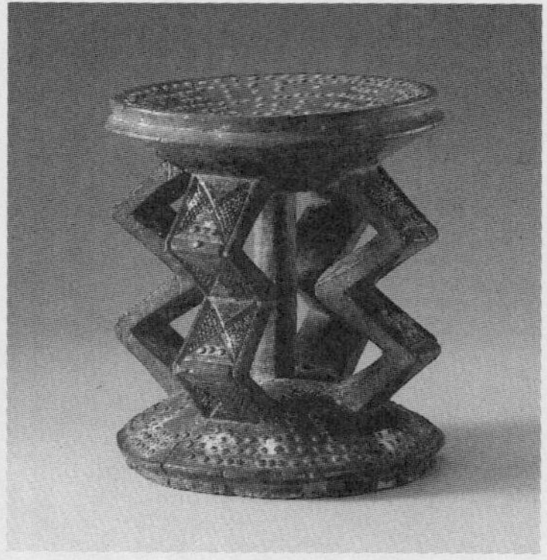

124 Stool
Kusu, Zaire
Wood, brass tacks, height 31, diam. 25 cm
Private collection, Brussels
Plate on p. 138

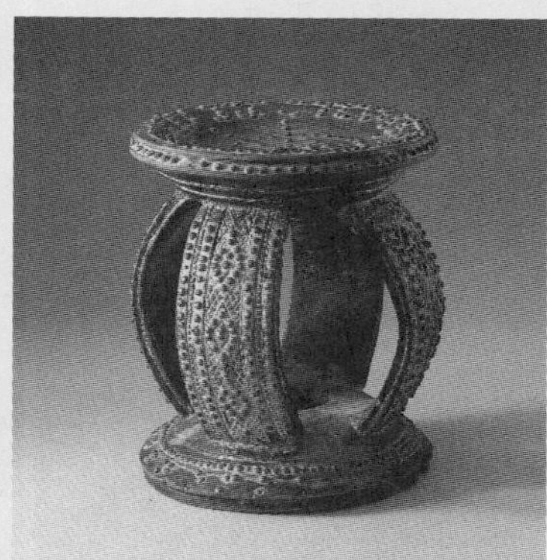

125 Stool
Hemba, Zaire (Kasongo)
Wood, brass tacks, height 34, diam. 27 cm
Private collection, Brussels
Plate on p. 122

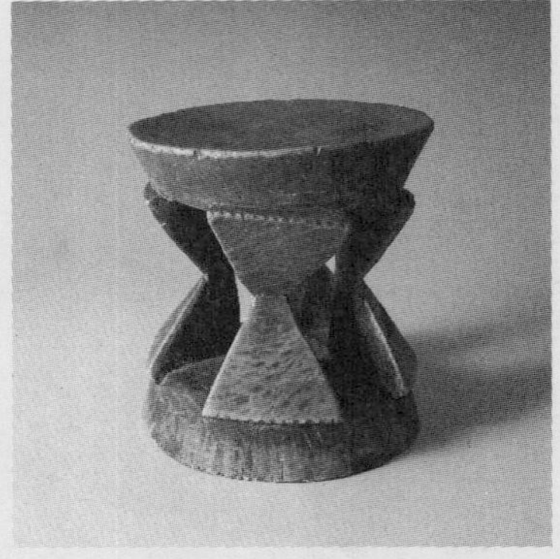

126 Stool
Songye, Zaire (Kwango)
Wood, height 22.5, diam. 22 cm
Africa Museum, Tervuren
Inv. 35795
Plate on p. 137

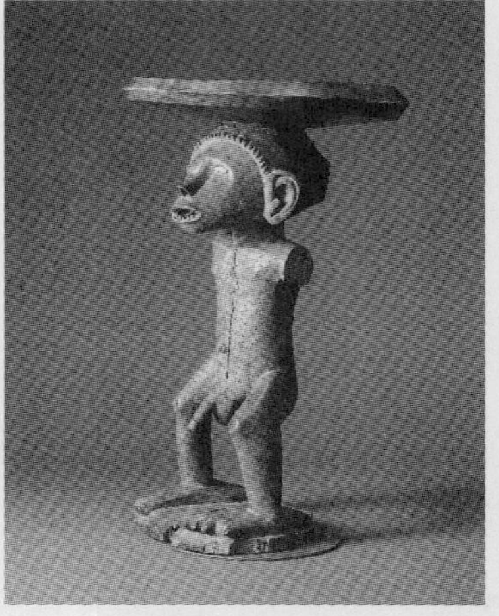

127 Caryatid stool
Zaire (probably Zimba region)
Wood, cowrie shells for the eyes, height 47, diam. 30.5 cm
Museum Rietberg, Zurich
Inv. RAC 306 A; plate on p. 117

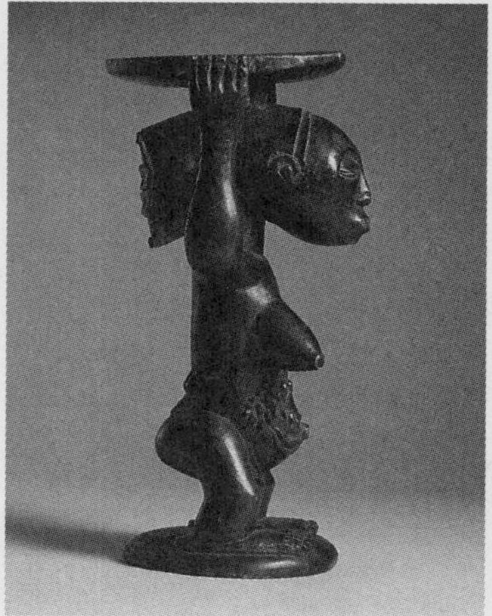

128 Caryatid stool
Luba, Zaire
Wood, height 41.5, diam. 19 cm
Collection of Udo and Waltraud Horstmann, Zug; plate on p. 112

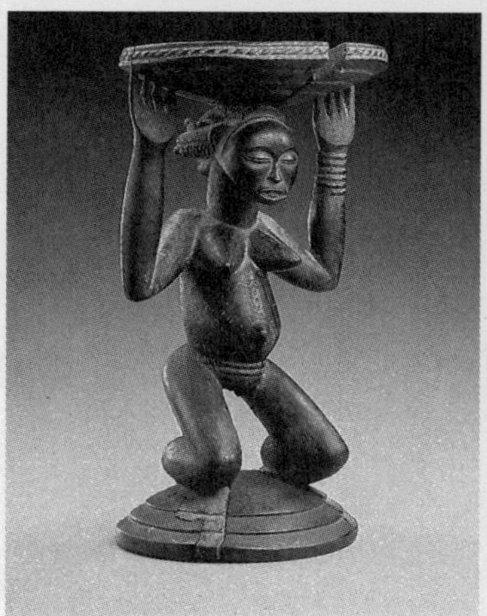

129 Caryatid stool
Hemba, Zaire
Wood, 46 x 26 x 23.5 cm
Collection of Comte Baudouin de Grunne, Sablon
Plate on p. 114

Through their coiffures and tattoos, the female bearer figures of the stools of the Hemba and the neighbouring Luba are recognizable as representatives of the upper class of society. As such, they may be understood to represent ancestors, the founding members of a clan or a tribe. It was previously assumed that they were female slaves. We now know this not to be the case. Caryatid seats were reserved for the use of the chiefs and embodied the notion of the continuity of power. (cf. Szalay 1986, pp. 147–150; Flam 1971.) This stool may be described as one of the greatest masterpieces of its type. The base was formerly damaged and was later repaired.

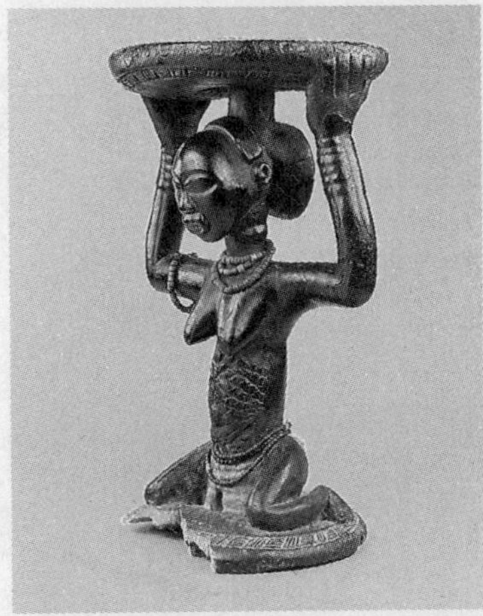

130 Caryatid stool
Hemba, Zaire
Wood, beads, height 53 cm
Private collection, Brussels
Plate on p. 115

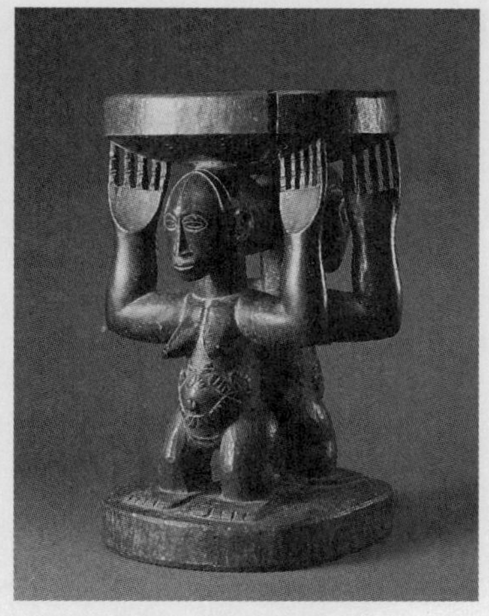

131 Caryatid stool
Hemba, Zaire (Shaba, Kasai)
Wood, height 53, diam. 32 cm
Museum Rietberg, Zurich
Plate on p. 113

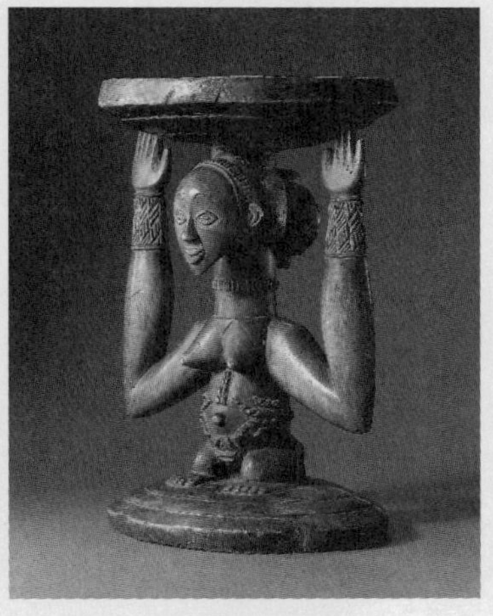

132 Caryatid stool
Luba-Hemba, Zaire
Wood, height 48.5, diam. 30 cm
Africa Museum, Tervuren
Inv. 17193; plates on pp. 120, 121

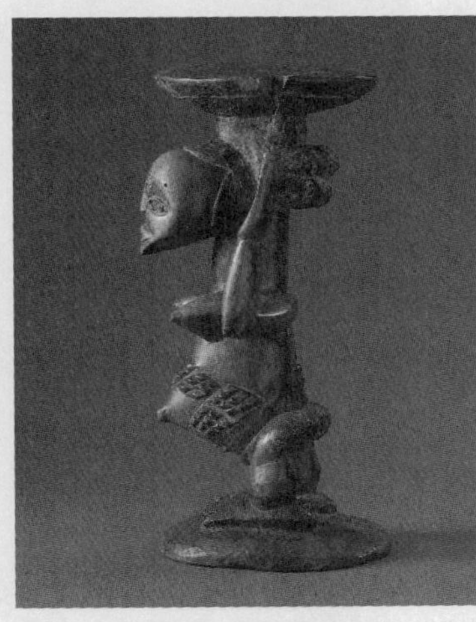

133 Caryatid stool
Luba, Zaire
Wood, 43 x 21.5 x 21.5 cm
British Museum, London
Inv. AF 1949,46.479, acquired in 1949; plate on p. 119

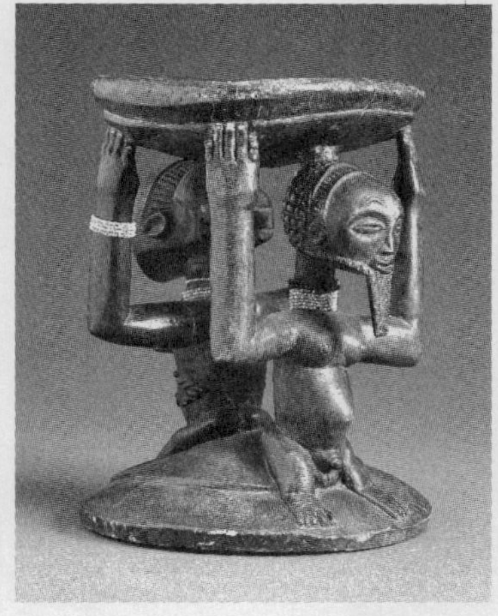

134 Caryatid stool
Luba-Katanga, Zaire (Kikumba)
Wood, beads, 37 x 27 cm
Africa Museum, Tervuren
Inv. 14354, acquired before 1907
Plate on p. 118

One of the few stools with a pair of supporting figures, a woman and a second figure with the mixed characteristics of a hermaphrodite – the beard and sexual organs of a man, but the breasts of a woman.

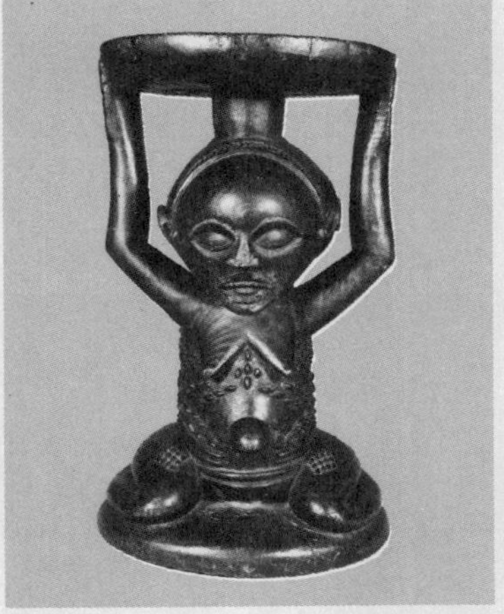

135 Caryatid stool
Luba, Zaire (Katanga)
Wood, height 57.3, diam. 32.5 cm
Africa Museum, Tervuren
Inv. 132

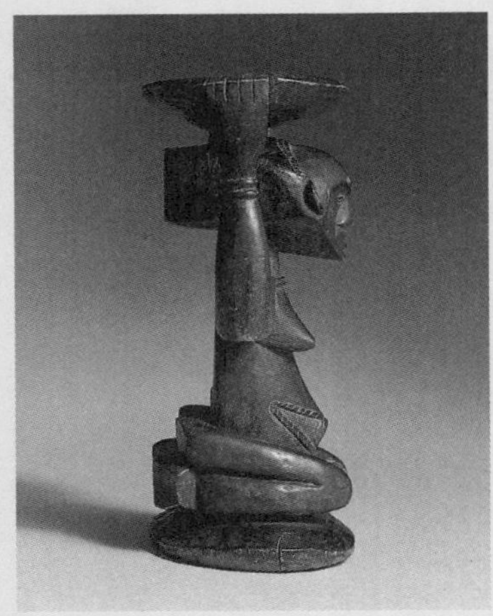

136 Caryatid stool
Luba, Zaire
Wood, height 48, diam. 24 cm
Staatliches Museum für Völkerkunde, Munich
Inv. 25-18-15, acquired in 1925
Plate on p. 116

'A figure squatting on its heels. The diamond shape of the face and the angular contours of coiffure, shoulders and upper arms are evidence of a tendency to the "cubistic" – a rare occurrence in the predominantly idealizing tradition of female figures. Despite the geometrization, the face is not without expression. The hairband and the tattoo patterns are conveyed through simple scratched lines and are without any suggestion of plasticity.' (Kecskési 1982, p. 366.)

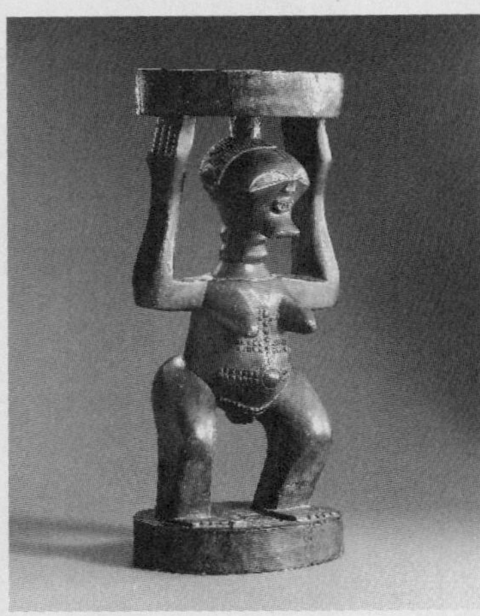

137 Caryatid stool
Songye/Luba, Zaire (Haut-Lualaba)
Wood, height 59.8, diam. 23 cm
Africa Museum, Tervuren
Inv. 53.85.27
Plate on p. 124

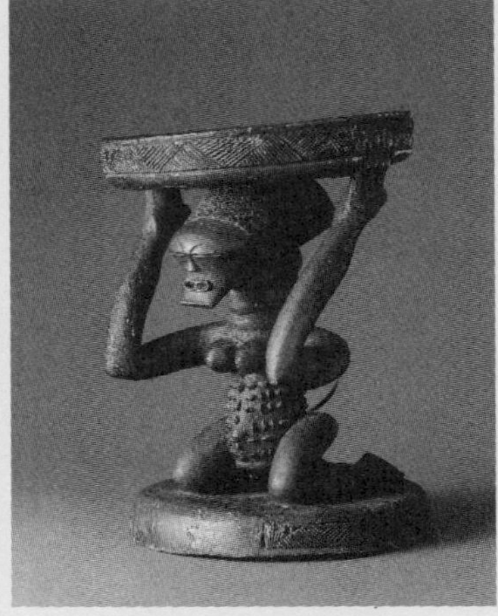

138 Caryatid stool
Songye, Zaire
Wood, height 51.5, diam. 36 cm
Völkerkundemuseum der Universität Zürich (Sammlung Han Coray)
Inv. 10159
Plate on p. 125

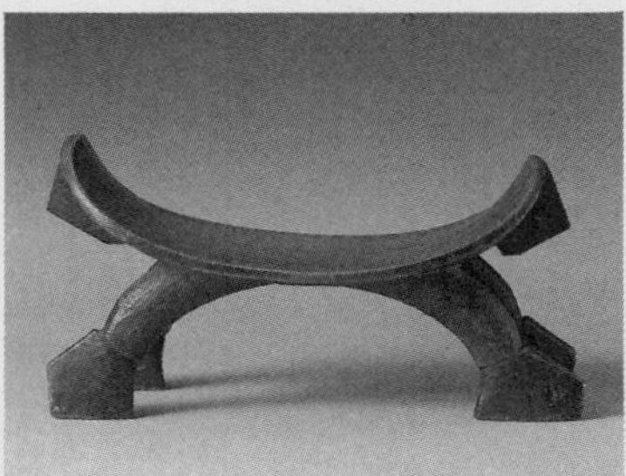

139 *Hegba* stool
Bongo, Sudan
Wood, width 47 cm
Musée Barbier-Mueller, Geneva
Inv. 1027-21
Plate on p. 168

In 1873 Schweinfurth wrote of the four-legged stools of the Bongo, or *hegba*, that were found in every household. (cf. Jack 1991, p. 29.)

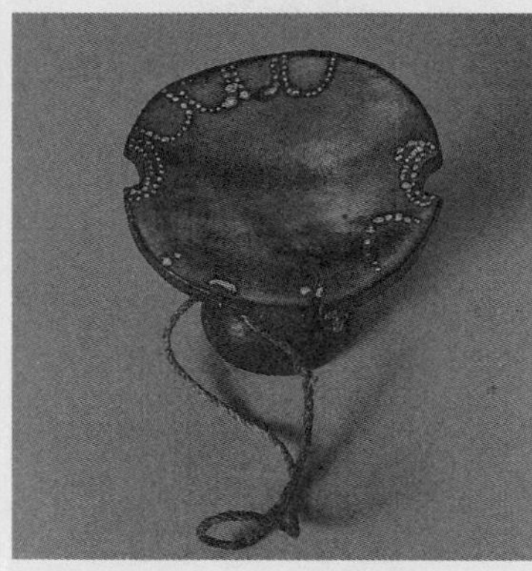

140 Stool
Gurage, Ethiopia
Wood, metal, cord, height 12, diam. 13 cm
Private collection, Zurich
Plate on p. 162

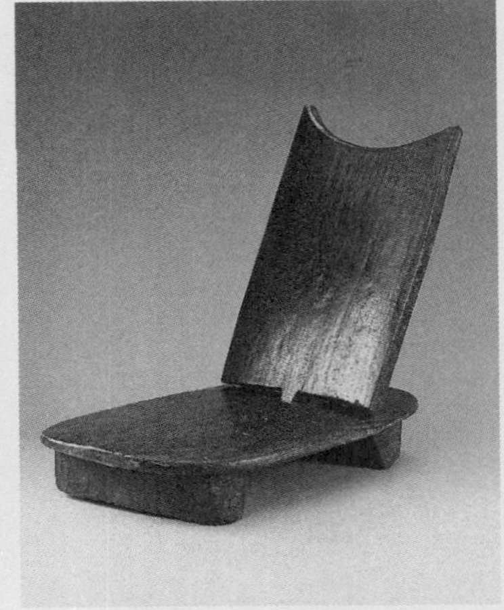

141 Semi-reclining chair
Ethiopia
Wood, 76 x 49 x 76 cm
Ghysels Collection, Brussels
Plate on p. 167

This type of chair, where the back can be removed, is unusual for Africa as a whole but is widely found in Ethiopia.

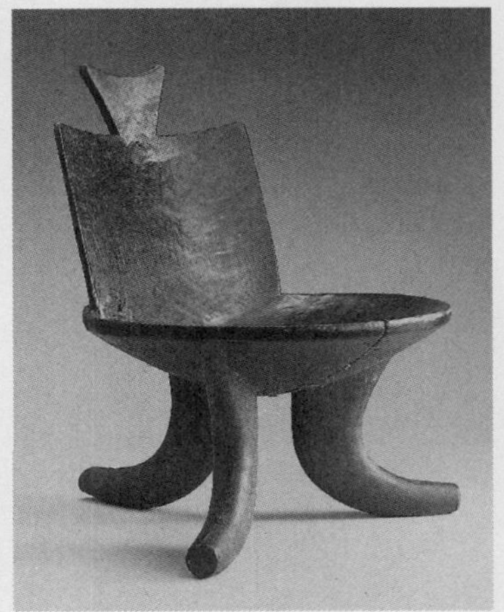

142 Chair
Galla (?), Ethiopia
Wood, iron, height 88, diam. 67 cm
Private collection, Brussels
Plate on p. 166

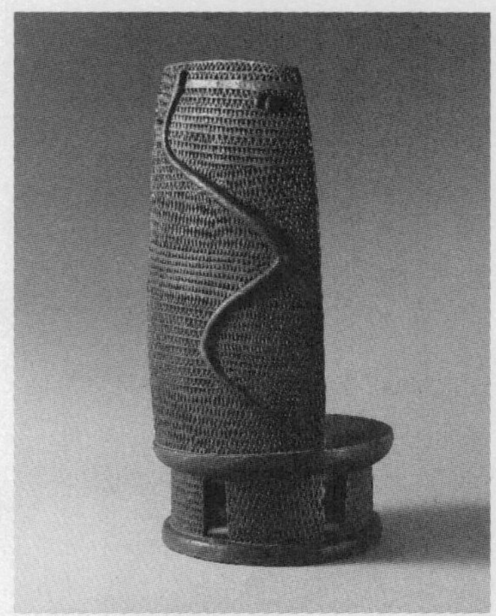

143 Chief's chair
Tabwa, Zaire
Wood, height 77, diam. 37 cm
Linden-Museum, Stuttgart
Inv. 42498, acquired in 1906
Plate on p. 140

Among the Tabwa, giant snakes represent *ngulu* (earth spirits). A chief's privileges were legitimized through his identification with the *ngulu* or with their mediation between man and nature. The motif of the giant snake thus appears in representational art, for example on this throne, and indicates the legitimate claim to exercise power. The two circular shapes to the right of the snake represent *kafwabubela* (beetles), to which special magical powers were ascribed. (cf. Maurer and Roberts 1985, p. 189.)

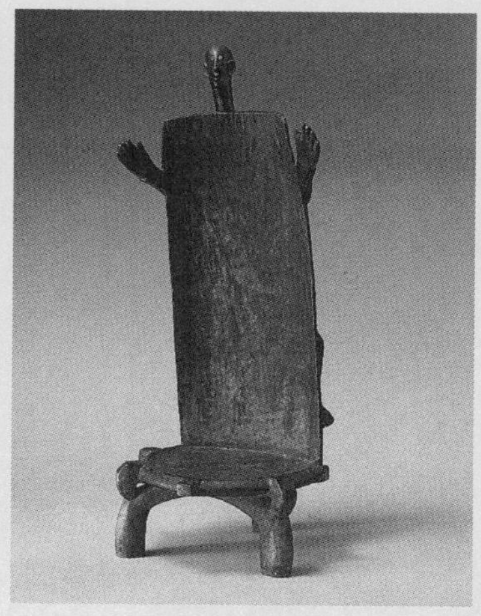

145 Chief's chair with back in the form of a human figure
Nyamwezi, Tanzania
Wood, 107 x 43 x 37 cm
Museum für Völkerkunde, Berlin
Inv. III E 6720, acquired in 1898
Plate on p. 158

While everyday stools are regarded as quite ordinary objects in Tanzania, the chiefs of certain peoples have specially carved seats of the most various forms, including those with high backs. As in the Tabwa chairs, this Nyamwezi throne has a figure carved into the back that appears to embrace the sitter. (cf. Maurer and Roberts 1985, p. 187.) 'These thrones, in the form of high-backed chairs, were used by the leaders when they convened to resolve disputes and during the course of initiation ceremonies.' (Felix 1990, p. 370.)

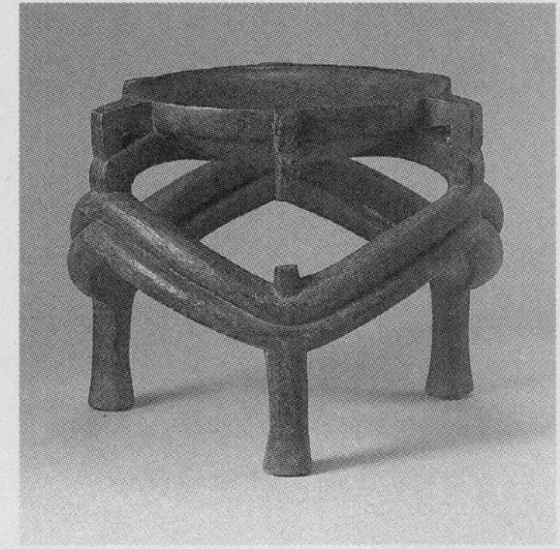

147 Stool
Zaramo, Tanzania
Wood, height 35.7 cm
Musée Barbier-Mueller, Geneva
Inv. 1027-101

'The stools that are to be found throughout the region are not part of the usual furnishings of a house. Most people prefer to sit on mats. There was a recognized hierarchy of sitting, and the type of seating furniture used by each person was a token of his or her rank or status. Stools were part of a family's treasures, which would be passed down from generation to generation, and were used only for ceremonies and rituals. They were a token of leadership and, as it was not permitted to lay sacred objects on the ground, they were always placed on a stool.' (Felix 1990, p. 364.)

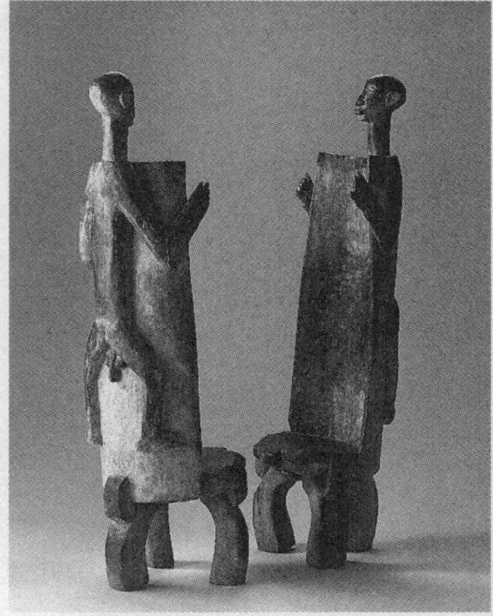

144 Pair of chairs
Nyamwezi, Tanzania
Wood, each 134 x 34 x 41 cm
Musée National des Arts Africains et Océaniens, Paris
Invs. A 933.1 and A 933.2

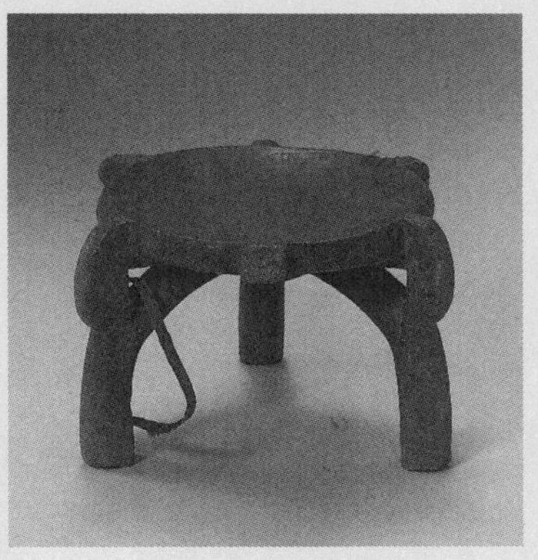

146 Stool
Hehe, Tanzania
Wood, leather, height 22, diam. 28 cm
Linden-Museum, Stuttgart
Inv. 78030, acquired in 1912
Plate on p. 159

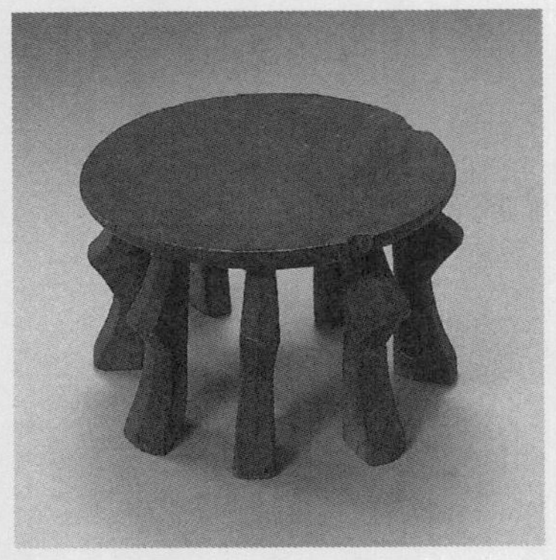

148 Stool
Hehe, Tanzania
Wood, height 25, diam. 35 cm
Linden-Museum, Stuttgart
Inv. 78029, acquired in 1912
Plate on p. 159

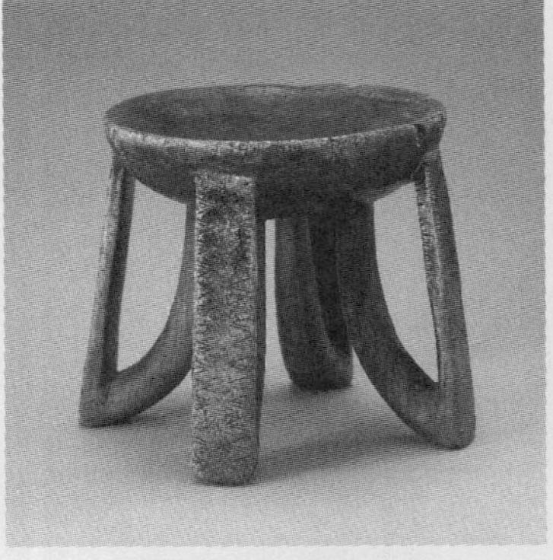

151 Stool
Zambia
Wood, height 24.5, diam. 24 cm
Private collection, Zurich
Plate on p. 137

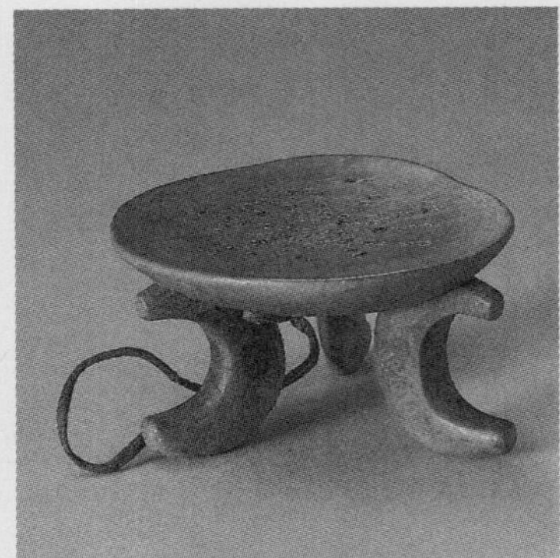

154 Stool
Kamba, Kenya
Wood, copper, iron, leather, height 9, diam. 18 cm
Museum für Völkerkunde, Berlin
Inv. III E 289, acquired in 1876
Plate on p. 163

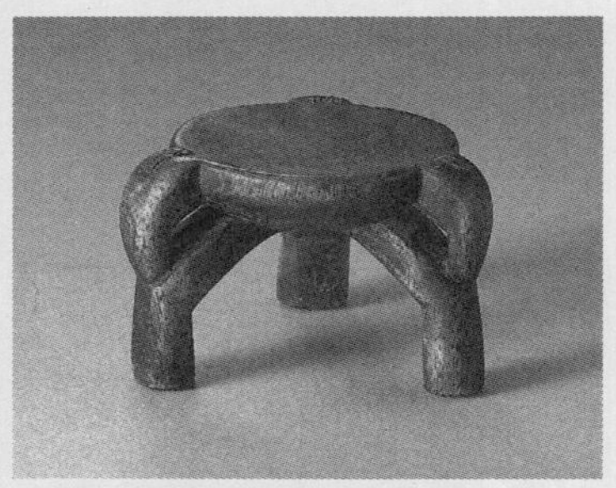

149 Stool
Safwa/Nyamwezi, Tanzania
Wood, brass, 9.5 x 14.5 x 11.5 cm
Museum für Völkerkunde, Berlin
Inv. III E 8856, acquired in 1900

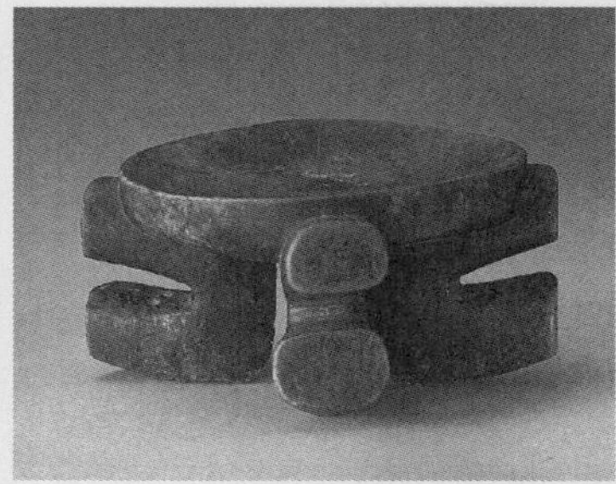

152 Stool
Malawi (Lake Chilwa)
Wood, height 14.3, diam. 24 cm
Museum für Völkerkunde, Berlin
Inv. III E 9611, acquired in 1900

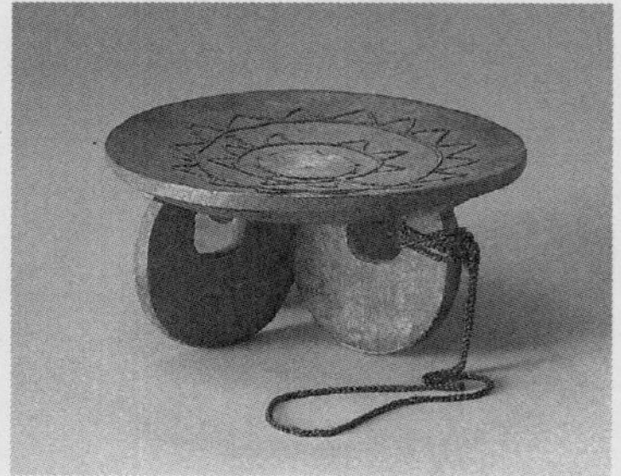

155 Stool
Kamba, Kenya
Wood, copper, iron, brass, height 9.5, diam. 22 cm
Museum für Völkerkunde, Berlin
Inv. III E 16427, acquired in 1916
Plate on p. 163

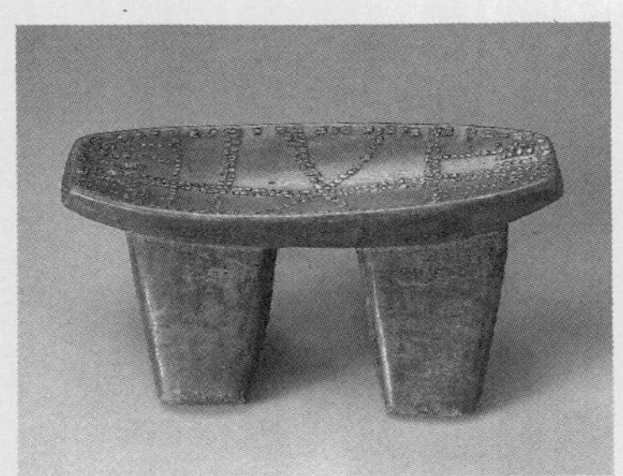

150 Stool
Safwa/Poroto, Tanzania
Wood, iron, brass, 15.5 x 36 x 22 cm
Museum für Völkerkunde, Berlin
Inv. III E 8855, acquired in 1900
Plate on p. 160

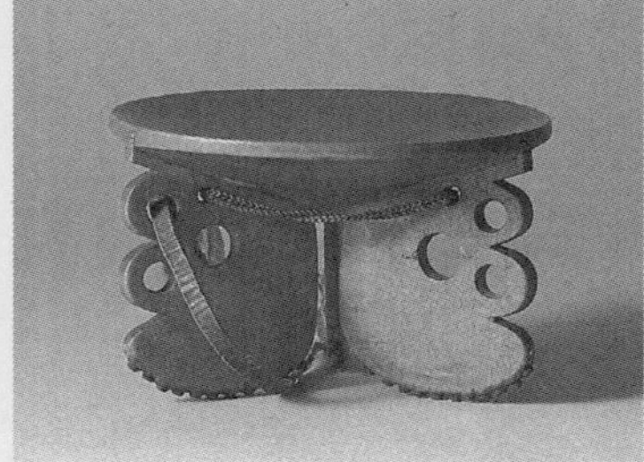

153 Stool
Kamba, Kenya
Wood, leather, iron wire, height 14, diam. 21 cm
British Museum, London
Inv. AF 1925, 1123.3, acquired in 1925

The older men of the Wakamba possessed small, finely worked seats that they carried with them when going to visit friends. These seats were reserved for those men well advanced in years and became a symbol of the oldest age group. (cf. R. M. Gramly, in: Vogel 1988, p. 36.)

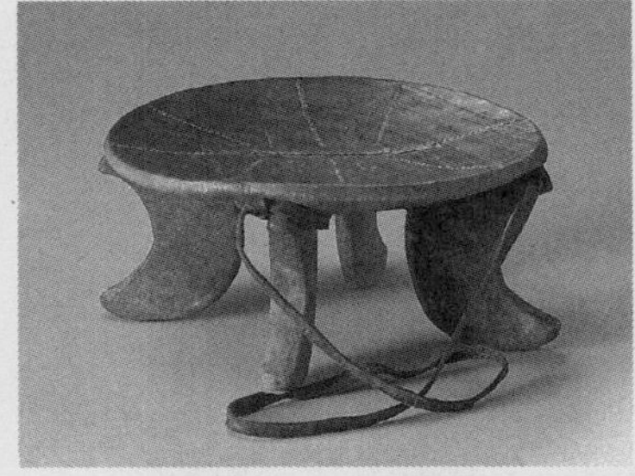

156 Stool
Kamba, Kenya
Wood, iron, copper, leather, height 11.2, diam. 22 cm
Museum für Völkerkunde, Berlin
Inv. III E 11349, acquired in 1905
Plate on p. 163

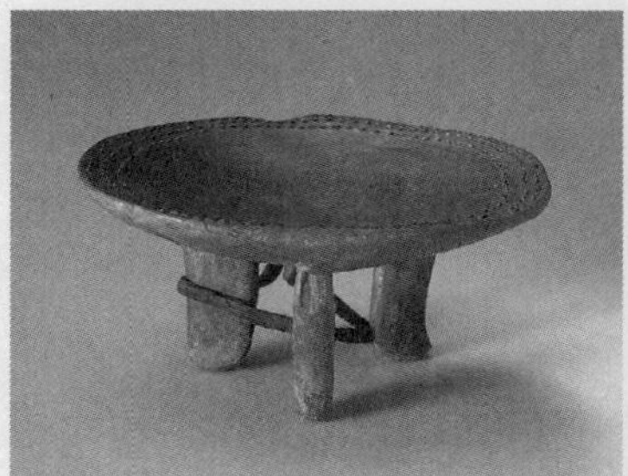

157 Portable stool
Kamba, Kenya
Wood, iron, leather, height 10, diam. 19.7 cm
Museum für Völkerkunde, Berlin
Inv. III E 288, acquired in 1876
Plate on p. 163

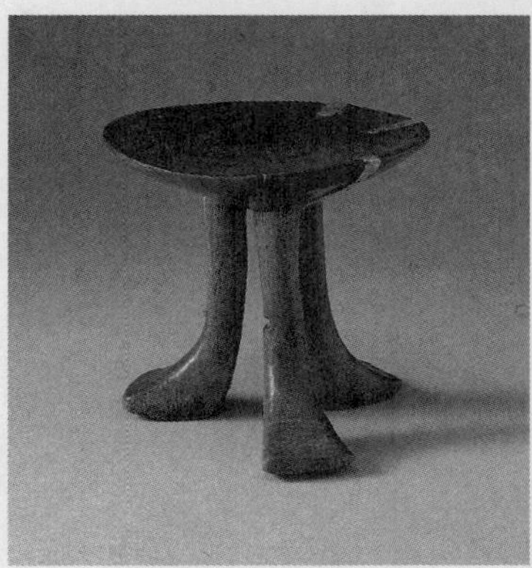

158 Stool
Maasai, Kenya
Wood, height 18, diam. 18.9 cm
Africa Museum, Tervuren
Inv. 74.73.2
Plate on p. 164

During meals men and women sat on stools called *origa*. As they were frequently travelling, they took such stools with them. (Information kindly supplied by the Africa Museum, Tervuren.)

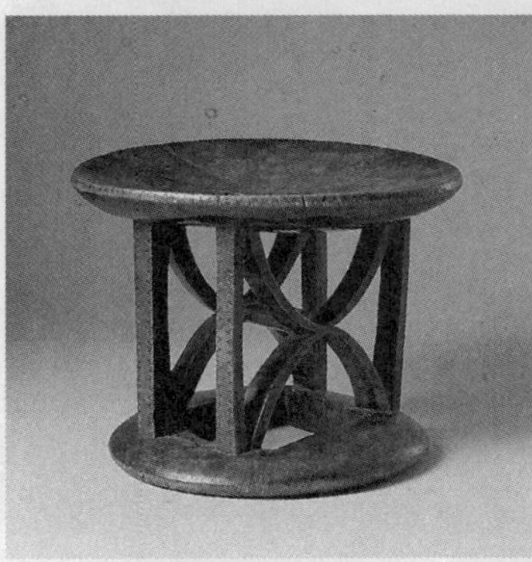

159 Stool
Shona, Zimbabwe
Wood, glass jewellery, height 28.5, diam. 33 cm
Collection of Udo and Waltraud Horstmann, Zug

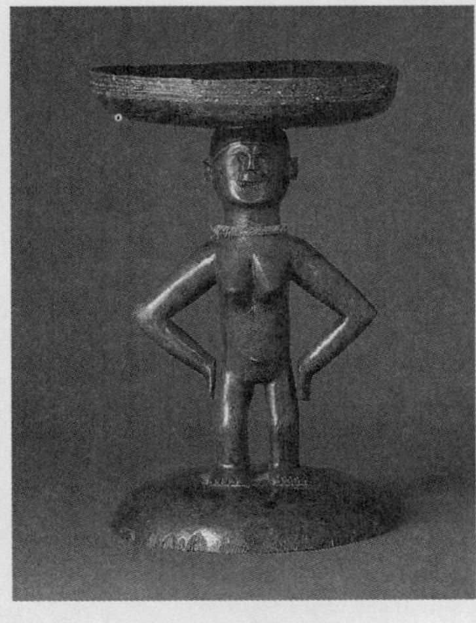

160 Caryatid stool
Makonde, Tanzania
Wood, glass jewellery, height 48 cm
Musée Barbier-Mueller, Geneva
Inv. 1027-6
Plate on p. 165

'This figure exhibits specific traits of Makonde sculpture: a spherical head, an ornamental lip peg (*ndona*), tattoo patterns on the temples and pierced ears. The severely vertical body appears even more powerful, on account of the diamond shape created by its arms and visually balancing the heavy seat. Interestingly, the hands do not touch the body!' (Enrico Castelli, in: Schmalenbach 1988, p. 300.)

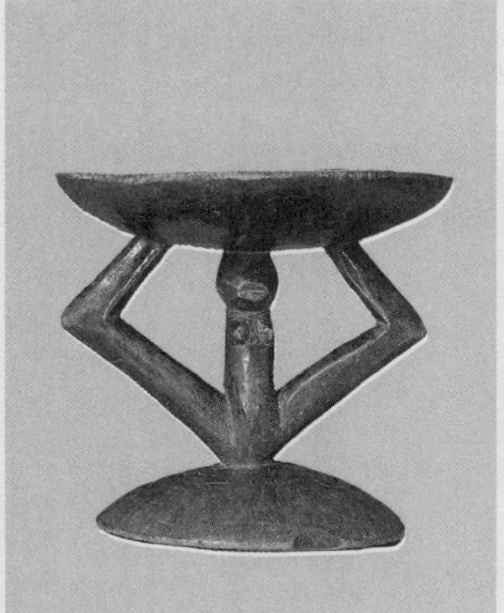

161 Caryatid stool
Thonga, South Africa (Transvaal)
Wood, height 28, diam. 29.5 cm
Africa Museum, Tervuren
Inv. 78.76.2

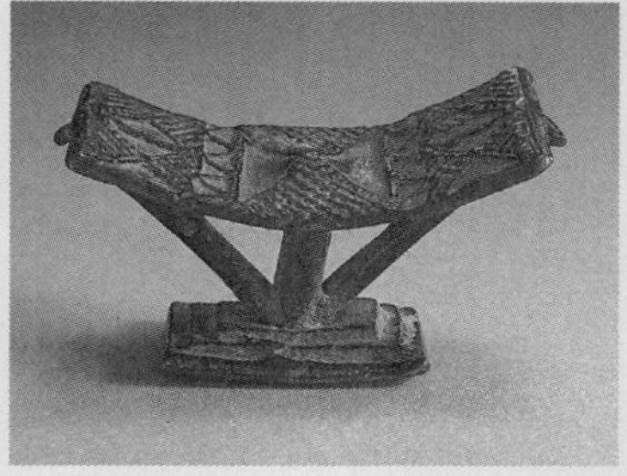

162 Goldweight
Asante, Ghana
Cast brass, height 3.2 cm
R. & D. David, Kilchberg
Plate on p. 85

The region of the Akan – which included the Asante, the Baule and others – was known for its rich reserves of gold. In Ghana gold dust was used as payment as late as the twentieth century. It was measured with the help of small weights. As only the owner knew the precise weight of the individual pieces – they were not standardized – both buyer and seller had first to agree on a price through mutual comparison of their respective weights. Most objects for weighing gold had a geometric form. There were also many figurative representations: scenes from everyday life or miniature renderings of plants, animals or objects of everyday use, such as stools and chairs. The figurative designs were regarded as interpretations of sayings. These goldweights were produced by the lost-wax process, so each one is unique.

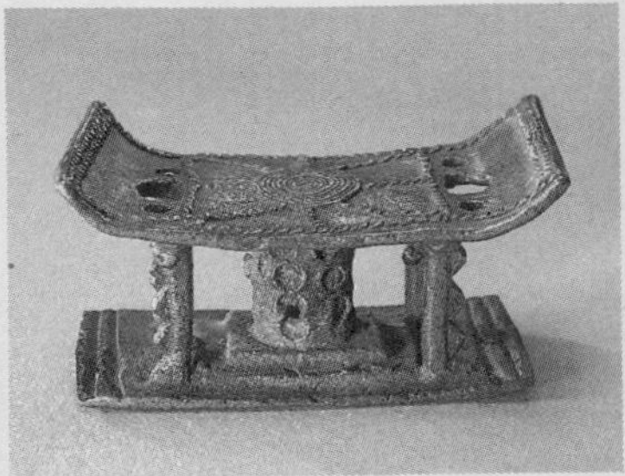

163 Goldweight
Asante, Ghana
Cast brass, height 2.7 cm
R. & D. David, Kilchberg
Plate on p. 85

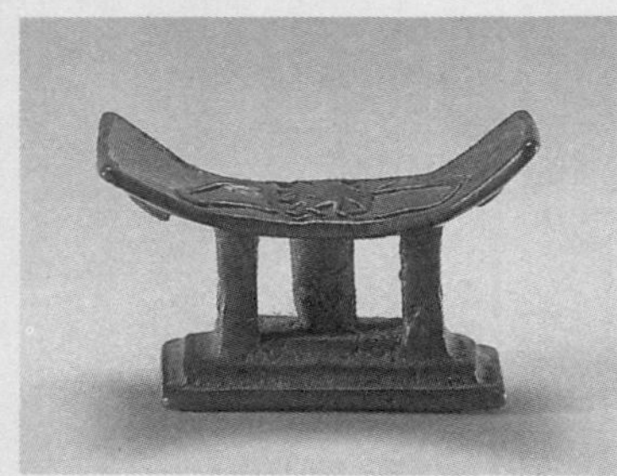

164 Goldweight
Asante, Ghana
Cast brass, 3 x 4.5 x 3 cm
Ingrid Hansen Collection, Zurich

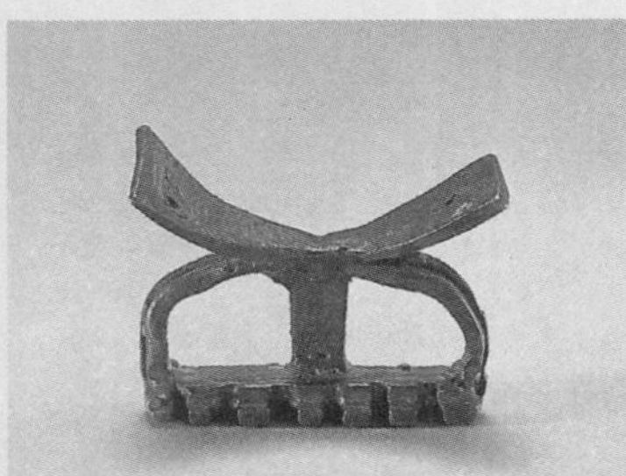

165 Goldweight
Asante, Ghana (Kyebi)
Cast brass, 4 x 3 cm
Bernisches Historisches
Museum, Berne
Inv. Z 350, acquired in 1910

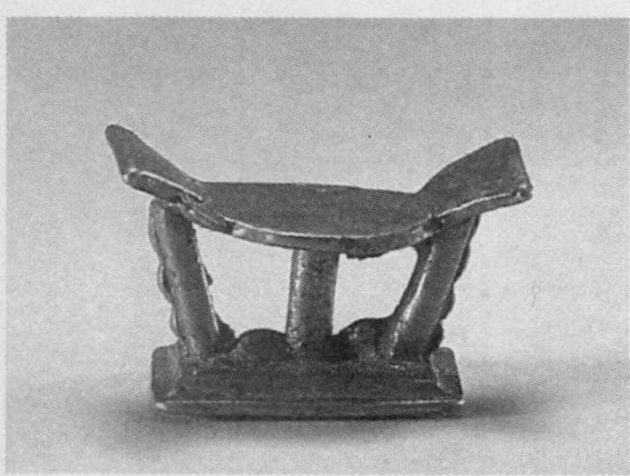

166 Goldweight
Asante, Ghana
Cast brass, height 3 cm
Ingrid Hansen Collection, Zurich

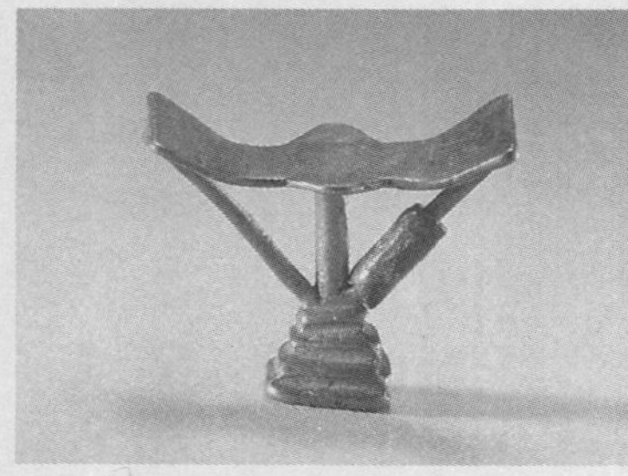

167 Goldweight
Asante, Ghana (Akem-Kotoku)
Cast brass, 4 x 3.5 cm
Bernisches Historisches
Museum, Berne
Inv. Z 273, acquired in 1909

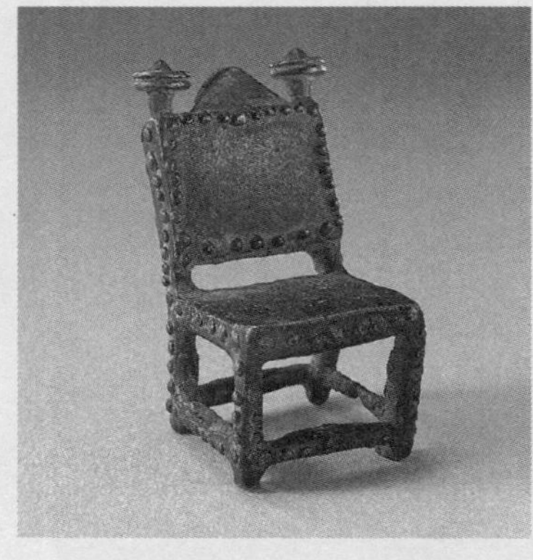

168 Goldweight
Asante, Ghana
Cast brass, height 4.4 cm
R. & D. David, Kilchberg
Plate on p. 84

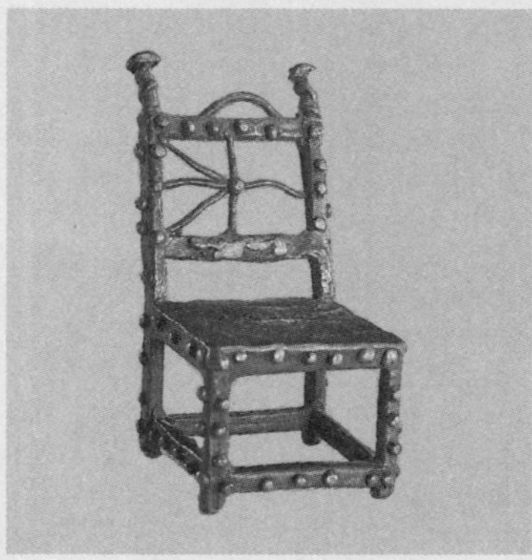

169 Goldweight
Asante, Ghana
Cast brass, height 6.4 cm
R. & D. David, Kilchberg
Plate on p. 85

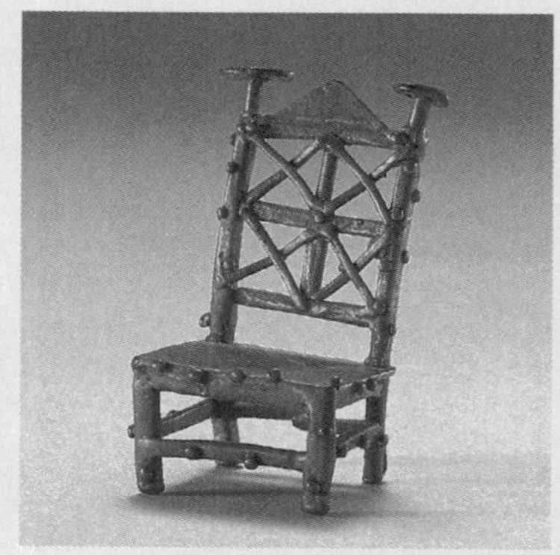

170 Goldweight
Asante, Ghana
Cast brass, 5.5 x 2.5 x 4 cm
Ingrid Hansen Collection, Zurich

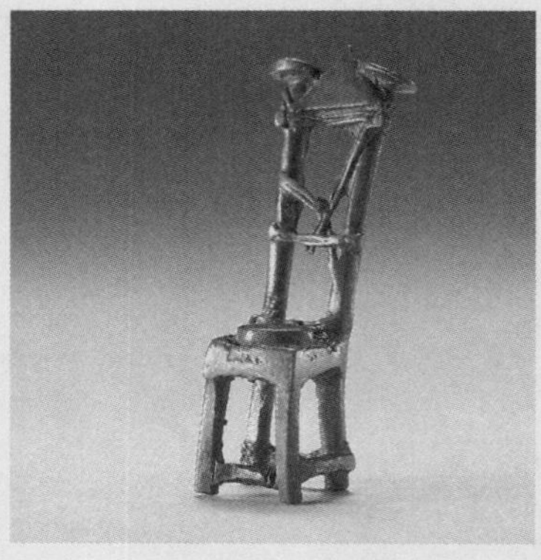

171 Goldweight
Asante, Ghana (Accra)
Cast brass, 8.5 x 2.7 cm
Bernisches Historisches
Museum, Berne
Inv. Z 115, acquired in 1903

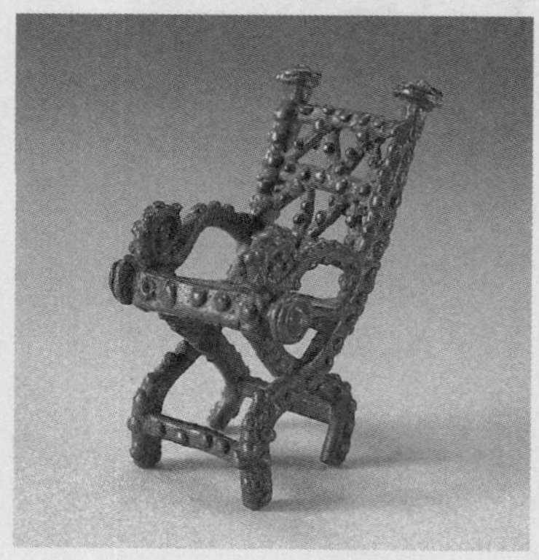

172 Goldweight
Asante, Ghana
Cast brass, height 4.4 cm
R. & D. David, Kilchberg
Plate on p. 85

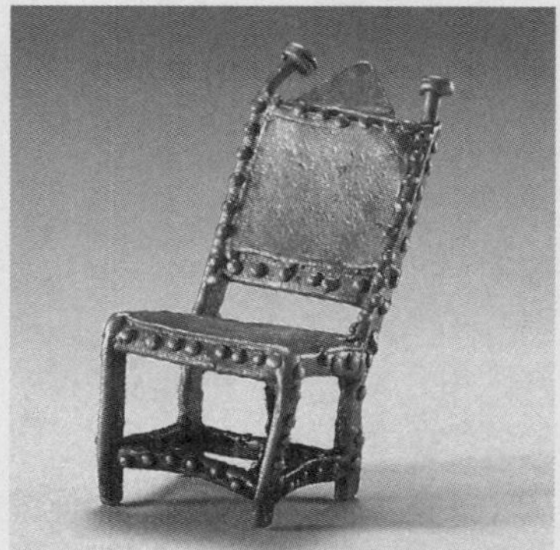

173 Goldweight
Asante, Ghana
Cast brass, height 5 cm
Ingrid Hansen Collection, Zurich

Appendix

Contributors

Ezio Bassani

Born in 1924. In 1973 commissioned by the Centro Studi per la Museologia in Florence to catalogue African sculpture in Italian museums (published 1977). Since 1977 has taught African art history at the Università Internazionale dell'Arte in Florence. In 1980 co-founder, and since then director, of the Centro Studi di Storia delle Arti Africane in Florence. Numerous guest professorships and memberships of academic committees. Has organized various conferences and exhibitions on African art and has contributed to many scholarly publications, including *'Primitivism' in 20th Century Art* (1984) and *Circa 1492 – Art in the Age of Exploration* (1991). Is the author of a number of important volumes on African art, including *Africa and the Renaissance: – Art in Ivory* (1988) and *La grande scultura dell'Africa Nera* (1989).

Sandro Bocola

Born in Trieste in 1931. Grew up in Italy, Libya and Switzerland and has lived in Switzerland since 1970. Initially worked as a painter, sculptor, exhibition designer and commercial artist. From 1970 co-editor, and from 1971 to 1973 director, of the multiples publishers Xartcollection. Attended the Psychoanalytisches Seminar in Zurich. In 1981 established and installed the Museo de Arte Popular in Horta de San Juan, Spain. Since 1981 theoretical publications and articles on social psychology and the psychology of art. Has published two books – *Die Erfahrung des Ungewissen in der Kunst der Gegenwart* (1987) and *Die Kunst der Moderne: Zur Struktur und Dynamik ihrer Entwicklung* (1994).

Hans Himmelheber

Born in Karlsruhe in 1908. Studied ethnology in Berlin, Munich and Tübingen. In 1933 made own expedition to the Ivory Coast, where he was the first to carry out studies in the field on the carvers of two African tribes. In 1934 doctoral dissertation 'Negerkünstler' at the University of Tübingen. Twelve further expeditions to Africa, some of these together with his wife, Ulrike Himmelheber, and his stepson, Eberhard Fischer. In 1936–7, ten-month stay in Alaska. In 1948 qualified as a medical doctor at the University of Heidelberg. Numerous publications, including *Die Dan – Ein Bauervolk im afrikanischen Urwald* (1958, co-authored with Ulrike Himmelheber), *Negerkunst und Negerkünstler* (1960), *Eskimokünstler* (1938).

Lorenz Homberger

Born in 1949. Studied law in Zurich. From 1976 to 1981 worked as a lawyer in Zurich. Since 1981 has been curator at the Museum Rietberg, Zurich. Extensive fieldwork among the Guro (Ivory Coast), studying traditional techniques of art production and divination. President of the Museumskommission der Schweizer ethnologischen Gesellschaft, member of the committee of ICOM for Switzerland and the Swiss Society for African Studies. Has organized various exhibitions on the art of West Africa, including *Die Kunst der Guro* (1985), *Die Kunst der Senufo* (1988), *Spoons in African Art: Emblems of Abundance* (1990), *Yoruba: Art and Aesthetics* (1991), and edited the accompanying catalogues.

Andrea Knecht Oti-Amoako

Born in Zurich in 1960. Studied ethnology in Zurich, taking her degree in 1987. Since then has worked as a free-lance ethnologist and has contributed to several exhibitions and publications.

Piet Meyer

Born in 1953. From 1972 to 1979 studied ethnology and art history in Munich and Basle. Extensive ethnological fieldwork among the Lobi in Burkina Faso, studying soothsaying, art and religion. In 1981 organized the exhibition *Kunst und Religion der Lobi* at the Museum Rietberg in Zurich (where he spent two years on the curatorial staff) and edited the accompanying catalogue. Spent two years working as an artist in Basle and New York. Since 1993 has been Chief Curator of the African department of the Rautenstrauch-Joest-Museum für Völkerkunde in Cologne.

Heini Schneebeli

Born in 1943. From 1960 to 1964 studied at the Kunstgewerbeschule, Zurich. From 1964 to 1972 worked as a photographer at the Atelier Joseph Müller-Brockmann in Zurich, at GGK in Basle and at Pentagram in London. From 1973 to 1979 taught at St Martin's School of Art in London and also at the Bath Academy of Art. Since 1973 has worked as a free-lance photographer, based in London. Has collaborated with leading design studios and has also carried out photo reportage assignments in Africa, the Middle East, the Far East and America. Has contributed to various journals and books, including *People of the Golden Triangle* (1984), *Shoowa Design* (1986), *The Tiger Rugs of Tibet* (1988), *The Nagas* (1990) and *Africa – Relics of the Colonial Era* (1991).

Roy Sieber

Born in Wisconsin in 1923. In 1957 obtained his Ph. D. at State University of Iowa. In 1957–8 received a grant from the Ford Foundation to carry out research at the British Museum, London, and in Nigeria. In 1964 taught at the University of Ghana. Since 1964 has taught at the University of Indiana at Bloomington, Indiana, initially as Professor of Art History and from 1974 as Rudy Professor of Fine Arts (from 1993 as Emeritus). Has also held various guest professorships. From 1983 to 1993 was Associate Director for Collections and Research at the National Museum of African Art, Smithsonian Institution, Washington, D. C. Has organized numerous exhibitions, including *Sculpture of Northern Nigeria* (1961), *African Textiles and Decorative Arts* (1972), *African Furniture and Household Objects* (1980–1), *African Art in the Cycle of Life* (1987–8), and edited the accompanying catalogues.

Dieter Thiel

Born in Hamburg in 1947. Studied design at the Hochschule für Bildende Künste, Hamburg. Worked in design studios in Zurich and Milan. Freelance work for Mario Bellini, collaborating with him on designs for products by Erco, Lamy and Vitra. Adviser to Vitra and Lamy on the development of products and of concepts for trade fair and exhibition displays. Has received a number of international awards for his product designs and for his exhibition and showroom installations.

Bibliography

Allison, Philip A. *African Stone Sculpture.* London, 1968

Ardener, Edwin. *Coastal Bantu of the Cameroons.* London, 1956

Astley, Thomas, ed. *A New General Collection of Voyages and Travels, Consisting of the Most Esteemed Relations, Which Have Been Hitherto Published in Many Languages: Comprehending Everything Remarkable in its Kind, in Europe, Asia, Africa and America.* 4 vols. London, 1745–7

Barbier, Jean Paul, ed. *L'Art de la Côte d'Ivoire de la Collection du Musée Barbier-Mueller, Genève.* 2 vols. Geneva, 1992

Barbot, John [= Jean]. 'A Description of the Coasts of North and South-Guinea; and of Ethiopia Inferior, Vulgarly Angola,' in: vol. v of Awnsham and John Churchill, *A Collection of Voyages and Travels, Some now first Printed from Original Manuscripts. Others Translated out of Foreign Languages, and now first Publish'd in English ... With a General Preface, giving an Account of the Progress of Navigation from its first Beginning. ...* Vols. I-IV: London, 1704; vols. V-VI: London, 1732

Bascom, William R. *The Yoruba of Southwestern Nigeria.* Case Studies in Cultural Anthropology. New York and London, 1969

Bassani, Ezio. *Un cappuccino nell'Africa Nera del seicento.* Quaderno Poro no. 4. Milan, 1987

Bassani, Ezio. *La grande scultura dell'Africa Nera.* Florence, 1989

Bassani, Ezio, and William B. Fagg. *Africa and the Renaissance: Art in Ivory.* Exh. cat., The Center for African Art, New York, 1988; Houston, 1989. New York and Munich, 1988

Bastin, Marie-Louise. *La Sculpture Tschokwe.* Meudon, 1982

Bastin, Marie-Louise. *Introduction aux arts d'Afrique noire.* Arts d'Afrique noire. Arnouville-les-Gonesse, 1984

Baum, Peter (ed). *Ursprung und Moderne.* Exh. cat., Neue Galerie der Stadt, Wolfgang-Gurlitt Museum, Linz, 1990. Linz, 1990

Berjonneau, Gérald, and Jean Sonnery. *Chefs-d'œuvre inédits de l'Afrique noire.* Paris, 1987

Beumers, Erna, and Hans-Joachim Koloß. *Kings of Africa: Art and Authority in Central Africa. Collection of the Museum für Völkerkunde, Berlin.* Exh. cat., Netherlands Foundation, Maastricht, 1992. Utrecht, 1992

Biebuyck, Daniel. *Lega Culture: Art Initiation and Moral Philosophy Among a Central African People.* Berkeley, 1973

Biebuyck, Daniel. *Symbolism of the Lega Stool.* Working Papers in the Traditional Arts, 2. Philadelphia, 1977

Bocola, Sandro. *Die Erfahrung des Ungewissen in der Kunst der Gegenwart.* Zurich, 1987

Bocola, Sandro. *Die Kunst der Moderne: Zur Struktur und Dynamik ihrer Entwicklung.* Munich, 1994

Born, Klaus. *Skulpturen aus Kamerun: Sammlung Thorbecke 1911/12.* Bildhefte des Städtischen Reiß-Museums, Mannheim, Völkerkunde Sammlung, no. 2. Mannheim, 1981

Bosman, William [= Willem]. *A New and Accurate Description of the Coast of Guinea, Divided into the Gold, the Slave, and the Ivory Coasts: Containing a Geographical, Political and Natural History of the Kingdoms and Countries ...* London, 1705; 2nd edn., 1721. Reprint London, 1967

Cavazzi, Giovanni Antonio. *Istorica descrizione de' tre regni, Congo, Matamba et Angola ...* Bologna, 1687

Cole, Herbert M. 'Ibo Art and Authority', in: Douglas Fraser and Herbert M. Cole (eds.), *African Art and Leadership,* pp. 79–97. Madison, 1972

Cole, Herbert M., and Doran H. Ross (eds.). *The Arts of Ghana.* Exh. cat., Frederick S. Wight Gallery, University of California, Los Angeles; Walker Art Center, Minneapolis; Dallas Museum of Art, Dallas; 1977–8. Los Angeles, 1977

Cornet, Joseph. *Art Royal Kuba.* Milan, 1982

Crowley, Daniel J. 'Chokwe: Political Art in a Plebeian Society', in: Douglas Fraser and Herbert M. Cole (eds.), *African Art and Leadership,* pp. 21–39. Madison, 1972

Dagan, Esther A. *Man at Rest / L'Homme au repos.* Ex. cat., Centre Saidye Bronfman, Montreal, 1985. Montreal, 1985

Dagan, Esther A. *Asante Stools.* Ex. cat., Galerie Amrad African Arts, Montreal, 1988. Montreal, 1988

Dalzel, Archibald. *The History of Dahomey, an Inland Kingdom of Africa.* London, 1793

Dark, Philip J. C. *An Introduction to Benin Art and Technology.* Oxford, 1973

Dark, Philip J. C., with W. and B. Forman. *Benin Art*. London, 1960

Dewey, William J. *Sleeping Beauties: The Jerome L. Joss Collection of African Headrests at UCLA*. Los Angeles, 1993

Dibie, Pascal. *Ethnologie de la chambre à coucher*. Paris, 1987

Drewal, Henry John. 'Ife: Origin of Art and Civilization', in: Henry John Drewel, John Pemberton III and Rowland Abiodun, *Yoruba: Nine Centuries of African Art and Thought*, pp. 44–75. New York, 1989

Duquette, Danielle Gallois. *Dynamique de l'art Bidjogo (Guinée-Bissau): Contributions à une anthropologie de l'art des sociétés africaines*. Lisbon, 1983

Einstein, Carl. *Negerplastik*. Leipzig, 1915; 2nd edn., Munich, 1920; reprint, Berlin, 1992

Eyo, Ekpo, and Frank Willett. *Treasures of Ancient Nigeria*. Exh. cat., Detroit Institute of Arts, Detroit, and eight other US venues: 1980–2. New York, 1980. Nasjonalgalleriet, Oslo; Royal Academy of Arts, London, 1982–3. London, 1982

Ezra, Kate. *Art of the Dogon: Selections from the Lester Wunderman Collection*. New York, 1988

Fagg, Bernard. *Nok Terracottas*. London, 1977

Fagg, Bernard, and William B. Fagg. 'The Ritual Stools of Ancient Ife', in: *Man* CLV (1960), pp. 112–15

Fagg, William B. *Nigerian Images*. London, 1963

Falgayrettes, Christiane (ed.). *Support de rêves*. Exh. cat., Musée Dapper, Paris, 1989. Paris, 1989

Felix, Marc L. *Mwana Hiti: Life and Art of the Matrilineal Bantu of Tanzania / Leben und Kunst der matrilinearen Bantu von Tansania*. Munich, 1990

Fischer, Eberhard, and Lorenz Homberger. *Die Kunst der Guro, Elfenbeinküste*. Exh. cat., Museum Rietberg, Zurich, 1985. Zurich, 1985

Flam, Jack D. 'The Symbolic Structure of Baluba Caryatid Stools', in: *African Arts* IV/2 (1971), pp. 54–9, 80

Forster, Till. *Die Kunst der Senufo aus Schweizer Sammlungen*. Exh. cat., Museum Rietberg, Zurich, 1988. Zurich, 1988

Freeman, Richard Austin. *Travels and Life in Ashanti and Jaman*. New York, 1898

Freeman, Thomas Birch. *Journal of Various Visits to the Kingdoms of Ashanti, Aku and Dahomi, in West Africa*. London, 1844

Gardi, René. *Auch im Lehmhaus laßt sich's leben (Über traditionelles Bauen und Wohnen in Westafrika)*. Berne, 1973. French trans. *Maisons africaines (L'art traditionnel de bâtir en Afrique occidentale)*. Paris and Brussels, 1974

Geary, Christraud M. 'Bamum Thrones and Stools', in: *African Arts* XIV/4 (1981), pp. 32–43, 87–8

Geary, Christraud M. *Things of the Palace: A catalogue of the Bamum Palace Museum in Foumban (Cameroon)*. Wiesbaden, 1983

Geary, Christraud M. 'Old Pictures, New Approaches: Researching Historical Photographs', in: *African Arts* XXIV/4 (1991), pp. 36–9, 98

Gilot, Françoise, and Carlton Luke. *Life with Picasso*. New York, 1964; London, 1965

Gramly, Richard Michael. 'Art and Anthropology on a Sliding Scale', in: Susan Vogel, *ART/artifact: African Art in Anthropology Collections*, pp. 33–40. New York and Munich, 1988

Hart, Paul E. H. (ed.). *Barbot on Guinea: The Writings of Jean Barbot on West Africa*. 2 vols. London, 1992

Harter, Pierre. *Arts anciens du Cameroun*. Arts d'Afrique noire. Arnouville-les-Gonesse, 1986

Heintze, Beatrix. 'A cultura material dos Ambundu segundo as fontes dos seculos XVI e XVII', in: *Revista Internacional de Estudios Africanos* X–XI (1989), pp. 15–63

Himmelheber, Hans. *Negerkünstler: Ethnographische Studien über den Schnitzkünstler bei den Stämmen der Atutu und Guru im Innen der Elfenbeinküste*. Stuttgart, 1935

Himmelheber, Hans. 'Die Großvater-Stühlchen der Guéré', in: *Baessler-Archiv*, Neue Folge, XIII (1965), pp. 539–44

Himmelheber, Hans. *Zaire 1938/39: Photographic Documents on the Arts of the Yaka, Pende, Tschokwe and Kuba / Fotodokumente zur Kunst bei dem Yaka, Pende, Tschokwe und Kuba*. Exh. cat., Museum Rietberg, Zurich, 1993. Zurich, 1993

Homberger, Lorenz (ed.). *Eßgerät – Kultobjekt: Löffel in der Kunst Afrikas / Spoons in African Art: Emblems of Abundance*. Exh. cat., Museum Rietberg, Zurich, 1990. Zurich, 1990. English edn., Zurich, 1991

Homberger, Lorenz (ed.). Rowland Abiodun, Henry John Drewel and John Pemberton III, *Yoruba: Kunst und Ästhetik in Nigeria / Yoruba: Art and Aesthetics*. Exh. cat., Museum Rietberg, Zurich, 1991. Zurich, 1991

Imperato, Pascal James. *Dogon Cliff Dwellers: The Art of Mali's Mountain People*. New York, 1978

Jack, Anthony. *Africa: Relics of the Colonial Era*. London, 1991

Jones, Gwilym Iwan. *Ibo Art*. Aylesbury, 1989

Kaplan, Flora S. (ed.). *Images of Power: Art of the Royal Court of Benin*. New York, 1981

Kauenhoven-Janzen, Reinhild. 'Chokwe Thrones', in: *African Arts* xiv/3 (1981), pp. 69–74, 92

Kecskési, Maria. *Kunst aus dem alten Afrika: Sammlungen aus dem Staatlichen Museum für Völkerkunde München*. Vol. 2. Innsbruck, 1982

Kochnitzky, Leon. *Negro Art in the Belgian Congo*. New York, 1948

Koloß, Hans-Joachim (ed.). *Art of Central Africa: Masterpieces from the Berlin Museum für Völkerkunde*. Exh. cat., Metropolitan Museum of Art, New York, 1990. New York, 1990

Kreide-Damani, Ingrid. *Kunstethnologie: Zum Verständnis fremder Kunst*. Cologne, 1992

Kyerematen, A. A. Y. *Panoply of Ghana*. London, 1964

Kyerematen, A. A. Y. 'The Royal Stools of the Ashanti', in: *Africa* xxxix/1 (1969), pp. 1–10

Laude, Jean (ed.). *African Art of the Dogon: The Myths of the Cliff Dwellers*. Exh. cat., Brooklyn Museum, New York, and eight other US venues; 1973 onwards. New York, 1973

Leuzinger, Elsy. *Afrikanische Skulpturen: Beschreibender Katalog / African Sculpture: A Descriptive Catalogue*. Museum Rietberg, Zurich, 1978

Luschan, Felix von. *Die Altertümer von Benin*. Veröffentlichungen aus dem Museum für Völkerkunde, viii–x. Berlin and Leipzig, 1919

Mack, John. *Emil Torday and the Art of the Congo 1900–1909*. London, 1990; Seattle, 1992

Maurer, Evan M., and Allen F. Roberts (eds.). *Tabwa: The Rising of a New Moon*. Ann Arbor, 1985

McLeod, Malcolm D. *The Asante*. London, 1981

Meyer, Piet (ed.). *Kunst und Religion der Lobi*. Exh. cat., Museum Rietberg, Zurich, 1981. Zurich, 1981

Northern, Tamara. *The Art of Cameroon*. Washington, D. C., 1984

Pemberton III, John. 'The Stone Images of Ife', in: Henry John Drewel, John Pemberton III and Rowland Abiodun, *Yoruba: Nine Centuries of African Art and Thought*, pp. 77–89. New York, 1989

Perrois, Louis. *Art Ancestral du Gabon*. Geneva, 1985; English trans., *Ancestral Art of Gabon from the Collections of the Barbier-Mueller Museum*. Exh. cat., Dallas Museum of Art; Los Angeles County Museum of Art; 1986–7

Picton, John, and John Mack. *African Textiles*. London, 1979; 2nd edn., 1989

Ravenhill, Phillip. *The Art of the Personal Object*. Exh. cat., National Museum of African Art, Smithsonian Institution, Washington, D. C., 1992. Washington, D. C., 1992

Rubin, William (ed.). *'Primitivism' in 20th Century Art*. Exh. cat., Museum of Modern Art, New York, 1984. New York, 1984. German trans., *Primitivismus in der Kunst des 20. Jahrhunderts*. Munich, 1984

Schildkrout, Enid. 'The Spectacle of Africa Through the Lens of Herbert Lang: Belgian Congo Photographs 1909–1915', in: *African Arts* xxiv/4 (1991), pp. 70–85, 100

Schildkrout, Enid, C. A. Keim et al. *African Reflections: Art from Northeastern Zaire*. Exh. cat., American Museum of Natural History, New York, 1989–90. New York, Seattle and London, 1990

Schindlbeck, Markus (ed.). *Die ethnographische Linse: Photographien aus dem Museum für Völkerkunde Berlin*. Exh. cat., Museum für Völkerkunde, Berlin, 1989. Berlin, 1989

Schmalenbach, Werner. *Die Kunst Afrikas*. Basle, 1953. English trans., *African Art*. New York and Basle, 1954

Schmalenbach, Werner. *Afrikanische Kunst aus der Sammlung Barbier-Mueller, Genf*. Munich, 1988

Schmalenbach, Werner. 'Grundsätzliches zur Ästhetik der afrikanischen Kunst', in: Miklós Szalay (ed.), *Der Sinn des Schönen: Ästhetik, Soziologie und Geschichte der afrikanischen Kunst*, pp. 49–62. Munich, 1990

Schweinfurth, Georg. *Im Herzen von Afrika: Reisen und Entdeckungen im zentralen Äquatorial-Afrika während der Jahre 1868 bis 1871* ... Leipzig, 1874; 2nd edn., 1878; 3rd, rev. ed., 1918); English trans., *The Heart of Africa: Three Years' Travels and Adventures in the Unexplored Regions of Central Africa from 1868 to 1871* ... 2 vols. London, 1873; 3rd, rev. ed., 1878

Shaw, Thurstan. *Igbo Ukwu: An Account of Archaeological Discoveries in Eastern Nigeria*. 2 vols. London, 1970

Sieber, Roy (ed.). *African Textiles and Decorative Arts*. Exh. cat., The Museum of

Modern Art, New York, 1972. New York, 1972

Sieber, Roy (ed.). *African Furniture and Household Objects*. Exh. cat., Indianapolis Museum of Art; Nelson Art Gallery, Atkins Museum, Kansas City; The Fine Arts Museum of San Francisco; Brooks Memorial Art Gallery, Memphis; The Brooklyn Museum, New York; 1980–1. New York, Bloomington and London, 1980

Stevens Jr., Phillips. *The Stone Images of Esie*. Ibadan, 1978

Szalay, Miklós. *Die Kunst Schwarzafrikas: Werke aus der Sammlung des Völkerkundemuseums der Universität Zürich*, Part I: *Kunst und Gesellschaft*. Ethnologische Schriften, 5. Zurich, 1986.

Szalay, Miklós (ed.) *Der Sinn des Schönen: Ästhetik, Soziologie und Geschichte der afrikanischen Kunst*. Munich, 1990

Tagliaferri, Aldo. *Stili del potere*. Milan, 1989

Theye, Thomas (ed.). *Der geraubte Schatten · Eine Weltreise im Spiegel der ethnographischen Photographie*. Munich and Lucerne, 1989

Thompson, Robert Farris. *African Art in Motion: Icon and Act in the Collection of Katherine Coryton White*. Exh. cat., Frederick S. White Gallery, University of California at Los Angeles; National Gallery of Art, Washington, D. C.; 1974. Los Angeles, 1974

Torday, Emil, and T. A. Joyce. *Notes ethnographiques sur les peuples communément appelés Bakuba, ainsi que sur les peuplades apparantées: Les Bushongo*. Brussels, 1910

Underwood, Leon. *Bronzes of West Africa*. London, 1949

Vallées du Niger. Exh. cat., Musée National des Arts Africains et Océaniens, Paris, 1993; Leyden, 1994; Philadelphia, 1994; and six other venues. Paris, 1993

Vogel, Susan (ed.). *ART/artifact: African Art in Anthropology Collections*. New York and Munich, 1988

Willett, Frank. 'Ife and its Archaeology', in: *Journal of African History* I/2 (1960), pp. 231–48

Willett, Frank. 'The Ritual Stools of Ancient Ife', in: *Man* CLXXXVI/CLXXXVII (1961), pp. 162–3

Willett, Frank. *Ife in the History of West African Sculpture*. London, 1967

Willett, Frank. 'A missing millennium? From Nok to Ife and beyond', in: Ezio Bassani (ed.), *Arte in Africa*, pp. 87–100. Modena, 1986

Wood, Revd John George. *The Natural History of Man; being an account of the manners and customs of the uncivilized races of men* ... 2 vols. London, 1868–70; 2nd edn., Hartford, Conn., 1871

z. B. Stuhle, ein Streifzug durch die Kulturgeschichte des Sitzens ... Exh. cat. (ed. Deutscher Werkbund), Badischer Kunstverein, Karlsruhe; Kunstmuseum, Düsseldorf; 1982. Gießen, 1982

Photographs: Sources and Acknowledgements

The colour photographs in the plate section (pp. 54–168) as well as the photographs in the catalogue (pp. 170–92) were mostly taken by Heini Schneebeli. The publisher and authors would also like to thank the following photographers, photographic archives and copyright holders for providing material for the illustrations (figures indicate page numbers; catalogue numbers refer to the catalogue section):

Africa Museum, Tervuren: 34 (photo S. Molin; neg. 26269), 111 (photo Thevoz; neg. 1336), 128 (photo Thevoz; neg. 5807), 151, cat. 120 (neg. G.3045), cat. 135 (neg. 111459); © 56–8, 59 bottom, 60, 78, 107, 118, 120, 121, 124, 127, 130, 131, 133 top, 134, 137 bottom, 144–7, 149, 152, 161, 164, cats. 3–6, 11, 27, 28, 43, 66, 85, 89, 90–93, 95, 96, 98–103, 105, 107, 109, 110, 115, 120, 126, 132, 134, 135, 137, 158, 161
American Museum of Natural History, New York; Courtesy Department of Library Services: 109 (photo Herbert Lang; neg. 111980), 110 top (photo Herbert Lang; neg. 111841), 110 bottom (photo Herbert Lang; neg. 111920)
artek, Helsinki: 21 top
Roger Asselberghs, Brussels: 114, cat. 129
Jean Paul Barbier, Geneva: 21 bottom, 70, cat. 79
Monique Barbier-Mueller, Geneva: 33 top
Archiv Barbier-Mueller, Geneva: 87 (photo Eberhard)
Basler Mission Archiv: 32 (photo Fritz Ramseyer; neg. QD-30.41.104), 53 (photo Fritz Ramseyer; neg. QD-32.027.0320), 86 (photo Helene Oldenburg; neg. E-30.29.d8), 88 bottom (photo M. Göhring; neg. E-30.26.51), 89 (photo Anna Rein-Wuhrmann; neg. E-30.31.61)
Bildarchiv Foto Marburg: 15 bottom (neg. 1.160.693)
© Sandro Bocola and Vitra Design Museum: 54, 55, 59 top, 61–4, 67, 69, 71–3, 75–7, 79, 80, 82, 84, 85, 90–3, 95, 97, 103–5, 112, 113, 117, 119, 122, 123, 125, 129, 132, 133 bottom, 136, 137 top, 138–40, 143, 148, 150, 153, 155, 159, 162, 165–7, cats. 2, 7–10, 12–23, 25, 26, 29–38, 40, 41, 45–55, 57–63, 65, 67, 69, 70, 75–77, 82–84, 87, 88, 94, 104, 106, 108, 114, 116–119, 122–125, 127, 128, 131, 133, 138, 140–144, 146–148, 151, 153, 159, 160, 162–173
The British Museum, Museum of Mankind, London: 38 top
Jean Christen, Mannheim: 106, cat. 68
R. & D. David, Kilchberg: cat. 42
Pierre-Alain Ferrazzini, Geneva: 93 bottom, cat. 61
Frobenius-Institut, Frankfurt am Main: 98 (by kind permission of the Stadt- und Universitätsbibliothek, Frankfurt am Main)
René Gardi: 66
Ghana Information Service: 31
E. Ablade Glover, University of Science and Technology, Kumasi: 44, 45
Grund & Flum, Basle: 154, cat. 121
Jeffrey Hammer, Los Angeles: 65, cat. 56
Luc Hautecœur, Paris: 100, 101, cat. 71
W. H. Hilton-Simpson: 108
Hans Himmelheber: 23, 42, 43 top, 50, 142
Foto Hinz, Basle: cat. 30
Lorenz Homberger: 27 bottom, 52
Udo Horstmann: 25 middle
Andrea Knecht Oti-Amoako: 24 bottom, 36 top
Hans-Joachim Koloß: 96
Hélène and Philippe Leloup, Paris: cat. 112 (photo Hughes Dubois)
By kind permission of Galerie Albert Loeb, Paris: 14
Malcolm D. McLeod: 74
Piet Meyer, Zurich: 22
Monzino Collection: 41 top
Archives Musée Dapper, Paris: 115, cat. 130 (photo Hughes Dubois)
Musée de l'Homme, Collection Photothèque, Paris: 51 (photo Aubert de la Rue; neg. C 39.1037.18), 88 top (photo F. Christol; neg. 66.4367.730), 94 (photo F. Christol; neg. D 66.4395.730)
Museum Rietberg, Zurich: 24 top, 25 top, 27 top, 29 (3 figs.)
National Museum, Lagos: 39 left (photo André and Ursula Held; neg. E 13624-14055), 40 top (photo André and Ursula Held)
National Museum of African Art, Eliot Elisofon Photographic Archives, Smithsonian Institution, Washington, D. C.: 30, 35 (photo Casimir d'Ostoja Zagourski; series 1, no 59), 36 bottom, 37 (photo Roy Sieber)
Österreichische Nationalbibliothek, Bildarchiv, Vienna: 28 bottom (photo Paul Schebesta; neg. 59677)
Réunion des Musées Nationaux, Paris: 16 top, 40 bottom (photo Denis Rouvre)
Sammlung Museum für Völkerkunde, Vienna: 156 (photo Mösenbacher)
Heini Schneebeli: 15 top, 17 left, 17 right, 18 top, 18 bottom, 19 left, 19 right, 20 (figs. 12–18), 26 left
The Seattle Art Museum, Nasli and Alice Heermaneck Collection, Seattle: 25 bottom (photo Katherine C. White), 41 middle
Staatliche Museen zu Berlin, Preußischer Kulturbesitz, Museum für Völkerkunde: 26 middle (neg. III C 19454), 26 right (neg. III C 18544), 38 bottom (neg. VIII A 15283, Inv. III C 20296); © 68, 81, 99, 102, 141, 158, 160, 163, cats. 1, 44, 74, 78, 113, 145, 149, 150, 152, 154–157
Staatliches Museum für Völkerkunde, Munich: 41 bottom; © 83, 116, cats. 39, 64, 80, 136
Serge Veignant, Paris: cat. 97
Erhard Vessely, Vienna: 97, cat. 77
Frank Willett, Glasgow: 39 right (neg. 1964-12-36)